Passage of the Ship *Empress of China*
New York – Canton

FEBRUARY 22 – AUGUST 28, 1784

THE *EMPRESS OF CHINA*

PHILIP CHADWICK FOSTER SMITH

The
Empress of China

1984

PHILADELPHIA MARITIME MUSEUM

OTHER BOOKS BY PHILIP C.F. SMITH

A History of the Marine Society at Salem in New-England, 1766-1966
(1966)
Portraits of the Marine Society at Salem in New-England
(1972)
The Frigate *Essex* Papers: Building the Salem Frigate, 1798-1799
(1974)
Captain Samuel Tucker (1747-1833), Continental Navy
(1976)
Fired by Manley Zeal: A Naval Fiasco of the American Revolution
(1977)
The Artful Roux, Marine Painters of Marseille
(1978)
More Marine Paintings and Drawings in the Peabody Museum
(1979)

EDITED BY PHILIP C.F. SMITH

The Journals of Ashley Bowen (1728-1813) of Marblehead (2 vols.)
(1973)
Seafaring in Colonial Massachusetts
(1980)
Sibley's Heir, A Volume in Memory of Clifford Kenyon Shipton
(1982)

Copyright © 1984 by the Philadelphia Maritime Museum
Library of Congress Catalogue Card Number: 83-62393
I.S.B.N. 0-913346-08-X (Hard cover edition)
I.S.B.N. 0-913346-09-8 (Soft cover edition)

TABLE OF CONTENTS

	LIST OF ILLUSTRATIONS	*ix*
	FOREWORD	*xv*
I	Western Eyes Turn Eastward	*3*
II	A Scheme of Furs and Ships	*14*
III	In Search of the *Panax quinquefolia*	*31*
IV	Shedding the Fur Scheme	*43*
V	Most Serene, Puissant, and Illustrious	*57*
VI	Aweigh at Last	*74*
VII	An Unexpected Stopover	*84*
VIII	Doubling the Cape	*103*
IX	The Flight of Daniel Parker	*115*
X	In the Sunda Strait	*127*
XI	Canton Cumshaw and Commerce	*147*
XII	Learning to Trade with the Hong Merchants	*172*
XIII	Chinese Justice	*189*
XIV	Bound for Home	*201*
XV	Sales and Selling Out	*220*
XVI	The Long Limbs of Litigation	*235*
	APPENDICES	
A	A Fragmentary Abstract Log of the *Empress of China*	*253*
B	F. Molineux's Accounts of Purchases at Canton	*259*
C	Captain John Green's Accounts of Purchases at Canton and his Abstract Manifest of the Return Cargo	*267*
D	Eighty-Five Historic Imports and Exports of Canton	*301*
	NOTES	*305*
	SELECT BIBLIOGRAPHY	*317*
	INDEX	*321*

LIST OF ILLUSTRATIONS

1. Fort George and The Battery, New York   7
   Peabody Museum of Salem, Massachusetts

2. Nootka Sound   15
   British Library, London

3. View of Unalaska   16
   Peabody Museum, Harvard University

4. Northwest Coast Sea Otter   17
   Library of The Academy of Natural Sciences, Philadelphia

5. Robert Morris   21
   Historical Society of Pennsylvania

6. John Holker   22
   Vose Galleries of Boston, Inc.

7. Eighteenth-century Philadelphia   24
   Philadelphia Maritime Museum

8. Plan of the *Bellisarius*   28
   Historical Society of Pennsylvania

9. William Turnbull   32
   Historical Society of Pennsylvania

10. Botanical engraving of ginseng (*Panax quinquefolia*)   34
    Library of The Academy of Natural Sciences, Philadelphia

11. Root ginseng   35
    Author's photograph

12. Interior Western Pennsylvania and Virginia   37
    Author's map

13. Samuel Shaw   45
    Philadelphia Maritime Museum

14. Major General Henry Knox   48
    Independence National Historical Park Collection, Philadelphia

15. James Nicholson   50
    Philadelphia Maritime Museum

16. Mill Prison, Plymouth, England   53
    Essex Institute, Salem, Massachusetts

17. John Barry   54
    Philadelphia Maritime Museum

18. Continental frigate *Alliance* passing Boston Light   *55*
   Peabody Museum of Salem, Massachusetts

19. Signatures of *Empress of China* owners and officers   *59*
   Holker Papers, Library of Congress

20. Thomas Truxtun   *61*
   Philadelphia Maritime Museum

21. Unidentified eighteenth-century Philadelphia vessel   *63*
   Philadelphia Maritime Museum

22. New York State clearance paper for the *Empress of China*   *64*
   Philadelphia Maritime Museum

23. Governor George Clinton of New York   *65*
   New-York Historical Society

24. New York State sea-letter for the *Empress of China*   *66*
   Philadelphia Maritime Museum

25. Congressional sea-letter for the *Empress of China*   *71*
   Philadelphia Maritime Museum

26. John Green's sea chest   *75*
   Philadelphia Maritime Museum

27. View of New York from the northwest   *76*
   Peabody Museum of Salem, Massachusetts

28. Sandy Hook and the lighthouse   *77*
   Peabody Museum of Salem, Massachusetts

29. View of Porto Praya   *92*
   Peabody Museum of Salem, Massachusetts

30. An insurance certificate for the *Empress of China*   *131*
   Library of Congress, Washington, DC

31. Detail map of the Sunda Strait   *136*
   Author's map

32. Mew Bay, Java   *137*
   Peabody Museum of Salem, Massachusetts

33. Map of the South China Sea   *146*
   Author's map

34. Shore profiles in the South China Sea   *148*
   Peabody Museum of Salem, Massachusetts

35. Comparative maps of the Delaware and Pearl Rivers   *150-151*
   Author's maps

36. View of Macao   *160*
   Philadelphia Maritime Museum

37. The Bogue Forts at the Boca Tigris, Pearl River   *163*
   Peabody Museum of Salem, Massachusetts

38. Chinese fan of the *Empress of China* in Whampoa Reach *164*
   Historical Society of Pennsylvania

39. Whampoa Reach   *166*
   Peabody Museum of Salem, Massachusetts

40. The approaches to Canton (1)   *169*
   Peabody Museum of Salem, Massachusetts

41. The approaches to Canton (2)   *168*
   Peabody Museum of Salem, Massachusetts

42. The approaches to Canton (3)   *169*
   Peabody Museum of Salem, Massachusetts

43. The foreign factories at Canton (4)   *168*
   Peabody Museum of Salem, Massachusetts

44. Dutch Folly Fort, Canton   *175*
   Peabody Museum of Salem, Massachusetts

45. Medicine shop at Canton   *178*
   Peabody Museum of Salem, Massachusetts

46. Sea Otters on the Northwest Coast of America   *181*
   Library of The Academy of Natural Sciences, Philadelphia

47. Chinese fur seller   *182*
   Peabody Museum of Salem, Massachusetts

48. The packing of tea at Canton   *187*
   Peabody Museum of Salem, Massachusetts

49. Shipping porcelain to Canton   *190*
   Peabody Museum of Salem, Massachusetts

50. Porcelain shop at Canton   *191*
   Peabody Museum of Salem, Massachusetts

51. Silk culture   *193*
   Peabody Museum of Salem, Massachusetts

52. Trial of the *Neptune* sailors at Canton   *196*
   Peabody Museum of Salem, Massachusetts

53. Spanish trade and chopped dollars   *199*
   Thomas P. Curtis; photograph by Robert McCoy

54. A Grand Chop　　　　　　　　　　　　　　　　203
Peabody Museum of Salem, Massachusetts

55. Map of Whampoa Reach　　　　　　　　　　　204
Author's map

56. Cape Town and Table Mountain　　　　　　　205
Peabody Museum of Salem, Massachusetts

57. Jonathan Ingersoll of the *Grand Turk*　　　206
Peabody Museum of Salem, Massachusetts

58. Elias Hasket Derby　　　　　　　　　　　　207
Peabody Museum of Salem, Massachusetts

59. *Empress of China* Hong bowl　　　　　　　213
Private Collection

60. *Empress of China* / John Green Bowl (side view)　　216
New Jersey State Museum Collection, Trenton

61. *Empress of China* / John Green Bowl (top view)　　217
New Jersey State Museum Collection, Trenton

62. John Morgan *Empress of China* cream pitcher　　222
Mystic Seaport Museum

63. John Morgan porcelain bowl　　　　　　　223
Mystic Seaport Museum

64. John Morgan porcelain bowl　　　　　　　224
Mystic Seaport Museum

65. John Morgan porcelain bowl　　　　　　　225
Mystic Seaport Museum

66. Gouverneur and Robert Morris　　　　　　227
Pennsylvania Academy of the Fine Arts, Philadelphia

67. William Constable　　　　　　　　　　　　229
National Gallery of Art, Washington, DC

68. Arch Street Ferry, Philadelphia　　　　　　233
Philadelphia Maritime Museum

69. Andrew Craigie　　　　　　　　　　　　　241
American Antiquarian Society, Worcester, Massachusetts

70. The Continental frigate / China trader *Alliance*　　247
Peabody Museum of Salem, Massachusetts

71. The China trader *Massachusetts*　　　　　249
New York Public Library

ON THE FIRST AMERICAN SHIP
That explored the Rout[e] to CHINA, and the EAST-INDIES
after the Revolution

By Philip Freneau
(1752-1832)

With clearance from BELLONA won
She spreads her wings to meet the Sun,
Those golden regions to explore
Where George forbade to sail before.

Thus, grown to strength, the bird of Jove,
Impatient, quits his native grove,
With eyes of fire, and lightning's force
Through the blue ether holds his course.

No foreign tars are here allow'd
To mingle with her chosen crowd,
Who, when return'd, might, boasting, say
They show'd our native oak the way.

To that old track no more confin'd,
By Britain's jealous court assign'd,
She round the STORMY CAPE shall sail
And, eastward, catch the odorous gale.

To countries plac'd in burning climes
And islands of remotest times
She now her eager course explores,
And soon shall greet Chinesian shores,

From thence their fragrant TEAS to bring
Without the leave of Britain's king;
And PORCELAIN WARE, enchas'd in gold,
The product of that finer mould.

Thus commerce to our world conveys
All that the varying taste can please:
For us, the Indian looms are free,
And JAVA strips her spicy TREE.

Great pile proceed!—and o'er the brine
May every prosperous gale be thine,
'Till, freighted deep with eastern gems,
You reach again your native streams.

FOREWORD

SOMEONE ONCE OBSERVED that history is only rumor solidified. Such eminent wordsmiths as Voltaire, Gibbon, and Shelley considered it to be little more than a tableau of human crime, folly, and misfortune. Henry Ford, supposedly, defined it as "bunk."

If elements of history sometimes seem bejeweled in fairy-tale imagery, it is because they are equally as much the products of the chroniclers' predilections as of the individual reader's strength of imagination. Like the rough gemstone subjected to the abrasive whirlings of a lapidary's tumbler, raw history tends to assume an unnatural polish over the course of time.

Such has been the case in the telling and retelling of the story of the *Empress of China*, the first vessel of the United States of America to initiate trade with the Chinese. With monkish duplication, one historian after another has repeated a standard account of the voyage, nearly always within the space of several paragraphs. The human beings who formed the links in the chain of that bold experiment have become faceless and fugitive. Flesh and blood have paled to shadows, and substance has been reduced to gloss.

This book makes no claim to have puffed the figures out again into the full round, but it has been undertaken to restore a measure of life and credibility to the shadows and to commemorate the two-hundredth anniversary of the *Empress of China*'s trailblazing venture.

Its genesis was the acquisition in 1981 by the Philadelphia Maritime Museum of the Captain John Green (1736-1796) Papers from several Philadelphia-area descendants. Among the manuscripts, which largely deal with Green's Revolutionary War naval service and captivity, is his journal as captain of the *Empress of China* during her initial voyage. It was not a new discovery: it had been exhibited, when still privately owned, at the Philadelphia Maritime Museum for a few months in 1962 and a dozen years before that had been published by the late, noted maritime historian, William Bell Clark, in the quarterly journal *The American Neptune*. Until then, however, Josiah Quincy's work of 1847, *The Journals of Major Samuel Shaw the First American Consul at Canton*, had been the principal source of information about the *Empress of China*'s 1784-1785 voyage to the Orient. Captain Green's journal complimented it handsomely.

Clark's involvement with the ship, nevertheless, was of the glancing blow variety, a spinoff from his principal scholarly endeavor: the collection of naval documents of the American Revolution for a monolithic publication series of the same name. John Green's journal he merely introduced and annotated lightly. The same held true for Green's instructions from the owners, a document Clark submitted for publication in *The American Neptune* a few years later. Only Clarence L. Ver Steeg's "Financing and Outfitting the First United States Ship to China," published in the February 1953 issue of the *Pacific Historical Review*, has, to date, gently cracked the Pandora's box of jealousies, arrogance, and misrepresentation that made up the enterprise.

By building upon the work accomplished by others in the past, it has been possible to put forward a clearer picture of the *Empress* epic than has been presented before, even though many mysterious corners yet await illumination. A smelting of a wide range of manuscript sources—some of them already well mined, while others barely have been assayed—has enabled refinement of this book's narrative sections into what may be described, loosely, as a social and logistical history of that first voyage.

As I have done in the past with works of a similar nature, I have encouraged the cast of characters to do most of their own talking, and I make no apology whatever for having done so. After all, they were there. In general, the extent of my twentieth-century meddling has been to make John Green's eighteenth-century journal readily comprehensible to its current readers: the words, if not necessarily the orthography, are his.

Every attempt was made, but to no avail, to discover the whereabouts of a contemporaneous portrait of Captain Green, last heard of—save by the present, elusive owner—more than a generous lifetime ago. It was then owned by a direct descendant of Captain Green, Joseph Minnick Williams, an attorney variously described as resident of Olustee, Oklahoma, and of Nashville, Tennessee. The painting, presumably an oil, measured approximately thirty-six inches high by twenty-nine wide, "the work apparently of a good artist, is much faded and in only by sponging [!!] could we determine the color of the coat which appears to be buff or old gold . . . The ship in the corner . . . seems to be a full-rigged three-master vessel."

Most of the actors in the *Empress* drama were young men, eager to make their mark in an uncertain world as citizens of an infant republic not yet taken too seriously elsewhere. What they did began the maturing process of worldwide statesmanship. Samuel Shaw, the ship's all-important supercargo, for instance, was only twenty-nine years of age when he set sail the first time for the South China Sea. As a guide to readers who may ponder such matters as they travel along with him, John Green, and the others, it seems convenient to give the birth and death dates of the principal *dramatis personae* they will encounter:

John Barry (1745-1803)
George Clinton (1739-1812)
William Constable (1752-1803)
Andrew Craigie (1754-1819)
Samuel Clarkson (1762-1832)
William Duer (1747-1799)
Thomas Fitzsimons (1741-1811)
John Green (1736-1796)
John Green, Jr. (1766-1831)
John Holker (1745-1822)
Peter Hodgkinson (unknown)
Dr. Robert Johnston (1750-1808)
Henry Knox (1750-1806)
John Ledyard (1751-1789)

Frederick Molineux (unknown)
Gouverneur Morris (1752-1816)
Robert Morris (1734-1806)
James Nicholson (c.1736-1804)
Daniel Parker (unknown)
John Peck (1725-1790)
Thomas Russell (1746-1796)
Thomas Randall (-1811)
Samuel Shaw (1754-1794)
John White Swift (1749/50-1812)
John Swift (1720-1802)
James Swan (1754-1830)
Winthrop Sargent (1753-1820)
William Turnbull (1751-1822)

In addition to the various private and institutional sources which kindly granted permission to publish here illustrative material from their collections, acknowledged in the List of Illustrations, thanks for significant help in other areas is most gratefully given to: James Daland Lannon, Wiscasset, ME; Kathleen A. Major, Keeper of Manuscripts, American Antiquarian Society, Worcester, MA; Irene Norton, Reference Librarian, Essex Institute, Salem, MA; Robert V. Sparks, Senior Assistant Librarian, Massachusetts Historical Society, Boston, MA; Dorothy W. Bridgwater, Assistant Editor, Papers of Benjamin Franklin, Sterling Memorial Library, Yale University, New Haven, CT; Philip R. Budlong, Registrar, Mystic Seaport Museum, Mystic, CT; John Catanzariti, Editor, Papers of Robert Morris, Queen's College, Flushing, NY; Francis James Dallett, Archivist, University of Pennsylvania, Philadelphia, PA; Roy E. Goodman, Reading Room Librarian, American Philosophical Society, Philadelphia, PA; Jean Gordon Lee, Curator of Far Eastern Art, Philadelphia Museum of Art, Philadelphia, PA; Clifford Lewis, III, Immediate Past President, Pennsylvania Society of the Cincinnati, Media, PA; Frances Johnston Markle, Ardmore, PA; Martha Shipman Andrews, Coordinator, Inventory of American Paintings, National Museum of American Art, Washington, DC; and Galen R. Wilson, Manuscript Curator, William L. Clements Library, University of Michigan, Ann Arbor.

Staffers of the following institutions also provided assistance and are warmly thanked: National Maritime Museum, Greenwich, England; State Paper Office, Dublin, Ireland; Peabody Museum of Salem, MA; The Massachusetts Archives and The Athenaeum of Boston; the Widener, Houghton, and Baker

Libraries of Harvard University, Cambridge, MA; The Museum of the American China Trade, Milton, MA; The New-York Historical Society and the New York Public Library, New York City; The Academy of Natural Sciences, Philadelphia; The Athenaeum of Philadelphia; The Historical Society of Pennsylvania, Philadelphia; The Library Company of Philadelphia; Historical Research Branch, Department of the Navy, Washington, DC; Library of Congress, National Archives, and the National Headquarters of the Society of the Cincinnati, Washington, DC.

Expressions of gratitude are also extended to Peter F. Wyer and to Sam and Kathy Smith for hospitality during research stints in New York City and Washington, DC, respectively.

Finally, it would be impossible not to acknowledge my debt to Klaus Gemming of New Haven, CT, for his design of the book and overseeing its production, as also to two very capable associates at the Philadelphia Maritime Museum, John M. Groff, Assistant Curator/Registrar, and Jane Ettinger Allen, Curatorial Research Assistant. These two were indefatigable in their quests for leads and in their monumental support to me in running a department while I was otherwise occupied with the writing process.

To the above and to all others who have provided useful insights, I express great appreciation. Lastly, but of major importance, the Philadelphia Maritime Museum acknowledges its debt to the Andrew W. Mellon Foundation which provided the funding for the publication of this volume.

PHILIP CHADWICK FOSTER SMITH

Philadelphia

THE *EMPRESS OF CHINA*

I

Western Eyes Turn Eastward

A chill, winter wind gusted fitfully out of the west-northwest, roiling the surface of New York's ice-flecked East River and moaning dolefully among a score of wharves long atrophied by war. It was Sunday, the twenty-second of February 1784: George Washington's fifty-second birthday, according to the revised Gregorian calendar, and John Green, Jr.'s eighteenth—an historic day for the young midshipman and the moment of truth for his boisterous captain father, John Green, Senior.[1]

Shortly after 5 A.M., a wan glow began to arise in the eastern sky. Aboard the black-hulled *Empress of China* and upon the dusky pier at which she lay, stirrings of life began to be felt and heard. Weeks of impatient waiting for the harbor ice to clear and unstopper the bottleneck at the Narrows had ended. Five days ago, a long-overdue rise in the thermometer and thawing winds had signalled a brief respite in one of the coldest, dirtiest winters within living memory.[2] Finally, yesterday, the great part of the ice, its stiff spine broken, had begun its inevitable retreat. And this Sabbath morning was dawning with a fresh, fair-weather sailing wind.

No one was more relieved than Captain John Green, a Philadelphian and a veteran officer in the now virtually defunct Continental Navy, from which he was, technically, on leave of absence. The *Empress of China*'s unusual cargo, consisting almost entirely of ginseng roots and Spanish silver dollars, had been on board since the eighteenth of January; he had signed the bills of lading on the twenty-fifth; and that same day, the ship's owners had handed him definitive orders respecting the conduct of the voyage. His instructions had come just as the harbor of New York glazed over, congealed, and brought all inward and outward bound shipping to a standstill. It had been rotten timing.

John Green was all too aware of those persons who were grumbling not so quietly behind his back, tending to blame him for what seemed like endless delays in putting to sea before the freeze came, yet there had been little or nothing he could have done about them. Maybe too many people were involved. Certainly, due to the venture's untried and experimental nature, many suggestions had been bandied about during the months, and a plethora of contradictory opinions had been voiced. Now, disagreements were becoming more frequent and more obvious. Resentments were growing, and several of the backers had begun to bicker amongst themselves. The withdrawal of the Boston merchants, who at first had been highly enthusiastic about the scheme, had nearly killed it off. Only last-minute apoplectic financial sleights of hand in both Philadelphia and New York had somehow saved it. If that, in itself, had not been enough, the difficulties of supply had been nearly unbearable: no cornucopia of material resources was a new nation not yet six months at peace with its estranged mother country; nor, either, was a city which ravenous British occupying forces had only reluctantly vacated within the last three.

Before the peace, no Americans had ever attempted to plan and then execute a trading voyage from North America to China, half a world away. Never before had the mercantilistic canons of their jealous parent allowed them to try. It was a bold scheme without domestic precedents to follow or experienced advisors to consult, but a knowledge of the customary trading season—when fleets of magisterial British and European East Indiamen swam northward through the South China Sea towards Canton, was not one of the unknowns. The success or failure of the *Empress of China*'s voyage depended to no small degree upon her timely arrival in the Orient, lest the volatile Chinese markets already be glutted with Western imports. The ice blocking New York from the sea threatened to make a mockery of the best laid plans.

Captain Green surely must have been struck by the irony of the situation. After all, one of the compelling reasons why the owners had decided to begin the voyage from New York rather than from Philadelphia, whence derived the bulk of the financing, was because of the Delaware River's notorious penchant for freezing early and thawing late. A winter's transit of treacherous river waters downstream for almost one hundred miles to the open sea was infinitely less desirable than the fifteen-odd-mile run from the tip of Manhattan to the long ocean rollers off Sandy Hook. Their foresight proved to be acute. During this filthiest of winters, the Delaware River at Philadelphia froze solid on the day after Christmas 1783 and remained that way until nearly mid-March 1784, by which time the *Empress of China* would find herself in sight of the island of Palma, in the Canaries, some 120 miles off the west coast of Africa.

While gangs of the *Empress of China*'s forty-two-man crew worked on deck in the pre-dawn light to clear away the last-minute raffle of unstowed gear and stores, hencoops, and sheep pens, others under the direction of the second—or backup—captain and the two mates, laid aloft onto the yards to throw off the gaskets, loosen the sails in their buntlines, and set every thing to rights before the order came to cast off from the wharf. From time to time, a horseman or a carriage clattered noisily through the half-light onto the pier, when Captain Green stepped to the gangway and welcomed aboard a visitor of influence. Seven such would accompany the ship out of the harbor as far as Sandy Hook.

With the exception of a Mr. Porter, who no longer can be identified with any precision, the others consisted of master shipwright Ebenezer Young, New York ship chandler Peter Schermerhorn, and four men, each of whom was a member of an exclusive fraternity recently organized, the Society of the Cincinnati.[3]

Named after the fifth-century B.C. Roman citizen-soldier Lucius Quinctius Cincinnatus—who lay down his plow to serve the state, only to return to his fields once the enemy had been vanquished—the Society of the Cincinnati had been organized formally, with George Washington as its President-General, in May 1783, shortly before the disbandment of the Continental Army.[4] Membership was restricted to officers of the Continental forces who had served at least three years during the Revolutionary War. Thereafter, successively, the right descended to the eldest living male. Roundly vilified in some republican circles as an inappropriate, undemocratic "aristocratic military nobility" within the United States, the Society's original purpose had been to continue and strengthen the bonds of friendship that had developed between officers during the war. Judging from the number of Cincinnati concerned with the *Empress of China* enterprise, they also were dedicated to each other's enrichment, welfare, and personal comfort.

The four Cincinnati to see her off consisted of Daniel Parker, who, with Robert Morris of Philadelphia (an honorary member of the Society), was one of the four principal owners of the vessel; Jonas Simonds of Pennsylvania;

Dr. Andrew Craigie, formerly Apothecary General of the Continental Army and one of Parker's personal cronies; and Captain James Nicholson, senior captain of the Continental Navy. Nicholson had been Parker's choice over Green to be commanding officer of the *Empress of China*; that had not worked out, so Nicholson had been appointed to the command of another of Parker & Company's vessels, the *Comte d'Artois*.

Strengthening the bond were five of the ship's officers, also Cincinnati: John Green, captain; Samuel Shaw and Thomas Randall, supercargoes; surgeon Robert Johnston; and surgeon's mate Andrew Caldwell. Both supercargoes hailed from Massachusetts; the remainder from Pennsylvania. Truly, the pioneer American expedition to China was bound together by a band of disparate brothers.

At 6:35 A.M., a sparkling winter sun rose out of the sea beyond Long Island and within minutes thrust its golden rim over the heights of Brooklyn. Nearby, in the river, a brig and three ship-rigged vessels began to show scraps of sail in anticipation of the turning of the tide and their own departures. One was the ship *Edward*, cleared for London, on board which were "the public dispatches of Congress, for the respective courts, containing the ratification of the Definitive Articles of Peace."[5] It was a poignant reminder of the short span of time since hostilities had ended, as also a mute tribute to the *Empress of China* venturers who, despite tremendous odds, severely depressed times, and the foibles of human nature, had nonetheless risen miraculously to the occasion.

At daylight, the *Empress of China* was hove from the wharf into mid-river, allowed to drift with the current a short distance upsteam until the anchor bit ground, and then swung to her moorings while the seamen left on shore to manhandle the hawsers dockside were rowed out to her and the boat swayed aboard.

High water at New York would occur during the middle of the morning.[6] At the time of slack water, the ship shook out her sails, hove short on the anchor cable, and filled away down the East River towards the Battery at the toe of Manhattan Island. Atop this "prodigious mound of earth," as one observer described it, an array of spectators had assembled spontaneously to bid her farewell. Heavily bundled against the raw wind, they lined the broad stone glacis built up from the water's edge—in warmer weather a favored place by the gentlemen and ladies of the city for an evening's promenade— and dotted the walls above as well as the ramparts of old Fort George within.[7]

It must have been a sight no one on board the *Empress of China* could likely forget: the colors of the United States snapping from the flagstaff,

1. "A View of Fort George with the City of New York from the SW," a mid-eighteenth-century view by J. Carwitham. The saluting British ship is about to enter the East River, from which the *Empress of China* sailed to the Orient several decades later.

which only a few months ago had been fouled and greased by the departing British to delay a final striking of their Union flag; a great concourse of hat-waving well-wishers; and, as the ship drew abreast of the fort, a sound carried on the wind of a resounding three cheers from the gathered multitude.

Captain Green had the foresight earlier to prepare for such an eventuality. His portside cannon, charged with powder but unshotted, boomed out a salute of thirteen guns. As the bluish haze of his gunsmoke drifted rapidly away to leeward, the fort answered the compliment gun for gun. Green replied with one last parting shot, shook out more sail, and steered a course for the Narrows and the boundless horizons beyond.

"On Sunday last," one Philadelphia newspaper purred, "sailed from New York, the ship *Empress of China*, Captain John Green of this port, for Canton in China. On passing the garrison at Fort-George, she fired with great regularity, the United States salute, which was returned from the fort. This handsome, commodious and elegant ship, modelled after, and built on the new invented construction of the ingenious Mr. Peck of Boston, is deemed an exceeding swift sailer. The Captain and crew, with several young American adventurers, were all happy and cheerful, in good health and high spirits; and, with a becoming decency, elated on being considered the first instruments, in the hands of Providence, who have undertaken to extend the commerce of the United States of America, to that distant, and to us, unexplored, country."[8]

Nearly a century before Lucius Quinctius Cincinnatus offered himself to the Roman state, the Greek philosopher-mathematician Pythagoras and his followers concluded that all relationships in the universe could be expressed by numbers. Four hundred years passed. Lü Pu-wei, prime minister of the Chinese state of Ch'in, is then known to have expressed accurately the Pythagorean musical scale and the immortal theorem concerning the square of the hypotenuse of a right triangle.[9]

Surely, this must have been one of the first instances of Western civilized thought to have touched China. Another millennium and a half passed before Far East and Far West finally met on terms other than the most tenuous and glancing. Even then, only scattered writings of the occasional missionary and the published adventures of the late-thirteenth-century Venetian traveler, Marco Polo, painted for Renaissance Europeans their remarkable images of mysterious Cathay and the fabled East Indies.

The commodities of those faraway dominions—spices, gemstones, gold, pearls, and silk—for generations had filtered slowly westward along the interminable caravan routes of eastern Asia, Persia, Mesopotamia, and Turkey. To the West, the exotic "Indies" conjured up fabulous images of wealth but very little else; the "Indies" were comprised of vast, amorphous regions that defied description. Not until the late fifteenth century did the perceptual blur come into focus as an area encompassing roughly the sub-continent of India, Malaysia, Indonesia, China, and adjacent quarters. Even then, the generic term "Indies" died hard. As late as 1784, Captain John Green wrote on the flyleaf on his seagoing blankbook: "A Jurnal of An Intended Voyage on Board the Ship Empress of Chinea Bound from New York to Canton In India".

Spices—cloves, pepper, mace, nutmeg, and cinnamon—especially spices used to preserve perishable foodstuffs as an alternative to salting or smoking, were the magnets that drew European traders towards the East. It was Portugal's Prince Henry the Navigator who, in 1418, set in motion the first, tentative probes along the west African coast into the dreaded "green sea of darkness" imagined to lurk beyond the far side of Cape Bojadore. Thanks to his initiative, such expeditions led not only to the European discovery of India but also to Portuguese domination of the East Indies trades as well.

No less bound up in the quest for sea routes to the Orient were many of the bold voyages into the unknown western seas, which culminated in the discovery and colonization of the Americas. That Columbus in 1492 believed he had reached the fringes of Asia is no more clearly demonstrated than by his naming the natives he found "Indians". From Columbus through the voyages of the Cabots, Verrazano, Cartier, Davis, and a half score of others during the next hundred years, a common thread united their efforts: the fruitless search for a commercially viable "Northwest Passage," the ultimate shortcut from West to East.

For a time, Portuguese influence in the Indies luxuriated in unrivaled sway. It did not endure. In 1580, King Philip of Spain inherited the throne of Portugal. The following year, the seven northern provinces of the Netherlands, worn down by Spanish rule and the terrors of the Inquisition, declared their independence. By so doing, their entrée into the spice markets of Lisbon was lost. The English sacrificed theirs, too, when later they came into the fray on the side of the free Dutch. Finally, when Philip sent his "Invincible Armada"—130 vessels, 3,165 cannon, 30,000 men—against England and was roundly trounced in July 1588 by a combination of English preparedness and the intercession of Nature's own elemental fury, the East Indies fell open to the ravages of the most powerful taker.

Dutch penetration of them was determined and swift. By mid-seventeenth century, they had effectively pushed the Portuguese aside and had established trading posts—known at that day as "factories"—from Cape Town, South Africa, to Nagasaki, Japan. At the heart of the burgeoning empire lay Batavia, present-day Djarkarta, on the island of Java at the side of the strategic Sunda Strait.

The Dutch may have taken an early lead, but the English were no laggards. In 1600, two years before the establishment of a comparable Dutch company, Queen Elizabeth I issued letters patent incorporating "The Governor and Merchants of London Trading into the East Indies". This was the earliest ancestor of Britain's prestigious East India Company, to which the Queen granted an exclusive monopoly for the space of fifteen years. James I made it perpetual, Cromwell reinforced it during the Protectorate, and Charles II upheld it again later. But just at the end of the century, a rival company came into being: "The English Company Trading to the East Indies". The two were merged in 1708. "Two East India Companies in England," grumbled the directors of the old company, "can no more subsist without destroying one the other, than two kings, at the same time regnant in the same kingdom."

For England, the greater part of the seventeenth century was fraught with unreasonable vicissitudes of life: two wars with France, one with Spain, three with the Netherlands, two civil wars, the Commonwealth government and the subsequent restoration of the monarchy, the devastation of London by bubonic plague and by fire, and shattering internal ruptures almost too great to bear. It is a wonder that far-flung voyages to unfamiliar corners of the globe could have been undertaken at all, let alone contemplated. For the fledgling company, these were decades of trial and error, advancement and retrenchment, short thrusts and larger parries. During them, it became clear that Dutch roots in the Spice Islands had grown so tough, so deep, and so parasitic that no others could tap the same soil and survive. The British East India Company turned its immediate attention to the Coromandel and Malabar Coasts of India, the serrated Ganges delta of Bengal, and, in due course, to China. But soon, the exigencies of war and the prosecution of trade compelled Britain to formulate new rules lest the billowing Dutch carrying trade around the world beggar the shipping merchants of England.

The first of the infamous Navigation Acts, the British Acts of Trade, was enacted in 1651 and precipitated the first of the three sea wars fought with the Dutch during the seventeenth century. It was the root cause why another *Empress of China* had never sailed from America before independence had been won.

An extension of prevailing mercantilistic policies calculated to assure England of the most accumulation of bullion possible, the Act of 1651 strictly prohibited the importation of "plantation" (colonial) commodities from Asia, Africa, or America except in ships owned, commanded, and primarily manned by Englishmen. Goods from Europe could only be transported in English bottoms or those that were the property of the subjects of the country from which the articles originated, were produced, or were first shipped.

The Staple Act of 1663, when combined with the monopoly enjoyed by the East India Company, effectively excluded inhabitants of North America from attempting legal penetration of such distant seas. None had, save for a few audacious pirates and freebooters who, from time to time, had extended their range in Caribbean and European cruising grounds to include the western rim of the Indian Ocean. Essentially, the Staple Act most affected the trade of the Thirteen American Colonies by the mandate that all foreign goods shipped to them must first pass through one of the home ports of Britain.

So it was that for more than a century American merchant mariners were obliged to trade within strictly defined limits. Coasting voyages between colonies served to exchange local produce, such as salt fish, rum, and lumber from the North; grain and flour from the Middle Atlantic region; indigo, rice, and tobacco from the South. In the West Indies and the Catholic ports of Spain and Portugal they traded in timber products, grain, flour, salt fish, sugar, molasses, and rum; in the Wine Islands they loaded pipes of delicate local wines and full-bodied Madeiras. In England, they completed ladings of raw materials, manufactured goods, and articles of luxury meticulously gathered together from the entrepôts of the world. Beyond ever-chronic smuggling activities, no other commercial innovations had been possible.

Had American shipowners been at liberty to seek avenues of trade with the Orient on their own, they probably would have achieved little or nothing with China until deep into the eighteenth century. Unlike so many other peoples whose dominions ringed the South China Sea, the Chinese perceived little virtue in opening their ports to outsiders. To them, Westerners were the "Fan Kwae": foreign devils, barbarians, tributary creatures deserving of contempt. "Their clothes and their hair were red," suspicious Chinese officials described the Dutch at first encounter, "their bodies tall; they had blue eyes sunk deep in their heads. Their feet were one cubit and two-tenths long; and they frightened the people by their strange appearance."[10]

Of all the European kingdoms which had become a presence in the Indies prior to the beginning of the eighteenth century—the Portuguese since mid-fifteenth, the Dutch and English from the beginning of the seventeenth, and the French from the year 1664—only the Portuguese had managed to establish a direct commercial relationship with China. It had crystallized in 1557 with the Portuguese settlement of Macao, a peninsula and two islands below the mouth of the Pearl River in Kwangtung province. They were kept in a state of rigid submission, nevertheless, by the Cantonese mandarins upriver, who supervised and regulated their activities as suited the whims of officialdom. The Dutch had attempted their own entrée into Canton as early as 1604 but had failed. The first English thrust, which occurred in 1635, proved equally abortive, as did a more determined sortie two years later by an expedition under the command of Captain John Weddell.

All European aspirants to the trade, excepting the Portuguese, were compelled to acquire Oriental merchandise from East India ports visited by big Chinese trading junks from the mainland. Among the items the junks carried for sale was quantities of dried leaves from the *Camellia thea*.

Even though tea had been around the British Isles in small amounts for a decade or more as a curiosity carried home by sailors, it made its official London debut in 1664, when the Directors of the East India Company presented a two-pound two-ounce tin of it to King Charles II. The Dutch had been aware of tea for much longer: "hay water," they sneered, preferring the stouter beverage brewed from Java coffee beans. Having won princely favor in England, however, the taste for tea proliferated rapidly and spread to the American colonies by the 1680's. All the same, to use it one had to know what to do with it. In 1685, for instance, the widow of the Duke of Monmouth sent a supply to relatives in Scotland. They boiled the tea, threw away the water, and, after consuming what remained of the leaves, wondered what on earth all the fuss was about in polite society down south![11]

As the demand for tea widened and imports grew from almost nothing to nearly 100,000 pounds weight per annum within fifteen years of the King's first sip, the East India Company resolved to pursue anew direct trade with China. During the remaining years of the seventeenth century it engaged in numerous furtive commercial forays to the port of Amoy on the Formosa Strait and to the buffer state of Tonkin (North Vietnam); in 1682 failed yet again to open Canton, but, betimes, gained invaluable experience about the prerequisites for dealing with the Chinese: patience, watchfulness, fortitude, and, above all, the liberal sowing of bribes.

In 1699, Emperor K'ang-hsi was at last persuaded to relax China's traditional prohibition of foreign trade within its harbors and permitted the English to establish a factory post at Canton. Within a little more than three decades, the British were joined by the Dutch, the Danes, the Swedes, and the Austrian Imperials based in the Flemish port of Ostende. Both sides, East and West, were learning to deal with the other. To maximize profits and minimize social contact by the Fan Kwae with their people, the Chinese in 1757 restricted all Western trade to Canton and a foreign compound built upon the banks of the Pearl River. So the state of affairs remained until 1842, eight years after the East India Company's monopoly on British trade with China came to an anticlimactic end.

For Captain John Green, his comrades aboard the *Empress of China*, and her financially hard-pressed owners, the success of their voyage was scarcely less risk-filled than the initial sorties of their British counterparts three and four generations before.

It is quite possible that such a bold vision might not have been devised quite so soon had not the euphoria caused by the end of the Revolution numbed many a man to the economic vacuum that surely would follow. Old markets were gone. Lucrative industries like the cod and whale fisheries had been ravaged. Coasting traffic had become but a thin shadow of its former self. Ancient overseas trade routes in eight short years had fallen into such disuse that it appeared doubtful if they ever again could be revived. The British West Indies, so crucial to the prewar trade of the colonies, had slammed shut to vessels of the new United States of America. No longer were the old colonies shielded by Fortress Mercantilism; no longer, either, were they hobbled by it. Suddenly, Americans truly belonged to the world and were rudely compelled to compete in it. Those interconnecting spider-webs of traditional commerce begged to be respun.

Potential investors in an untried, precarious voyage such as that of the *Empress of China* had to be men of substance, influence, or enormous self-confidence. No single merchant could have pulled it off on his own; the daunting sums required to engineer such a gamble could only be tapped by powerful men working in concert.

Once begun, there was no turning back for the principal actors. Too much capital had been laid out to permit withdrawal. Too many interlocking lines of credit, some of them reaching across the Atlantic into the banking houses of France, had been pledged to entertain retreat.

What follows is the saga of their uncommon reconnaissance of the fabled dominions of the Celestial Empire.

II

A Scheme of Furs and Ships

"There is now no doubt but a good Voyage might be made to China, but to do it to advantage will require at least 1,200,000 Livres. . . ."[1]

So wrote Matthew Ridley of the Baltimore mercantile house of Ridley & Pringle to correspondents in France on the eighteenth of March 1783. His optimistic outlook stemmed from the welcome infusion of strength by news that had reached the United States just six days before and was spreading throughout the country like a wind-driven grass fire: on November 30, 1782, preliminary articles of peace had been signed in Paris.

On land and at sea the long, bitter struggle of the American Revolution was over at last. The armistice joined with the articles assured that.

Even though the definitive treaty would not be signed until the following September and the last of the British occupying forces—those in the city of New York—would not finally embark for home until almost the end of November 1783, the shipowners and merchants of America in the meantime began to lay the groundwork for a resumption of prewar trade. The initial flush of confidence in future prosperity was infectious. Out of it sprang the voyage of the *Empress of China*.

Who first planted the seed may never be known, but like so many innovative ideas that seem to sprout full-grown in several places at once, the prospect of an American China voyage undoubtedly germinated virtually spontaneously in the consciousness of a variety of shipowners well scattered along the 9,000 mile coastline between the Piscataqua River in New Hampshire and the Severn in Maryland.

Judiciously watering it wherever he went, however, was a thirty-two-year-old adventurer from Groton, Connecticut, the incomparable John Ledyard.

Early in May 1783, Ledyard showed up in New York City with a strange tale to tell and an astonishing scheme festering in his brain.[2] In 1776, he informed anyone who might be induced to patronize his plan, he had sailed from London as a corporal of marines on the third and final voyage of discovery by the celebrated explorer and navigator, Captain James Cook. Cook, as was common knowledge, had been slain by natives of the Sandwich (Hawaiian) Islands, and the expedition had terminated in London, via Canton and the Cape of Good Hope, late in the year 1780. The scientific nature of Cook's work had transcended the politics of war, but once Ledyard again set foot on British soil he found himself liable for further service in the Royal Navy with the probability of having to fight against his own countrymen. He refused and so remained in barracks for two years before being assigned

2. Captain James Cook's ship *Resolution* lies in Nootka Sound on the Northwest Coast of America during his third voyage of discovery. American-born John Ledyard, a member of the expedition, quickly realized the value of the furs available in the area. Painting by expedition artist John Webber (1750-1793).

3. Unalaska Island in the Aleutians was also visited by John Ledyard during Captain Cook's third voyage. Russian fur operations there convinced him that pelts from the region would find a ready market in China. Painting by expedition artist John Webber (1750-1793).

to duty aboard a naval vessel ordered to join the North American squadron. At the end of 1782, he found himself in Long Island Sound, off the Connecticut coast and virtually within a stone's throw of his mother's residence. Authorized shore leave turned into unsanctioned French leave, which concluded his connection with the Royal Navy. After making himself known to his mother, Ledyard repaired to his boyhood stomping grounds of Hartford, Connecticut, where for the next four months he prepared for publication his book, *A Journal of Captain Cook's Last Voyage to the Pacific Ocean.*

In reliving his experiences as pen crossed paper, Ledyard was struck anew by observations he had made with Cook while exploring Nootka Sound, just west of what is now Vancouver Island, British Columbia.[3] Here, the Indians had produced for inspection some of the richest pelts the English had ever examined, including the most luxurious of all, the rich, umber-gloss sea otter. The lushness and abundance of furs later encountered at the Russian trading post on Unalaska Island in the Aleutians reinforced Ledyard's growing conviction that unimaginable fortunes were there just for the taking by any entrepreneur who could early exploit the American Northwest Coast. All doubt was removed when he observed the going rate in Canton for prime furs.

Ledyard's plan, which he flogged unmercifully in New York, was essentially that a suitable vessel or vessels should be fitted out for an expedition to the Northwest Coast, where he would acquire land from the Indians, establish a trading factory, and encourage the natives to supply him with pelts in return for an assortment of commodities valuable to them but of little intrinsic value to the promoters. Once a sufficiently large cargo had been assembled, it would be sent off to Canton while other ladings were being collected. By buying low and selling high, anyone connected with the enterprise should clean up handsomely.

Although to all intents and purposes the war was over, New York still was an occupied city. That fact cast a pall over whatever spirit of enterprise was beginning to reawaken in the breasts of local merchants. "Not meeting with encouragement adequate to his sanguine expectations," a biographer of Ledyard wrote, "he hastened onward to Philadelphia."[4]

4. A Northwest Coast sea otter. Upper class Chinese were attracted by its sumptuous pelt for use in clothing. Plate no. 37 from Audubon's *Viviparous Quadrupeds of North America* (New York, 1848).

The journey between New York and Philadelphia was a long and arduous one at the time: several days by stagecoach and considerably longer by water, especially if winds and currents were uncooperative. Ledyard arrived in Philadelphia disheartened, nearly broke, and looking for some seafaring employment to tide him over, but in that he was also disappointed. "The most of the shipping here," he reported his lack of progress in a letter, "are foreigners. Sixteen sail of seven different maritime powers arrived a few days ago. Fourteen sailors went out to the northward the morning I arrived, for want of employ, and numbers are strolling the docks on the same account. There is at present little home navigation."[5]

Not unlike the legendary Johnny Appleseed, who in years to come would roam the interior of the country planting apple orchards, John Ledyard's glib tongue sowed the germs of his grand design from the Delaware River docks to the Indian Queen Tavern uptown and to the banks of the Schuylkill beyond. At length, it won for him an audience with the richest and, perhaps, most influential man in the nation, Philadelphia's Robert Morris, the "Financier of the American Revolution" and currently Superintendent of Finance of the United States. Morris was impressed by what he heard.

"I have been so often the sport of fortune," Ledyard wrote in high spirits to a friend, "that I durst hardly credit the present dawn of bright prospects. But it is a fact, that the Honorable Robert Morris is disposed to give me a ship to go to the North Pacific Ocean. I have had two interviews with him at the Finance Office, and tomorrow I expect a conclusive one. What a noble hold he instantly took of the enterprise! I have been two days at his request drawing up a minute detail of a plan, and an estimate of the outfits, which I shall present him with tomorrow; and I am pleased to find, that it will be two thousand pounds less than one of his own. I take the lead of the greatest commercial enterprise, that has ever been embarked on in this country; and one of the first moment, as it respects the trade of America. If the affair is concluded on, as I expect it will be, it is probable I shall set off for New England to procure seamen, or a ship, or both. Morris is wrapt up in the idea of Yankee sailors."[6]

It had happened with neither hoopla nor fanfare. A plan was agreed upon which involved two or more ships to be fitted out for the Orient: one to load a cargo and sail directly for Canton via the Cape of Good Hope; the other or others to double Cape Horn, proceed to the Northwest Coast for a lading of furs, and then continue across the Pacific to China. Both should sail from America at approximately the same time: the Chinaman in early winter, so to reach the Canton market at the proper trading season, and the furman so that the doubling of Cape Horn would be accomplished during the summer weather months of the Southern Hemisphere.

Finding suitable ships should not have presented particular problems. In every harbor and stream up and down the coast lay a multiplicity of sleek privateers built during the war but now idled by its conclusion. Designed for speed to outpace the enemy; constructed for strength, endurance, and self-sufficiency at sea for weeks or months at a time, the majority of these private engines of war were nevertheless unsuited to the purposes at hand. Nothing appropriate could be found in Philadelphia or in adjacent parts of the Delaware River; relatively few ship-rigged vessels with sufficient stowage capacity had been built there during the Revolution, and those that had been were either already employed in commercial voyages or were destined to be. The privateer owners of the Revolution had preferred handier sloops, schooners, brigs, and brigantines: smaller, nimbler craft calculated to nip and run; then turn under a cloud of canvas and pounce again. Cargo capacity in a privateer had not always been a virtue.

While John Ledyard, heady in the flush of success, journeyed north-eastward to New England, the future collaborators in the China scheme, like droplets of quicksilver brought into contact, quickly merged into a conglomerate.

Lest anyone suppose that the prodigious distances between population centers of eighteenth-century America, or the slow communications between them, in any way promoted insularity between regions, let it be known that, commercially, nothing could be farther from the truth. The merchants of Philadelphia maintained intimate business connections with their counterparts in Boston. Bostonians were closely linked to Charleston, South Carolina; Carolinians with New Yorkers; New Yorkers with Virginians; Virginians with Marylanders; Marylanders with Pennsylvanians. Extending the whole, American shipping merchants preserved incredibly complicated networks of personal credits and debits with scores of shipping houses and banking establishments from Göteborg to London to Paris to Cadiz and Lisbon; to and beyond the Windward and Leeward islands of the Caribbean.

The immediate quicksilver pool for the China venture was the aggregate of several eminent Philadelphians, Robert Morris leading the pack; two Philadelphia French emigrés; a formidable New York speculator; and a slick-talking transplant from Massachusetts presently operating out of New York City. A handful of Boston merchants also was expected to become associated with the others but to date remained uncommitted. Perhaps Ledyard's gift for convincing gab would speed them into the fold once he arrived in Boston.

The original plan called for a proportional sharing of expenses, which, even allowing the most Spartan of budgets, were bound to be shocking. Robert Morris would put up one-third. Daniel Parker & Company of New York, consisting of Daniel Parker, William Duer, and, by late summer, another partner, would provide the second third. The "sundry merchants of Boston," probably including such stalwarts as James Swan, Samuel Breck, Thomas Russell, and Joseph Barrell, were expected to come up with the capital for the final third.

Robert Morris's tentacles, owing to his position as Superintendent of Finance, spread predictably in every direction. Among the houses with which he was more than a little connected was the Philadelphia partnership of Turnbull, Marmie & Company, composed of Scottish-born William Turnbull, who came to Philadelphia just before the Revolution and became Commissary for the Continental troops of Pennsylvania during it; and Peter Marmie, said by some to have made his way from France to America in the service of the Marquis de Lafayette. Also involved in a partnership with Morris was thirty-eight-year-old John Holker, fils, an English-born Frenchman whose father had fled from Scotland after taking part in the Rebellion of 1745 and now operated a textile mill in Rouen.[7] The younger Holker first appeared in Philadelphia in 1778, where he became Agent for the French Royal Marine (Navy) in North America and French Consul-General for Pennsylvania, Delaware, New Jersey, and New York, posts from which he was eventually removed because of his numerous private and conflicting business speculations. He and Morris had gone into partnership in 1781 and involved themselves in farther speculations in tobacco, flour, grain, and other commodities; the whole waxing so complex as to defy total clarification during their own lifetimes let alone from the vantage point of several centuries later.

An equal portion of the financing was the responsibility of Daniel Parker & Company, with Parker himself acting as Agent and Cashier for the outfitting of the vessels to come under the firm's control. A resident of Watertown, Massachusetts, where his family continued to dwell, Parker had spent the last year or so of the Revolution in and around New York State as a contractor supplying rations for the American garrisons. With him as co-contractors were William Duer of Albany and New York and Walter Livingston of "Manor Livingston", New York. From August to November 1783, these three held the contract to provision General George Washington's private retinue at Rocky Hill, including the General, his foot and horse guards, and his wagoneers. English-born and Eton educated, Duer had inherited a share of his father's extensive plantation holdings in Antigua and

5. Robert Morris (1734-1806) of Philadelphia, the "Financier of the American Revolution". Morris owned a half-interest in the *Empress of China* and originally was attracted to the idea of a China voyage by John Ledyard's Northwest Coast fur scheme. Portrait by Edward Savage (1761-1817), *circa* 1790.

6. John Holker, Jr. (1745-1822), the son of a British emigré to France, came to Philadelphia during the American Revolution. He became the principal financial backer of the half-share in the *Empress of China* owned by Daniel Parker & Company, of which he was a partner. Portrait by Gilbert Stuart (1755-1828).

Dominica, had served as Lord Clive's aide-de-camp in India, and most recently had been a delegate to the Continental Congress. Despite his credentials, wealth, and subsequent entrepreneurial importance, he nonetheless, in opposition to Parker, was a soft-spoken, somewhat sickly visionary with fingers in an infinite variety of financial and land speculation pies. Walter Livingston, who formerly had been concerned with equipping and supplying the Northern Army, aided and abetted Duer in his various enterprises.[8]

In a postwar reorganization of Daniel Parker & Company (this time without Livingston), Parker and Duer added to the partnership during the late summer of 1783 the very same John Holker who was in partnership with Robert Morris. "I have very probably established another house in New York," Holker bragged to his father on September 4, 1783, having already explained the liaison with Morris, "on an equally respectable footing, under the house of Parker, Duer & Company, two merchants of the first reputation on the continent. . . ." With them during the past year he, too, had contracted supplies for the Continental Army as before he had done for the French Navy. The connection seemed to be a happy one. "These gentlemen," Holker continued in the original French, "acquitted themselves of it with great intelligence."[9]

Truly, a tightly woven fabric had begun to loom large in the initial formation of what one interested party appropriately, if inaccurately, referred to as "the American India Company".[10]

Although the precise timetable and detail of John Ledyard's fur scheme remains clouded, it is clear enough that the search for suitable vessels was begun during the summer of 1783 and that the onus of it devolved upon Daniel Parker & Company. Ledyard, presumably, was combing the Boston waterfront and the North and South Shores of Massachusetts for a suitable hull. Whether or not he was the one who actually found it is immaterial. Word has a way of leaking out very quickly about curious undertakings, and this was no exception.

On August 21, 1783, a Salem, Massachusetts, newspaper printed news of a rumor going the rounds. It was picked up and repeated three weeks later by the *Pennsylvania Packet* in Philadelphia.[11] "We hear," it read, "that a ship is fitting out at Boston for an intended voyage to China; that her cargo out, in money and goods will amount to 150,000 L. and that she will sail the ensueing fall. Many eminent merchants in different parts of the Continent are said to be interested in this first venture from the new world to the old."

Over the years, there have been those who have maintained that this news item concerned the sloop *Harriet* of Hingham, Massachusetts, owned by

7. "Second Street North from Market St. wth. Christ Church. Philadelphia." When John Ledyard arrived in Philadelphia from New York, armed with introductions to its leading merchants, he found the second largest English-speaking city in the world struggling to regain her prewar vitality. Engraving by William and Thomas Birch, 1799.

Colonel Sears of Boston, which sailed during the early winter of 1783-1784 with a cargo of ginseng destined for China. Upon reaching the Cape of Good Hope, the story has been told, the *Harriet*'s Captain Hallett encountered several officers of the British East India Company. They were so shocked at the thought of Yankee competition in China that to prevent it in this instance they bought the *Harriet*'s entire cargo for double its value in Hyson tea.[12]

But, no. The article *must* have referred to the vessel that would become the *Empress of China*, for no eighteenth-century newspaper editor would have written of a "ship" when the vessel was a "sloop." By no means could the *Harriet*'s cargo have been large enough to account for the £150,000 cited, nor were there "many eminent merchants in different parts of the Continent" concerned in her.

Daniel Parker himself explained the *Harriet*'s mission in a letter written the following February to Robert Morris. He had taken great pains to discover the price of ginseng in Europe, he told Morris, and "Colo Sears assures me that Mr. Loderstrom in Gottenburg wrote him in September last, that 10,000 lb weight would sell in that place at 8 dollars per pound, provided it arrived there before the 20th of February—the time when their Ships sailed for China, & he desired Colo Sears to purchase and Ship for their Joint a/c the above quantity. Colo Sears bot 9,000 lb, but not being able to Ship it from Boston before the 17th December last, he feared it would not arrive in time, in consequence of which he has sent the Vessel which is a Sloop of about 50 Tons to the Cape of Good Hope & there sell it [the ginseng] to the Ships bound to China."[13]

Obviously, despite local tradition to the contrary, Sears never intended to send a vessel to China at all and only decided at the last minute to dispose of the ginseng at Cape Town when the season had passed to assure its timely arrival in Sweden. The ship fitting out in Boston for a China voyage, therefore, could only have been the *Empress of China*, or, as she seems to have been called originally, the *Angelica*.

Over the years, too, claims have been made that she was a Baltimore privateer. She definitely was not. A "true Copy as Pr Record," signed by Nathaniel Barber, late Custom House Naval Officer for the port of Boston, and dated March 21, 1787, attests to the fact that the *Empress of China* was a square-sterned ship of 300 tons built at Boston in 1783. As of November 21, 1783, the date of the original registration certificate, her captain was John Green, and the owners were "Benj. Guild, Daniel Parker & others."[14] Guild and Parker had been involved in numerous joint business ventures before Parker had left Massachusetts.

It seems likely that the ship was bought by Daniel Parker & Company right off the stocks or that she had been recently launched but not finished or rigged. It is also probable that she had been intended for a swift-sailing letter of marque—a cargo-carrying privateer—but that the end of the war had thwarted the need for her and the owners had been prompted to sell out.

The *Empress of China*'s tonnage was, even then, reported variously: 360 tons, carpenter's measure, according to one of the supercargoes; 368¼ tons, by certificate of a later day when she was sailing under another name; 400 tons, according to Parker and the policy of insurance written on her; and 500 tons recorded in the sea-letter provided by the United States Congress. She had a square-stern, quarter-galleries, a woman figurehead, copper sheathing on the hull, and measured 104.2 feet in overall length, 28.4 feet in breadth, and had a draft of sixteen feet.[15]

"This Ship," Daniel Parker apprised the insurers shortly after her departure from New York, "is about four hundred Tons Burthen commanded by John Green, navigated by 42 Seamen & armed with 10 Nine Pounders &

4 Six Pound Cannon with Small arms, Cutlasses, Powder & Shot Sufficient for that number of Men. She was Built in Boston under the direction of the Celebrated Mr. Peck on a Model that is universally acknowledged in this Country, to be greatly superior to any other, both for fast Sailing & good Qualities as a Sea Boat; she is entirely New, Stout, Staunch & Strong—her Bottom was Coppered in Boston with great attention & Care & her Hull is as fully Strongly & Compleately finished as this country is capable of doing it—she has fine Cables & Anchors, her Standing & Running Rigging new & good with a great Quantity of spare Rigging of all Sizes on board, fully Sufficient & Suitable for a Compleat set of standing & running Rigging. She has two new Suits of Sails compleat & 14 Bolts of Duck of Different Qualities and 5 Months water and 14 Month Provisions for her Crew with a good Surgeon who is supplied with every Article required by him and she is as fully & amply equipped as can be necessary for a Vessell bound on any Voyage whatever."[16]

The "celebrated Mr. Peck" was John Peck (1725-1790) of Boston, who frequently has been described as "the first American naval architect" at a time when formal, drafted plans for a vessel were more the exception than the rule and ships were designed by the old-fashioned eyeball method which relied on the master shipwright's experience, intuition, and sense of proportion.

Something of an enigma in his own time, John Peck is hardly less so two hundred years later. He was the son of a Boston glazier, and at a tender age was sent to a "Mathematical School," where he developed an interest in ship design. Later, he entered the employ of a merchant and performed several voyages as a "supercargo," the owners' business representative afloat. Then he went into business as an apothecary-grocer, but the design of ships continued as a hobby. There being no one within reach to teach him the rudiments of either drafting or of the established conventions for rendering a vessel's lines on paper, he developed his own methods, methods barely intelligible to Peck himself as he grew older and more sophisticated. According to his son, Peck had never seen a ship's draft when he began his labors, and the only book on naval architecture he possessed during his entire life was the 1711 edition of William Sutherland's *The Shipbuilder's Assistant*. "This gentleman," his obituary notice pointed out, "after a long series of study and application, reduced naval architecture to system and science, founded on philosophick principles."[17]

To Francisco de Miranda, a traveling Venezuelan and son of a prosperous Caracas linen merchant, we owe a somewhat greater knowledge of Peck's "philosophick principles." Miranda spoke with him at length on the twentieth of October 1784.

"This morning I had Mr. Peck's visit," he recorded in his Spanish language diary, "and we had a long talk about his new plan of construction, a section of which was sketched by him on the margin of my table. His principles are practical and scientifical as well. The form, said this ingenious artist, is the principal feature of a vessel. One sees that a whale, after death, and therefore without movement in itself, when a strong gale is blowing, the boats that are towing it are compelled to cut the cable for fear of capsizing with the violence with which they are dragged along. The dead body of the whale is dragging them along, notwithstanding the boats are of the strongest construction. In modern construction vessels are made thin at the bows, and the keel in the interior forms a multitude of inflected curves not to be found in the works of Nature, particularly in fishes; consequently, there must be the same adaptability to the body of a vessel, &c. This is the main thesis of his theory and which, I confess, caused an impression on me superior to all others on this subject. When this artist, after infinite opposition, constructed his first vessel in Boston, the people called it 'Peck's Folly,' until they saw by their own eyes that it would not capsize by the force of the wind, as their narrow intelligence taught them. This construction unites advantages which other constructors and all others in general believed incompatible, that is, not only being the best sailers known, they also load more than other vessels of the same tonnage, and they have less balance than those of other construction. He already has constructed seven vessels since the [beginning of] the last war, each one better than its predecessor. I have seen two which are the *Empress of China*, belonging to Mr. Parker of New York, and she sailed for China; and the *Leda*, of Mr. Swan, in this city [Portsmouth, New Hampshire]. They both reunite all the qualities that I am mentioning."[18]

The model upon which the *Empress of China* was based, mentioned by Parker in his letter to the insurers, was "the Model of the Ship *Bellisarius*, which ship was acknowledged to be the fastest Sailing Ship in the [British] Navy. . . ."[19] Not to be confused with a vessel of the same name owned by George Crowninshield & Sons of Salem, Massachusetts, and built there in 1794, John Peck's *Bellisarius* had been built by Mr. Paul in Plymouth, Massachusetts, as a privateer during the Revolution. That she wound up as a twenty-gun ship in the Royal Navy was through no fault of her designer or of her sailing abilities: in 1781 she had been sent to sea without sweeps and had been captured during a calm. So innovative had she been that Philadelphia's leading ship designer, Joshua Humphreys, who became the

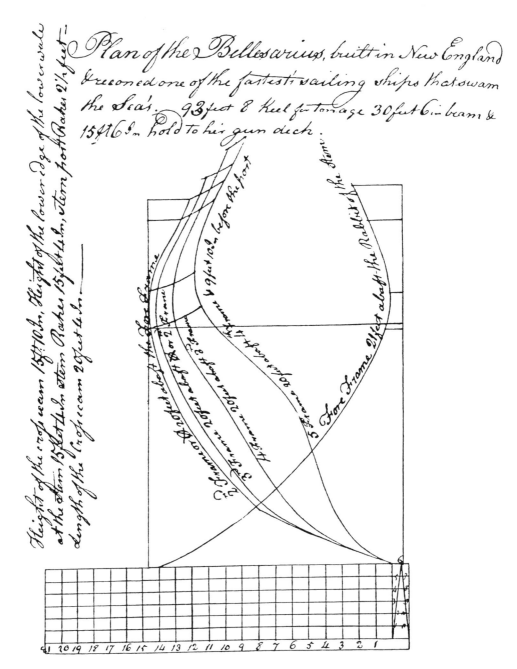

8. The ship *Bellisarius*, designed by John Peck of Boston, was Peck's own model for the *Empress of China*. Joshua Humphreys of Philadelphia, the first United States Naval Constructor, obtained her lines and copied them into one of his workbooks, from which this illustration derives.

United States' first Naval Constructor, got hold of a draft of her lines and copied them into one of his workbooks. The *Bellisarius*, he remarked, had been "rec[k]oned one of the fastest sailing ships that swam the Seas" and measured 93′8″ on the keel for the determination of tonnage, 30′6″ beam, and 15′6″ depth of hold to the underside of the gundeck.[20]

The *Empress of China* was by no means the only vessel to concern Parker & Company during the autumn of 1783, for John Ledyard's fur adventure required three: one to sail directly to Canton and the others to go first to the Northwest Coast for sea otter pelts. Seven others occupied their attention throughout the latter months: the *Bourbon*, authorized in 1777 by the Continental Congress to be built as a twenty-eight-gun frigate for the Continental Navy but not launched until midsummer 1783 and so sold out; the ship *Comte d'Artois*, a large Frenchman acquired in New London, Connecticut; the ship *Columbia*; the *Contractor*; and three whaling vessels.[21] It appears from the evidence available that the *Empress of China*, the *Bourbon*, the *Comte d'Artois*, and the *Columbia* were the four from which the China traders would be chosen, yet throughout the autumn of 1783 their respective roles remained airborne like a juggler's apples and oranges.

In an attempt to commit the Boston merchants to their one-third share in the enterprise, Daniel Parker had written during the last week of September to James Swan, urging him and the others around him to begin providing their share of the capital. Available monies and lines of credit had shriveled almost to nothing. A native of Fifeshire, Scotland, Swan had been a participant in the Boston Tea Party, had been twice wounded at the Battle of Bunker Hill, held various posts around town including that of adjutant-general of the Commonwealth, and lived very well on his wife's inheritance. In him, Parker saw someone who could help to bail out a venture at the brink of stumbling.

"I recd your favor 26th Ulto," Swan replied on the fourth of October, "and am very willing to hold the third allotted me in the Ships to Canton, provided I can raise the money either by a loan in the Bank or from my debtors—the latter, altho' very numerous & large Sums yet can't be come at speedily. I am still of the mind, that your Ship here [the *Empress of China*] is best calculated for the first plan of the South Sea after Furrs & that the *Bourbon*, with the *Count de Artoise*, since the *Hague* would not answer, will be the best, since they will fetch so much more Tea than the *Angelica*, & that ought to be our principal stay.[22] Would not one Ship do (the *Bourbon*) to go directly to Canton & the Furrman to follow,—This will be a sufficient entering wedge, & if it suits, shall then go largely into it next year? This only for your consideration, and I should think too, would be sufficient for the Continental supply, especially as many India Goods will be introduced, indeed I know it personally thro the Island of St Helena & Assention, by Whalemen, taken out of Indiamen stopping there.

"I am very sick," he told Parker, "Therefore propose meeting you at Newport on Fryday the 17th Instant—and if the Wind be contrary, pray you to take horse and come by land—Would meet you at New London, but the D[oct]or will not let me ride, & very nearly you can get to N'wport as quick as to the other. Shall then bring loan office notes to the Amount I want to borrow, for you to get the loan for me for 60 days—I'll renew it myself or get Nesbit & Co to do it, provided I don't pay it. Do use every exertion in getting the *Bourbon* ready—The *d'Artoise* can soon [go]. It is nearly time they were gone. In all Trades the Ship here ought to be deck'd & her Guns carried on the uppermost—say light Brass pieces."[23]

No matter which of these vessels ultimately would be deemed the most fit and appropriate for the direct passage to Canton, a cargo had to be assembled for her in the meantime. The process was to consume much of the late summer of 1783 and most of the autumn. There was not much in the United States of value to the Chinese. To find an article of trade, the China venturers took to the woods.

III

In Search
of the *Panax quinquefolia*

"We are in want of 10,000 lb. Ginseng," Daniel Parker apprised Philadelphia's Messrs. Turnbull, Marmie & Company on August 28, 1783, "which we are informed may be had with you. We therefore request you to procure that Quantity if to be had at your Market, or to adopt such Measures for obtain'g it, as shall appear most Eligible. We pray your Exertions to procure this Article as it is a matter of great moment to us."[1]

The importance of ginseng was incalculable indeed; in fact, by the time the *Empress of China* sailed, almost thirty tons of it would have been procured. It was no simple task. Ginseng was not cultivated; it grew naturally on northern and eastern mountain slopes and deep in the rich, shady soil of backcountry hardwood forests.

Why ginseng? The choice of it for the major portion of the ship's cargo was hardly accidental, because the dried root of the *Panax quinquefolia*, as both the English and the French had discovered three-quarters of a century before, was one of the few products of the New World for which the Chinese seemed to have an insatiable appetite. Until a sufficient quantity of sea otter pelts and other furs could be accumulated on the Northwest Coast there was little else from America useful as a medium of trade at Canton.[2] No market existed there for salt fish, rum, flour, barrel staves or lumber as did in many other parts of the world. And, in a novel, untried speculation like this, other alternatives such as edible sea slugs from the Fijis and sandalwood from the Hawaiian Islands, were not yet known.

31

9. William Turnbull (1751-1822), born in Scotland, became a partner in the Philadelphia house of Turnbull, Marmie & Company, which was instrumental in obtaining the thirty tons of Western Pennsylvania and Virginia ginseng shipped to Canton in the *Empress of China*. Portrait by Rembrandt Peale (1778-1860).

Ginseng, remarked *The Chinese Repository* a number of years later, "is obtained in Tartary, and also in America, from which latter country it is exported to China. It is generally considered by the Chinese physicians as a panacea. All the ginseng growing in Tartary is the property of the emperor, and he sells a quantity yearly to his faithful subjects, who have the privilege to purchase it at its weight in gold! Enormous quantities are consumed by the Chinese who consider no medicine good, if this not be a constituent. The roots are about the size and length of a man's little finger, and when chewed have a mucilaginous sweetness; and, if good, will snap when broken. They should be sound, firm and free of worm holes. The Chinese consider that which comes from Tartary to be the best, even when they can see no difference. When first brought from America"—in the *Empress of China* and the vessels following her—"the profits were 500 or 600 per cent."[3]

For the ordinary Chinaman who had no access to the emperor's coveted supply, American ginseng was the next best thing. It was believed to soothe nerve irritation, improve the workings of the brain, and cure either high blood pressure or low. It lengthened life, aided the diabetic, strengthened the blood, and cleared up boils, pimples, or rashes. Appetites were promoted by its ingestion and digestive complaints cured. Ginseng, Chinese doctors were convinced, remedied anemia, dysentery, malaria, cancer, sciatica, and lumbago. It was recommended to stop dizziness and relieve headache, to restore serenity, retard senility, and stimulate sexual passion. In short, there was little the root was incapable of achieving.[4]

It seemed for a time that ginseng was not only a panacea for bodily imperfections but also for business. The March 1790 issue of *The American Museum* predicted its enduring value: "It was generally supposed that forty or fifty peculs [about 600 pounds, averaged] were equal to the annual consumption [in China]. Experience has proved the contrary. Upwards of four hundred and forty peculs [58,665 pounds] were carried thither by the first American ship in 1784, which did not equal the quantity brought from Europe [via North America] the same season, the greater part of which must have been previously sent thither by citizens of the United States. In 1786, more than one thousand eight hundred peculs [240,000 pounds] were sold there, one half of which was carried in American vessels. Notwithstanding this increased quantity, the sales were not materially affected: and it is probable there will always be a sufficient demand for this article, to make it equally valuable."[5]

Unfortunately, the native supply was not inexhaustible. At approximately one-half ounce per cured root, the number of roots carried by the *Empress*

I[1333]

PANAX QUINQUEFOLIA. FIVE-LEAVED
PANAX OR GINSENG.
****
Class and Order.
POLYGAMIA DIŒCIA. (PENTANDRIA DIGYNIA Persoon).
Generic Character.
Cal. 5-dentatus. Cor. 5-petala. Bacca infera, cordata, 2-fperma.
Cal. in flore mafculo integer.
Specific Character and Synonyms.
PANAX quinquefolia; foliis ternis: foliolis quinis petiolatis,
pedunculo petiolis breviore, radice fufiformi.
PANAX quinquefolium; foliis ternis quinatis. Sp. Pl. 1512.
Reick. 4. p. 362. Kalm. it. 3. p. 334. Blackw. t. 513.
Regn. Bot. Zorn ic. 155. Woodv. Med. Bot. 270. t. 99.
Gron. Fl. Virg. 35. ed. 2d. 162. Mart. Mill. Dict.
PANAX quinquefolium; caule herbaceo, foliis ternis, foliolis
quinis ovalibus acuminatis petiolatis. Michaux Fl.
Bor-Amer. 2. p. 256. Persoon Syn. 1. p. 298.
GINSENG. Jartoux; Lettres edifiantes et curieuses, v. 10. p.
172. Philofoph. Tranf. v. 28. p. 237. t. 5.
AURELIANA canadenfis, Lafiteau Ginf. p. 87. c. tab. Catefb.
Carol. app. t. 16. Breyn. Prod. pl. 2. p. 35. t. ad. p. 52.
ARALIASTRUM, Quinquefolii folio; majus, Ninzin vocatum
D. Sarrazin. Vaill. ferm. 43.
ARALIASTRUM foliis ternis quinquepartitis, Ginfeng f.
Ninfen officinarum. Trew Ehret. t. 6. f. 1.

GINSENG has been a famous remedy among the Chinefe
from time immemorial; it is underftood however to be
found only in Chinefe Tartary. In the year 1709 Father
JARTOUX, a miffionary at Peking, was fent by the Emperor
of China to make a map of that country. Whilft engaged in
this bufinefs he fell in with an army of Tartars who were employed in collecting this highly valued root for the emperor;
which gave him an opportunity of defcribing and making a
drawing of the plant, and tranfmitting the fame to Paris, in a
letter to the procurator-general of the miffions of India and
China; a tranflation of which was publifhed in the 28th vol.
of the Philofophical Tranfactions.
JARTOUX fays that the Ginfeng is found between the thirty-
ninth and forty-feventh degree north latitude, where there is
a long tract of mountains covered with wood. It grows on
the declivities of the mountains, on the banks of the torrents,
and

10. Ginseng (*Panax quinquefolia*) as illustrated and described in John Sims,
ed., *Curtis's Botanical Magazine* (London, 1811), vol. 33.

of China on her first voyage alone must have approached two million spec-
imens.

The presence of ginseng growing wild in North America was first noted
in 1717 by Father Joseph Francis Lafitau, a missionary among the Iroquois
Indians, who began looking for it following the suggestion by Jesuit Father
Jartoux in China that a species of ginseng might possibly be found in Canada.
"After spending three months looking for the ginseng," Father Lafitau wrote,
"by accident I found it. It was ripe, and the color of the fruit attracted my
attention. I pulled it up, and with joy took it to an Indian I had engaged to
help me hunt for it. She recognized it at once as one of the plants the Indians
used" in their medicine.[6]

Within three years, a company was formed to gather, cure, and ship the Canadian ginseng, through France, to China. For a time, it was an article of trade surpassed only by pelts. For the backwoodsman, frontiersman, itinerant peddler, and friendly Indian in need of staple products or manufactured goods, ginseng was as good, or better, than currency. "The sang diggers," reported one authority on the subject, "go into the woods with a small mattock, a sack and a lunch and the hunt for the valuable plant begins. Ginseng usually grows in patches. This is not because the plant is by nature a bedding plant but for the reason that the seeds fall near the parent plant . . . In the early days, hunters found very large patches where for hundreds of years the parent plant and its progeny had increased without molestation. Sometimes as high as one hundred pounds of root would be secured from one such plot. Women as well as men and boys hunt for the root. The plant is well known to all mountain lads and lasses and few are the mountain cabins that have no ginseng in them waiting for market."[7] Migratory buyers worked their way through the deep country from Indian village to trapper's shack to valley farmhouse buying whatever the people had collected.

Peter Kalm, the Swedish botanist who traveled through parts of North America during mid-eighteenth century, described how it was prepared for sale. The freshly dug roots, he recorded, "are spread on the floor to dry,

11. Young ginseng roots. After several years, the roots become thick and gnarled, assuming a humanoid shape, a fact which fostered the belief that the root was an aphrodisiac and panacea without equal.

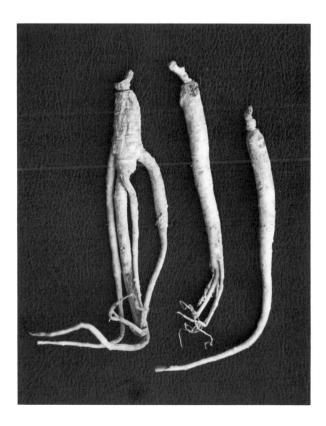

which commonly requires two months or more, according as the season is wet or dry. During that time they must be turned once or twice every day, lest they should spoil or moulder."[8] The root, one trader cautioned, should be taken from the ground during the month of September, and no later than the beginning of October, because the juice is then in the plant and the root will be free from unsightly wrinkles. In order to keep shipments pure, the harvested roots must also be subjected to "garbling"—picking them over to remove earth, pebbles, and other extraneous rubbish.[9]

If the estimated time for the China ship to depart American waters had been planned for the first several weeks of the new year 1784, as seems to have been the case, then Daniel Parker had initiated the quest for ginseng only in the nick of time. The harvesting season was nearly at hand. In the meantime, his investigations of its commercial value abroad had resulted in contact with Colonel Sears of Boston, whose sloop *Harriet* would take a load as far as the Cape of Good Hope. Sears, he advised Robert Morris later, "as well as others who have had advices from Europe on this Subject, are very Sanguine that it will command a *very* great price in China, provided the Quality is good & to this end, I have caused the Quantity Shiped in the *Empress* to be very carefully inspected & have detained a considerable Quantity of Inferior quality, lest the Sales of the good, should be affected by it."[10]

Turnbull, Marmie & Company, having received Parker's ginseng order of August 28, 1783, lost no time. Recruited for the arduous journey into the remote hinterlands of the country to search out the supply was a thirty-three-year-old doctor named Robert Johnston.

Johnston, described by a contemporary as "a Man possessing a very Noble and Philanthropic mind," had been born near Greencastle, Pennsylvania, and graduated in 1770 from the College of Philadelphia (afterwards known as the University of Pennsylvania). His medical education completed in England, he returned to the colonies and set up a practice in the Conococheague Valley of Pennsylvania until the Revolutionary War found him Surgeon of the Sixth Pennsylvania Battalion. In 1781, he was ordered to leave the regimental service and to assist the wounded of the American army who were prisoners of war in the British hospital at Charleston, South Carolina. Johnston was a member of the Society of the Cincinnati and was destined to become the surgeon of the *Empress of China*.[11]

On September 3, 1783, Johnston received one thousand dollars from Turnbull, Marmie & Company, on account of Daniel Parker & Company, and that day started out from Philadelphia "with full directions regarding his embassy" and expectations of being heard from again after his arrival at

12. Map of the interior regions of Pennsylvania and Virginia illustrating the travels of
Dr. Robert Johnston during his quest for the *Empress of China*'s ginseng cargo.

Fort Pitt in about a week's time.[12] On the twelfth, however, he arrived at
Bath Town and the following day reported back to Philadelphia. "After a
most tiresome Journey across the Frontier of Pennsylvania," he wrote, "yesterday I arrived at Bath in Virginia: as yet my success has not been equal to
my Expectations. I have not been able to procure more than 400 weight of
Ginseng on my way to this Place for which I gave 3s/9d pr. lb.

"I have adopted such Measures as I think will secure all that may come down from the back woods between this & the 1st of Novr at the same rate.

"I am informed that large Quantities has passed on to Baltimore & Alexandria within this Month. I would advise you to employ some Person to secure that which may have gone to those Places: I fear it will not be in my power to provide the Quantity wanted, the Season being so far advanced.

"I have got the promise of 2000 weight to be delivered to me in Cumberland on or before the 14th of October at 3s/9d p lb. Also I am promised about 1500 weight to be delivered at this place for 3s per lb. I will want about Two Thousand Dollars in Cash on or before the 14th of Octr.

"I have a Brother in the Assembly (Col. James Johnston) to whom I have wrote & enclosed an Order in his Favor . . . for Two Thousand Dollars which Sum if you can give to him in Gold there will be no doubt of my getting it safe, in proper time—He will deliver you this letter. Bank Notes will not do in these parts. I have got 500 Dollars of them. The Country People will not receive them, neither can I get Store keepers to exchange them. Tomorrow I set out for Stantown [Staunton] & Augusta, where I am informed large Quantities of Ginseng has been sent from the Frontier parts of this State."[13] Johnston was in the heart of the Appalachian Mountains, the perfect environment for virgin ginseng growth.

Notwithstanding the tedious nature of his business and the formidable distances he was obliged to travel through wilderness and sparsely settled regions, Dr. Robert Johnston returned to Philadelphia on September 30 and paused to report to Turnbull, Marmie & Company before pushing on to confer with Daniel Parker in New York. His brother, Colonel James, had the day before received £740.11.0, the equivalent of the two thousand dollars required to honor the commitments in Bath Town and Cumberland.[14]

"You will receive this by Doctor Johnston," Turnbull, Marmie wrote on the thirteenth to Parker, "who arrived here to day from his Tower [tour] into the back parts of this State and Virginia, and believe he has been very diligent in accomplishing the commission he was sent on. We received a letter from the Doctor a day or two ago directing us to forward him Two Thousand Dollars by his Brother, which was complyed with and his Brother left this [Philadelphia] early in the morning.

"The Doctor will make you acquainted of his success, and as we should have been under the necessity of sending an Express, the Doctor thought it would answer as well to proceed himself, as the Bank has found it necessary to lessen their discounts—it has occasioned some difficulty to us to accomplish the last Two Thousand Dollars that was sent to the Doctor, obliges us to make you acquainted with this circumstance. Mr Holker is at present out of Town for some days and Mr Morris could not supply us with the sum the Doctor will want for his engagements. . . ."[15]

Although not yet clearly felt by most of the participants, the last lament inadvertently forecast the squally financial climate that increasingly came to threaten the China venture: in dispensing credit or operating cash, John Holker was the most liberal, Robert Morris tended to be stingy, and Daniel Parker, according to himself, at least, was nearly penniless.

Dr. Robert Johnston was indefatigable. Fresh from a month of gruelling travel in almost inaccessible regions of the interior, he departed almost immediately for New York and then returned to Philadelphia by the eighth of October, only once more to set off for remote regions of Virginia.[16] At Fredericksburg, he paused on October 13 to deliver from Parker instructions to the firm of Callender & Henderson. The urgency of securing a sufficiency of ginseng had grown more acute as the season advanced. Johnston had even offered a dramatic increase in price.

"We yesterday received from our friend Daniel Parker," the Fredericksburg agents informed Turnbull, Marmie & Company, "directions of purchasing a quantity of Ginsang and to draw on your House for the amount. We have already (from his former letters) 7000 or 8000 wt and it will be Ship'd for New York by the last of this week. We have also contracted for about as much more."[17]

Had Callender & Henderson been informed of the actual quantities required when their representative had been in Philadelphia, they continued, "the whole might have been procured before this and at a much earlier date, for Doctor Johnstons coming here and offering 4/3p. lb has been the means of Raising the price all over the Country. We have Just purchased of Mr Brownlow 3000 lb @ 3/9, the same Ginsang that the doctr offered 4/3 for. If we cou'd have had two months notice this article cou'd have been bought at 2/6 or 2/9 at most. All we have purchas'd except the 3000 of Brownlow is @ 3/6.

"Mr Parker writes that it must be entirely Clear of all Fibres & burls but this is Impossible except we pick it over after purchasing but will get it as Clean as possible. We have drawn on you of this date at 20 days Sight, in favor of John Brownlow for Eighteen hundred Seventy five Dollars it being for 3000 lb of Ginsang purchas'd of him.

"My Partner Mr Henderson will be with you in a day or two after the Receipt of this. He can give every information respecting this Article . . . and if you can wait until Xmas we can procure a large quantity of Ginsang."

Two days later, October 16, 1783, Dr. Robert Johnston was writing to Turnbull, Marmie & Company from his home in Conococheague, near Antrim, Pennsylvania: "The Bearer of this Mr Jas Shansy has about 300 lb of Ginseng which he has promised to let you have at the Market Price & take Goods—He offered it to me @ 5s/- per lb. I would not give it on account of the Precident in this Settlement. Mr Shanasy is a Gentleman of Landed property, a Store Keeper in this Settlement of Repute & very worthy of Credit.

"My prospects are good: I think I can count on at least 8000 lb this trip. It will not cost more than 4s/6d in Baltimore. I received the Cash which you sent me By my Brother. I will be under the necessity of drawing on you when I return to Baltimore, which I expect will be in another ten days."[18]

True to his prediction, Johnston's laborious travels brought him to Baltimore on October 27. The next morning, he brought Turnbull, Marmie & Company up to date: "I arrived in this Town Yesterday Evening from the back part of Virginia—in my last jaunt I have secured about 14,000 weight of the best Ginseng which I have seen: It has cost me from 3s/9d to 5s/- per lb. delivered in this Town." Its delivery in Baltimore was to be expected before the tenth of November; at least $5,000 would be needed within the next two weeks to pay for it. "From some Conversation with Mr Pringle," Johnston went on, "I apprehend great difficulty in raising the above Sum in this Town on Bills, the Cash being so scarce. At Winchester I drew on you for £63.13.9 in favour of Mr Willm Baker of this Town. I beg you to write me next Post & let me know when you think the Ship will be ready to sail."[19]

Cash was virtually nonexistent. Neither was it forthcoming. By November 11, Johnston was becoming alarmed. "You cannot conceive," he wrote to Turnbull, Marmie, "how much I am distressed for want of Cash: Ginseng is coming on dayly & I am engaging it on Credit. I expected to have been supplied with Cash before now. Mr Pringle has been so obliging as to borrow Money for me, for which he has been this day denied. Messrs McEldrie & McHendrie has been so good as to advance Cash & Goods to the Amount of Three Hundred & Twenty nine Pounds 1s/4d: for which sum they have this Evening called upon me for the cash or a Bill on you. Mr McEldrie being under the necessity of going to New York Tomorrow Morning, therefore I have taken the liberty of drawing upon you for £327.1.4 payable ten Days after sight, it being the longest time they would allow.

"This day Mr Pringle has chartered a Vessel which will set out next Sunday with 60 or 70 Hogsheads of Ginseng for New York."[20] The delay in receiving the cash was causing "great Uneasiness." Unless it arrived soon, he would have to stop purchasing "as not only my own but my Friends Credit is likely to suffer." Three or four other Baltimore purchasers of ginseng had already tried to outbid him by offering five shillings sixpence the pound weight to his inflated five.

To Parker in New York he wrote one week later. "I can with propriety keep up the price in this Town so long as I can Stay here by purchasing a few pounds of the first quality—this much I advertize that I will give six Shillings p. lb for ginseng & the first quallity, I know it will produce the desired effect. This day the Schooner *Betsy* Captn Blunt will sail for New York with fifty four Hhds, nine Bbls & four Cases Ginsang. The cases are all marked & numbered in amount as to distinguish the quallity—all that are marked thus # are of the first quality, # of the second, # the third, X that of the most inferior—my time would not admit of the separation notwithstanding there is a very great difference between each class—there may be many good roots picked from the worst Classes—I thought there would be no possibility of selling off in Cases if picked as Close—There will remain about 10,000 lb when I receive all that I have contracted for, the last of which will be in this week—I flatter myself altho I gave some people who I contracted with until the first of next month agreeable to your former instructions—immediately on receipt of your last letter I wrote to every person in the back Country employed by me to receive ginsang on my account to [   ] they were limited to 4/6 per lb and to deliver it in this Town before the first next month—there are a company in this Town who have given 5/6 per lb which I rejected before—I am informed they buy for a company lately formed in Phila. Shall I sell to them, or Shall I send what yet remains to New York, there will sail a Vessel for that port the last of next Week— Should I not hear from you before that I will Ship what remains to that place—inclosed you have an invoice of what I have put on Board the *Betsy*, there is one Hhd of Snake root marked R.S.V. which I was obliged to take with a quantity of ginsang, at 3/8 per lb. If you think it will not answer to Ship I beg you will sell it to the best advantage there are three or four Bbl &ca marked R.E. dried Apples &ca for Sea Stores—the large cask no. 56.501 & the nine Bbls were put in on accounts of Stowage they were not sorted. I have had them opened the root appears very good I will not have time to get what comes in now properly sorted the quallity in general better than what I have now sent that from the Vicinity of Pitts. . . ."[21]

Between mid-November and mid-December 1783, more than thirty tons of Virginia and Western Pennsylvania ginseng had been shipped to New

York aboard the coasting vessels *Betsy*, Captain Blunt; *Brothers*, Captain Whiting; *Sally*, Captain Killum; and *Black Duck*, James Morgan; insured by Parker's order between Baltimore and New York by payment of a two percent premium. Smaller, additional quantities were acquired wherever found, including six hogsheads weighing 2020 pounds from Dr. Benjamin Parker, Daniel's brother.

When all was said and done and the amassed supply had been picked over, 242 casks weighing 57,687 pounds of root remained ready for shipment to China. Its purchase was dear. In terms of the times, approximately one percent of the ginseng's cost would have had its equivalent in a one-way passage by ship for one person from New York to London.[22]

Despite Daniel Parker's habitual cheery overexaggeration, his optimistic outlook about sales of the ginseng in China was excusable and, no doubt, warranted: "We feel ourselves warranted," he echoed, "to assert that no part of this Business is estimated upon uncertainty except the Sales in China, which are very far below the prices Current at that Market by the latest & best Information, especially in the Article of Ginseng, which from the great difficulty that has attended the extraction of it from America, for Several Years past, hath increased the Value of that root to Fifteen Dollars per pound, these accounts we have received from London, Gottenburgh & Lisbon and thro' such channells as renders them authentic, but we have grounded our estimate on the most Substantial Basis, in that of the Price actually paid by the Companys of England & Sweden for the Two Years last past, Twenty Shillings Sterling per pound was the price current paid in London in the year 1782, to this price the charges of Inspecting and Shipping are to be added which cannot be less than Five Shillings & Six pence per pound from Gottenburgh & Ostend it was shipd at a much higher price & as we have every reason to suppose that our Ship will be in China some months before any of the European Ships with that Article, it is very just to suppose that she will arrive at a great market."[23]

About the time the last ladings of ginseng were being received in New York, the "*Queen of China*," as Turnbull, Marmie & Company was wont to call her in the beginning, arrived there as well after a tempestuous fifteen-day passage from Boston, battered by the blizzard of November 28 and 29, but safe.[24]

IV

Shedding the Fur Scheme

John Ledyard's Northwest Coast fur scheme gradually, but inexorably, fell apart. The exact causes cannot be defined precisely, yet one thing is certain: it probably was doomed to failure almost from the very beginning. Its demise clearly was speeded by worsening economic times and second thoughts about prosecuting such a grandiose plan without first testing the waters on a simpler scale. There can be no doubt that it suffered severely from the delays in outfitting the vessels and an apparent inability on the part of Daniel Parker to marshal his forces decisively or effectively. The emergence of wounded feelings, uncertainties, and philosophical rifts among some of the partners dealt it a body blow. The failure of the Boston consortium to come forward with its third share—obliging Robert Morris to assume a full half interest and John Holker, William Duer, and Daniel Parker the other half—finished off the pipe dream about furs once and for all.

That John Ledyard finally threw up his hands in frustrated despair is hardly surprising. For a time, perhaps, he may have continued to harbor faint hopes that, even if the present season had passed, the plan might be resurrected the following spring. But, when the time came, so much evidence of wheeling and dealing and outright dishonesty surrounded the *Empress of China*'s autumnal outfitting that there was scant interest left in what "the mad, romantic, dreaming Ledyard" continued to propound. Several of the owners, furthermore, by that time had ceased speaking to each other and another was at the threshold of fugitive flight.

Thus, in June 1784, while the *Empress of China* was thrashing her way eastward through the Indian Ocean, Ledyard decamped for Europe. In Paris, he eventually befriended Thomas Jefferson, who succeeded Benjamin Franklin in 1785 as United States minister to France, and the redoubtable John Paul Jones, in Europe attempting to collect prize monies for enemy vessels captured and sent into port for condemnation during the war. Both men offered encouragement, but each time Ledyard's aspirations seemed to be on the brink of fulfillment they were dashed. Finally, in a mad gesture, he proposed to walk across Siberia, find a vessel at the far side to carry him over the Bering Sea, hike down to Nootka Sound and then traipse the length of the North American continent to Virginia.[1] The Empress Catherine, however, took a dim view of what she took to be a foreign reconnaissance of her Russian fur operations and ordered his arrest. "Apart from his having been once with Cook," one noted historian has harshly remarked, "his chief claim to fame seems to be the fact that he was probably the first American citizen deported from Russia for spying."[2] Ledyard died at Cairo in 1789 from the aftereffects of a violent rage into which he flew when the departure of the caravan scheduled to guide him towards the darkest interior of Africa was unexpectedly delayed.

His idea of the Northwest Coast-Canton link had great merit, but 1783 was just too early a date for it to be fully embraced in the United States. An expedition with many similarities of purpose was, indeed, mounted by a group of merchants in Bombay, India, in 1785, but it remained for others in Boston a few years later truly to open the way for Americans to "New Albion" and the nutrient ground for several thriving financial empires Ledyard had so correctly predicted.[3]

Exactly when the fur proposal began to implode cannot now be determined, but it had to have been sometime during the last several months of 1783. By late summer, the *dramatis personae* for the ships themselves was beginning to assemble. One early member of the cast was William Duer, who, as a partner of Daniel Parker & Company, expected to go along as principal supercargo and attend to the firm's business affairs afloat. Duer, Parker informed John Holker in Philadelphia on September 16, 1783, "is very unwell not able at present to attend to any Business what ever. I think by attention to himself which he is now resolved on that he will in a short Time be in health—he will go to China & is pleased with the plan—pray request Mr. Morris to answer my Letter to him Respecting the Ship for the Furr Trade if he has not already done it."[4] Duer was *not* pleased with the plan—far from it—and with each passing day became more and more disenchanted by the way it was moving. Parker was exaggerating for private purposes best known to himself.

Second supercargo under him was to be twenty-nine-year-old Major Samuel Shaw of Boston, who had served in the war since 1775 and from June 1782 to November 1783 had been aide-de-camp to Major General Henry Knox, one of the highest ranking officers in the Continental Army next to George Washington himself, and in civilian life a former Boston bookseller. Shaw was Secretary of the committee of officers which organized the Society of the Cincinnati and was instrumental, with Knox, in the disbandment of

13. Major Samuel Shaw (1754-1794), a former officer of the Continental Army and aide-de-camp of Major General Henry Knox, became the principal supercargo (businessman afloat) of the *Empress of China*. Shaw traveled to the Orient four times and was the United States' first consul at Canton. Engraving by J. Andrews after J. Johnston.

the Army.[5] But, by November 9, 1783, he had become totally disillusioned by the prospect of making a China voyage. It had turned into something far removed from what he had understood at the beginning. "I don't go to China," he wrote that day from West Point to his comrade, Major Winthrop Sargent of Gloucester, Massachusetts, "—*Parturiuntmontes, nasutus mus* ['The mountains are giving birth to an absurd mouse']—The intended voyage has been so altered that it scarcely retains an original feature. It is now barely an object for a single gentleman, and [Thomas] Randall goes second to Duer, merely because he has at present no prospect more promising. Your baggage is still here, owing to my having been absent to Philadelphia five weeks, under the idea that I should have been gone only eight days. . . ."[6]

William Duer's aggravation, not only about the planning of the voyage but also about his own part in it, was expressed with complete candor to his friend and Philadelphia partner, John Holker. Duer was not one of the more forceful personalities in the proceedings, but he was not lacking in opinions. "I transmit you a Copy of a Paper transmitted not long since from France to a Gentleman in this Country, and Communicated to me Confidentially by a Friend—I have Every Reason to think the Authenticity of the Intelligence may be depended on—You will see that the Golden prospects of Ginseng and Furs are by this Intelligence much obscur'd—With Respect to the Ship destined for the NW: Voyage: I am Convinced, the Season for Cape Horn is past, and that the Ship is not of Sufficient Strength for the Adventure—And if the Concern (in Spite of all the Reasons which can be offered for a Preference to the Passage at this Season by the Cape of Good Hope) for the two Ships destined immediately for Canton, persist in the first Route I must decline going—for the State of my affairs and that of a Young Family will not justify me in adding a dangerous Experiment in Navigation, to one of Commerce. It is in vain to reason with Mr Parker on this Subject, as well as some other Matters of Importance to the Success of the Adventure.

"I must, my dear Friend, Confess to you that the Treatment I have received from some of the Parties makes me Undertake the Voyage with rather a heavy heart—Nothing but a Conviction that if matters are properly arranged it would prove of great Benefit both to you & myself would Induce me to Undertake it—The Same Influence of GM [Gouverneur Morris?] and D:P: [Daniel Parker] which is working against me (and I am sure from the same Motives in General,) will be constantly operating—You on my Return would be absent, and if for Want of proper Arrangements to Secure a Right to Trade at Canton, the Ships Should Return without a Cargoe, Ill Success would be Imputed to me and you and RM: [Robert Morris] would be censured for Suffering an ill founded attachment to determine your Choice of me as principal agent—The Confidence of all Parties appears to me absolutely Essential to the Trust reposed.

"I must, my dear Friend, Entreat you to consider candidly the Situation I am placed in—My acceptance of the Trust, after the Steps taken by the Parties, appears to me like offering myself in the Concern, merely in the Love of having some Information on the Plan of Business—My feelings are distrest beyond all you can Conceive—How would you, my dear Friend, act under such Circumstances? Place yourself in my Situation, and give me your candid opinion.

"I have been lately looking over some of R Ms Letters to me on the Subject of our present Plan—and his Expressions are so different from the late Treatment I have received that the Comparison afflicts me—To make me Dependent in the Original Appointment, on a Person with whom he had a Short Acquaintance [Ledyard] and whose Consequence is derived from myself, to decline a Conference with me on the Business to be Entrusted to my Management, and on the Situation the Company meant to place me under the Pretext of not having Time for such Discussions, and afterwards, when I had agreed on the terms with Mr. P:, to find Time for making a Proposition of a Nature far from pleasing, to induce me to forego the first appointment are Circumstances that I cannot Reflect on without Pain—Mr. Morris is a Person of Spirit, and Delicacy—he must know that I have had pretty broad hurts given me by the Parties. . . ."[7]

As Superintendent of Finance, beset by a chronic shortage of revenue with which to pay the country's debts, Robert Morris had scant time to give to personal concerns. "The want of time to Bestow on private Pursuits," he wrote, "more especially on the Collection of Monies due to me, on settlement of Old Accounts &c which I cannot expect untill I shall be so happy as to get clear of my present Troublesome and Disagreeable Office . . ." severely limited his attention to the China venture or any other.[8] It is obvious that what little thought he could spare to it obliged him to make snap judgments not always based on complete or unbiased information, decisions often expressed hastily without the appropriate cushion of diplomacy. Great latitude for misunderstanding accrued.

In pouring out his soul to Holker, William Duer sought not only a sympathetic ear but also a cathartic explanation about why he was being treated shabbily. Certainly, he could not confide in his other partner, Daniel Parker, because Parker was suspected of being one of the voices whispering against him; or, if not actually whispering, at least making surreptitious noises in

14. Major General Henry Knox (1750-1806) at the end of the American Revolution was the highest ranking officer after George Washington. He was a steadfast friend and supporter of *Empress of China* supercargoes Samuel Shaw and Thomas Randall. Portrait by Charles Willson Peale (1741-1827).

favor of Samuel Shaw's appointment over Duer as the chief supercargo.

Why this should have been so is confusing unless one assumes that Parker was angling for economic and political favor. Samuel Shaw, unlike Duer, tended to be gregarious and outwardly flamboyant. William Duer, unlike Shaw, was quiet and easily wounded. Both men were highly influential, but, in weighing one against the other, it may be that Parker judged Shaw to be of the most immediate use owing to his particularly intimate friendship with Henry Knox. A good word from Knox could be most helpful for business. Indeed, Knox was to provide Parker with a letter to New York Governor

George Clinton, soliciting his favor to help Parker open an auction room in New York City for the sale of merchandise: "He served with reputation in the Corps of Artillery until 1779," the General assured the Governor, "when he resigned his commission. His family and connections which are respectable are in Boston, but it is his intention to reside in this state."[9]

With the demise of the Northwest Coast expedition, the choice of the vessel still destined directly for Canton boiled down to one, but the selection of that one appears not to have taken place until nearly mid-December 1783 when the fur plan was buried once and for all. More than three months after Parker had written to Robert Morris posing questions about the fur ship, Morris finally replied. For reasons that would become manifest much later, the tenor of it was deeply disturbing to Parker, who could not well afford the upset caused by such drastic changes of plan. In bemoaning his plight to John Holker, in his turn, he placed the blame for the failure on any shoulders other than his own.

"I have recd from Mr. Morris," he wailed, "an Answer to the Letter wrote him respecting the Ship Destined for the South Sea. He does not think the Reasons sufficient to justify the Delay & I am Exceedingly hurt at his not being Convinced that the delay was occasioned by a fault in the first plan given by Mr Ledyard & by the delay of Capt Small in Boston. Attention was not wanting in me—God knows I made every Effort to obtain some person here to command the Ship, but no one I could trust her with could be obtain'd—& for my own part I am fully Convinced that had she gone as we proposed Originally we should have failed the Object. The Expedition requires a better Ship than we Expected & very differently Equiped—I beg you to confer with Mr Morris on this Subject & to be so good as to send me your mind & his, on this Business. . . ."[10] Parker was out of funds. Send more money, if you please. At Christmastime, he was in Philadelphia, lodged at the Indian Queen Tavern on Fourth Street, to plead his case. The response was unswerving. The fur plan was off. One vessel, the *Empress of China*, would proceed with the ginseng to China as quickly as possible.[11]

The choice of the *Empress of China* clearly derived from her newness, her size, strength, and nearly complete state of readiness. The others simply were unsuitable or could not be hurried along to sea before the season for sailing to China had passed. Even so, there must have been doubts and many dissenting opinions. John Holker, for one, had received a letter from Baltimore's Matthew Ridley of Ridley & Pringle, who was in Paris settling business affairs. Cautioned he: "I have seen Messrs. Wadsworth & Carter, & I have been hinted that an Expedition is on foot for China. It is necessary

15. James Nicholson (*circa* 1736-1804), senior ranking officer of the Continental Navy, was at one time considered for the captaincy of the *Empress of China*. Subsequently, he accepted the command of another vessel belonging to Daniel Parker & Company. Portrait from Gardner W. Allen, *Naval History of the American Revolution* (Boston, 1913), vol. II.

to inform you of one Circumstance, attending those Voyages, all ships large or small pay a certain [fixed] duty of Forty Thousand Livres; and therefore no persons send any but those of 800 or 1000 Tuns. If a ship only of 300 is sent, so considerable a duty makes a great addition to the Cargo."[12] Reasoned heads probably argued that the largest of the Daniel Parker & Company ships, the ex-frigate *Bourbon*, could not possibly be completed in time; if the ginseng cargo reached Canton early, on the other hand, the expected profit margin was sufficiently elastic to absorb the duty. All the more reason for haste. They were right. At the beginning of the 1784 trading season at Canton ginseng was selling for $2,000 a pecul (133 pounds). Once all the European ships had arrived with their own supplies of North American ginseng the price dropped to between $200 and $300 a pecul![13]

During the early months of the new year, 1784, the other vessels acquired by Daniel Parker & Company were dispatched on commercial voyages of a more routine nature: the *Bourbon* to Cadiz; the *Columbia*—the one intended for the Cape Horn passage—to Amsterdam by way of Charleston; and the *Comte d'Artois* to France, where she was sold. The captains for three of the company's vessels were recruited from the Continental Navy: Commodore James Nicholson, the navy's senior officer, for the *Comte d'Artois*; Thomas

Read, eighth ranking navy captain for the *Columbia*; and John Green, thirty-first captain on the navy list, for the *Empress of China*.[14]

Notwithstanding Daniel Parker's opinion of Green, whom he felt should not have been appointed over James Nicholson, Green was an experienced mariner in whom Robert Morris placed every confidence. Born in Ireland in March 1736, supposedly to an Irish father and an English mother, with one uncle a member of Parliament and another a bishop of the Church of England, Green went to sea while he was still in his teens and wound up in Philadelphia by the year 1764 when he was employed by Robert Morris and his partner, Thomas Willing, as master of a vessel in their trade between Philadelphia and New York.[15] On June 13, 1765, a few weeks before sailing on a three-month voyage to Jamaica and Honduras, he married at Christ Church, Philadelphia, twenty-one-year-old Alice ("Alcie") Kollock of Lewes, Delaware. The following decade of voyages for Willing & Morris took him to Quebec, along the Middle Atlantic and Southern colonies from Pennsylvania to Georgia, throughout the Caribbean, to Madeira, Spain, Portugal, France, and England.

A strapping figure weighing well over two hundred pounds and standing six feet four inches tall, John Green was not a man to be crossed.[16] Charles Biddle, master of the brig *Ann*, from the bay of Honduras bound for Philadelphia, recollected his behavior just before they sailed for home in August 1769:

I had this voyage four masters of ships passengers, Captain [John] Green, [Robert] Shewell, and two of the name of Welsh . . . Green had a dispute with one Samuel Jones, of New York, whom he struck. Jones stuck up an advertisement at the tavern that Green presuming on his bodily strength, had struck him and refused to give him satisfaction. He therefore published him as a coward and a rascal. As Green was going with me, and belonged to Philadelphia, I took down the advertisement and gave it to him. He immediately called on Jones and agreed to fight him. They prepared a boat, and, as I was not present, Green spoke to a Captain Sinnot to be his second. Sinnot was one of the magistrates, but before he set off he resigned his commission. There was at this time a sloop-of-war commanded by a Mr. Jackson lying there, and the boat happening to be at the [St. George's] Key with Jackson, some persons informed him that Jones and Green were just put off with an intention of going to the next Key to fight, and begged he would send his boat and bring them back. He immediately sent his boat. When she got near and Jones understood their errand he swore he would fire into the boat if they attempted to come alongside. Finding they paid no regard to what he said he fired a pistol into the boat and wounded one of the boat's crew slightly in the thigh. They however pulled alongside, and the bowman, if he had not been prevented, would have driven the boat-hook through Jones. They carried him on board the man-of-war, and he was kept there until we sailed. There were a good many duels fought at this time in the Bay. Captain Shewell was wounded in the breast by one Brockholst, of New York, and the celebrated [Benedict] Arnold, who was here at this time, fought and wounded one of the Bay men. It was said that Arnold frightened his antagonist, who agreed that he should fix the distance, by naming five yards. They were more turbulent at this time in the Bay than I had ever known them before.[17]

One individual, whom Green met in France during the Revolution, described him as "the most Violent [patriotic] American I ever met with. His daily toast is: 'Success to Washington and downfall of the British Arms.' "[18] To his friends, he was a man "of unblemished integrity, of great cheerfulness and good nature, candid, friendly, generous and hospitable to an uncommon degree."[19]

Early in the Revolution, Green commanded the 200-ton Willing & Morris ship *Pomona*, which the fortunes of war obliged him to abandon in the Thames. Crossing the Channel to France, he set about to secure for himself "a Ship of some force," which one pro-British observer felt assured he would get, because "he is highly esteemed here, and not without reason, putting aside his [patriotic] principals he is one of the finest fellows I have ever met with. . . ."[20]

His reward for his diligence came in the form of a captain's commission in the Continental Navy, issued by the American Commissioners treating with the French Court in Paris, and the old French East Indiaman *La Brune*, armed with twenty-four six-pounders, sporting "an Indian Woman Head, Neck, Breast and Legs naked," and laden with clothing and stores to bolster the American war effort at home.[21] "A Bundle Rubbish she is," the Navy Agent in Boston exclaimed to Robert Morris after her arrival at that port.[22] But political favoritism replaced Green with Captain Joseph Olney. Complained another former Willing & Morris shipmaster to John Paul Jones: "Green was flung out of his Ship in a low manner."[23] *La Brune* was taken into the Continental Navy as the *Queen of France* and ended her days at the bottom of the Cooper River in Charleston, South Carolina, as part of the defensive boom vainly sunk to prevent the entry of the British fleet in May 1780.

In August 1778, however, Green was temporarily appointed to the Continental brigantine *Retaliation* and ordered to cruise off Capes May and Henlopen in Delaware Bay. The following April, having taken a leave of absence from the Continental Navy, he assumed command of the Pennsyl-

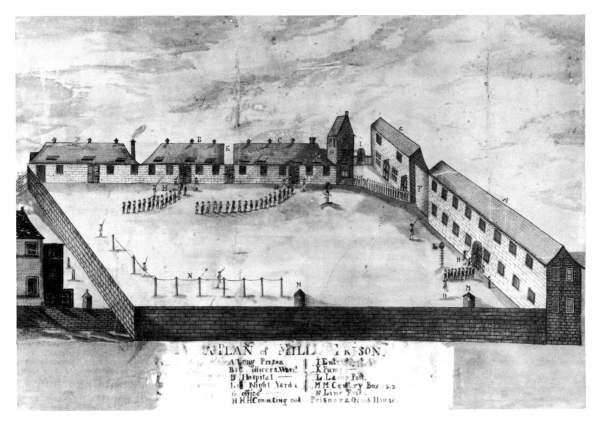

PLAN of MILL PRISON.

A Long Prison.   I Entry Post
B&C officers Ward   K Pump
D Hospital ——   L Lamp Post,
L.f Night Yards.   M M Centry Box :s.s
G office   N Line Post.
H H HCounting out   Prisoners.Cook House.

16. Mill Prison, Plymouth, England. This rare drawing by an unknown prisoner depicts the place where Captain John Green was incarcerated for nine months as a prisoner of war during the American Revolution. Mill Prison and Forton Prison (Portsmouth, England) became the miserable abodes for many an unfortunate American seaman during the war.

vania letter of marque and reprisal brig *Nesbitt*, owned by Messrs. Morris and Nesbitt, and sailed from Philadelphia for France with a load of tobacco. En route, he was captured by the British cutter *Liberty* and carried into Falmouth, England.[24] Green fled to France, where eventually he secured another vessel, the *Patriote*, which almost immediately was cast away and lost in the River Loire from the negligence of the pilot.[25] He then took command of the new, eighteen-gun ship *Lion*, built at Lorient, and in March 1781 sailed with a cargo for Port-au-Prince, St. Domingo. On the way back to France, when only some fourteen leagues to the westward of Belle Ile off the coast of Britanny, Green was again overpowered and captured, this time by the British frigate *La Prudent*. On the eleventh of September 1781, he found himself committed as a prisoner of war to Mill Prison on the outskirts of Plymouth, England.

There he remained for nine-and-a-half months, writing dozens of letters soliciting assistance or exchange for himself and his fellow sufferers, all the while building miniature models of ships—"the mains of pasing manney a

17. Captain John Barry (1745-1803) was an Irish-born Philadelphian who frequently has been called the "Father of the American Navy." Among the Continental Navy vessels he commanded during the Revolution was the frigate *Alliance*. The engagement which he and John Green fought after their departure from Havana was the last fought by the Continental Navy during the war.

tadious hour hear"—for two or three London merchants who had gone out of their ways to be helpful.[26] Then, on June 22, 1782, as the war was beginning to come to an end, there was a general liberation. He and 215 other men from Mill Prison were put aboard the flag-of-truce cartel vessel *Symmetry* and sent home to Philadelphia.

The Independent Gazetteer paid Green many a tribute upon his return:

The feelings of this gentleman for his unfortunate and distressed countrymen in captivity augmented by the very essential services he rendered them, must ever be acknowledged with the utmost gratitude. He clothed the naked, fed the hungry, and administered comfort to the sick and afflicted . . . He was not less attentive to the improvement of their morals, and the instruction of their youth, as through his application, assiduity, and attention, several reverend, respectable dissenting Clergymen were permitted to visit them, and preach the gospel in the prisons of Sunday . . . In short, in every apparent respect, where the honor or credit of our republic were concerned, under whose flag he bears a commission, he always demeaned himself in such a manner as justly entitles him to the good-will and thanks to his country. The circumstances of most of those people are so reduced as to render it immediately impracticable for them to make any return for favours received, other than a dutiful, thankful and public acknowledgement of the many obligations they are under to that very worthy and respectable fellow-citizen.[27]

Freedom and idleness were not synonymous for John Green. On the seventeenth of October 1782, Robert Morris gave him command of the twenty-gun Philadelphia-built ship *Duc de Lauzun*, purchased by the Continent from Captain Thomas Truxtun, his partner Thomas Randall (later the *Empress of China*'s junior supercargo), and Don Francisco Rendon, an emigré Philadelphia merchant.[28] At the end of November, he set sail for Havana with a cargo of flour and beef, with orders to rendezvous there with Captain John Barry in the frigate *Alliance*, take aboard some $200,000 negotiated on bills for the account of the United States and return with it at all hazard. The two vessels sailed from Havana, after lengthy opposition by the local governor, on March 6, 1783, and at once ran afoul of a British squadron. The fiery engagement to ensue was the last naval skirmish of the American Revolutionary War.

At nearly the same moment the *Alliance* reached Newport, Rhode Island, in safety and the *Duc de Lauzun* anchored in the Delaware River, word reached America of the signing of the preliminary articles of peace.

To all intents and purposes, the war was over. John Green was out of a job.

By May of 1783, Green was beginning to toy with the idea of having a ship built for himself to put into regular trade between the United States and

18. The Continental frigate *Alliance* passing Boston Light, 1781. The *Alliance* was designed and built at Salisbury, Massachusetts, in 1777-1778 by William Hackett, who in 1798-1799 also designed the United States frigate *Essex*. The *Alliance* was one of only two frigates remaining in service at the end of the Revolution. Painting by Captain Matthew Park, USMC, who served on board.

France. But, then, along came John Ledyard, filled with visions of sea otters, silks, porcelains, and pelts.

In mid-August, Green purchased of James Penrose a house and estate in Bristol Township alongside the banks of Neshaminy Creek in Pennsylvania's Bucks County.[29] To this place from their residence "in Frunt Street Near South Street," Philadelphia, he was making preparations to remove his family when duty intervened. At the end of the month, he was on his way to Boston, there to sit on the courts-martial called upon four fellow naval officers whose past conduct had warranted investigation, if not necessarily censure.[30] There, he first set eyes on the *Angelica*, coming into flower as the *Empress of China*.

Did he know at the time what Morris had in mind for him? The chances are good that he did and that the second journey to Boston to sit on more courts-martial that autumn was also calculated to help him keep tabs on the outfitting of his future command.[31]

The courts were still in session when, on November 22, 1783, the *Empress of China*, under a surrogate master, cleared Boston Harbor bound for New York City.[32] Green paused there briefly on his way back to Philadelphia. The *Empress of China* had reached port on December 7 after a fifteen-day, storm-driven passage. "I arrived here a few days past," he wrote on December 18, "& found my ship had got here before me, she had very bad weather during her passage but behaved as well as it was possible."[33]

With the collapse of John Ledyard's dream and the selection of the ship to perform the voyage to China, John Green applied to Morris, in the latter's capacity as Agent of Marine, for another leave-of-absence from the now lifeless Continental Navy. So, too, at the same time did Captains James Nicholson of the *Comte d'Artois* and Thomas Read of the *Columbia*. Permission for the three "to engage in private Business" until such time as they were called upon to resume the public service was granted on January 14, 1784.[34]

V

Most Serene, Puissant, and Illustrious

By the time Captain Green returned to New York, his officers had been selected and for the most part were hard at work on board.

Serving as "back-up" captain, in the event of Green's incapacity or death, was Philadelphia shipmaster Peter Hodgkinson, another employee of Willing & Morris who, most recently, had commanded their letter of marque brigantine *Virginia*. He and Green were brothers-in-law, Hodgkinson having married Hester Kollock, Alcie's younger sister. As a result of the experience gained during the *Empress of China* voyage, in later years he would command the India-China trader *Washington*, owned by Constable, Rucker & Company of New York.[1]

Purser was John White Swift of Philadelphia and Bensalem Township, Bucks County. A 1767 graduate of the College of Philadelphia (the University of Pennsylvania) and the recipient of a Master's degree from the same institution three years later, Swift became a merchant in Quebec until the outbreak of the Revolution when he participated in the 1775 expedition against that city and was wounded. Disliking the Declaration of Independence, however, he withdrew from the army and took no further part in the war. He, too, was related to Green through intermarriages with the Kollocks.[2]

Ending the family circle aboard was Midshipman John Green, Jr., known familiarly as "Jack," who turned eighteen the day the *Empress of China* left New York. During the latter part of 1781, he had sailed with his Uncle

Peter Hodgkinson in the *Virginia* privateer and had been captured. Only within recent months had he been able to make his way home from Europe. In time, he came to command, among other vessels, the Philadelphia China trader *Pigou*, owned by the Walns.[3] The second midshipman on board was Samuel Clarkson, nephew of the influential Philadelphian Matthew Clarkson, who lately had been first marshal of the Pennsylvania Court of Admiralty and in the next decade would become a director of the Bank of the United States and Mayor of Philadelphia. Samuel's father, Gerardus Clarkson, became surgeon for the Board of War and founder and first president of the College of Physicians. In time, the young midshipman would become the Reverend Samuel Clarkson, D.D., M.D.[4]

Of the first and second mates, Robert McCaver and Abel Fitch, respectively, little is known except that McCaver entered the Continental Navy in 1776 as a midshipman and served throughout the war.[5]

Acting as Captain's Clerk was Frederick Molineux, an enigmatic figure who appeared in Philadelphia, swore an oath of allegiance to Pennsylvania on August 31, 1777, and later served as an officer in the privateer sloop *Comet*. The sloop was captured on October 3, 1780, and he was thrown into Mill Prison, preceding John Green there by nine months. Upon their release, Molineux set himself up as a merchant in Philadelphia until persuaded to sail in the *Empress of China*. There is tenuous evidence to suggest that he was already familiar with East Indian waters, perhaps owing to service in the employ of the East India Company. In any case, upon his return from China, he provided New York merchant William Constable with a lengthy dissertation describing in detail the directions of winds and monsoons in the East as well as an intricate plan for a voyage to the area. For a simple captain's clerk it is a highly unusual document.[6]

The ship's Surgeon was Dr. Robert Johnston, the same tireless traveler who had coaxed to the coast from interior Virginia and western Pennsylvania the thirty tons of ginseng. Assisting him as Surgeon's Mate was Andrew Caldwell, whose father had been Commodore of the Pennsylvania Navy for a short term in 1776 and subsequently was a member of the State Navy Board and an owner of a fleet of privateers.[7]

By this time, William Duer, perhaps influenced by Lady Kitty, his wife of four years and the daughter of Lord Stirling, had definitely made up his mind not to accompany the ship as a supercargo or in any other capacity. At that, Major Samuel Shaw was induced to change his mind. "There is a fatality attends the movement of your friend," Shaw wrote at Christmastime from Boston to his friend Winthrop Sargent. "I am now certainly destined

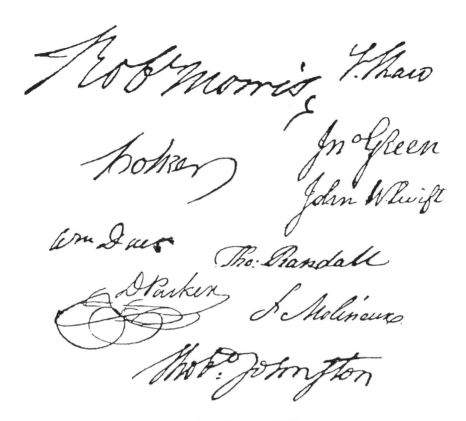

19. Signatures of owners and officers of the *Empress of China*.

to India—I come to shake hands with my father, have been three days in town and set out the day after tomorrow for New York, whence we shall sail by the 15 of next month . . . God bless you, my dear friend—wherever I go, you will be ever near the heart of your / S. Shaw." Similarly, he bade farewell to his brothers William and Nathaniel. To William, a resident of Goldsborough, Maine, he wrote: "My prospect of seeing you in the course of the winter is at an end. I shall sail for China by the 15th of January, from New York. The terms on which I go promise something clever, and I hope to shake you by the hand in two years. Though fortune has dealt rather hardly with you, it will never do to give out. Things may take a favorable turn in the spring. If Heaven prospers my present undertaking, it will be in my power to help you. Therefore, keep up a good heart, and be assured that in me you have a brother who will cheerfully share with you his last penny. . . ."[8]

Second supercargo under him, as had seemed likely before, was Shaw's intimate friend, Thomas Randall, a Bostonian who went into the Revolutionary forces immediately after the battles of Lexington and Concord as a second lieutenant in Gridley's Regiment of Massachusetts Artillery. Both he and Shaw entered Henry Knox's Regiment of Continental Artillery in December 1775, Randall as a first lieutenant and Shaw as a second. Two years later, they simultaneously transferred to Crane's Third Continental (Massachusetts) Artillery, by which time Randall had been promoted to captain and Shaw to first lieutenant. Then, their paths diverged for a time when Randall was taken prisoner at the Battle of Germantown, above Philadelphia, in October 1777.[9] "In the above surprise," remarked Shaw, "my friend Randall, after getting one of his pieces away, was taken while he was anxiously exerting himself for the security of that, and another, which, under cover of the night, was also got off. On finding himself in their hands, he endeavoured to escape, but the enemy prevented it by knocking him down and stabbing him in eight places. His wounds not admitting of his being carried with them, they left him at a house near the scene of action, and took his parole to return when called for, unless exchanged. It is no less true than remarkable, that a continued series of ill-luck has constantly attended poor Randall; who, no sooner than he finds himself at liberty to oppose the enemies of humanity and justice, has, by some perverse trick of Fortune, been thrown into their hands, and bound, by the strongest tie that can affect a man of honor, not to act against them."[10]

Although exchanged the following December, Randall appears not to have taken any significant further part in the fighting and resigned his commission in 1779. It would seem that after the British occupation of Philadelphia ended in June 1778 he returned thence and became involved with privateering and West Indian commercial ventures with Thomas Truxtun, Andrew and James Caldwell, and a young French emigré, Stephen Girard, who later became one of Philadelphia's richest merchants and most celebrated sons.[11] By war's end, Randall and Truxtun were linked by a formal partnership as Thomas Randall & Company, with a place of business in Front Street a few doors above Market. The combination was dissolved in May 1783, Truxtun continuing the business.[12]

During the time the ship's officers were converging on New York, the *Empress of China* was taking in her sea stores and cargo. Daniel Parker, as usual, was making a show of tearing his hair. The expenses to date, he declared to John Holker, "amount at this moment to upwards of 80,000 Dollars: *Actually* paid . . . The money that is necessary for her to take [to

20. Thomas Truxtun (1755-1822), onetime partner in Philadelphia of supercargo Thomas Randall, and Revolutionary privateersman. Truxtun subsequently became one of the early and important figures in the United States Federal Navy of the 1790's and was the first commanding officer of the frigate *Constellation*.

China] must be raised from such Bills or advanced by the Company I must pray you to take some Arrangements on this Business as all the Funds I have (& more) is absorbed. I am very unhappy in being obliged to trouble you on this Subject. Your Goodness will I hope Excuse it my whole Time is not enough for the Business I am Obliged to attend to here or I would be at Philad to make these arrangements. . . ." To this letter, at a later day, when Parker's name was anathema to Holker, the latter added bitterly: "here he is beging for more money: all the funds he had & more are exhausted: he is unhappy to trouble holker . . . Laughing in his sleeve at the time . . . sending madeira to China & making holker drink pump water."[13]

The actual complete cost of the ship and the cargo was $119,000, Parker & Company and Robert Morris each paying $59,500. The money "necessary for her to take" referred to $20,000 in silver coin, which, next to the ginseng, was the most important item of trade on board. Holker's caustic note about madeira arose from eleven pipes of brandy and Teneriffe wine Parker had all but purloined from Turnbull, Marmie & Company and had disposed of for his own advantage to the ship's unsuspecting but wine-loving officers.[14]

Back on the thirteenth of December, Parker had predicted that the *Empress of China* would be ready to sail within twenty days, or sometime before the second of January 1784. But, during those twenty days, he had been forced to travel to Philadelphia for money and to appeal in vain for a continuing commitment to Ledyard's fur scheme; John Green had passed through New York from Boston on his way to Philadelphia to secure his leave-of-absence from the Navy; Supercargo Shaw had gone to Boston to spend Christmas with his father; and the winter of 1783-1784 had begun to bear down with a vengeance, dumping twenty inches of drifting snow over coastal New York and New Jersey on December 30 and 31.[15]

On January 17, 1784, Parker, who had long since returned to New York, apprised Holker that "the Ship *Empress* is Compleatly Loaded all the Dollars are procured & I shall be wholly ready for her to Sail in 2 days so far as respects me, I hope Capt Green will be here tomorrow . . . The very uncommon Frost delays every thing."[16]

Green, whose leave-of-absence was delivered to him on January 15, was hurrying back to his ship. Thirteen more inches of snow fell between the eighteenth and the twentieth.

Samuel Shaw and Thomas Randall, confident the vessel was about to sail, on January 22 jointly bid adieu to their Massachusetts friend, Major Winthrop Sargent: "Before, my dear Sargent receives this letter," Shaw wrote in his most fulsome fashion, "probably his friends will be ploughing the watry element. Wherever we go and whatever circumstances attend us, the remembrances of the pleasing hours we have spent in his company and the assurance that we possess his friendship and good wishes will ever warm our hearts. We bid you farewell, our dearest friend, till we have the happiness to see you again, which we expect will be within the compass of eighteen months. That Heaven may bless you, and make your path through life easy and delightful, is sincerely the prayer of, dear Sargent . . . ," and on it went.[17]

Little did they know that the *Empress of China* would not depart for another month. She "will sail the moment that Captain Green can ship three or four men that are wanted to complete her Crew," Parker assured Holker on January 26. "Nothing but the ice can prevent her from going to Sea this week when the Invoice of her Cargo the Inventory & description of the Ship &c shall be instantly sent to you. I only wait for Captain Green to sign the Inventory of the Ship or I could send to you all the papers by this conveyance."[18] During that night and the next day another eighteen inches of snow sifted out of the sky.

The bills of lading had been signed the day before, January 25, by Green, with Purser John White Swift adding his signature ten days later. The wording of each was identical, save for the articles described and the cargo marks illustrated in the margin:

Shipped in good order and well conditioned by Daniel Parker in and upon the good Ship called *Empress of China* whereof is Master for this present Voyage John Green now riding at Anchor in the Harbour of New York and bound for Canton in China to say Eleven pipes of Wine and Brandy Thirty eight barrels containing Tar and Turpentine And Seven Boxes Containing Twenty thousand Dollars in Specie being marked and numbered as in the Margin and are to be delivered in the like good Order and well conditioned at the aforesaid Port of Canton (the danger of the Seas only excepted) unto Samuel Shaw or Thomas Randall or to their Assigns, he or they paying freight for the said Goods Nothing Being Owners Property with Primage & average accustomed. In witness whereof the Master or Purser of the said Ship hath Affirmed to six bills being accomplished and the others to stand void. Dated in New York the 25th day of January 1784.

| | (signed)   Jno Green |
| Februa 4th 1784 | (signed)   John W. Swift Purser[19] |

21. An unidentified Philadelphia merchant vessel of the period immediately following the American Revolution rides to moorings in this painting by an unknown English artist. Except for the lack of gunports, the ship closely resembles in design and size the probable appearance of the *Empress of China*.

22. Health and sailing clearance granted to the *Empress of China* by Governor George Clinton of New York State.

Unbeknownst to anyone on board except Samuel Shaw, Daniel Parker had secretly withheld $2,300 of the specie from its boxes without amending the bills of lading. Shaw said nothing because Parker, as an owner, had asked him not to and also had assured him that the shortfall of funds was necessary to cover a note due. The sum, furthermore, would be made good before the *Empress of China* sailed. The matter was to give Shaw many an uneasy thought not only during the months between the sealing of the boxes in New York and their reopening at Canton but also for the rest of his life.

That same day, January 25, two important documents were signed by New York Governor George Clinton and delivered to the ship. One was a clearance permission; the other, a passport or sea-letters.[20]

By His Excellency George Clinton
Esquire, Governor of the State of New York, General
and Commander in Chief of all the Militia, and Admiral
of the Navy of the Same.
To All Whom it may Concern

Permission is granted to John Green Esquire, Master, of the Ship *Empress of China*, of the burthen of Five hundred Tons or thereabouts, mounting Eighteen Carriage Guns, laden with Dollars, Cordage, Ginseng and other Articles of Merchandize, and Navigated by forty Hands, all on the departure of the said Ship free from every Pestilential disease, and Epidemical disorder; to depart this State with the Said Ship and Cargo, to proceed to the port of Canton, in the Kingdom of China, unmolested.

Given under my Hand and Seal at Arms at the City of New York, this twenty fifth day of January in the Year of our Lord One thousand seven hundred and Eighty four, and in the Eighth Year of the Independence of the Said State.

By His Excellencys
Command

(signed) Robt Benson Secry   (signed) Geo; Clinton

* * *

23. George Clinton (1739-1812),
Governor of New York. Portrait
by Ezra Ames (1768-1836), 1814.

24. Sea-letters for the *Empress of China* from Governor George Clinton of New York. This
document was intended as a passport requesting foreign governments to provide the ship with all
lawful aid and protection.

His excellency George Clinton Esquire, Governor of
the State of New York, General and Commander in Chief
of all the Militia, and Admiral of the Navy of the Same.

To all Emperors, Kings, Princes, Potentates, States,
Republics, and Powers; being Friends and Allies to the
United States of America, and all Others to Whom these
presents Shall come, Sendeth Greeting.

Know ye

That the Ship or Vessel called the *Empress of China*, burthen about Five hundred
Tons, and commanded by John Green Esquire, being about to depart the Port of

New York on a trading Voyage to China, is the property of Daniel Parker Esquire and Others, Inhabitants and Citizens of this State and of other, the United States of America.

I therefore do pray and desire, that all Aid, Assistance and Succour in your power, may be given to the said John Green, without doing or Suffering to be done to him, any Wrong, Trouble, or Hindrance; Offering to do the like when thereunto desired.

In Testimony

Whereof, I have with my hand Signed these Presents, and caused them to be Sealed with my Seal at Arms. Dated at the City of New York the Twenty fifth day of January, in the Year of our Lord, One thousand seven hundred and Eighty four, and in the Eighth Year of the Independence of the Said State.

By his Excellency's Command
(signed)   L.R. Morris secy

Also on January 25, 1784, Captain Green received his detailed and very specific orders from the ship's owners respecting the conduct of the voyage:[21]

To John Green Esqr: Captain in the Navy of the United States, and now Commanding the private Merchant ship, called the *Empress of China*, bound on a Voyage from the port of New York, to the port of Canton and from thence to return to the port of New York. The following Instructions are given on the part and behalf of the Owners of the said Ship.

It being of very great Consequence to arrive in Canton before any other Vessel which can go from Europe with fresh Ginseng, every attention has been paid, as you know, to procure a Ship particularly calculated, both for fast sailing and to encounter rough Weather, and as she has upon severe experiment, in her very Stormy passage from Boston to New York proved equal to both these Objects; is well man[n]ed and found agreeably to your own wishes: it is expected from your diligence, and attention that your passage will be very short. In order that you may not be under a Necessity of waiting for the Westerly Monsoons you will run down your Longitude in the high Latitudes, and for this purpose you will make all expedition from New York to the Cape de Verd Islands; thence keeping as well to the Eastward as circumstances will permit, you will run Southward to the Latitude of forty degrees South, and keep in that Latitude Eastward as far as the Island of St Pauls; thence Eastward & Northward to the Island of Clote, thence to the Island of Java being carefull to make this Island sixty leagues to the Westward of Princes Island, lying in the mouth of the Streights of Sunda and proceed thence thro' the Streights of Sunda to Macao, the Charts of that Coast with Dunns directions, herewith delivered to you, will afford usefull matter of instruction on the Subject.

It is expected that you will go the whole voyage without putting into port, for as your Vessel is very Stout and Sheathed with Copper, and there is no doubt of your own and your Officers care and Attention, it is conceived that (Extraordinary accidents excepted) nothing but sickness among your people can Necessitate you to seek a port. Your owners have provided you with a Skilfull and attentive Surgeon, who has had long experience, and therefore it is presumed, that if the due attention be paid to keeping your Ship Clean and sweet and your Crew well fed & well employed, they will avoid the Diseases which sometimes happen in long Voyages. But as unforeseen accidents may Oblige you to seek a port, You will as Circumstances shall direct, either go to the Cape of Good Hope, the Island of Mauritius or some convenient port in the Island of Java. You have Letters both from the French and Dutch Ministers here, which will secure you a friendly reception in the ports of their Respective Nations. When in port you will be under the directions of Samuel Shaw Esquire or in case of his death Thomas Randall Esquire, who are appointed Supercargoes of the Ship and who will provide and pay for such repairs or other articles as may be needfull, but in all such cases we recommend to you as well as to them, the Strictest regard to Oeconomy, for we hope not only this present Voyage may turn out to such profit as to prompt a new expedition of the same Kind, but that you yourself may both give and receive such satisfaction as by your own desire, to be employed in it again. Your care and attention to the discipline and health of your men is not to be intermitted either at Sea or in port, particularly the latter, for you Know that seamen are most likely to be debauched when in port, and that the rivers of warm Climates are unfavorable to health. You will stay at Macao or proceed onward according to the orders you shall receive from your Supercargoes, to whose direction this is confided, and they are instructed to assist you in the disposition of your property to the best advantage, which we doubt not may be Usefull; as the Chinese are very great Rogues, and you will not have the Same good Opportunities of dealing with them.

This instruction is intended also for the benefit of your Officers as well as of yourself, Should they or you incline to take advantage of it.

The Supercargoes will be furnish[e]d with Documents as to the Stowing your return Cargo which they will communicate, & you and they will adopt the best means for doing that business well. For this purpose you will also as occasion offers, make Observations and Enquiries.

Voyages like the present are attended with great expence, it is therefore highly important to the Owners to make use of all the room in the Ship which can with any convenience be Stowed. They have been liberal in the allowance of Forty Tons privilege to you & your Officers, and they expect this Conduct on their part will meet a suitable return on yours; which your Integrity of Disposition gives every reason to rely on. You will therefore take on board as much goods as the Ship will hold, and it will be better to touch at the Cape of Good Hope for Provisions & Water on your return if needfull, than by the Quantity of those things to prevent the Ship from bringing as much as she otherwise might. You will sail from China as soon as circumstances will permit, and of those Circumstances your Supercargoes will be best able to judge—whose orders you will Obey, but upon the time of your sailing must depend the route which you are to take, and therefore Nothing shall be said on that subject. You will use your discretion, for your Interest and that of your Owners is intimately connected and indeed the same. Other expeditions are fitting out on the same errand and it is clear that the Vessel which first arrives in this Country will come to the best market provided always that her Commodities are good. No Vessel that can be sent has in this respect equal advantages with yours, for you will probably arrive in China by the begin[n]ing or at most the end of May. If you should get your Cargo on board so as to come away by the begin[n]ing or even the End of August and return by the same Route as you go, you will be able, of the Stop[p]ing at the Cape, to get back to New York by January, or if you should not be able to leave China untill after the easterly Monsoons set in or even as late as the end of November, Your Ship being so good a Sailer will doubtless arrive before any other Vessel.

It is earnestly recommended to you as well on board as on Shore to cultivate the good will & friendship of all those with whom you may have dealing or Connections. You will probably be the first who shall display the American Flag in those distant Regions, and a regard to your own personal honor will induce You to render it respectable by integrity and benevolence in all your Conduct and dealings; taking the proper precautions at the same time not to be yourself imposed on.

So soon as you shall arrive at Newyork, you will announce your arrival to your Owners or their Agent, and you will take very particular care that no article whatever be landed untill you shall receive their further Orders.

You have delivered to you herewith not only the declaration of Independence, but Copies of the several treaties made with the different European powers, and also a Sea Letter from this State Signed by the Governor thereof. You will show these things as Occasion may require and avoiding all Insult to others you will consult your own Honor and that of the Country whose Commission you bear; if any are Offered to you.

We heartily wish you a Secure and prosperous Voyage and recommend you to the protection of Heaven.

Dated, New York January 25 1784,   Danl Parker, for himself and
                                     Owners of the Ship *Empress of China*

One further document considered critical to the undertaking had not yet arrived. As it turned out, it was unnecessary, but at this earliest day of the American China trade no one knew exactly what formalities might have to be observed with the Chinese or if, indeed, the mandarins at Canton would even permit a ship of the fledgling United States to trade there at all. It seemed best to be prepared with documentation of legitimacy. To that end, while in Philadelphia at Christmastime, Parker had requested from the Continental Congress, then sitting at Annapolis, Maryland, official sea-letters.

New Yorker Gouverneur Morris, old friend and confidant of Robert Morris but no relation, wrote a supporting letter to Charles Thomson, the Secretary of Congress. "Mr. Parker," he stated, "informs me that he makes application to Congress for Letters to Captain John Greene of the navy now about to proceed in a few days for the Port of Canton in China. You will oblige me and others of your friends by taking Care to have this Being couched in such ample Terms as may procure a respectful Notice of the Bearer. As Greene is one of their Officers who has faithfully served . . . it is of Importance by opening this direct Trade to prevent the Europ Powers from draining us as they now do of our Specie in Exchange for the Superfluities of the East the Design itself deserves some Countenance."[22]

The sea-letters were taken under consideration by a committee of Congress consisting of Mr. James Monroe of Virginia, Mr. George Partridge of Massachusetts, and Mr. Hugh Williamson of North Carolina, which, on January 30, 1784, resolved that the document be granted in the form following:

Most Serene, Serene, most puissant, puissant, high, illustrious, noble, honorable, venerable, wise and prudent Emperors, Kings, Republicks, Princes, Dukes, Earls, Barons, Lords, Burgomasters, Councillors, as also Judges, Officers, Justiciaries & Regents of all the good Cities and places whether eclesiastical or secular who shall see these patents or hear them read, We the United States of America in Congress Assembled make known that John Green Captain of the Ship call'd the Empress of China is a Citizen of the United States of America and that the Ship which he commands belongs to Citizens of the said United States and as we wish to see the said John Green prosper in his lawful affairs, our prayer is to all the beforementioned, and to each of them seperately, where the said John Green shall arrive with his Vessel & Cargo, that they may please to receive him with goodness and to treat him in a becoming manner, permitting him upon the usual tolls & expences in passing & repassing, to pass, navigate and frequent the ports, passes and territories to the end to transact his business where and in what manner he shall judge proper: whereof we shall be willingly indebted.
                    In Testimony whereof we have caused the Seal of the United
                    States to be hereunto affixed—Witness His Excellency
                    Thomas Mifflin President this thirtieth day of January in
                    the year of our Lord one thousand seven hundred and Eighty four
                    and in the Eighth Year of the Sovereignty and Independence of
                    the United States of America.[23]

The Congressional parchment, impressive for the copperplate hand and resplendent seal of the United States with pale green ribbon flowing under

25. Sea-letters for the *Empress of China* from the Congress of the United States. Not knowing what form of documentation would be required for a ship of a new nation entering the China trade, the Congress provided this parchment for Captain John Green's use.

it and across the sheet, reached Parker during the morning of February 8. In acknowledging its receipt to Holker, he launched into a heart-rending catalogue of his various afflictions:

"The extreme Severity of the weather," he began, "has rendered it Impossible for the Ship to Sail, altho' she was Loaded on the 18th Ulto. My whole attention has been paid to these Ships since I had the pleasure of seeing you in Philadelphia and on your looking Over the Inclosed Accounts I am fully Convinced that you will readily believe no Time has been lost by me, I hope the Accounts will meet your Approbation. Nothing has been wanting on my part to render them less Expensive, but I am Constrained to say, that had the command of this Ship for China been given to Commodore Nicholson that she would in all probability have been at Sea 25 Days agone, and saved an Expense of at least 2,000 Dollars that we are now Oblidged to pay. Capt Green has received his Orders Signd his Bills of Lading and *shall* Sail the first moment that the Ice and Wind will permit.

"You will also find Inclosed a Statement of the Accounts of the Concern. It was impossible for me to send them compleat, as many of the Bills are not Obtaind and Expenses are hourly made. Neither can I call for all the Bills at present, not having Cash to discharge them but you will see very nearly the State of the concern with Mr R Morris, and of our own company accounts by which you will see the great advance that I am now in. And by the Estimate of the Value of the Ship *Empress* and Cargo, in London (which you may be assured is founded upon the latest Advices from London, and the Opinions of the best Judges here, and which I am confident will be thought low by the Merchants in that City) an Advance of more than 40,000 Dollars is made upon the Sale of our part of that Adventure only, beside leaving us one third of the Ship and Cargo, which on that estimate is worth 68,000 Dollars, all this Advantage is made by me for the Companys account, without having one Dollar in cash for the purpose, but on the Contrary I am in advance 16,000 Dollars for the other concerns as you will perceive by the Account Inclosed which is as nearly as can be Ascertaind a true Statement of our Concern.

"I am fully Convinced that upon the Examination of this Statement you will readily believe that I am in a very Distressed Situation for money and unless the Amount of one third part of the Value of the Ship *Empress* and Cargo is drawn for by Mr Morris, and that I do receive one half of the same, together with the Balance due In Mr Morris's accounts, I shall be under the necessity of stopping payment of the monies that I owe in this place, but as that measure was agreed upon by us, and Mr Morris I rest with full assurance, not doubting it will be done. I think you will find herewith all the Documents necessary to effect this Business, viz, the Description of the Ship, with an Inventory of her numerous Stores and Invoice of her Cargo, and Bills of Lading for the same. I am very unhappy that it is not in my power to be with you in Philadelphia, it is Impossible for me to leave this place before the Ship for China has Saild, and the *Comte de Artois* ready for Sea—I must therefore Intreat you to lay before Mr Morris the accounts and papers, and agree with him to draw the Bills of Exchange for one third part of the amount estimated at £45,934.12/ Sterling, one half of the third part would be £7,650 Sterlg from this my draft on you for 1795 Dollars may be paid, and my acceptance on John Codmans draft of 1000 Dollars due him on the 17th Inst. payable at Bank."[24]

On it went for pages more, filled with references to bills to be bought, cash to be borrowed, accounts to be settled, and monies owed. "By the return of this Express," it concluded, "I *pray* you to send me relief from my present Disagreeable Situation."

Three days later, on February 11, he wrote to Holker again, yet again acknowledging receipt of the sea-letters, and promising to send the accounts and bills of lading of the *Empress of China* provided the ice did not prevent the messenger from crossing the river. "I am at this time quite unwell having a bad cold & full of Pain," he complained. To Robert Morris, he wrote much the same thing but omitted mention of his indisposition.[25]

Pity it was he was feeling poorly just then. The eleventh of February was not only a day and night of even more snow for New York City, but it also was George Washington's true birthday by the old calendar system under which he had been born in 1732. The occasion prompted much joy. "The same was celebrated here," one newspaper reported, "by all the true friends of American Independence and Constitutional Liberty, with the hilarity and manly decorum ever attendant on the Sons of Freedom. In the evening an entertainment was given on board the East-India Ship in this harbor, to a very brilliant and respectable company, and a discharge of 13 cannon was fired on the joyful occasion."[26]

VI

Aweigh at Last

"Tomorrow, if the weather permits," Thomas Randall wrote to Major General Henry Knox, "my friend Major Shaw and myself shall take our departure for China—we have every pleasing prospect before us, and I trust that the Providence that has in many instances so manifestly favored us, will continue its divine protection in this—should I reside in that Country I shall honor myself by soliciting your correspondence.

"Present my most respectful compliments to Mrs. Knox, and be pleased to assure her, my sense of the politeness I have received in her family will ever be gratefully remembered." To this, Shaw added a line or two in the same vein, closing: "Adieu. May Heaven bless you."[1]

The perfectly atrocious winter carried on into February 1784 with such continuous, severe cold that its equal scarcely remained within the memories of those who had to endure it. "In some places the fir trees cracked with the sound of cannon shots from the cold," one country observer noted in his journal.[2] Another in New York City, awaiting passage to Europe, catalogued day after day of continuous cold, producing prodigious amounts of ice which first clogged the Narrows and then gradually backed up to freeze the North River, too. No ship could sail.

While Captain John Green awaited a rise in the thermometer, he took the occasion to communicate with John Swift, the father of his purser, on matters of mutual concern.

"The Hurrey of business and not Inatention to you will I hope plead an

Excuse for my not Wrighting you Sooner—but this is a fittaguing Business and new to us all. I hope our Next outfitt will be more Fammiller you Sun John has Shuen more Industry that I Ever New him have before is much Esteemed by all His brouther offisurs, Mr Parker and the Supercargos I lave you to Judge of my hapiness in my offisurs & Hope all will End in harmoney & to our Satisfacktison as well to open a New doore for Commerce at a futour day— I have on board and Conserved to geather about 12 tousand dollars, I have Wroght Mrs Green to have a pollisey opend at Philada and gitt Insured on goods on board Ship *Empres of Chiner* from New York to Canton and Back to york by good men the Survey £1200 the Premeam here out and home is 15 Pr Ct but no money advansed as Premiam, if the Premiam is pd at opning the Pollisey it would be dun a 12 Pr Ct this for your Goverment—we have Seavare Winter here Every thing is now on board and we only waight For a fair wind which hope will Come Soone I must Request your Euseal attentison to Mrs Green & the Children I hope to See you all in May or June 1785 May you your Good Ladey & Children Inioy good Health and Hapiness to whome pray Make my Respecktful compliments. . . ."[3]

The most moderate weather in weeks finally made a welcome appearance on February 17. It continued during the next four days. By the twenty-first,

26. Captain John Green's sea chest. Said to have been made by the ship's carpenter, it has since been the recipient of some replacement and additional hardware.

thawing had cleared away the worst of the ice, and shipping began to move in and out of New York Harbor again. The Delaware River, at Philadelphia, in contrast, continued to be closed.

As the *Empress of China* took on board during the dawning hour of Sunday, February 22, 1784, the seven influential visitors who were to go in her as far as Sandy Hook, the sun rose over the heights of Brooklyn and the ship was hove from the wharf into midstream. With the turn of the tide, she shook out her sails, hove short on the anchor cable, and filled away towards the Battery at the toe of Manhattan Island. There, with spotless timing, ship and fort saluted each other, the crew dressed ship in the yards, and cheers arose from the assembled onlookers. The first American vessel to make the attempt of trading with China steered her course for the Narrows and the open sea beyond.

"Yesterday morning," reported *The New York Packet*, "several vessels left the Wharves, bound for the several places of their destination; among others was the *Empress of China*, Captain Green, for China. The morning being pleasant drew a large party of gentlemen to the Battery, congratulating each other on the pleasing prospect of so many large ships being under sail in the bay, after so long a suspension of trade by the severity of the season; and if we may judge from the countenances of the spectators, all hearts seemed glad, contemplating the new source of riches that may arise to this city, from

27. "A View of New York from the North West," from J.F.W. DesBarres' late-eighteenth-century chart series, *The Atlantic Neptune*, demonstrates that the city from which the *Empress of China* sailed was still little more than a town.

28. "The Light House on Sandy Hook, S.E. one mile," from J.F.W. DesBarres' chart series, *The Atlantic Neptune*. The *Empress of China* lay at anchor off Sandy Hook during the night of her departure from New York Harbor.

a trade to the East-Indies; and all joined their wishes for the success of the *Empress of China*, with thanks to the concerned who thus early and nobly stood forth the friends of commerce and their country."[4]

A few days later, *The Independent Gazette* echoed similar sentiments with words of approbation for Captain Green: "A correspondent remarks, that notwithstanding the many difficulties he may have to encounter with, as being the first ship from this new nation, to that rich and distant part of the world, from his character as an able and spirited navigator, we may form a pleasing presage of that success which every friend to his country wishes him, and to the gentlemen, whose ambition to discover new resources of wealth, by forming new channels for the extensions of our commerce, a contemplation of the services they are rendering their country, must sufficiently compensate for the risque to their property."[5]

Between 4:30 and 5:00 o'clock that afternoon, the flood tide began to make. The *Empress of China* let go her anchor to await the light and the morning ebb tide, riding within the bay, guarded by the tall, octagonal lighthouse erected on Sandy Hook, New Jersey, twenty years before.[6]

During the hours of waiting, Captain Green began the journal he would keep during the voyage. As witnessed by his letter to John Swift, he wrote much the way he spoke. The result was that his orthography left, by more modern standards, much to be desired. For the ease of modern readers, therefore, his spelling has been silently corrected, abbreviations expanded, and the daily navigational entries arranged in a uniform fashion.[7]

The entry for the day of departure from New York, February 22, commenced using civil time. But, in good sailorlike fashion, Green's February 22 ended at noon, after which the new day, February 23, began.

The most important time of day aboard a vessel at sea was the meridian passage (noon), when the sun reached its maximum altitude in the sky, because it was at that instant that navigational observations were taken to determine the ship's daily latitude position. The day at sea, in consequence, officially ran from noon to noon, whereas civil time began and ended at midnight. Thus, Green's subsequent references to "the fore part" generally dealt with events occurring from noon to approximately 8 P.M.; "the middle part," from 8 P.M. to 4 A.M.; and "the latter part" from 4 A.M. to the following noon.

A Journal of an Intended Voyage
on Board the Ship
EMPRESS OF CHINA
Bound from New York to Canton
in India
John Green Commander

FEBRUARY 1784

Sunday, 22. This morning commenced with pleasant weather. The winds at WNW. At daylight, hove the ship from the wharf into the stream. Got all hands on board. Mr. [Daniel] Parker, Simmonds, Scamhorn [Schermerhorn], Porter, Doctor [Andrew] Craigie, Captain [James] Nicholson, and Mr. Young all went in the ship as far as the Hook. At passing the Grand Battery, a great number of inhabitants saluted us by giving three cheers, which we returned. We also saluted the Fort with 13 guns, which they returned with 12. Several vessels in company with us, bound to Europe. At noon, the wind dies away.

Monday, 23. The fore part, came to anchor in eight fathom, Sandy Hook ENE. Calm. At 9 past meridian, the wind comes to ENE. The middle part at North, and at daylight the wind at NNE. The tide of flood running, prevented our getting under way. At ½ past nine, hove up in company with several other vessels bound to sea. At ½ past 11, abreast of the Hook after making several tacks. At ½ past 12, light winds [and] the pilot left us with all the above-named gentlemen. Saluted the company with nine guns and three cheers, which they answered with three cheers.

Tuesday, 24. Commences with light winds. Got up the topgallant yards. Bent several staysails.

Got out fore-topmast steeringsail. The winds at NE. At ½ past 3 calm, the lighthouse on the cape NW about 4 leagues in latitude 40ᵈ-27ᵐ North latitude. Longitude 74ᵈ-5ᵐ W[est] from [London]. At 7 P.M., dark and overcast attended with some snow. The tide of flood setting us much in to the Hook, we had all clear for coming to anchor when a small air sprang up from the SW and soon deepened our water from 10 fathom to 13 ditto.

Course made good this 24 hours, from the
     departure South 42ᵈ E, distance 108ᵐ.
Difference of latitude 51ᵐ.
Departure 72ᵐ.
Latitude per account 40ᵈ06ᵐ.
Meridional distance 72ᵐ.
Difference of longitude 92ᵐ.
Longitude in 72ᵈ33.

At noon, gloomy weather. Employed removing our sails and other stores from out of the cabin into the main hatchway in order to bring the ship more by the head. Stowed the anchors and unbent the cables. Two sail in sight a long way astern. A sheep lambed with one lamb. Seems well. Thermometer 34ᵈ [Fahrenheit].

Wednesday, 25. The fore part, pleasant. The middle part, less wind from NW. The latter, light winds from WNW, W, and SW. At noon, light wind [and] drizzling rain. Steeringsails set and ditto royals.

Course made good this 24 hours by dead
reckoning SE½E, distance 130ᵐ.
Difference of latitude 83ᵐ.
Departure 101.
Latitude per account 37ᵈ43ᵐ.
Meridional distance 173.
Difference of longitude 128.
Longitude in 70ᵈ25ᵐ.
Thermometer 42ᵈ.

Captain Hodgkinson saw a tropic bird this
morning. Several of our seamen seasick. Mr.
[Thomas] Randall and the purser both sick but
eat very much and throw it up again.

Thursday, 26. The former part, light winds and
some fine rain. The winds to the NE. The wind
variable at 4 o'clock and very bad weather. Sent
down the topgallant yards. Hands the mainsail.
Close-reefed the topsails and struck the topgallant masts. At 9 past meridian, the wind flies
out of the West. Hard rain, much lightning.
Blows very hard. Hands the topsails. Scuds under the foresail, at 2 A.M., set the close-reefed
fore-topsail. A heavy sea. The ship makes much
water and keep one pump continually working.
Ships a great deal of water. The latter part,
much hail and rain.

Course made good by dead reckoning South
62ᵈE, distance 111ᵐ.
Difference of latitude 52ᵐ.
Departure 98.
Latitude per account 36ᵈ51.
Meridional distance 271.
Difference of longitude 123.
Longitude in 68ᵈ22ᵐ.
At noon, thermometer at 33ᵈ.

Friday, 27. Hard gale and a high sea. Ships
much water. Pump a great deal. The rigging
chafe much. A great deal of rain and some hail.
At 6 P.M., handed the foresail. Scuds under the
fore-topsail close-reefed. At 4 A.M., moderate.
Set the foresail, and at eight set the close-reefed
main-topsail.

Course made good ESE, distance 185ᵐ.
Difference of latitude 71.
Departure 171.
Latitude per account 35ᵈ40ᵐ North.
Meridional distance 442.
Difference of longitude 211.

Longitude [in] 64ᵈ51.
Thermometer 51½ᵈ.

Saturday, 28. At meridian, the gale moderates.
Out 3ᵈ reefs fore- and main-topsails. Pumps much
water. The ship ships a great deal of water. At
4 P.M. set the reefed mizzen-topsail. Winds
WNW. At 7, found the iron tiller had worked
itself off in the rudder head against the lining
of the rudder case and almost off the sweep in
the cabin. Clewed up the main- and mizzen-
topsails and handed them; also the foresail. Laid
the ship to under the reefed fore-topsail on the
cap. Shipped the wooden tiller in the roundhouse[8]
and unshipped the iron tiller and hauled him
in his proper place. Wedged him and put pre-
venters on him to keep him in his place there.
At 11 P.M., completed this business. Wore ship
after reeving new wheel rope and set the topsails
and foresail. The morning moderates. Swayed
up the topgallant masts. Out reefs the topsails.
The wind veers to the SW. Set the mainsail,
jib, and staysails. People employed repairing the
rigging.

Course made good: EbS, distance 130ᵐ.
Difference of latitude 25.
Departure 128.
Latitude per account 35ᵈ15ᵐ.
Meridional distance 570.
Difference of longitude 159ᵐ.
Longitude in 62ᵈ12.

The ship makes much water. The sick begin
to come on deck. Some gulls in sight and a
school of porpoise round us. Thermometer 56ᵈ.

Sunday, 29. The fore part, variable winds. The
middle and latter part, blowing a strong wind
from West. Mostly the close-reefed topsails set.
Ship continues to make much water. At daylight got the spritsail yard fore and aft and sent
down the mizzen-topgallant mast.

Course made good E¼North, distance 193.
Difference of latitude 9.
Departure 193.
Latitude observed 35—22.
Ditto per account 35—25.
Meridional distance 763.
Difference of longitude 235.
Longitude in 58ᵈ17ᵐ.
Thermometer at 57ᵈ—½.

During the time the *Empress of China* was thrashing her way east with nearly everyone on board consumed by the task of stopping the leaks in her upper-works, the partnership in Philadelphia between Robert Morris and John Holker was itself foundering. The situation had nothing to do with the China venture, because their respective shares in the vessel did not derive from activities of the partnership. The animosity that developed was the first of several major afflictions which altered the intended characteristics of the voyage by the time it came to an end.

The formalization of the Morris-Holker business connection had occurred in 1781, some three years after Holker's arrival in America from France. Having presented himself to the Congress as the "Royal Agent of France," Holker eventually won recognition as a Consul and as Agent of Marine. His positions, together with the temptations the offices brought with them, soon led him into currency speculations, futures in flour and grain, and numerous other commercial ventures from provision contracting to privateer cruising. Morris, even more, was a man with incredibly complex financial responsibilities, both public and private, so it was quite natural for the two to have come into close contact whether they wanted to or not. They did, although for Morris it was a reluctant alliance.

On February 26, 1784, four days after the *Empress of China* departed New York Harbor, Robert Morris caused to be delivered to John Holker a twelve-page, 6,500-word, foolscap-size letter, together with a statement of their accounts, the whole in response to letters written by Holker the previous month demanding to know why their affairs for the past three years had not been settled. Morris had been incensed by their tone and the "groundless assertions" they contained, "charges & Suspicions which I have only discovered of late were in your mind."[9]

For some weeks, letters passed back and forth between them demanding vouchers, denying vouchers, claims and refusals of depreciation on all or any accounts, hopes for settlement, and threats of litigation. By March 25, Morris threw up his hands in disgust. "Sir," he wrote to Holker, "I think you will not be surprised to learn that your conduct has determined me to have no further connection in business with you. . . . You or I must withdraw ourselves from the partnerships of Turnbull Marmie & Co and also from that of Harrison junr & Co. [of Richmond]. The choice of both or either shall be with you. . . ."[10] Holker opted to maintain his association with Turnbull, Marmie.

"I most cheerfully Consent to an immediate dissolution of the partnership with Mr Robt Morris, on any grounds," Holker fumed to Turnbull, Marmie, "I should certainly degrade myself for his opinion should I wish to remain

Connected in Business one Instant, with a Merchant, who on a settlement of accounts with me in any Private or public capacity refuses all communication (not only of the Vouchers relative to his transactions, his receipts and expenditures, But also to those made by myself in the City of Boston, which were Entrusted afterwards by me, to his Care and Keeping, and obliges me by such unparalleled conduct to sue him to account).

"You must therefore Gentlemen, Immediately take such steps and measures as will be necessary for the general safety, attending particularly to the Interest of those persons abroad, whose concerns are confided to your attention and Management.

"So soon as the accounts of the Original Company are settled, which I hope will be done also without delay & the heavy sums due to the former Company are paid by Mr Robt Morris, & the whole finally liquidated, I shall without doubt Enter with you into the necessary arrangements in order to Continue the house with you on a proper footing & to general satisfaction.

". . . Mr Morris Engaged to place in the house a capital of £200,000 & to throw in a Large share of his Business and Concerns, In order to compensate for the advantages he was to reap from the Connexion: however, far from giving any advantage, very soon after the Commencement of the Partnership, finding a full Employment for the monies of the house, he took out of it the original stock & moreover various sums nearly Equal to 6000 specie one half whereof I presume are yet due by him to the former partnership.

"Such was the Conduct of Mr Morris that I Complained of to himself, & these Complaints are, I must suppose, the only grounds of his objection against a Continuance of the partnership with me. . . ."[11]

The continuing fracas between Holker and Morris had no immediate effects on the voyage of the *Empress of China*, for she was out of range of communications. But, by the time she returned to the United States, the spoils of the enterprise had been diluted in a way no one could have calculated in the beginning.

Continuation of John Green's Journal

MARCH 1784

Monday, 1. Strong gale at WbS. Much hail and rain. At 5 P.M., handed the foresail and at 6 handed the main-topsail. The ship leaks much and ships a deal of water. The seamen were obliged to bring their bed in the roundhouse and great cabin to prevent water going down the fore hatchway. At 6 A.M., the starboard fore-topsail sheet gave way. Clewed up the topsail and bent a new sheet. The rigging chafes much. All hands employed repairing ditto. At 8 set the foresail.

Course made good E¼North, distance 205.
Difference of latitude 11.
Departure 205.
Latitude observed 35ᵈ34.
Meridional distance 968.
Difference of longitude 250.
Longitude in 54ᵈ07.
Thermometer 56ᵈ.

Tuesday, 2. A strong gale. High sea. Much hail and rain. Ships much water. Pumps a great deal, and at 9 P.M. the 2d ewe lambed. Obliged to keep the ewes and lambs in the roundhouse. The decks continually full of water. At 8 A.M., set the main-topsail and mizzen ditto. Winds at WbS.

Course made good E½North, distance 211ᵐ.
Difference of latitude 20ᵐ.
Departure 210.
Latitude observed 35ᵈ54ᵐ.
Meridional distance 1,178.
Difference of longitude 256.
Longitude in 49ᵈ51ᵐ.
Thermometer [   ].

Wednesday, 3. All this 24 hours a strong wind from West. Ships much water and pumps much. The ship makes a deal of water in the run. Damaged several bolts canvas and some of the purser's beds and stores. At 11 P.M., the sea pooped us. Stove a cabin window and broke a globe lamp. Removed the ewes and lambs from the roundhouse to a pen made for them on the quarterdeck. Our larboard pump choked with chips. The carpenters soon removed the damage. Some heavy showers of rain.

Course made good EbS¾S, distance 202.
Difference of latitude 68.
Departure 190.
Latitude observed 34ᵈ46ᵐ.
Meridional distance 1,368.
Difference of longitude 232.
Longitude in 45—59.
Thermometer 64ᵈ½.

Thursday, 4. A fresh of wind and some rain. The winds at West. Mostly the 3 topsails set, Reefed topsails. At 8 A.M., out all reefs. All hands employed. Some repairing the rigging. Others overhauling the water [casks] and some

repairing main- and mizzen-topmast staysails, At 10 P.M., the First Mate, Mr. McCaver, fell down in an apoplectic fit but received no damage. At 7 A.M., the ship rolling much, threw me with violence from the starboard side on the quarterdeck and bruised my arm and hurt my head much.

Course made good EbS, distance 200ᵐ.
Difference of latitude 39ᵐ.
Departure 196.
Latitude observed 34ᵈ07ᵐ.
Meridional distance 1,564.
Difference of longitude 230.
Longitude in 42ᵈ09ᵐ.
Thermometer 68ᵈ.

Friday, 5. All this 24 hours moderate and pleasant. The winds WbNorth to WbS. At 6 P.M., the main-topsail tie gave way. Repaired ditto. Single-reefed the topsail. At 6 A.M., got up maintopgallant yard. Set the sail. Set the lower steeringsails forward. Got up several of our new sails from the 'tweendecks to dry. All the sails wet. Messrs. [Samuel] Shaw and [Thomas] Randall, in company with Captain Hodgkinson, visited all parts of the 'tweendecks, orlop and bread room, and find all places much damaged by wet and the leaking of the ship.

Course made good E½S, distance 197ᵐ.
Difference of latitude 19.
Departure 196.
Latitude observed 33ᵈ46ᵐ.
Meridional distance 1,760.
Difference of longitude 236.
Longitude in 38ᵈ13ᵐ.

Saturday, 6. Pleasant weather. People employed drying our new sails which were damaged in the 'tweendecks. The middle part, squally and some rain. At 7 P.M., handed the maintopgallant sail. At 3 A.M., set the topgallants and mainsail and staysails. Wind at WSW. At daylight, set lower and topmast steeringsail. Observed the slings of the foreyard broke. Replaced him with a new one. Got up main topmast steeringsail booms. Some showers of rain. Winds at noon SW.

Course made good EbS, distance 199.
Difference of latitude 39.
Departure 195.

Latitude per account 33—07.
Meridional distance 1,955.
Difference of longitude 232.
Longitude in 34ᵈ41.

Sunday, 7. Blowing fresh and hazy. The wind at WSW and variable. Set the topgallant sails and steeringsails. People employed drying our new sails which have been wet ever since we left New York and had no opportunity to dry until now.

Course made good EbS¼S, distance 189.
Difference of latitude 46.
Departure 183.
Latitude observed 32—21.
Meridional distance 2,138.
Difference of longitude 218.
Longitude in 31ᵈ03.
Thermometer 68ᵈ.

Monday, 8. Fresh breezes and hazy weather. Winds at SW. Steeringsails and topgallant sails set. The people employed drying sails and repairing rigging. Got the spritsail yard athwart.

Course made good EbS, distance 128ᵐ.
Difference of latitude 25ᵐ.
Departure 126.
Latitude observed 31ᵈ56.
Meridional distance 2,264.
Difference of longitude 150.
Longitude in 28ᵈ33ᵐ.

N.B.—find the ship's distance on the log to be 207ᵐ and to be steered ESE by the compass. Imagine the distance on the log too much or the course quite different from that made.

Tuesday, 9. The fore and middle part of this 24 hours blowing strong. The reefed topsails set. Winds at SWbS. The ship makes a deal of water. At 6 A.M., less wind. Set the jib and staysails.

Brought up many of our sails to dry. Shifting the topgallant yards and bending the proper sails, we find that fore-topgallant sails had been bent in the room of the main-topgallant sail. This day Mr. Randall took sick. The doctor gave him a vomit. At noon, let a reef out of the topsails.

Course made SE, distance 151.
Difference of latitude 107ᵐ.
Departure 107.
Latitude observed 30ᵈ09ᵐ.
Meridional distance 2,371ᵐ.
Difference of longitude 124.
Longitude in 26ᵈ29.

Wednesday, 10. Light winds and pleasant weather. The winds from SWbS and SSW. Mostly all sail set. At meridian, bent the spritsail and ditto topsail. Up mizzen-topgallant sail. This day used 4 pieces of cordage belonging to the cargo for our small sails. Employed drying our sails and lashing our small spare spars on the quarters between the main and mizzen channels.

Course made good ESE southerly, distance 149.
Difference of latitude 57.
Departure 138.
Latitude observed 29ᵈ04ᵐ.
Meridional distance 2,509.
Difference of longitude 158.
Longitude in 23ᵈ51ᵐ.
Thermometer 71ᵈ.

N.B.—this day corrected my longitude my middle latitude from the time of my departure and find that the meridional distance is 2,509ᵐ which gives me 2,961ᵐ. Difference longitude observed 49ᵈ21ᵐ taken from long Sandy Hook makes the ship in longitude 24ᵈ54ᵐ.

VII

An Unexpected Stopover

Prior to the sailing from New York, Captain John Green had been commissioned by various merchants in Boston, New York, and Philadelphia to acquire in China an assortment of merchandise for their personal accounts (see Appendix C). Altogether, including what he had been able to scrape together for himself, Green had on board some $12,000 in trade goods and specie. Alcie Green, presumably, was having that insured by underwriters in Philadelphia.

As for the *Empress of China* herself and the owners' cargo on board, no policies had been opened before her departure—at least, not by Daniel Parker & Company. What final arrangements Robert Morris made to protect his own half interest have not yet surfaced.

Due to John Holker's considerable influence with highly placed officials and bankers in France, as well as to the extensive lines of credit he had established there, Daniel Parker & Company resolved to cause insurance on its half share to be underwritten through the merchant-banking firm of LeCouteulx & Compagnie, consisting of Messrs. Laurent-Vincent leCouteulx de la Noraye, Jacques-Jean leCouteulx du Moley, and Barthélemy-Jean-Louis de la Noraye in Paris; Antoine leCouteulx de Verclives and Jean-Barthélemy leCouteulx de Canteleu in Rouen; and branches in Havre-de-Grâce and Cadiz.[1]

On the tenth of March 1784, Parker prepared a packet of exhibits for transmission to Paris: an invoice of the *Empress of China*'s cargo; her inventory; the instructions given to Green, Shaw, and Randall; a power of attorney; copies of the bills of lading; an estimate of the voyage; a copy of the account current of Daniel Parker & Company, with Holker as agent for LeCouteulx & Cie.; and a list of bills drawn on the account of the ship.[2] Two letters from Parker accompanied the documents: a general letter containing a statement of facts, accompanied by a French translation of the same, and another calling specifically for insurance to be made.

"By the papers herewith Inclosed," wrote Parker in the former, "you will be made acquainted with an Adventure to China, Originally entered into by Robert Morris Esq Danl Parker & Co and Several Merchants in Boston, each agreeing to be interested one third, but in consequence of the failure on the part of the Gentlemen in Boston, the whole has developed upon Mr Morris and our House who now hold the one half of this Ship and Cargo, the amount of which being much larger than is Convenient for us at this Time to be in advance for, we have entered into an agreement with John Holker Esq. of Philadelphia to reserve ourselves from that advance, which we have very unhappily been under the necessity of making; Mr Holker has agreed to draw Bills upon your House payable at Six months Sight, to the amount of Sixty Thousand Dollars, & in order to Induce your acceptance of those bills, we have herewith Transmitted to you a power of attorney, authorizing you to sell such part of this Ship & Cargo at the Price therein mentioned as will raise the sum of Three hundred and Fifteen Thousand Livres which is the amount of the Bills drawn by Mr Holker for our Account, but in case a sale cannot be effected we have impowered you to borrow the money necessary to take *up these Bills on the best Terms for our Interest*, and for your Security we have by the above power of attorney enabled you to Mortgage and assign to the persons from whom you may borrow this money the whole of our half of the Ship *Empress of China* & Cargo, which we have valued at Twenty four Thousand One hundred & fifteen pounds . . . agreeable to the inclosed estimate. You will perceive that this Ship will return to a better & more Advantageous Market than can be found in any part of Europe. The several prices affixed to the Articles that are to form her return Cargo are the lowest prices ever known in this Country. By the estimate of the Value of this Ship and Cargo in London (which market we are most acquainted with) compared with the sum that the return Cargo will sell for shows the advantage that this Voyage will afford."

After explaining about the cargo of ginseng and detailing the *Empress of China*'s design, measurements, crew, and armament, he continued:

"The Gentlemen who are intrusted with the Business as Super Cargoes are men of great Probity and Abilities in whom all Confidence may be placed. By the orders to the Captain you will perceive that he is not to touch at any port untill he arrives at Macao unless from necessity and from the extraordinary Qualities of the Ship as a Sea Boat, as was proved on her passage from Boston to New York, and the Plentiful manner in which she is supplied with every Necessary for the Health and Sustinence of the Crew. We are fully in the belief that she will not touch at any place before her Arrival at that port.

"Before the Bills now drawn by Mr Holker will become due either Mr Holker Mr Duer or Mr Parker will be with you to take such arrangements as may be necessary in case you are not able to effect the Sale of that part of the Ship & Cargo that is mentioned in the Power of Attorney viz One half of the moiety [half share] belonging to us or to borrow money on the security of the whole of our property in the Ship & Cargo. You will find every Document necessary for your Government in this Transaction inclosed herewith and Mr Holker will write you also fully on the Subject. If you should be Oblidged to take the Money on Bottomry we hope you will be able to effect it at a rate not exceeding Twenty five to Thirty pr Cent Including the Premo of Insurance as that is to be paid by us. You will in all cases where you sell a part of the Ship or receive the money on Bottomry calculate the Premo on the amount sold or Conveyed. If the money is procured on Bottomry we hope the Time that will elapse from the Sailing of the Ship, to the Time that the money is Actually Advanced will be reduced nearly by Eight months.

"We inform you also, that the Ship *Empress of China* or Cargo on their Return Home will be Sold at Public Vendue within the Space of two months after her arrival for ready cash, & we shall if necessary undertake to make from the proceeds immediate Remittance in good bills on France at 30 or 60 days Sight. But if it was Judged proper In consequence of your order Gentlemen Messrs LaCara & Mallet, Messrs Prager Liebart & Co or any other house you will think proper, Shall be authorized with the Interest of these & to make remittance to such persons as will be willing to purchase in this expedition or to Loan on Bottomry. . . .

"On account of the Quick Sailing of this vessel and the nature of the evidence here given, she must be here by the month of June or July 1785 & as we dont doubt but that she will arrive at a proper Season in Canton & that the Sale of the Ginseng will be instantaneous because this precious article of Luxury to the Chinese is immediately wanting. We are convinced She will be soon Dispatched there on her return home. . . ."[3]

The letter requesting insurance contained many of the same ingredients but also explained why it was being sought in France, rather than elsewhere.[4]

"We had the honor to address you under this Date [it read] on the Subject of our Ship *Empress of China* . . . the present is to request you to cause Insurance to be made on one half of that Ship her tackle apparel and Cargo from the Port of New York in the United States of America, to such Ports in China as she may touch at, being bound to Canton & from such port or ports to the aforesaid Port of New York, with Liberty to touch at such places for refreshment, repairs or supplies as the Captain may deem necessary. . . .

An Estimate of the Value of the ship *Empress of China* and her Cargo, founded upon the best Information from London.[5]

			Sterling
The Ship Completely finished with 2½ suits of Sails, 5 Cables 5 anchors, 14 Months provisions, 5 Water, & 2 months advance pay to officers & men			8,000.
Pursers stores to be sold for the Owners acct		150.	
Carpenters stores &cs not Included In the Ship Inventory above		400.	
			550.
97,445 lb french cordage at	45/	2,192.10.	
57,687 lb Ginseng of ye 1st quality culled	10/	28,843.10.	
69 Kegs tin in sheets	60/	207.	
63,595 lb Bar 5 sheets Lead	21/	667.15.	
437 yards Broad Cloths	16/	349.12.	
			32,260. 7.
1 Box Camp Kettles Dishes &ca		40.	
2 Hhds Iron wire 660 lb		16.10.	
4 Pipes teneriff Wine £12		48.	
5 Pipes London Madeira £33		165.	
1 Pipe Old particular dito for the Owners		52.	
1 Pipe Brandy 124 Galls	5/	31.	
1 Pipe Old Jamaica spirits 109 Galls	5/	27. 5.	
25 Bblls tar	20/	25.	
13 Bblls turpentine	30/	19.10	
2,395 feet Plank		20.	
1 Box furs		60.	
17,325 Ounces silver	5/4	4,620.	5,124. 5.
		£	46,934.12.
Commission at 5 Pr Ct			2,296.14. 7
		Total £	48,231. 6. 7

"She Sailed from New York on the 22d Feby and on the 23 was seen 15 Miles without Sandy Hook and as a brees of strong westerly winds prevailed immediately after her departure she no doubt has had a very quick run to the eastward. We are anxious to have this Insurance made as soon as possible, and it has been a matter of concern to us that it was not done before she left the Port of New York, but the arrangements first made by Mr Morris and our selves to effect this Business Jointly this in London was on more mature Consideration objected to. We have but lately agreed, to make the Insurance on our Separate Accounts, we have prefered having the Insurance made on our parts in France for several reasons, one of which is that the Amt is not paid in hand as in London and also the Prem demand may be Larger. . . ."

The estimate enclosed had been based on information received from correspondents abroad, who were in a position to evaluate the *Empress of China* and cargo, based on long-standing European experience in the China trade. The copy above, dated March 20, was probably a fair copy of the one sent to LeCouteulx & Cie. on the tenth. The last item, 17,325 ounces of silver, does not tally with the actual amount on board, even taking into account the sum diverted by Parker and never replaced.

Continuation of John Green's Journal

MARCH 1784

Thursday, 11. Moderate weather and a smooth sea. Winds variable in the southern quarter. All hand employed: the seamen with the rigging, the gunner making cartridges for great guns and small arms. At noon, inclining to be calm.

Course made good EbS, distance 66^m.
Difference of latitude 13^m.
Departure 65.
Latitude observed 28—51.
Meridional distance 2,574.
Difference of longitude 73^m.
Longitude in 23^{d}41.
Variation West 11^{d}24^m.
Thermometer at noon 73^d.

Friday, 12. Light airs of wind and smooth water. The winds from the SW quarter. This day rigged the spanker. Unbent the mizzen. All sail set. This day for the first time got up all hammocks. Got up all our store of potatoes and turnips to dry. The carpenters preparing horses for our

scuttlebutts, making crutches for the spanker boom and saddles for the topgallant studding-sail booms. Unbattened the lower hatches to get up some water. Find the 2d cask we looked at was leaked entirely out.

Course made good EbS, distance 56^m.
Difference of latitude 11.
Departure 55.
Latitude observed 28^{d}40^m.
Meridional distance 2,629.
Difference of longitude 63.
Longitude in 22^{d}38^m.
Thermometer at noon 73^d.

Saturday, 13. Light winds and pleasant weather. The winds varying in SW quarter. Heavy clouds rising and threatening for rain the same as they generally do amongst the Islands. Pulled down the pantry in the middle steerage to make room for the gunner, boatswain, and carpenter who are much crowded below forwards.

Course made East Southly 67ᵐ.
Difference of latitude 2ᵐ.
Departure 67.
Latitude observed 28ᵈ38ᵐ.
Meridional distance 2,697.
Difference of longitude 76.
Longitude in 21ᵈ22ᵐ.
Thermometer at noon 69ᵈ.

Sunday, 14. All this 24 hours light winds and variable, the clouds flying as they generally do amidst high land. At 6 A.M., got up the top-gallant steeringsail booms. Set the sails. The wind at NNW. At ½ past 10, saw the island of Palma bearing ENE. Catched a large alba-core. Wore ship and steered to the SSW. Made all sail. At noon, the island bore ENE to EbS, distance 14 or 15 leagues. Latitude observed at noon 28ᵈ13ᵐ. Made much Southing this 24 hours owing to a current setting that way. Thermom-eter at 68ᵈ. Through course made per log: EbS 58ᵐ. Distance [   ] by latitude observed SEbE¾E, distance 59ᵐ. The through course made allowing for currents is EbSouth, distance 128ᵐ and departure 126ᵐ, which makes the lon-gitude in, at noon, 19ᵈ00. Meridional distance 2,822.

Monday, 15. All this 24 hours fine weather and a good wind from the NW and NNW.

Course made good SbW¾W, distance 161ᵐ.
Difference of latitude 152.
Departure 54.
Latitude observed 25ᵈ41ᵐ.

Meridional distance 96.
Difference of longitude 60.
Longitude in 19ᵈ37ᵐ.

People employed making points, drying new canvas, clearing and scraping the boats. Ther-mometer 68 degrees.

Tuesday, 16. Variable winds and pleasant. All sails set. The winds from Northwest and WbN. All hands employed.

Course made good SbW¼W, distance 109.
Difference of latitude 106.
Departure 27.
Latitude observed 23—55.
Meridional distance 123.
Difference of longitude 29.
Longitude in 20ᵈ06ᵐ.
Thermometer 71ᵈ.

Wednesday, 17. Light winds and smooth sea attended with a long swell from the NNW. Winds from WNW.

Course made good SbW½W, distance 152.
Difference of latitude 146.
Departure 44.
Latitude observed 21ᵈ29.
Meridional distance 167.
Difference of longitude 48.
Longitude in 20ᵈ54ᵐ.

All hands employed as usual; seamen merry as the custom on St. Patrick's [Day]. Thermom-eter 72ᵈ.

Narrative by Samuel Shaw[6]
[From his Journal]

March 17th. Having in yesterday's run passed the northern tropic, the usual cere-monies were observed this afternoon by the crew. Those of them who had never before passed being confined below, about three o'clock our ship was hailed by the Old Man of the Tropic, who, being desired by the officer of the deck to come on board, entered over the bow, attended by his wife, whence they were drawn in their chariot (one of the gratings) by a number of sailors, as Tritons, to the quarter-deck, where the captain and gentlemen received them. Their appearance was truly lu-dicrous, having their faces blacked and painted, a blanket over their shoulders, by way of robe, and a large swab on their head, instead of a crown, the long strands of which, hanging down to their waist, served for hair. After paying their compliments to the captain, and welcoming the ship to their dominion, they observed, that she was a new ship and had never been there before, and that they saw a number of faces about them who were in the same predicament. The captain having given his word that both the ship and the gentlemen should be properly entered, they returned forward and proceeded to business. The jolly-boat being previously filled with water, and a bucket containing a mixture of tar and grease placed alongside, the men who had never passed the tropic were brought up, singly and blindfold. They were welcomed with great ceremony by the old man, who told them that he was glad to see them, and should take the liberty to have them shaved before they went any farther. The candidate is then placed on a seat across the boat, and his feet kept from the water, where, still blindfold, he is lathered with the tar and grease, and shaved with a notched stick. As soon as this is done, the oath is administered to him, namely,—That he will, to the best of his ability, prove himself a good fellow,—never drink small beer while he can get strong, unless he likes the small better,—nor eat brown bread while he can get white, but under the same proviso,— never kiss the maid when he can kiss the mistress, unless he likes the maid best,— never go in an old ship when he can get a new one, unless he knows he is born to be hanged,—and, in fine, never suffer any man, where he may be, to pass the tropics or equator, for the first time, without going through the same ceremonies. A speaking-trumpet is now put into his hand, and he is told to hail the tropic. As soon as he gets the trumpet to his mouth, with an almost perpendicular elevation, a bucket of water is thrown into it, and, at the same instant, the seat on which he is placed being pulled from under him, he falls backward into the boat filled with water, where he is very handsomely washed by the bystanders, which closes the ceremony. About half a dozen went through this operation, which was conducted with great good-humor, and followed by the parties joining in drinking the grog given for the ship and the gentlemen who had crossed the tropic for the first time.

This being also St. Patrick's day, proper attention was paid by the gentlemen to the memory of the patron of Ireland.

Continuation of John Green's Journal

Thursday, 18. Moderate weather and smooth water. All hands employed on sundry jobs. This day drying our corn for the stock and painting the barge.

Course made good SbW½W, distance 99ᵐ.
Difference of latitude 95.
Departure 29.
Latitude observed 19ᵈ54ᵐ.
Meridional distance 196.
Difference in longitude 31.
Longitude in 21—25.
Thermometer 72.

Friday, 19. Moderate weather and variable winds from NNW to NNE. All sail set. At 8 A.M., set up all the standing rigging fore and aft and served it in many places. The ship makes very little water in her bottom. Find the rigging of an inferior quality, the hemp bad, and now we are in fine weather the tar runs much.

Course made good SbW½W, distance 106ᵐ.
Difference of latitude 101.
Departure 31ᵐ.
Latitude observed 18ᵈ13ᵐ.

Meridional distance 227.
Difference of longtitude 34.
Longitude in 21ᵈ59ᵐ.
Thermometer 72ᵈ½.

Saturday, 20. Moderate and pleasant. Winds from NEbNorth and very light breezes. Steeringsails and all other sails set. Carpenters employed. The ship's company quartered to their guns. Saw some petrels and several red Portuguese men-of-war.

Course made South, distance 97ᵐ.
Difference of latitude 97ᵐ.
Departure 00.
Latitude observed 16ᵈ36ᵐ.
Meridional distance 227.
Difference of longitude 00.
Longitude in 21ᵈ59.

Sunday, 21. Moderate and pleasant weather. All hands employed on sundry occasions. At ½ past one, saw the island of Boa Vista bearing WSW, distance about 8 leagues. Down steeringsails and hauled the ship up WbN½North. At 6, the isle of Sall NNW½W, 6 leagues. The body of Bonavista WbS, distance [   ]. At 6 A.M., saw St. Nicholas NW about 8 or Nine

leagues distant. Bonavista SE 7 or 8 leagues. At 6¼, saw the island of St. Jago bearing SWbS, distance 13 or 14 leagues.
Latitude observed 15ᵈ40ᵐ.
Thermometer 74ᵈ.

Monday, 22. Moderate and pleasant. All sails set. The winds at NE. At 7 P.M., close in with St. Jago. Bent our cables and run down between the Isle of May, which bore at 8 o'clock East, distance 3 leagues, until the Isle of May bore ENE and then took in our small sails and hauled the ship to the NE under her fore- and mizzen-topsails full, her main ditto aback. At 12, wore and laid the ship's head in SE until 4 A.M. Now being about 3 miles off the land, stood off until daylight and made all sail to the Westward. Soon saw some vessels laying at anchor. We hoisted our ensign, and one of the vessels, a Portuguese snow, fired a gun and hoisted her ensign. Cleared our anchors and stood into the harbor. Got a pilot on board. Came to an anchor at ½ past 7 in the morning in 9 fathom, seemingly good ground. The wind at NE. At 10, I went on shore. Saw the Commander of the port and made the proper arrangements for getting our ship soon fit to depart this place.

Of their arrival, Samuel Shaw penned the following record, to which he annexed copies of his letter explaining to Parker why the unexpected stopover had been necessary and Randall's covering letter of transmission of the papers to Philadelphia via Stephen Girard's brother in the West Indies:[7] "Came to anchor at 7 oclock this morning in Port Praya, at St Jago, one of the Cape de Verd Islands—at 10, Captain Green and the supercargoes went on shore and paid their complements to the Commandant of the Fort, and informed him of their motives for putting in at their island. The Governor being at the town of St Jago, nine miles distant, and the day too far advanced to allow of visiting him, they returned to the ship about 12. Having learned that a French vessel in the harbor was to sail in the evening for Hispaniola (Cape François) the supercargoes sent a copy of the aforegoing [following] letters and remarks to Mr Danl Parker, together with the following letter, the whole enclosed to the care of Messrs Girard & Co. Merchants in Cape François, to whom they wrote a letter, of which the annexed is a copy."

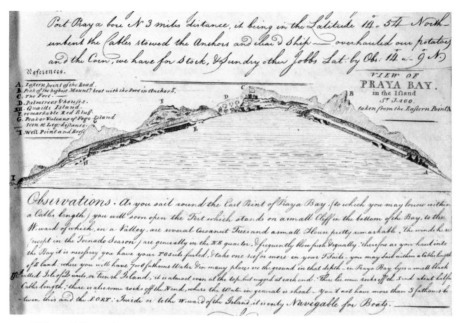

29. "View of Praya Bay in the Island [of] St. Jago . . ." was copied into a sea journal
from the original engraving on an eighteenth-century chart of the Cape Verde Islands.
Here, the *Empress of China* was obliged to pause in order to recaulk the hull and
replenish stores of drinking water.

Samuel Shaw to Daniel Parker, March 22, 1784

The reasons for our being in this place are contained in the enclosed papers. Our
passage hitherto has been very pleasant, but every day after examination had of
the ship's upper works convinced us of the necessity there was for their being
caulked before she ought to proceed—added to which several of our water casks
had leaked out, and it was essential to examine the state of that article very
critically, and make up the deficiency.

We cast anchor here about 7 oclock this morning and are now getting everything ready to set the caulkers to work—no artificers of any kind are to be had
on the island—but there are two Portuguese brigs here bound for Africa that
will lend us four men that understand caulking, who in addition to our own
people will be able to do the needful in the course of three or four days. While
this is doing, the most minute attention will be paid by Mr Randall and myself
to the state of the ginseng between decks, which we are apprehensive must have
suffered in some degree, though we hope not much. We write now by way of
Cape François, to which place a French brig, with slaves from Senegal, sails this
afternoon. In four days Capt Green says we shall be ready to sail, and we shall
have the pleasing satisfaction to know that every thing is in order and (extraordinary and unforeseen accidents excepted) that there can be no obstacle to our
proceeding directly, without our making any port, till we get through the Streights
of Sunda. The ships company are all in health and we have not since our departure
had a man unable to do his duty.

Thomas Randall to Messrs. Girard & Company,[8] *March 22, 1784*

As I formerly [corresponded] with you from Philadelphia, under the firm of Thos Randall & Co I have taken the liberty to request your forwarding the enclosed letters agreeable to their address, I am now on a voyage to China, on board the ship *Empress of China*, which sailed from New York last month. On my return I shall settle in America, and shall be happy in the continuance of your correspondence.

"Mr Randall," Shaw continued, "carried the aforegoing letters on board the French brig [on March 23], named *La Jengut*, commanded by Capt Pecote owned by Monsieur Dorea at Havre de Grâce and addressed to Monsieur Torterelle at Cape François. The French brig in passing us this morning at 7 o Clock gave us a salute with four swivels and *Vive le Roi!* which we returned by three cheers from the poop."

Continuation of John Green's Journal

Tuesday, 23. At daylight, hove up and warped close under the weather shore. Winds at NE. Got into a good berth and moored with the small bower to the NE and the stream to the South. The carpenter and his mate caulking. Unstowed the water casks in the main hold to examine them. Find them leaked out in the upper and middle tier. Sent the longboat on shore for a load of water. She returned at evening. Set the watch—4 men and an officer on the watch. Condemned one of our water casks.

Wednesday, 24. Moderate and pleasant this day. Got two Portuguese carpenters belonging to a snow in the road. Overhauled the starboard side of the main hold. Find several casks leaked out. Hoisted them on deck. The cooper overhauling them and when done we stowed them away. The longboat returned this day with two trips of water. In the evening, cloudy and some fine rain. Got off several fowls, some goats, a sow and boar, some oranges.

Thursday, 25. Moderate and pleasant. We had no Portuguese caulkers this day, it being a holiday. Our carpenters employed the people in the hold overhauling water casks. The longboat

brought off several casks water. Stowed eight of our nine-pounders as low down as we could in the fore hold and removed some casks of ginseng from the main hold to the fore ditto.

Friday, 26. A fresh trade wind. Our Portuguese returned this day to caulk. We finished at night. Paid them and sent them off. Our people very busy in overhauling the larboard side of the main hold which we find the casks in bad order. Almost finished. The longboat brings a load of water on board.

Saturday, 27. Squally. At daylight, employed some men in starting some casks into empty ones below in the hold. Others breaking up the carpenters' float stages and getting them on board. Sent the longboat on shore for the last load of water, and on her return we unmoored ship. Stowed all our water. Hoisted in the longboat and at 2 ditto in barge. Sent the yawl on shore for some necessaries. Cleared ship. Reefed our topsails, and at sundown hove up and got under way. Hoisted in the yawl and stowed our anchors. Latitude Porto Praya 15ᵈ00 North latitude.

Samuel Shaw to Daniel Parker,[9] *March 27, 1784*

You have herewith transmitted you a particular account of our situation, from the time we left New York till our arrival at this place, the 22d instant. Since then, all hands have been constantly employed in making the arrangements previous to pursuing our voyage. They are now completed, and we shall put to sea this evening. The event has convinced us of the expediency of the measure. For besides the necessary repairs in the ship's upper works, such was the condition of the water, from the badness of the casks, that it is more than probable we should have wanted that essential article before we could have reached the Cape of Good Hope, which would have obliged us to have stopped there—whereas the precautions now taken will enable us to proceed without stopping till we make the port of Canton. Besides which, the improvement that has been made of the stowage in the ship and putting ten of her guns below, has so much bettered her trim as will probably make one sixth part odds in her sailing. Some of the ginseng between decks was a little touched with the mould, but not materially injured. It is where it can be come at easily, and as soon as we get out, will be properly taken care of. For every hand has been constantly employed, and the decks occupied in such a manner as to render a minute attention to it, under present circumstances, impossible—unless we would incur a longer delay at this place.

I send this letter to the care of your correspondent, Mr Le Fevre, in Lisbon, by a vessel that will sail from this port in a few weeks, and I shall put a duplicate on board the other, that will follow soon after.

Samuel Shaw to Le Fevre, March 27, 1784

The ship of which I am supercargo having put in at this place for water, on her passage from New York to Canton, and there being two vessels here that will sail shortly for Lisbon, I have done myself the honor of recommending to your care the enclosed packet for Daniel Parker Esq, one of the principal owners. Previous to my leaving America, he informed me that he was acquainted with your house, and directed that my letters, via Lisbon, should be forwarded to you for conveyance. I have therefore to request you would transmit the enclosed by the earliest opportunity which may offer for any of the American ports—which favor will be gratefully acknowledged, as well by Mr Parker as by Sir, your most obedient servant. . . .

Narrative by Samuel Shaw[10]
[From his Journal]

On the 20th, we saw Boavista, at three, P.M., and, during that and the next day, the remainder of the Cape de Verde islands. Between six and seven o'clock, on the morning of the 22d, being close in with the island of St. Jago, we fired a gun, on which two pilots came on board, who soon after brought us to anchor in Port Praya. We found here a snow and two brigs, a boat from one of which came on board with the captain and supercargo, who informed us that the snow and one of the brigs belonged to Portugal, and were waiting for a third, daily expected, on whose arrival, they should all three proceed to the coast of Africa for a cargo of slaves, with which they should come back to these islands, for account of a company who have the trade of them, and thence return to Lisbon. There was also here a French brig, on her way to Cape François, with a cargo of slaves, from Senegal, the captain of which, who likewise came on board, told us that he belonged to Havre de Grâce, and had one hundred and twenty-three slaves, that cost him, on an average, about five crowns a head, who he hoped would come to a good market at the Cape, whither he intended to sail this evening. The gentlemen did us the honor to take breakfast with us,— and it was not a bad caution which our captain gave the people, to have a good lookout after the sailors who brought them on board. "These fellows," said he, "are St. Peter's children,—every finger a fish-hook, and their hand a grapnel."

At nine o'clock, the captain, Mr. Randall, and I, went ashore in the pinnance. We were met on the beach by a negro, rigged in second-hand clothes, quite *à la militaire*, namely,—a blue navy-coat, faced with the same, anchor buttons; a scarlet cloth vest, crimson plush breeches, black silk stockings, and a long brass-mounted sword. "How do do?" was the only English he could speak; however, he conducted us to the fort, where we paid our compliments to the commandant, who is a Portuguese. He received us with much formality, and asked, in French, the reason of our stopping at the island. Being answered, that it was to take in water, some live stock and fruit, and get our ship new calked in her upper-works, he told us that the former was very easy to be accomplished, but that for the latter we must depend on ourselves, as he did not know a single calker in the whole island. He demanded five dollars as a fee for anchorage, which we paid him; and added, that, when we came on shore again, we must make him a *compliment*, after which we might trade for such articles as we wanted. We gave him a list of what we had occasion for, and he promised they should be ready in the morning, as soon as we should come on shore. After drinking a glass of grog with him, we took leave.

It being too late in the day to go to St. Jago, the capital, nine miles distant, to pay our compliments to the governor, or viceroy, we went to see the next officer in the port. He is also a Portuguese, genteel in his manners, gave us a glass of wine, and appeared very happy to see us. On telling him, by the interpreter, a negro, that we were Americans, he discovered great satisfaction, and exclaimed, with an air of pleasure and surprise,—"Bostonian! Bostonian!" In his apartment was a woman, who we supposed might be his wife. She was by no means handsome;—her complexion, whatever it might have been, was exceedingly sallow; added to this, her hair was cut all round, as close as possible, and, instead of a cap, or garland, her head was bound with a fold of white cloth, about four inches in width; a calico petticoat, and a piece of calico thrown over her shoulders by way of mantle, composed her dress. Her whole appearance was entirely different from that of the fair of our own country, and I believe she did not excite in any of us an idea that would militate with the tenth commandment, though she did not seem to be past five-and-twenty.

We returned on board at noon, and employed ourselves in writing letters to go by the French brig. To Mr. Parker I wrote an account of our transactions, respecting ship and cargo, from the time of our departure till our arrival here, taken from my journal kept for that purpose, and added a private letter, inclosing one for my friend in New York. Mr. Randall carried them on board and delivered them to the captain, having put them under cover to Messrs. Girard & Co., merchants at Cape François, with whom he had corresponded from Philadelphia. The brig is called *La Jengat*, Captain Pécot, consigned to M. Tartarel, and owned by M. Dorea, at Havre de Grâce.

The French brig sailed the next morning, and in passing gave us a salute of four swivels and *Vive le Roi!* which we returned with three cheers. A number of the naked blacks were on deck,—poor creatures, going to a state of hopeless slavery, and, torn from every tender connection, doomed to eat the bread and drink the water of affliction for the residue of their miserable lives! Good God! and is it man, whose distinguishing characteristic should be humanity and the exercise of every milder virtue, who wears sweet smiles and looks erect on heaven,—is it man endowed by thee with a capacity for enjoying happiness and suffering misery, to whom thou hast imparted a knowledge of thyself, enabled him to judge of right and wrong, and taught to believe in a state of future retribution,—is it man, who, thus trampling upon the principles of universal benevolence, and running counter to the very end of his creation, can become a fiend to torment his fellow-creatures, and deliberately effect the temporal misery of beings equally candidates with himself for a happy immortality?

After breakfast we went on shore, and made our *compliment* to the commandant, consisting of a round of salt beef, a cheese, and some apples. He demanded a dollar, for watching some of our water-casks, which was paid him,—and begged for some wine. The market-people being assembled about his hut, we there made our purchases of goats, pigs, poultry, and fruit, which he superintended in person, and assigned as a reason, that the king received an impost on every thing that was sold. After visiting the second officer, to whom we gave a cheese and some apples, for which he seemed very grateful, we returned on board to dinner.

The mate of the Portuguese brig came on board. He had commanded a topsail schooner from Lisbon, which foundered at sea. Two of his people were lost, and an English vessel took him and the remaining six up at sea, in an open boat, forty leagues from land, and brought them here, about three weeks ago;—the boat now lies on the beach, is very old, and not eighteen feet long. How innumerable are the mischiefs to which seafaring people expose themselves! Well might Horace say,—

> "Illi robur et æs triplex
> Circa pectus erat, qui fragilem truci
> Commisit pelago ratem
> Primus."

Towards sunset, the captain called me to look at a whale, which, at the distance of about five miles, appeared to be striking the water very forcibly with its tail. The people on board said it was attacked by the sword-fish and thresher, and gave this account of the combat. The sword-fish keeps under the whale, pricking him up, to prevent his descending, while the thresher, with his sharp tail, is cutting large pieces out of him, &c. This account is generally believed among seafaring people; though, on inquiry, I cannot find any of ours who have ever seen the thresher. It would seem that the tail of the whale striking the water is mistaken by them for this imaginary antagonist. Goldsmith, in his "Animated Nature," gives the following relation of the manner in which the sword-fish attacks the whale.

"The sword-fish is the whale's most terrible enemy. 'At the sight of this little animal,' says Anderson, 'the whale seems agitated in an extraordinary manner, leaping from the water, as if with affright: wherever it appears, the whale perceives it at a distance, and flies from it in the opposite direction. I have been myself,' continues he, 'a spectator of their terrible encounter. The whale has no instrument of defence except the tail; with that it endeavours to strike the enemy, and a single blow taking place would effectually destroy its adversary: but the sword-fish is as active as the other is strong, and easily avoids the stroke; then bounding into the air, it falls upon its great subjacent enemy, and endeavours, not to pierce with its pointed beak, but to cut with its toothed edges. The sea all about is soon dyed with blood, proceeding from the wounds of the whale; while the enormous animal vainly endeavours to reach its invader, and strikes with its tail against the surface of the water, making a report at each blow louder than the noise of a cannon.' "

We were not near enough to judge of all these circumstances, but we very plainly saw the tail of the whale striking the water, and distinctly heard the report of the blows.

"There is," continues Goldsmith, "another and more powerful enemy, called, by the fishermen of New England, the Killer. This is itself a cetaceous animal, armed with strong and powerful teeth. A number of these are said to surround the whale, in the same manner as dogs get round a bull. Some attack it with their teeth behind; others attempt it before; until, at last, the great animal is torn down, and its tongue is said to be the only part they devour when they have made it their prey. They are said to be of such great strength, that one of them alone was known to stop a dead whale that several boats were towing along, and drag it from among them to the bottom."

On the 25th, at sunrise, the proper arrangements having been made the evening before, the captain, Mr. Randall, the purser, doctor, and I, went on shore, mounted our horses, and proceeded for the town, or rather city, of St. Jago, with a negro guide on foot, who, notwithstanding, out-travelled our horses. There are crucifixes at small distances all along the road, and about half-way is a small stone church, in the yard of which is a crucifix surrounded by skull-bones. Our guide, in passing any of these crucifixes, always pulled off his hat. Near this church were a number of small huts, and a plantation, through which ran a small stream, from which we picked and ate a few water-cresses. At the edge of the high ground above the town are the ruins of an old fort, that appears to have been a regular fortification, flanked by four bastions, commanding the town, which is situated near the water. At the first hut after passing these ruins we saw some blacks, decently clothed, who told us, in Latin, that they were scholars, and designed for the church, could read Ovid, Virgil, Horace, and Cicero, but did not understand Greek. They directed us to the house where the viceroy lives, in point of elegance nearly equal to a good barn. His Excellency was confined to his bed by a fever, but, after being informed that we were Americans, he gave orders for us to be introduced into his chamber. Having announced our reasons for putting in at this island, which I was obliged to do in French, to one of his soldiers, of that nation, who served as interpreter, his Excellency bade us welcome, told us we had permission to go wherever we pleased, and made us a tender of his services in any thing we might have occasion for during our stay. He is a native of the country, and a mulatto, and appears to be about fifty-five years old; went to Lisbon in 1765, where he remained nine years; since when he has been viceroy of this and the other Cape de Verde islands. He inquired very particularly respecting the nature of our government, which I explained to him, and added that the Americans entertained a grateful sense of the good-will of the Portuguese towards them, manifested in the late decree of the queen, acknowledging their independence. He received the compliment as his due, and, in the course of conversation, mentioned the affair of Commodore Johnstone, who with his squadron was attacked, as he lay at anchor in Port Praya, by M. Suffrein, in the year 1780. The force on both sides was nearly equal; but the French, having the advantage by coming upon the enemy unexpectedly, did him considerable damage and sailed away. He spoke in very favorable terms of Johnstone, and appeared exceedingly partial towards the English. We mentioned a number of articles we had on board in the way of stores, and made him an offer of part, but he declined accepting any, except a few packs of cards, which, if we could spare them, he said he should be glad of. He treated us with wine, sugared almonds, fruits, and cheese, but no bread; after which, having thanked his Excellency for his civilities, we walked out to visit other parts of the city.

We went next to the convent, where are seven monks of the Franciscan order. There is a pretty chapel belonging to it, which we entered, and found a white priest with a black assistant, performing mass; the audience, exclusive of ourselves, consisting of about a dozen blacks, great and small. After staying a short time here, we went into the convent, saw the brothers, and visited the garden. It was very indifferent, and exceedingly hot, being open to the sun, and surrounded by excessively high rocks, that excluded every breath of air. On returning through the hall, we found the brothers had spread a table with some fruits, wine, preserves, and cake, of which having partaken, we thanked them for their hospitality, and gave them a few dollars for the use of their convent. All our conversation with these people was either in French, by the interpreter, or in Latin, which, though very bad on our part, they had the good manners perfectly to understand. After walking to several other parts of the city, we returned and took leave of the viceroy, who presented us with a watermelon.

St. Jago is a walled town, situated, to the south-west, on the low ground towards the sea, at the foot of a large hill, which keeps off the fresh breezes that are met with on the high grounds, and renders the place extremely hot. When the town was in its most flourishing state, there might have been about three hundred houses; but the greater part, and some of them the best, are now without inhabitants, and in ruins. This, I was told, is owing to the trade having been diverted from this to the neighbouring islands, and to the removal of many to the town of St. Domingo, a healthy and pleasant situation on the other side of the island. There are two prisons here, and several churches, one of which is large, has four bells, and, by its inscription, appears to have been built in 1696, and is still in good order. The buildings are mostly of stone, covered with brick tile, and have very little glass,—either the public or the private. Besides the gate by which we entered the town, there is another at the north-west extremity. These openings, for the gates are taken away, appear to be the only places of ingress or egress, by land; towards the water it is entirely open, and has nothing to defend it but the old fort on the hill and four small guns near the shore.

After ascending the hill, on our return, we sat down at the gate of the ruined fort, to enjoy the cool breeze and eat our watermelon. There is a fine view of the sea from this eminence, and a distant prospect of the island of Fogo, directly opposite, the base of it just visible,—then a cloud, and above that the high land appearing very plain. After a fatiguing ride, we got on board ship to dinner, about four o'clock, and sent the viceroy, as a present, some biscuit, half a dozen of *good* wine (for his own was very ordinary), a cheese, and three packs of cards, accompanied by a letter of acknowledgment, in French, for the attention he had shown us. These were delivered to the soldier that had served as our interpreter, who was sent by the governor to receive the cards we had promised him.

The next day, our captain, Mr. Randall, and the doctor, went ashore, after dinner, a shooting. During their absence, I wrote to my friend in New York, by the two vessels that are to sail for Lisbon after our departure. Our sportsmen returned on board at evening, with a few small birds, and a very excellent turkey, which the second officer, to whom we had given a cheese and some apples, had presented to the captain.

On the morning of the 27th, the captain and I went on shore and took leave of the commandant, to whom we gave four bottles of wine. This commandant appears in every respect foreign to the idea one would form of a gentleman. He does not seem to want sense, but is exceedingly deficient in good breeding and hospitality. Although we never went on shore without calling to see him, and made him two *compliments*, instead of one, he did not once, excepting the first day, when he gave us some grog, ask either of us to eat or drink; and yet, on our return from the city of St. Jago, he knew we had not dined, and told us that we looked very much fatigued. We returned on board about eleven o'clock, and, as it was determined the ship should sail in the evening, I employed the remainder of the day in writing letters. Duplicates of those that went by the way of Cape François, together with a detail of transactions since our arrival here, were addressed to Mr. Parker, in New York, with a private letter, enclosing what I had written to my friend. The packet was put under cover to Mr. Le Fevre, merchant in Lisbon, and, in duplicate, carried by Mr. Randall on board the two vessels intended for that place.

The island of St. Jago is about fifty miles long, and, in some parts, upwards of thirty wide, and is the largest of those called the Cape de Verde. It is exceedingly mountainous, and in those parts entirely barren; but the valleys are well cultivated from one end to the other, and produce abundance of fruits, such as oranges, cocoa-nuts, tamarinds, bananas, figs, pine-apples, and a few limes; also, very fine Indian corn and small beans. Plenty of live stock may be had here, namely, goats, pigs, sheep, horned-cattle, and poultry. There are, besides, small horses, asses, and little green monkeys with black faces. The inhabitants amount to about six thousand; one hundred and fifty of whom only are whites, the remainder blacks, mulattoes, &c.; of these, numbers are priests. Besides the city of St. Jago, already mentioned, there is a considerable inland town, St. Domingo, lying north-east from Port Praya, and about the same distance from it as St. Jago.

Port Praya, at the south end of the island, is in latitude 14°54′ north, and longitude 23°29′ west from London. Two points projecting towards the sea form the bay, nearly semicircular, where there is good water and safe anchorage for ships of any burden, the distance from one point to the other being about a league. Here the shipping take in water and refreshments, and may ride with safety nine months of the year, during which time the wind is northerly, and off the land. The months of June, July, and August are the rainy season, when the wind, being southerly, renders the bay very dangerous. On an eminence to the eastward, within the bay, is a fort that mounts about a dozen old iron guns, for the protection of the port. It is open in the rear and on both flanks. Its garrison consists of about forty whites and two hundred blacks, who live in miserable huts, built of stones and thatched with the leaves of the cocoa-tree. The only good buildings in it are the chapel, the prison, and a store-house. The non-commissioned officers are principally blacks. The uniform of the officers is blue, faced with red and trimmed with silver, with red underclothes. The trade of the island is conducted by a company, who have a factory not far from the fort. Their vessels arrive here from Lisbon, whence they go to the coast of Africa for slaves, which they dispose of in their other islands, and return here to complete their homeward cargoes.

Such vessels as put in here for refreshments only procure them from the negroes, many of whom are free. They are generally intelligent, more honest than the whites allow their color to be, and many of them write very well, and speak English. I was particularly pleased with the behaviour of a boy about thirteen or fourteen years of age, who wanted to buy a blanket. "If you sell him to me," says he, "I gib you de little pig, de chicken, de orange." I told him I had none to sell, and asked him if he had parents. His father, he answered, was gone to heaven from the coast of Africa, and his mother was still living on the island. I told him he was a good boy, and gave him a small piece of silver. "Ah, massa, you say me good boy, me no teef, me no tell lie," was his reply; and he seemed more grateful for my good opinion of him than for the money. The men discover much sagacity in their traffic,—one of whom, being told that he asked too much for his corn, answered, "No matter; me see last night in my sleep two English ships come here tree day more, buy much corn, and give one dollar bushel."

Our putting in at Port Praya was occasioned by the upperworks of our ship proving leaky, and a discovery that part of our water had been lost by the badness of the casks. This rendered an examination of the whole of that article necessary, and the event convinced us of the propriety of the measure; for, had we gone on without stopping, we must inevitably have wanted it, before we could have reached the Straits of Sunda. Vessels bound from America to China would do well to stop here, or at some of the neighbouring islands, where they may make small repairs, and take in water, live stock, and fruits, which conduce greatly to the preservation of health, in passing the warm latitudes. We accomplished all these objects in six days, stowed ten of our guns below, made room between decks, which rendered the men more comfortable, and put our ship in much better trim than she had been in before; and at seven o'clock this evening we came to sail, with a fair wind and pleasant weather.

Continuation of John Green's Journal

Sunday, 28. At nine, the land or harbor of Porto Praya bore SSW, distance four or 5 leagues.

Course made good SouthbE½E, distance 142ᵐ.
Difference of latitude 136.
Departure 41.
Latitude observed 12ᵈ46.
Meridional distance 41.

Difference of longitude 42.
Longitude in 22ᵈ03ᵐ.

All sail set fore and aft. Unbent the cables and cleared ship.

Monday, 29. Moderate and pleasant weather. All sail set. Winds from ENE. All hands employed on sundry. The sailmakers making windsails. The cooper making buckets. The carpenters caulking the pump coamings and rack ditto. Seamen drying sails and repairing rigging.

Course made good SSE, distance 178.
Difference of latitude 165.
Departure 68.
Latitude observed 10—01.
Meridional distance 109 East.
Difference of longitude 69.
Longitude in 20ᵈ54ᵐ.
Thermometer 78 degrees.

Tuesday, 30. Moderate and pleasant weather. Winds from NE and NbW and NNE. All sails set fore and aft. All hands employed from eight in the morning until 4 in the afternoon on cleansing ship and overhauling her materials, drying sails and stores.

Course made SSE, distance 157ᵐ.
Difference of latitude 145.

Departure 60.
Latitude observed 7ᵈ36ᵐ.
Meridional distance 169.
Difference of longitude 60.
Longitude in 19ᵈ54ᵐ.
Thermometer 80ᵈ.

Wednesday, 31. The fore part, hazy, sultry weather and flattering winds from East, NE, and North. All sail alow and loft to catch what air possible to waft us to the Southward. Our people employed as usual—caulkers, cooper, sailmakers, seamen, and armorer each busied at his own works.

Course made good SbE, distance 62ᵐ.
Difference of latitude 60.
Departure 12ᵐ.
Latitude observed 6ᵈ35.
Meridional distance 181ᵐ East.
Difference of longitude 12ᵐ.
Longitude in 19ᵈ42ᵐ.
Thermometer 84ᵈ. Smooth water.

VIII

Doubling the Cape

Having taken a navigational departure from Porto Praya in the Cape Verde Islands, the *Empress of China* during the month of April 1784 slowly worked her way southward through the South Atlantic Ocean. At the beginning of May, while still some thousand miles to the westward of the Cape of Good Hope, she reached the Cape's latitude. Dropping several degrees farther south during the next few days, she then turned toward the east and for nearly a month never strayed farther north than latitude 36° South nor farther south than 40°.

The route was entirely novel and unfamiliar to Captain Green; in fact, no man on board, with the possible exception of clerk Frederick Molineux, had ever sailed these waters. Their guides, delivered to Green with his orders, were a set of charts and a copy of Samuel Dunn's *A New Directory for the East-Indies*, the latest edition of which, the fifth, had been published in London in 1780. The *Empress of China* was making a textbook passage.

On May 13, Green's calculations for longitude put him due south of the Cape. Three of his officers had been keeping their own reckonings as well: First Mate Robert McCaver nearly agreed with Green's own figures, only placing the ship twenty-eight minutes more westerly; Second Captain Peter Hodgkinson put her two degrees two minutes farther east than Green; while Second Mate Abel Fitch disagreed with them all. According to his estimate, they were fifty-four minutes east of the Cape, but the latitude position placed the ship a comfortable 180 nautical miles from the tip of Africa.

"When you take your departure from the Cape of Good Hope, or from the soundings of the bank," the *Directory* warned, "increase your latitude to 37° S. or 38° S. to make advantage of the westerly winds, which are more constant there than in a lower latitude, and which generally blow from NW. to WSW. Though they mostly blow the strongest in the months of June, July, and August, it happens, that in April and May (which in those parts should be looked upon as the end of autumn) you sometimes have violent squalls of wind. These gales are generally foreseen by black clouds which obscure the horizon from NW. to W.

"As soon as you perceive these presages, prepare for their reception, because they come on apace, and are sometimes accompanied with whirlwinds. They begin to blow violently from WNW. to W. then they shift with fury to the SW. but when they get to the south, the wind abates, and it falls calm all of a sudden; but the sea (agitated and raised by the boisterous winds) is not so soon composed; this is frequently of worse consequence than the height of the gale."[1]

The conditions experienced by the ship confirmed what Dunn had written; a good augury for the *Directory*'s accuracy farther along when the *Empress of China* would have to rely upon it explicitly while threading her way through the Sunda Strait and into the island- and reef-strewn South China Sea beyond.

Also in late April or early May 1784, the papers concerning the *Empress of China*'s insurance reached France. "We have received, and also in duplicate by way of London," LeCouteulx and Cie. wrote to John Holker on the eleventh of May, "all the papers relative to her with the order to insure £196,000 on the body of the vessel and £392,000 on her cargo, equivalent to the sum of 112/m dollars evaluation, which you give to Mr. Parker's half share. We have forwarded this order to the Normandy chambers which, for various reasons, they have refused to sign; among other things, the novelty of the risk in every respect; first, the voyage from an American port to the Indies with a return to America, the crew and the flag, which is making its debut in the trade; moreover, the small confidence they have, which we share with them, in the success of the expedition" due to a cargo of "very slender consumption" and the small stock of dollars which could not possibly purchase a return lading, made it unlikely to secure underwriters either in France or in England.[2] Besides, the vessel was too small to carry a cargo sufficient to cover the duties. For a ship of 400 tons or 1,000 tons the duties were the same. "*Tant pis, Monsieur!*" but these were the sad truths. Credit, furthermore, would be most difficult to secure for such a tenuous enterprise. "As for the insurance, we are going to forward your original papers to Nantes and Mr. DelaVille . . . it is all that we can do for you." Mr. DelaVille would inform them about what success he had in Nantes or if he would have to forward the papers on to others in Bordeaux or Marseilles.

Continuation of John Green's Journal

APRIL 1784

Thursday, 1. The former and middle part, moderate, close, sultry weather. Winds variable in the North quarter. Amplitude this evening 9^{d}52^m. At ½ past eight, hard squalls from NE to East. In all small sails. Reefed the topsails. Set the foresail and mainsail. Much rain and continued blowing strong. At noon, ESE.

Course made South, distance 66.
Difference of latitude 66.
Departure 00.
Latitude per account 5^{d}29^m.
Meridional distance 181^m.
Difference of longitude 00.
Longitude in 19^{d}42^m.
Thermometer 84^d.

Friday, 2. The fore part, light airs and calms. Winds varying from SE to NNE. At 4 P.M., the wind shifted to South. We tacked ship and stood to the Eastward. At 7, fell flat calm. At 10, a small air from North. At 2 A.M., out all reefs and set all the steeringsails and small sails. Some flying clouds and light rain with some lightning.

Course made good S½E, distance 47^m.
Difference of latitude 47^m.
Departure 5.
Latitude per account 4^{d}30.
Latitude observed 4^{d}42^m.
Meridional distance 186.
Difference of longitude 5.
Longitude in 19^{d}37^m.
Thermometer 84^d.

Saturday, 3. Dark, cloudy, uncertain weather attended with a deal of rain and some thunder and lightning. Got up our conductor, furled all small sails. Catched about three hundred gallons of rain water for washing with. This day gave orders for making a water sail for catching

water. At 6 A.M., set steeringsails and all small sails. Winds light and variable from NE to NW and NE.

Course made good SSE, distance 63.
Difference of latitude 58^m.
Departure 24.
Latitude observed 3^{d}44.
Meridional distance 210^m East.
Difference of longitude 24.
Longitude in 19^{d}13^m West.
Thermometer 80^d.

Sunday, 4. Heavy, cloudy weather attended with much rain and variable winds and calms.

Course made good South-westerly, distance 21.
Difference of latitude 21^m.
Departure 2^m West.
Latitude Observed 3^{d}23^m North.
Meridional distance 208 East.
Difference of longitude 2^m W.
Longitude in 19^{d}15^m W.

All hands clean and in good order, capable of eating their allowance. Brewed a barrel of spruce beer. Thermometer 83^d.

Monday, 5. Light airs, variable and calms. Continually bracing the yards round to catch every air. The sun's amplitude at setting 9^{d}00. People employed at their different occupations. The supercargoes requested to have an overhaul at some of the casks of ginseng, which lays in the 'tweendecks. The order granted, and 4 men and a midshipman with a mate appointed to assist in getting it up to dry agreeable to the request, but on opening the first cask find it better letting it remain in its present state rather than move it up where *they say* it would embroil the salt air and spoil it.

Course made good SEbS, distance 36ᵐ.
Difference of latitude 30ᵐ.
Departure 20.
Latitude per account 2ᵈ53ᵐ North.
Meridional distance 228 East.
Difference of longitude 20ᵐ.
Longitude in 18ᵈ55ᵐ West.
Thermometer 83ᵈ.

Tuesday, 6. Light winds and variable with some calms. The wind from ENE—SSW—SSE and EbS. All hands employed as usual from eight in the morning until four in the afternoon.

Course made good S-Westerly, distance 48ᵐ.
Difference of latitude 48ᵐ.
Departure 2ᵐ W.
Latitude per account 2ᵈ05ᵐ North.
Latitude observed 2ᵈ3ᵐ.
Meridional distance 226 [*sic*].
Difference of longitude 2ᵐ.
Longitude in 18ᵈ57ᵐ.
Thermometer 84ᵈ.

Wednesday, 7. Light winds, calms, and very sultry. The winds variable from SEbE—SSE—South and SbW. All sail set. The water smooth and all hands employed as customary. This day brewed a barrel of essence of malt beer.

Course made good SWbSouth, distance 52ᵐ.
Difference of latitude 43ᵐ.
Departure 28.
Latitude per account 1ᵈ20.
Latitude observed 1ᵈ21ᵐ.
Meridional distance 198.
Difference of longitude 28ᵐ W.
Longitude in 18ᵈ25ᵐ West.
Thermometer 86ᵈ.

Thursday, 8. Moderate and sultry. Light airs from the SE quarter. Our starboard tacks on board from noon until eight at night. Tacked ship, winds South, and stood to the SW. All hands employed as usual.

Course made good East, distance 11ᵐ.
Difference of latitude 00ᵐ.
Departure 11.
Latitude per account 1ᵈ—21.
Meridional distance 209.
Difference of longitude 11ᵐ.
Longitude in 18ᵈ14ᵐ.
Sun's amplitude 13ᵈ.
Thermometer 84ᵈ.

Friday, 9. A steady breeze all this 24 hours from the SE quarter. The larboard tacks on board and braced up sharp. Smooth water. All hands employed as usual.

Course made good SSW, distance 92ᵐ.
Difference of latitude 85ᵐ.
Departure 35ᵐ W.
Latitude observed 00—04ᵐ South.
Meridional distance 156ᵐ E.
Difference of longitude 35ᵐ W.
Longitude in 19ᵈ9ᵐ West.
Amplitude 10ᵈ West.
Azimuth 9ᵈ36ᵐ.
Thermometer 84ᵈ.

Saturday, 10. Some flying squalls and a fresh of wind from the SE quarter. Our larboard tacks on board and the yards braced up sharp.

Course made good SbW, distance 90ᵐ.
Difference of latitude 88ᵐ.
Departure 18.
Latitude observed 1ᵈ32ᵐ South.
Meridional distance 138 E.
Difference of longitude 18.
Longitude in 19ᵈ27ᵐ West.
Variation 9ᵈ52ᵐ West.
Thermometer 84ᵈ.

Sunday, 11. Strong squalls, at times intermixed with rain and dark clouds, the winds from the SE quarter. Often obliged to take in the topgallant sails and staysails and set them when the squalls passed. Our larboard tacks on board and the yards braced up quite sharp.

Course made good SbW, distance 100.
Difference of latitude 98.
Departure 20.
Latitude per observation 3ᵈ10ᵐ South.
Meridional distance 118 E.
Difference of longitude 20.
Longitude in 19ᵈ47ᵐ West.
Thermometer 84ᵈ.

Monday, 12. Steady breezes and smooth water. Our larboard tacks on board, the yards braced sharp. Winds from the SE quarter. All hands employed on different subjects. ⟨The water smooth considerably.⟩ Caulker employed on the roundhouse deck. Some new sails altering.

Course made good SbW, distance 122.
Difference of latitude 120.

Departure 24.
Latitude observed 5ᵈ10ᵐ S.
Meridional distance 94ᵐ E.
Difference of longitude 24.
Longitude in 20ᵈ11ᵐ West.
Thermometer 85ᵈ.

Tuesday, *13*. Fresh of wind and smooth water. All sail set. By the wind standing to the Southward. Winds from ESE.

Course made good South, distance 143ᵐ.
Difference of latitude 143.
Departure 00.
Latitude observed 7ᵈ33ᵐ South.
Meridional distance 116ᵐ.
Difference of longitude 00.
Longitude in 21ᵈ01ᵐ West.
Variation 8ᵈ West.
Thermometer 84ᵈ.

Used some rope of the cargo. See the log.

Wednesday, *14*. Fresh breezes and smooth water. This day fitted fore- and main-topsail ties. Overhauling the rigging and putting it in the best order in our power against our come up with the high latitude where we must expect bad weather and heavy gales. Winds from the ESE. Standing to the Southward with a press of sail.

Course made good South ½ West, distance 143ᵐ.
Difference of latitude 143.
Departure 7ᵐ.
Latitude observed 9ᵈ56ᵐ South.
Meridional distance 87ᵐ.
Difference of longitude 7ᵈ.
Longitude in 20ᵈ18ᵐ West.
Variation 7ᵈ02.
Thermometer 84ᵈ.

Dried some of our spare sails and made a large tarpaulin from some canvas taken out of the new fore- and main-topsails to cover our spare sails below and prevent any wet getting at them.

Thursday, *15*. Fresh of wind from SEbE. Some dark, cloudy weather. A press of sail all this 24 hours, a-standing to the Southward. All hands employed as usual. The caulkers caulking the larboard side of the roundhouse.

Course made good SbW, distance 136.
Difference of latitude 134.

Departure 27ᵐ.
Latitude observed 12ᵈ10ᵐ South.
Meridional distance 60.
Difference of longitude 28.
Longitude in 20ᵈ45ᵐ.
Thermometer 84ᵈ.

Friday, *16*. Fresh breezes and some squalls in the flying clouds. Find our lower and topmast rigging quite slack. At 6 A.M., hauled up the courses. Down all staysails and wore ship, her head to NE. Lay to. Winds at SE and ESE. Set up our rigging. Wore ship at eight o'clock and made all sail to the Southward.

Course made good SbW¼W, distance 137ᵐ.
Difference of latitude 133.
Departure 33.
Latitude 14ᵈ23ᵐ.
Meridional distance 27ᵐ.
Difference of longitude 34.
Longitude in 21ᵈ18 W.
Thermometer 82ᵈ1/2.

At noon, pleasant weather and a head sea.

Saturday, *17*. All this 24 hours a fresh of wind from the SE quarter. Mostly the topgallant sails handed and the small sails furled. A press of sail set. A-standing to the Southward. All hands employed on necessaries. Some at the rigging. Some making hammocks. The gunner, mate, and armorer cleaning the small arms.

Course made good SSW, distance 148ᵐ.
Difference of latitude 136.
Departure 56.
Latitude observed 16ᵈ39ᵐ.
Meridional distance 31ᵐ West.
Difference of longitude 58ᵐ.
Longitude in 22ᵈ—16ᵐ West.
Thermometer 83ᵈ.

At noon, topgallant sails and staysails set.

Sunday, *18*. Moderate breezes and smooth water with some flying squalls. All sail set standing to the Southward.

Course made good SbW¼W, distance 138.
Difference of latitude 134ᵐ.
Departure 34ᵐ.
Latitude observed 18ᵈ53ᵐ S.
Meridional distance 65ᵐ W.
Difference of longitude 35ᵐ.
Longitude in 22ᵈ51ᵐ.

Saw some shearwaters and many flying fish. Thermometer 80ᵈ. Winds from ESE to SE.

Monday, 19. Squally weather, as if near some land, and flying showers. The water smooth. The wind from SE to ESE. Expecting we were near the islands of Martin Vaz, St. Mary's, and Trinidad and, not having any knowledge of them further than their latitude and longitude, shortened sail at night and run close by the wind at the distance of 4 miles per hour and kept a good lookout, fearing we might fall in with them in the night.

Course made good SSW, distance 114ᵐ.
Difference of latitude 105.
Departure 44.
Latitude observed 20ᵈ38ᵐ S.
Meridional distance 109ᵐ W.
Difference of longitude 46ᵐ.
Longitude in 23ᵈ—37ᵐ West.
Thermometer 81ᵈ.

Tuesday, 20. Fresh of wind and smooth water. The winds from ESE and EbS. All sails set. A-steering to the Southward. All hands employed making mats. Carpenter fitting the air ports. Gunner a-cleaning the small arms.

Course made good South, distance 140ᵐ.
Difference of latitude 140.
Departure 00.
Latitude observed 22ᵈ58ᵐ S.
Meridional distance 109ᵐ W.
Difference of longitude 00.
Longitude in 23ᵈ37ᵐ W.
Thermometer 77ᵈ1/2.

Wednesday, 21. Moderate and pleasant. Some dark clouds but no wind to hurt anything. The water very smooth and all our sail set that would draw to advantage, the wind E to SEbE. All hands employed. The sailmaker making hammocks. The carpenter making a boobyhatch for the fore hatchway.

Course made SbE, distance 142.
Difference of latitude 40.
Departure 28ᵐ.
Latitude observed 25ᵈ18ᵐ S.
Meridional distance 81ᵐ West.
Difference of longitude 30ᵐ.
Longitude in 23ᵈ7ᵐ West.
Thermometer 77ᵈ.

Thursday, 22. Moderate and pleasant weather. All sail set. The water as smooth as glass, the winds from E—ENE and NE. All sail set alow and aloft. All hands employed as usual.

Course made good SEbS, distance 144ᵐ.
Difference of latitude 120.
Departure 1ᵐ W.
Latitude observed 27ᵈ18ᵐ S.
Meridional distance 23ᵐ East.
Difference of longitude 89ᵐ.
Longitude in 21ᵈ—58ᵐ West longitude.
The thermometer at sunset 71ᵈ; at noon 76ᵈ.

Saw a large bird made like a gannet in shape and color, named albatross.

Friday, 23. Moderate and pleasant weather. The winds from NE and NNW. All sail set alow and aloft. Ship standing to the SEward. The sea very smooth. All hands employed. A very heavy dew fell, which wet the sails as much as rain.

Course made good SEbS1/2South, distance 90ᵐ.
Difference of latitude 70.
Departure 57.
Latitude observed 28ᵈ38ᵐ.
Meridional distance 56ᵐ E.
Difference of longitude 64ᵐ.
Longitude 20ᵈ54 West longitude.
Variation 1ᵈ40ᵐ West.
Thermometer 75.

Saturday, 24. Moderate weather, light winds, and smooth sea. All sail set. Winds from NNW. All hands employed as usual from eight in the morning until 4 in the afternoon. One of our larboard main-topmast backstays broke. Spliced him and set him up again. Heavy dews fall every night.

Course made good SSE, distance 76ᵐ.
Difference of latitude 70.
Departure 29.
Latitude observed 29ᵈ49ᵐ.
Meridional distance 85 East.
Difference of longitude 33ᵐ.
Longitude in 20ᵈ21ᵐ West.
Thermometer at noon 74ᵈ; at sunset 74 ditto.

Sunday, 25. Light winds, smooth water. All sail set alow and loft.

Course made SEbE¾E, distance 81ᵐ.
Difference of latitude 35.
Departure 73ᵐ.
Latitude observed 30ᵈ24ᵐ S.
Meridional distance 158.
Difference of longitude 83.
Longitude 18ᵈ—56ᵐ.
Thermometer at noon 73ᵈ; at sunset 73.
Variation 1ᵈ30ᵐ.

Monday, 26. Fine wind from NE. All our stay-sails and topgallant sails set. Hauled down the steeringsails. Gloomy weather and a long swell from the SSW as if there had been much wind in this parallel.

Thermometer at noon 72ᵈ; at sunset 70 ditto.
Course made ESE, distance 159.
Difference of latitude 61ᵐ.
Departure 147.
Latitude observed 31ᵈ25ᵐ South.
Meridional distance 303.
Difference of longitude 171ᵐ.
Longitude in 16ᵈ5ᵐ West.

Tuesday, 27. Fresh of wind from NNE. A press of sail set. Gloomy weather. All hands employed knotting yarns and making points for the courses.

Course made EbS¾ South, distance 214.
Difference of latitude 72ᵐ.
Departure 202.
Latitude observed 32ᵈ37ᵐ South.
Meridional distance 507ᵐ E.
Difference of longitude 238.
Longitude in 12ᵈ07ᵐ West.
Thermometer 74ᵈ.

Wednesday, 28. All this 24 hours gloomy weather and variable wind. Steeringsail and all sail set. Winds in the NW quarter.

Course made good EbSouth, distance 100ᵐ.
Difference of latitude 20ᵐ.
Departure 98.
Latitude observed 32ᵈ57ᵐ S.
Meridional distance 605 E.
Difference of longitude 115.
Longitude in 9ᵈ32ᵐ W.
Thermometer 69ᵈ.

Thursday, 29. Gloomy weather and variable winds. Down all steeringsails. The winds varying from SSW to SSE. Uncertain weather and

a long swell from SW. At 6 A.M., the wind ESE. Tacked and stood to the Southward.

Course made good E½North, distance 73ᵐ.
Difference of latitude 7ᵐ.
Departure 73.
Latitude per account 32ᵈ50ᵐ S.
Meridional distance 678.
Difference of longitude 87ᵐ.
Longitude in 8ᵈ05ᵐ W.
Thermometer 67ᵈ.

Friday, 30. Gloomy weather and variable winds from SE quarter. A long swell from the SW. All hands employed at work.

Course made SE½E, distance 50ᵐ.
Difference of latitude 31ᵐ.
Departure 39.
Latitude per account 33ᵈ21ᵐ.
Latitude per observation 33ᵈ34ᵐ.
Meridional distance 717ᵐ E.
Difference of longitude 46.
Longitude in 7ᵈ—19ᵐ West.
Thermometer 67ᵈ.

May 1784

Saturday, 1. Gloomy weather and variable winds with a long swell from the SW. The wind vary from the SE to South. All hands employed.

Course made E½North, distance 93.
Difference of latitude 9.
Departure 93.
Latitude observed 33—24 S.
Meridional distance 810.
Difference of longitude 111ᵐ.
Longitude in 5ᵈ28ᵐ W.
Thermometer 67.

Sunday, 2. Gloomy weather. Variable winds. High swell from SW. All sail set. Some calms.

Course made EbS¾S, distance 42.
Difference of latitude 14ᵐ.
Departure 40.
Latitude observed 33—38.
Meridional distance 851.
Difference of longitude 47ᵐ.
Longitude in 4ᵈ41.
Thermometer 67ᵈ½; at sunset thermometer 65ᵈ.
Winds SSW to ENE.

Monday, *3*. Variable winds and gloomy weather. Winds from the NE and ENE. Find those winds to be of the same nature as the southerly winds are on the coast of America.

Course made good SEbE¾E, distance 168.
Difference of latitude 72.
Departure 152.
Latitude per observation 34ᵈ50ᵐ.
Meridional distance 1,003ᵐ.
Difference of longitude 179.
Longitude in 1ᵈ40ᵐ W.
Thermometer 66ᵈ.

Tuesday, *4*. Fresh of wind and a tumbling sea from the NE. Dark, cloudy weather and some fog. Winds at NNE. Mostly the reefed topsails set.

Course made good SEbE¼E, distance 195.
Difference of latitude 100.
Departure 167.
Latitude per account 36ᵈ30ᵐ.
Meridional distance 1,170.
Difference of longitude 204.
Longitude in 1ᵈ44ᵐ E.
Thermometer 66ᵈ.

Wednesday, *5*. Foggy weather and misty. Let the reefs out of the topsails. Set all small sails. Winds from NNW.

Course made good EbS, distance 94ᵐ.
Difference of latitude 18ᵐ.
Departure 92.
Latitude per account 36ᵈ48ᵐ South.
Meridional distance 1,262ᵐ E.
Difference of longitude 114.
Longitude in 3ᵈ38ᵐE.
Thermometer at noon 65ᵈ; at evening 66ᵈ.

Thursday, *6*. Foggy weather. Smooth water. All sail set. The winds NbE.

Course made E½South, distance 148ᵐ.
Difference of latitude 14ᵐ.
Departure 147.
Latitude per account 37ᵈ02ᵐ.
Latitude observed 37ᵈ06ᵐ.
Meridional distance 1,409.
Difference of longitude 182.
Longitude in 6ᵈ40ᵐ E.

Mr. Swift, purser, sick of the intermitting fever, and Mr. Randall, supercargo, complains of pain

in his stomach. Thermometer 66ᵈ.

Friday, *7*. Steady breeze and foggy. Set the lower and topmast steeringsails [and] all the staysails. The winds North and NNE and NW.

Course made E½S, distance 187.
Difference of latitude 18ᵐ.
Departure 186.
Latitude per account 37ᵈ20ᵐ S.
Meridional distance 1,596 E.
Difference of longitude 233.
Longitude in 10ᵈ33ᵐ E.
Thermometer 65ᵈ.

Saturday, *8*. At 5 P.M., took in the lower steeringsails. At 8, took in the topmast ditto. At nine, the wind flies out of the Southward. In all small sails. At 10, close-reefed the topsails. Blows strong and very thick attended with some small rain.

Course made EbNorth¾N, distance 162ᵐ.
Difference of latitude 55ᵐ.
Departure 153ᵐ.
Latitude per account 36ᵈ25ᵐ S.
Meridional distance 1,748.
Difference of longitude 191.
Longitude in 13ᵈ44ᵐ W [*sic*].
Thermometer 59ᵈ.

Sunday, *9*. Commences fresh gale and dark, cloudy weather. At sunset, moderates. Out a reef the topsails. At midnight, the wind veers to ESE. Wore ship to the South. At daylight, moderate. Set all the staysails and the topgallant sails.

Variation per amplitude 17ᵈ28ᵐ.
Course made: EbN½North, distance 43ᵐ.
Difference of latitude 12ᵐ.
Departure 41ᵐ.
Latitude per account 36ᵈ37ᵐ South.
Latitude per observation 36ᵈ40ᵐ.
Meridional distance 1,789.
Difference of longitude 51.
Longitude in 14ᵈ—35ᵐ East.

Monday, *10*. Moderate weather and gloomy, the winds from ENE. The steeringsails set.

The variation per amplitude 17ᵈ41ᵐ.
Thermometer at noon 67ᵈ; at sundown 64ᵈ.
Course made ESE, distance 97ᵐ.
Difference of latitude 37ᵐ.

Departure 90.
Latitude observed 37ᵈ17 South.
Meridional distance 1,879.
Difference of longitude 113.
Longitude in 16ᵈ28ᵐ E.

Tuesday, *11*. Moderate weather and variable winds from North to East. The latter part, squally and light winds. At nine, unbent the foresails and main ditto, the fore and main topsails, the fore-staysail and main-topgallant sail, and brought in new ones in their places.

Thermometer 66ᵈ.
Course made ESE, distance 92ᵐ.
Difference of latitude 36.
Departure 86.
Latitude observed 37—52 S.
Meridional distance 1,965.
Difference of longitude 107ᵐ.
Longitude in 18ᵈ15ᵐ E.

Wednesday, *12*. The former part, squally. Single-reefed the topsails. The middle and latter part, more settled weather. Out reefs and set the topgallant sail and all staysails. The wind variable from the NE to ENE.

Course made good SEbE¼E, distance 61ᵐ.
Difference of latitude 31ᵐ.
Departure 52.
Latitude observed 38—23.
Meridional distance 2,017.
Difference of longitude 66ᵐ.
Longitude in 19ᵈ21ᵐ E.

By the appearance of the water, it's likely to be a strong current here, which we have got into at noon.

Thursday, *13*. Uncertain weather. Winds variable and calms. Unbent the main-topmast-staysail to mend. The latter part, repairing the fore-topsail which was unbent the other day.

Course made good EbNorth¾North, distance 71ᵐ.
Difference of latitude 17ᵐ.
Departure 69.
Latitude per account 38ᵈ05ᵐ S.
Meridional distance 2,086.
Difference of longitude 87ᵐ.
Longitude 20ᵈ—58ᵐ.

Mr. Hodgkinson's longitude given in this day

23ᵈ E; his meridional distance from St. Jagos 2,380 miles.
Mr. McCaver longitude 20ᵈ30ᵐ E; meridional distance 2,167ᵐ.
Mr. Fitch longitude in 22ᵈ06ᵐ E; his meridional distance 2,222. Thermometer at noon 72ᵈ.

Friday, *14*. Uncertain weather. People employed repairing the fore-topsail and main-topmast-staysail.

Variation per amplitude 21ᵈ55ᵐ West.
Course made good SE¼S, distance 48.
Difference of latitude 36.
Departure 32.
Latitude per account 38ᵈ41ᵐ.
Meridional distance 2,412.
Difference of longitude 40.
Longitude in 21ᵈ28ᵐ E.

The latter part, got down the topgallant yards and reefed the fore- and main-topsails. Thermometer 69ᵈ and 64ᵈ.

Saturday, *15*. Dark, cloudy weather and has all the appearance of bad weather. Some sharp lightning. The winds varying in the southern quarter. The latter part, moderate. Out reefs and set the staysails. Our larboard pump split. Got him up and repairing ditto.

Course made EbNorth¼North, distance 132ᵐ.
Difference of latitude 32.
Departure 128.
Latitude observed in 38ᵈ09ᵐ S.
Meridional distance 2,540.
Difference of longitude 162.
Longitude in 24ᵈ10ᵐ E.

At noon, almost calm. Thermometer 69ᵈ.

Sunday, *16*. Pleasant weather. The middle and latter part, the winds varying to the E and NNW. Up topgallant yards. Set all the staysails and steeringsails.

Course made good E, distance 102ᵐ.
Difference of latitude 00.
Departure 102.
Latitude per account 37ᵈ50ᵐ S.
Latitude per observation 38ᵈ08ᵐ.
Meridional distance 2,640.
Difference of longitude 127ᵐ.

Longitude in 26ᵈ17ᵐ E.

N.B.—find a current which has set us to the North and whether to the East or West we can't ascertain.

The azimuth 23ᵈ18ᵐ West.
The amplitude at same time 22ᵈ36ᵐ West.

Monday, 17. The fore and middle part, cloudy and a steady wind from WSW. The latter part, calm for some time. The wind at noon NEb-North.

Sun's amplitude sun's setting 23ᵈ24ᵐ West.
Thermometer 69ᵈ and 71ᵈ.
Course made good E¼South, distance 102ᵐ.
Difference of latitude 6ᵐ.
Departure 102ᵐ.
Latitude per account 38—14; per observation 38—16.
Meridional distance 2,742.
Difference of longitude 129.
Longitude in 28ᵈ26ᵐ East.

Tuesday, 18. Pleasant breezes from NE to NW. All sail set fore and aft. People employed repairing fore-topsail.

Thermometer from 67ᵈ and 71ᵈ.
Course made good E½North, distance 174.
Difference of latitude 17ᵐ.
Departure 173.
Latitude observed 38ᵈ00.
Meridional distance 2,915.
Difference of longitude 219.
Longitude in 32ᵈ05ᵐ East.

One of our people informed the officer of the watch he saw a large turtle swimming close to leewards of the ship. Many small birds in sight, like pigeons, but they alight on the water and rise again.

Wednesday, 19. Pleasant breeze and some flying clouds. All the sail set. The winds from NEbN and NWbW. People employed repairing the main-topsail, having finished the fore ditto.

Thermometer 68ᵈ and 71ᵈ.
The azimuth 25ᵈ41ᵐ West.
The amplitude 25ᵈ17ᵐ West.

Rove new topgallant braces and shifted fore-topsail and main ditto braces end for end.

Course made good E½South, distance 200ᵐ.
Difference of latitude 20.
Departure 199.
Latitude observed 38ᵈ20.
Meridional distance 3,114ᵐ East.
Difference of longitude 252.
Longitude in 36ᵈ17ᵐ East.

Thursday, 20. Cloudy weather. At 4 P.M. fell into a cross heavy swell from the West NW round to ENE. The ship labors much. Took in the steeringsails and topgallant sails, reefed top-sails, and hands the mainsail. At midnight, the swell abated. Out all reefs and made sail. Find a strong current setting to the North. Winds from NNE to North.

Thermometer 64ᵈ and 66ᵈ.
Course made good EbN¾North, distance 134ᵐ.
Difference of latitude 45 North.
Departure 126.
Latitude per account 38ᵈ20ᵐ S.
Latitude per Observation 37ᵈ35ᵐ S.
Meridional distance 3,240.
Difference of longitude 160ᵐ.
Longitude in 38ᵈ57ᵐ E.

N.B.—added the difference latitude this 24 hours to the distance Immadging [*sic.*, imagined (?)]. She was driven as much to the East as she was to the North by the current.

Friday, 21. Fresh of wind from NW to W. All sail set.

The variation per amplitude 29ᵈ17ᵐ W.
Thermometer 65ᵈ.
Course made E2ᵈ North, distance 170ᵐ.
Difference of latitude 6ᵐ.
Departure 170.
Latitude per observation 37—30.
Meridional distance 3,410.
Difference of longitude 216ᵐ.
Longitude 42ᵈ33ᵐ E.

Saturday, 22. Variable winds and calms. The winds veering from NWbW to SE, E and NE.

Course made SEbE¾E, distance 45ᵐ.
Difference of latitude 20.
Departure 42.
Latitude per account 37ᵈ50ᵐ S.
Meridional distance 3,452.

Difference of longitude 53ᵐ.
Longitude in 43ᵈ36ᵐ South.
Thermometer 63ᵈ.

Sunday, 23. Commences variable winds and
some rain. The winds from SW to West and
NW.

Course made good E½North, distance 114ᵐ.
Difference of latitude 11ᵐ.
Departure 114.
Latitude observed 37ᵈ39ᵐ S.
Meridional distance 3,566ᵐ.
Difference of longitude 144.
Longitude in 46ᵈ00ᵐ E.
Thermometer 61ᵈ.

At noon, winds at SW. Blows strong and clear
weather.

Monday, 24. Fresh of wind and variable. The
fore part, winds at SSE. Middle part, ESE.
Latter part, ENE. The single-reefed topsails
set. All the staysails handed. Squally and a head
sea. Find the ship to make a good spell of water
every half hour.

Thermometer 59ᵈ and 62ᵈ.
Course made E¾North, distance 111ᵐ.
Difference of latitude 16ᵐ.
Departure 110.
Latitude per account 37ᵈ23ᵐ.
Latitude observed 37ᵈ07ᵐ.
Meridional distance 3,676.
Difference of longitude 138.
Longitude in 48ᵈ18ᵐ E.

N.B.—find a current setting to the North and
imagine the current is setting to the Eastward.

Tuesday, 25. Blowing fresh of wind from NE-
bE to NEbNorth. The reefed topsails set and
the staysails. Blowing in squalls, the water
smooth. The sky dark and gloomy. No sun appearing. The thermometer 63ᵈ. The ship makes
a good spell of water every half hour.

Course made good ESE, distance 197ᵐ.
Difference of latitude 75ᵐ.
Departure 182.
Latitude per account 38ᵈ22ᵐ S.
Meridional distance 3,858ᵐ E.
Difference of longitude 231.
Longitude in 52ᵈ09ᵐ East.

Wednesday, 26. Blowing strong from NNE and
North. The single-reefed topsails set, the topgallant sails and staysails. The air clear and not
so cloudy as has been for some days past. Thermometer 63ᵈ. Ship leaks much. The water
smooth.

Course made EbS¾South, distance 198ᵐ.
Difference of latitude 67ᵐ.
Departure 186.
Latitude per account 39ᵈ32ᵐ.
Latitude per observation 39ᵈ24ᵐ.
Meridional distance 4,044ᵐ E.
Difference of longitude 239.
Longitude in 56ᵈ08ᵐ East.

Thursday, 27. Fresh breezes and cloudy. The
winds at NNE and North. The reefed topsails
set.

At sunset azimuth 28ᵈ51ᵐ.
Amplitude 27ᵈ33ᵐ West.
Thermometer 62ᵈ and 64ᵈ.
Sunrising amplitude 27ᵈ27ᵐ.
Course made good North 85ᵈ E.
Difference of latitude 18ᵐ.
Departure 215.
Latitude observed 39ᵈ06.
Meridional distance 4,259.
Difference of longitude 276.
Longitude in 60ᵈ44ᵐ E.

Friday, 28. Commences a fresh gale and smooth
water. The winds NNW. The middle part more
moderate. The latter part the wind veers to SW
attended with gloomy weather. The staysails
and the main-topgallant sail set. Single-reefed
topsails set.

Course made EbNorth, distance 167ᵐ.
Difference of latitude 33.
Departure 164.
Latitude per account 38ᵈ33ᵐ S.
Meridional distance 4,423.
Difference of longitude 208.
Longitude in 64ᵈ12ᵐ East.
The winds at noon ESE.
Thermometer 59ᵈ.

Saturday, 29. Blows strong and some rain. Winds
from SSE and SE. Hands fore- and mizzen-
topsails. At nine, hands the mainsail. Blows very
strong. Sent down the topgallant yards. The
gusts of wind comes down [as] if from high

land. The water remarkable smooth for the wind that blows.

Thermometer 50^d and 55^d.
Course made good NNE, distance 70^m.
Difference of latitude 65^m.
Departure 27^m.
Latitude per account 37^{d}28^m S.
Meridional distance 4,450.
Difference of longitude 34^m.
Longitude in 64^{d}46^m.

Sunday, 30. Blows strong all this 24 hours. At 4 A.M., a little moderate. Set the mainsail and at 8 hands ditto. Hard squalls. Heavy sea. Ship leaks much. Winds from SEbS to ESE and some drizzling rain.

Course made good N, distance 86^m.
Difference of latitude 86.
Departure 00.
Latitude per account 36^{d}02^m S.
Meridional distance 4,450.
Difference of longitude 00.

Longitude in 64^{d}46^m.

Monday, 31. The fore part, blows strong. The winds ESE. The middle and latter part, less winds. At 8 P.M., wore ship to the South. A heavy sea from the SE. The latter part, hard rain. The wind veers to ENE. Set the fore- and mizzen-topsails and mainsail. Ship pitches much. Carried away our starboard upper rail of ship's head.

Course made good SE, distance 15^m.
Difference of latitude 11^m.
Departure 11.
Latitude per account 36—13^m.
Latitude per observation 36^{d}06^m S.
Meridional distance 4,461.
Difference of longitude 13.
Longitude in 64^{d}59^m E.

For several days past uncertain weather and variable winds.

Thermometer 63^d.

IX

The Flight of Daniel Parker

Since the very beginning of the China scheme, perhaps even before, Daniel Parker had been painting himself into a corner. The doors he had passed while backing into it had either closed or were no longer within reach without treading on sticky ground. Much of it he had done in darkness and secrecy so successfully that his motions had scarcely been noticed. Only Samuel Shaw, now well out of harm's way at sea, had any inkling of Parker's true nature whenever his mind was troubled by the $2,300 discrepancy in the boxes of specie. "There was something in his manners," Shaw told his old comrade Winthrop Sargent later on, "that stilled suspicion to sleep—I had been conversant only with the honest part of mankind and I even omitted taking a receipt or any kind of written voucher for the transactions."[1]

Even four months after the *Empress of China* left for the Orient, Parker still was crying poor to John Holker, who, by then, had every right and reason to poor-mouth back. Holker's confrontation with Robert Morris was sufficiently perplexing for anyone: two headstrong financial entrepreneurs locking horns over principles, stubborn recalcitrance replacing cooperation and mutual trust. With the Superintendent of Finance pressing hard on one side to settle immensely complex accounts compounded during the last two years of the war, and Parker bellowing for more money to settle current demands against Parker & Company on the other, Holker's patience and liquidity rapidly drained away. Something had to be done, and that something included squeezing the most benefit possible out of the equity already accumulated around the China venture. The embarrassments Parker claimed to be experiencing had become acute.

"The very unexpected and extraordinary advance," Parker complained to Holker, "that we have been under the necessity of making for the Ship *Empress of China* in consequence of a failure on the part of those Gentlemen who engaged to Advance the money for one third of that Ship and Cargo, has employed so much more of our Capital than we had any reason for expecting that we have been under the necessity of delaying the payment of our Obligation to you for £3900 Ster[lin]g Advanced us in Bills of Exchange on London.

"In Order to prevent any further delay of that payment we would propose to write to Messrs LeCouteulx & Co Paris to pass to your Credit one half of the Proceeds of the Ship *Comte de Artois* & Cargo which may remain in their hands agreeably to Letters wrote them by Robert Morris Esq on the 30th Decr last, copy of which you have herewith."[2]

The very serious problems mushrooming for Daniel Parker & Company intimately affected not only Parker and Holker but also, by association, William Duer, who had kept pretty much to himself following the political maneuverings for selection of the chief supercargo. Duer and Parker had been concerned, with Walter Livingston, in Parker & Company long before Holker had entered the picture and in early times had involved themselves in contracting for the army, provisioning, borrowing large sums to accomplish the same, and attempting to keep one step ahead of notes falling due by financing others. Now Holker, as a partner, was finding himself liable for the debts of the others for transactions that had taken place months before he entered the partnership.

Parker, not Duer, it was beginning to appear, was the chief offender: his creditors, including some of the very merchants in Boston who, it had been supposed, would take up the final third share in the *Empress of China* voyage, had also begun to lose patience. The more anyone learned about Parker's dealings with them, in fact, the more plausible it seemed that the Boston merchants' failure to come into the China venture was caused by Parker's participation in it and their understandable reluctance to throw good money after bad. "I have mortgaged my personal Estate," Holker fumed to Duer when Parker's true duplicity became clear, "& all these misfortunes happen [to] me through your introducing to me D[aniel] P[arker] as a worthy Caracter."[3]

Parker, endeavoring to persuade Holker to furnish even more money than he had already—"although Holker advanced almost double the amount of stock stipulated in the deed of Copartnership"—attempted to convince the influential Philadelphia merchant Thomas Fitzsimons that he, Parker, was indeed owed vast sums by the other partners. For evidence, he provided Fitzsimons with a copy of his accounts, transcribed in his own hand, which he had recently filed in court.[4]

By mid-May 1784, William Duer's dander was up. Parker's failure to make good on notes and bills when due was beginning to reflect on him, and Holker as well. Clearly, as Agent and Cashier of the Company, Parker was withholding information from the partners; he was inefficient, incompetent, dishonest, or all three. When, in May, Duer received a plea from Ebenezer Young, the master shipwright who had overseen the outfits of several of the Company's vessels, he could no longer restrain himself.

"There is four Hundred and thirty or forty Pound coming to me from Mr Parker for fiting his Vessels &c," Young wrote in desperation, "the greatest part of it I owe to Carpenters I Broat from Midletown [Connecticut] which have ben wating from March 10 to this day for thare money, now find thare is no prospect of geting it Since thay find Mr Parker is gon to the E[a]stward. Thay tell me that thay will wate no Longer and if I dont pay them this week thay will apply to a Lawer. I know of no one but your Self in this City to apply to for Relief. . . ."[5]

Duer foresaw the worst and took it upon himself to give Young his course of action.

"If during your Journey in Connecticut," Duer ordered, "you should discover that Mr Parker has any Idea of Embarking from any Port in that State you will Immediately apply to an Attorney of the first eminence to take out a Writ in the Name of John Holker and William Duer, against Danl Parker, for One Hundred and Fifty Thousand Doll[ar]s and get him held to Bail in the Sum of Twenty Thousand pounds lawful Money—you will get yourself deputed to serve this writ and take good care that he gives Bail before he is Released—I hereby Indemnify you, against all cost and damage which may attend this Business, and authorize you to show these instructions to the Council you Employ to Issue the Writ.

"If Mr Parker should have proceeded to Boston, which you will endeavor to discover, proceed thither without delay and deliver the letters given you herewith to Mr Oliver Smith at Boston, who will take such Measures as he shall deem adviseable in the Business.

"The Business Entrusted to you being of a Delicate Nature, and such as nothing but necessity would induce me to adopt, You will act in this matter with Caution, Secrecy, and firmness—In particular you will not Divulge the matter to any person (unless the writ is Served) without my permission."[6]

In point of fact, despite fears to the contrary, Daniel Parker had not run off. He showed up in Philadelphia, ostensibly to close the books of Parker & Company, which had been dissolved in May with Thomas Fitzsimons the trustee appointed to conclude its affairs. Holker instantly wrote to Duer requesting his immediate attendance, but, when day after day passed and he still had not arrived, Holker penned a totally uncharacteristic rebuke to his erstwhile friend:

"I cannot Conceive what can detain you so long in New York, you were to have returned here with Lady Kitty in ten days, and you are still in New York. Mr. Melancton Smith, Mr. Taylor's clark, Mr. Flint & Mr. Parker are all here to settle these accounts, waiting for you every hour: in the Name of God—what do you mean by such delays—are we never to finish, I hope the next Stage will Bring you here."[7]

One of the matters decided was that part of Daniel Parker & Company's shares in the *Empress of China* would have to be sold or, at least, mortgaged by bottomry, a mortgage executed to enable a ship to return to her port of registry. It had been discussed before but was essential now to clean the slate of debt. Parker drafted another proposal and passed it along to Holker on June 16:

If money cannot be obtained by selling one half of the Ship *Empress [of] China* at the rate of 100,000 dollars for the half we would prefer having the money borrowed on bottomry, even at a premo of 30 pr Cent—and in case this cannot be effected, we would wish that attempts might be made to take up the Bills drawn on Le-Couteulx & Co. by engaging other Houses in Amsterdam, or London, to come under acceptances for their drafts to the amount of J[ohn] H[olker]'s Bills, & for the House with whom you engage, to reimburse on LeCouteulx & Co.—this operation will give a sufficient Time for the Return of the Ship & the Commissions paid will be much less than the premo paid on bottomry—rather than suffer the Bills to return, we would sell two sixths parts of her & Cargo at the rate of one hundred fifty Thousand dollars for the whole, reserving the other sixth for ourselves—there is lately established at Canton an English House for the sole purpose of transacting business on Commission, from this house very probably every assistance that our Super Cargoes may want will be obtained—and we have every reason to believe that this adventure will be a profitable one.[8]

To Edward Bancroft, whom historians more than a century afterwards revealed to have been a British double-agent during the American Revolution, Holker wrote in a similar vein:

My dear friend.

Encouraged by your friendship for me, I have requested your interference respecting the sale of our share in the Ship the *Empress of China* on her way to Canton: you will find with Messrs LeCouteulx & Co. of Paris all the papers relative to this business, with instructions relative to our intentions thereon but as it is possible that delays may take place which may be injurious to us, as also it is absolutely necessary for my honor and reputation & Safety that my bills be duly accepted & paid, so as not to return under protest, for any possible reason, I must entreat your Very Serious attention to this Subject, & in consequence hereof, you are hereby authorized with Messrs LeCouteulx to do all that may be needful on such an occasion, as I Should rather sacrifice largely whats necessary, rather than an individual Should suffer thro' me, this being premised it will only remain to Express what we Should think most Eligible for our interests; if you can have the choice of the means when in Europe, if you can Sell at the limits Expressed in our power of attorney to Messrs LeCouteulx, we wish on these terms to part with two Sixths of the Ship out of the three we hold in our name, we wish to propose that Thomas Fitzimmons Esqr be employed to act for the purchasers, and for us jointly with Robt Morris or his representatives in New York on the arrival of the Ship *Empress* in that port from China. If we cannot sell on the Evaluation of 100,000 Dol., for the half of the Ship, then we wish to part with two Sixths of our Share, Valueing the whole Ship at one hundred & fifty thousand Dol. borrowing the remaining Sum that may be necessary on interest, giving a Sixth of the Ship as Security, or raising the money thro' negotiations in Europe to gain Ten or twelve months Credit So as to give me time to take up the engagements, or taking up the money at Bottomry, if impracticable on reasonable terms considering the period of the advances, & that of the return of the Ship, which must be in June, July, or August 1785 without we have great bad luck, indeed, if you find that great Sacrifices are to be made either on Loans at Bottomry, or on the Sales, I Should wish that a negotiation took place to take up my bills over for six months, So as I may turn ourselves in the Interval, & have leisure to dispose of the property to better advantage, rather than to part with it under our present unfavorable circumstances.

Such are our Ideas, Such our desires respecting this business, which by its nature & consequences is highly important to us, you are at liberty to act forthwith in all cases in conjunction with Messrs LeCouteulx, & we therefore trust to your Zeal & activity for us . . . and allow 5 p % Commission. . . .[9]

Parker was still in Philadelphia at the beginning of July.[10] He must have been having a gruelling time of it with the others, all pressing him to produce his books, to justify this or that account, explain why he had acted as he had on one occasion after another; why he was berift of funds. The pressure on him became unbearable. Then the truth came out. Daniel Parker had consistently and consciously falsified his books!

"There can hardly be traced a letter in which he has acknowledged the receipt of the sums remitted to him," Holker wailed in disbelief, "of the acceptances for him, or the Bills or drafts paid for him: he gave nothing but Notes to pay debts, & these he early ever took up . . . so many negotiations were transacted without any record, he left everyone in the Dark, & none had an opportunity to unravel them truely;—when this attempt was made, & when in Philada he found that Holker, Duer, & Fitzimmons were urging the settlement or payment upon, the unravelling his transactions, in order to look after the monies witheld or Concealed or misapplied by him, then to be sure he took to his heels, got on board ship & fled to Europe, leaving his unfortunate Copartners & friends to bewale their losses, & to pay the Creditors, with what he had not been able further to deprive them of."[11]

Parker had written a "valedictory" letter to Holker on July 12, 1784, and then abruptly disappeared. Thirty years later, Holker was still enraged by the duplicity of the man and frustrated in the settlement of their accounts. Over the course of time, some facts had emerged: in 1783, Parker had been associated with Benjamin Guild & Company of Boston; through that source the *Empress of China* had been found. Parker's books, such as they were, revealed almost nothing about the affairs of the company: no accounts had been opened for company stock; supplies for the army had not been credited; in all facets of its dealings no facts had been recorded nor had transactions been noted; "we can find no trace in the Company books," Holker wrote with mounting astonishment, "of the transactions between Duer and Parker & R. Morris SuperIntt of Finance—nothing about the sum of bills received from him, on whom drawn, the exchange allowed by said R.M. & agreed to by Duer—not one word of the sale of said Bills. . . ."[12]

Parker's former counting house clerk confirmed their worst fears when he deposed under oath that monies received on other accounts had been diverted by Parker for purposes which included covering his private expenses.[13]

"Let us now observe that his letter to Holker & to Turnbull Marmie and Co. in Decr 1783 & January 1784," Holker angrily summed it all up, "show that he was pleading at least utter distress in his outfitts of *Bourbon* & *Empress of China*—so exhausted that he could not borrow in New York 1000 dollars he had scarce any dollars at his disposal:—But how could this be—was this more, shere deception . . . an attempt at swindling?—what says the statements . . . he says that he was in advance for D:P. & Co. for $76,097½ what Says our statement: that he held in his hands $121,748 over & above all his expenditures stated as then known—we contend that the whole was decep-tion, as Fitzimmons says: imposition on his friends, evidently a downright swindling statement—untrue by a difference of $197,845 from facts."[14]

From his places of exile—London, Amsterdam, and Paris—Daniel Parker was to remain a festering thorn in many a side for decades to come.

Continuation of John Green's Journal

JUNE 1784

Tuesday, 1. The fore and middle part, fresh breezes and cloudy attended with some rain. The latter part, moderate. Set the mainsail and staysails. Winds from NE.

Course made SEbE½E, distance 109^m.
Difference of latitude 51^m.
Departure 96.
Latitude observed 36^{d}57^m S.
Meridional distance 4,557^m.
Difference of longitude 120.
Longitude in 66^{d}59^m East.
Thermometer 63^d and 64^d.

Wednesday, 2. Fresh breezes and cloudy. Winds from NNE. Variation per azimuth 23^{d}06^m. At 6 A.M., sent up the main-topgallant yard and set the sail. Carried away the slings of the main yard. Repaired ditto. The latter part, some light rain.

Course made good ESE, distance 136.
Difference of latitude 52^m.
Departure 126.
Latitude observed 37^{d}49^m.
Meridional distance 4,783.
Difference of longitude 157.
Longitude in 69^{d}36^m East.

Thursday, 3. Commences light winds and cloudy weather. Heavy dews and some fogs. Saw a seal close to the stern of the ship. The winds from NNE, veers to SSE and SSW. The latter part, foggy. Saw some clouds to the South as if appeared over the land but the weather so foggy can't see at a distance of more than 2 or three leagues.

Course made good E½North, distance 67^m.
Difference of latitude 7^m North.

Departure 67^m.
Latitude per account 37^{d}56^m.
Latitude observed 37^{d}42^m.
Meridional distance 4,850.
Difference of longitude 84.
Longitude in 71^d.
Thermometer 62^d.

Friday, 4. Commences moderate and some driz-zling rain. The winds at SW. The middle part, going under easy sail as the weather looked dark and hazy, fearing we might drop on the Island St. Paul's closer than I could risk in the dark. The winds at WNW. At daylight, squally. Hands the topgallant sail and at 7 set them and the fore-topmast steeringsail. At noon, the wind veers to NNW. A fresh gale and cloudy.

Course made good E¼S, distance 103^m.
Difference of latitude 3^m.
Departure 103.
Latitude 37—45.
Meridional distance 4,953.
Difference of longitude 129.
Longitude in 73^{d}09^m.

Saturday, 5. Commences fresh gale. At 7 P.M., the wind flies out of the WSW and becomes very thick and some rain. Blows strong. Hands all the small sails. Reefed the topsails and keep the ship more to the North, fearing to fall in with the Island St. Paul's and Amsterdam whilst the weather look so bad and it's so very dark and raining. Hands mainsail.

Course made good this 24 hours
    EbN¾North, distance 202^m.
Difference of latitude 70^m.
Departure 190.
Latitude observed 36^{d}35^m.

Meridional distance 5,143.
Difference of longitude 238.
Longitude in 77^{d}07^m East.
Thermometer from 53^d and 57^d.

Sunday, *6*. Commences a fresh gale. The wind from WbS. Mostly the reefed fore- and main-topsails set. The weather dark and gloomy. Carried away main-topsail tie. Reeve a new one and let out all reefs main-topsails.

Course made NE, distance 189^m.
Difference of latitude 132^m.
Departure 132.
Latitude observed 34^{d}23.
Meridional distance 5,275.
Difference of longitude 161.
Longitude in 79^{d}58.
Thermometer 60^d and 63^d.

High sea and ship leaks much. Obliged to pump every half hour.

Monday, *7*. Commences moderate gale. The winds at WbS. The sea abates. Set lower- and topmast-steeringsails and topgallant sail. Winds WbS. All through repairing fore-staysail. Observe ship makes less water going before the wind.

Course made good NE½E, distance 164^m.
Difference of latitude 104^m.
Departure 127^m.
Latitude observed 32^{d}37^m S.
Meridional distance 5,402.
Difference of longitude 151^m.
Longitude in 82^{d}32^m E.

Tuesday, *8*. Moderate weather and pleasant, the winds from WSW. All sail set alow and aloft. Unbent a mizzen topsail which was split and brought a new ditto to the yard. Thoss ⟨Richards⟩ Peter behaved ⟨ill⟩ seaman for threatening to beat the carpenter and using vile language to the boatswain, also beating James Marshall, a seaman. Sundry complaints appearing against ⟨thoss⟩ Peter Richards ordered him hands and feet in irons and chained to the mainmast with orders to keep him on half allowance for some time.

Course made good NE¼E, distance 182^m.
Difference of latitude 125^m.

Departure 135.
Latitude observed 30—32.
Meridional distance 5,537.
Difference of longitude 159.
Longitude in 85^{d}11^m E.

Wednesday, *9*. Moderate weather and pleasant. The winds from SSW and SW. All sail set fore and aft. Some hands employed painting the ship, others repairing sails, and the remainder of the crew overhauling the rigging.

Course made good NE½E, distance 168.
Difference of latitude 107^m.
Departure 130.
Latitude observed 28^{d}45^m S.
Meridional distance 5,667.
Difference of longitude 149^m.
Longitude in 87^{d}40^m.
Thermometer 67^d.

Thursday, *10*. Moderate winds and pleasant. The sea smooth. A swell from WSW. All sail set. The winds South and SSW. People employed painting the ship, repairing main-topgallant sail, and overhauling the rigging.

The course made good NE¾E, distance 136^m.
Difference of latitude 81^m.
Departure 109.
Latitude observed 27^{d}24^m S.
Meridional distance 5,776.
Difference of longitude 123.
Longitude in 89^{d}43^m E.
The thermometer 67^d and 71^d.
Amplitude sunrising 8^{d}30^m W.

Friday, *11*. Commences and continues fine weather and pleasant. Winds from SW. All sails set alow and aloft. People employed painting the ship. The water smooth and a long swell from SW. Got up the topgallant steeringsail booms.

Thermometer 69^d and 72^d.
Course made good NE¾E, distance 122^m.
Difference of latitude 73^m.
Departure 98.
Latitude per observation 26^{d}11^m S.
Meridional distance 5,874.
Difference of longitude 109.
Longitude in 91^{d}32^m E.

Saturday, 12. Moderate weather and fine winds. The water smooth and a long swell from the SW. The winds variable in the SW to NW quarter. The latter part, squally and some rains.

Thermometer 68^d and 71½^d.
Course made good NE¼E, distance 118^m.
Difference of latitude 78.
Departure 86.
Latitude observed 24^{d}53^m S.
Meridional distance 5,960.
Difference of longitude 94.
Longitude in 93^{d}06^m East.

Sunday, 13. Commences moderate and pleasant, the winds NNW and SW, azimuth sun's setting 4^{d}20^m W. Amplitude 4^{d}11^m W. The water smooth and a long swell from the SW. At 6, hands mainsail, staysails and down steering-sails. A good lookout for danger. At daylight, set all sails. A fresh breeze.

Course made good NE¼North, distance 179.
Difference of latitude 132.
Departure 119.
Latitude observed 22^{d}41^m South.
Meridional distance 6,079.
Difference of longitude 129.
Longitude in 95^{d}15^m East.

At noon, the winds SW. Hauled to the North in order to get to the north of Choates Island before dark—its latitude 22^{d}7^m S.

Monday, 14. The former and middle part, a fresh of wind from SW to SSE. Mostly all sail set. Thermometer 71^d and 70^d. People employed clearing decks and stowing the spars on the quarters as well on the belfry to make room on decks for the guns which are in the hold.

Course made NbE, distance 133^m.
Difference of latitude 133.
Departure 26^m.
Latitude observed 20^{d}28^m.
Meridional distance 6,105.
Difference of longitude 28.
Longitude in 95^{d}43^m East.

Tuesday, 15. Variable winds in the southern quarter and squally. Mostly the single-reefed topsails set. Got up some of our guns from the hold and about two tons of cordage from the fore end of the ship and put aft in order to bring the ship by the stern. Filled several casks of salt water in the hold to keep the ship stiff as she is already too crank.

Course made NE, distance 116^m.
Difference of latitude 82^m.
Departure 82.
Latitude observed 19^{d}06^m S.
Meridional distance 6,187^m.
Difference of longitude 87^m.
Longitude in 97^{d}10^m.
Thermometer 71^d.

Wednesday 16. Moderate weather. Winds from ESE. The latter part, set up the topmast shrouds and backstays. Gunner employed painting the guns and the carriages on the main deck.

Thermometer 70 and 75½ degrees.
Course made good NNE, distance 113.
Difference of latitude 105.
Departure 43.
Latitude in 17^{d}21^m.
Meridional distance 6,230.
Difference of longitude 45.
Longitude in 97^{d}55^m East.

Thursday, 17. A fresh of wind all this 24 hours from ESE and East. Mostly the reefed topsails set.

Course made good NNE¾E, distance 98^m.
Difference of latitude 84.
Departure 50^m.
Latitude observed 15^{d}57^m S.
Meridional distance 6,280.
Difference of longitude 52^m.
Longitude in 98^{d}47^m E.
Thermometer 67^d and 72^d.

Saw several flying fish and many clouds like land clouds.

Friday, 18. A fresh of wind all this 24 hours. At sunset, saw a large bird hovering over the mastheads resembling a bird named man-of-war in the West Indies. At 6, hands mainsail and all the staysails. Up foresail and run under the three topsails. At midnight, brought to under the fore- and mizzen-topsails full, the main-topsail aback. At daylight, made all sail. Saw several shore birds and some which flew like geese and was the color of our American gannets. Winds SEbE.

Course made good NNE½E, distance 125ᵐ.
Difference of latitude 111ᵐ.
Departure 59ᵐ.
Latitude in 14ᵈ06ᵐ South.
Meridional distance 6,339.
Difference of longitude 61.
Longitude in 99ᵈ48ᵐ.
Thermometer 77ᵈ and 79ᵈ.

Saturday, 19. Blowing fresh all this 24 hours from SE. At dark, shortened sail and at 10 at night hove to under fore-topsail full, main ditto aback. The latter part, all sail set. All hands employed at clearing small arms and putting the anchors on the gunwale.

Course made good NNE, distance 140.
Difference of latitude 130.
Departure 54ᵐ.
Latitude 11ᵈ56ᵐ S.
Meridional distance 6,393.
Difference of longitude 55.
Longitude in 100ᵈ43ᵐ East.
Thermometer 79ᵈ and 81ᵈ.

Sunday, 20. Blowing fresh all this 24 hours from ESE. Mostly the reefed topsails set, close-hauled by the wind. Saw numbers of fowls like gannets as to their plumage but fly like seagulls or a bird called boobys. Numbers of flying fish in sight as well as the tropic birds. At noon, saw a plank which had been in the water for some time by its appearance.

Course made good NNE½E, distance 140.
Difference of latitude 123.
Departure 66.
Latitude 9ᵈ53 S.
Meridional distance 6,456.
Difference of longitude 67ᵐ.
Longitude in 101ᵈ50ᵐ East.

Monday, 21. Moderate weather and clear. Mostly the winds ESE. Single-reefed topsails set. Carried away the jib traveler. Got a rope ditto in his place. Saw several pieces of wood and a piece of plank floating by the ship.

Course made good NE½E, distance 99ᵐ.
Difference of latitude 63ᵐ.
Departure 77ᵐ.

Latitude 8ᵈ48ᵐ S.
Meridional distance 6,533.
Difference of longitude 78.
Longitude in 103ᵈ08ᵐ East.

Tuesday, 22. Moderate weather and very sultry. Many birds hovering round us as well several pieces of wood passing by the ship. The winds from the SE. A long swell from the Southward.

Course made good NE, distance 49ᵐ.
Difference of latitude 34.
Departure 34ᵐ.
Latitude 8ᵈ14ᵐ S.
Meridional distance 6,567.
Difference of longitude 34ᵐ.
Longitude in 103ᵈ42ᵐ.

Wednesday, 23. Light winds from SSE and ESE. At midnight, tacked and stood to the Southward for three hours and tacked and stood to the NE. Hove to and sounded. Thought we saw the land in the NE quarter. No ground in 120 fathoms. Single-reefed topsails set.

Course made good NEbNorth, distance 49ᵐ.
Difference of latitude 41.
Departure 27ᵐ.
Latitude per observation 7ᵈ33.
Meridional distance 6,594ᵐ.
Difference of longitude 27ᵐ.
Longitude in 104ᵈ09ᵐ.
Thermometer 84ᵈ.

Thursday, 24. Fresh of wind and squally attended with some rain. The winds mostly from East to SE. A-beating to windward under single and reefed topsails. Split the jib. Unbent ditto and bent a new one in his place. At 6 A.M., set up lee main shrouds and backstays. Reefed jib and set ditto.

Course made good SbE¾E, distance 48ᵐ.
Difference of latitude 45ᵐ.
Departure 16ᵐ.
Latitude observed 8ᵈ18ᵐ.
Meridional distance 6,610ᵐ.
Difference of longitude 16.
Longitude in 104ᵈ25ᵐ E.
Thermometer 83.

Friday, 25. Very uncertain weather. Mostly reefed topsails set. Sent down the topgallant yards. The wind from SE and ESE. A-beating to windward. Saw several pieces of bamboo and driftwood going past the ship.

Course made good NE¾E, distance 51ᵐ.
Difference of latitude 22.
Departure 46.
Latitude per account 7ᵈ30ᵐ.
Meridional distance 6,656.
Difference of longitude 46ᵐ.
Longitude in 105ᵈ11ᵐ East.
Thermometer 83ᵈ.

N.B.—the ship has been given too much distance per log.

Saturday, 26. Hard squalls of wind and rain. Obliged to stand by the sails all this 24 hours. Hands mainsail. Reefed main-topsail. 3d-reefed fore ditto and close-reefed mizzen ditto. Heavy gusts of wind. Ship makes a great deal of water. Continually one pump a-working to keep ship free. At 8 A.M., struck the topgallant masts. Bent main-staysail and set ditto.

Course made good SSW, distance 80ᵐ.
Difference of latitude 74.
Departure 31ᵐ.
Latitude per observation 9ᵈ10ᵐ S.
Meridional distance 6,625ᵐ.
Difference of longitude 104ᵈ40ᵐ.

N.B.—the ship was given 33 miles too much in the last 24 hours per log or we must have a strong current setting this 24 hours to the South, which imagine is not the case. The log distance 120ᵐ. The distance 27ᵐ South think right but not the 93 miles which she is marked to the Eastward.

Sunday, 27. Strong winds and hard squalls of rain. The foresail set at times. Mostly close-reefed fore- and mizzen-topsails and reefed main ditto with fore-, main- and mizzen-staysails set. A heavy head sea. Ship makes much water in her upper works. Pumps continually going. Tacked ship at 8 P.M. and stood to the Southward. Winds ESE. Wore ship at midnight and stood to the NE.

Thermometer 83ᵈ.
Course made good NNE¼E, distance 64ᵐ.
Difference of latitude 58ᵐ.

Departure 27ᵐ.
Latitude per account 8ᵈ12ᵐ.
Latitude observed 8ᵈ12ᵐ.
Meridional distance 6,652ᵐ East of meridian St. Jago.
Difference of longitude 27ᵐ.
Longitude 105—07.

Monday, 28. Squally weather attended with much rain. Mostly the mainsail handed and no other sails set but 3d-reefed fore-topsail. Reefed main, ditto foresail, main-, mizzen-, and fore-staysails and mizzen-topsail. Standing to the NE and to the Southward as the winds would admit of our making most Easting.

Course made good NNE½E, distance 35ᵐ.
Difference of latitude 31ᵐ.
Departure 16.
Latitude per account 7ᵈ39ᵐ.
Meridional distance 6,668.
Difference of longitude 16.
Longitude in 105ᵈ22ᵐ East.
Thermometer 78ᵈ.

Tuesday, 29. Squally, rainy weather with thunder and lightning. A strong current setting to the South this 24 hours and imagine to the Westward. The wind in squalls veers to the North. The ship by the course and distance steered makes 12ᵐ North and is in per account latitude 7ᵈ27ᵐ, but latitude per observation 7ᵈ-50ᵐ South. Add the difference of latitude between account and observation makes difference 23ᵐ. That added to the Westward with the difference of latitude 23 makes ship course this 24 hours SW course, distance 32ᵐ.

Difference of latitude 23ᵐ.
Departure 23ᵐ.
Latitude per observation 7ᵈ50ᵐ.
Meridional distance 6,645ᵐ.
Difference of longitude 23ᵐ.
Longitude in 104ᵈ59ᵐ East.
Thermometer 81ᵈ.

Wednesday, 30. This 24 hours moderate than we have had for several days back. Swayed up the topgallant masts. Let the reefs out of the topsails to dry the sails which we find much mildewed from their being reefed so long. When dried, single-reefed ditto. Some hands in the hold overhauling our water. Others repairing sails split in the late bad weather, and some hands employed cleansing seamen's berths and drying spare sails. Many logs and pieces of bamboos floating by the ship. Saw many boobies. Catched 5 of them by their lighting on board.

Course made ENE, distance 22^m.

Difference of latitude 8^m.
Departure 20.
Latitude 6^{d}58.
Meridional distance 6,665.
Difference of longitude 20^m.
Longitude in 105^{d}19^m East.
Thermometer 83^d.

Narrative by Samuel Shaw[15]
[From his Journal]

On the 25th of June, being, by account at noon, in 7° 52' south latitude, and 105° 15' east longitude, we expected to make the island of Java,—having observed, the four preceding days, pieces of reed, bamboo-root, and other wood passing us, besides a species of birds differing from any we had hitherto seen. These birds are by the sailors called boobies. We killed one of them on the spritsail-yard, and another lodged upon the tafferel and was seized by our boys, who afterwards caught numbers of them by holding out poles, on which they alighted and were taken. They are generally gray, about the size of the tame duck, have a long, pointed beak, webbed feet, and long wings. They live upon flying and other small fishes, which, upon being caught, they instantly disgorge whole. They were lean, very fishy, and but indifferent food. There is also a large bird, called the albatross, that we have frequently seen during our passage. It is of the size of the goose, and very shy. We repeatedly attempted to take them,—particularly by baiting a hook with a piece of meat, and letting it go astern with a long line, floated by corks,—but without effect. They must be exceedingly strong, as common log-line was insufficient to hold them, and one of them, on being hooked, broke the deep-sea line of the ship, to which the hook was fastened, and carried part of it away with him.

X

In the Sunda Strait

On the fifth of June 1784, John Green had allowed the *Empress of China*, for the first time in a month, to veer north of the thirty-sixth parallel of south latitude. The ship's longitude reckoning suggested that the mid-Indian Ocean islands of St. Paul and Amsterdam were rising somewhere ahead. Dunn's *Directory* was specific on that point: "When you are in latitude 37° S. you must keep therein, steering east, for about 1100 leagues, or till you have made about 70° east longitude from the Cape of Good Hope. It will not be absolutely necessary to see the island of St. Paul or Amsterdam, though the sight thereof will greatly assist you in rectifying your account, and shaping your course afterward . . . when you have made 70° east longitude from the Cape, you may edge away by degrees to the northward, in such a manner as to be able to pass the Tropic of Capricorn in 83° E. Longitude. . . ."[1]

Captain Green had crossed the tropic one week later but in a longitude some ten degrees farther east than Dunn's recommendations. By the thirtieth of June, the western end of the island of Java lay just over the horizon; it must have, because he made no landfall that day, but the coordinates of his estimated position placed him—by the highly accurate standards of a modern chart—in imminent danger of ramming the volcanic island of Krakatoa in the middle of the Sunda Strait between Sumatra and Java.

The Sunda Strait had been the *Empress of China*'s navigational objective ever since the Cape Verde Islands had sunk from view ninety-four days before. Certain that land was not far away, wisely trusting neither the exactitude of his reckoning nor the accuracy of his charts but relying on Dunn's advice that "if you should fall in to the westward, and in 7°30′ south latitude you do not see the land, haul upon the wind, to get to the eastward till within sight of it," Green steered a course to the south and then to the east.[2] On July 17, Java Head rose like a thundercloud out of the sea to greet them. The ship rounded First Point into the Sunda Strait and the Mew Bay anchorage.

From here, Purser John White Swift wrote to his father in Philadelphia.[3]

Mr Dear Father

At last I address you from the East Indies We came too in this Bay last Ev'ning after a Passage of three months & 18 Days from the Island of St Jago, (our first halt, & from whence I address'd Letters to you—) We have had no agreable passage. It has been one dreary waste of Sky & water, without a pleasing Sight to cheer us. I am heartily tired of so long a Voyage, more especially as we are not yet at our Journeys End by about Sixteen hundred Miles. We are employ'd Wooding & Watering & expect to sail in about four Days, in Company with a French Ship of Sixty four Guns, which we found riding at Anchor here, & employ'd in the same business. In about a Month more we have a prospect of being at Canton.

I send this to Batavia by a ship bound to that Port, (which we also found here) under a promise from a Dutch merch't on board, that he wou'd forward it to Holland. I am in tolerable good health—tho exposed to hotter sun than I ever before experienced. The Thermometer stands Commonly at 86°. We are constantly visited by the Malayans—Inhabitants of Java & Princes Island, & have got a fresh supply of Stock including a Dozn or two of fine green Turtle, (I wish you had the largest) Make my Love & Compts to all my friends. Capt Hodgkinson who is along side of me, offers his likewise, he is very hearty but does not write by so precarious & long opportunity, but lest I shou'd never have another, I embrace it, with this only view, to tell you how much, how often I think of you & how ardently I wish to see you again in America. Canton next, and then, O Ye Gods! how happy shall I be when I am returning.

I am most affectionately & Most sincerely yours &c M.D.H.

John W. Swift

This Opportunity being Uncertain I have Only to Inform you I am in Perfect health, & wish this may meet you so. I could wish to say or write you a long letter but this Conveyance will not admitt of it for Reasons I cannot at Present make mention of—I will only add that I hope in the Course of Twenty days to Arrive at Canton, the most Tedious Part of our Passage being now Compleated, & After three or four Months Detention thear, we shall then take our leave of this Eastern part of the Whorld & Bend our Course for America, & believe it is my Ardent Wishes to meet You Once more on Green Bank. Until then I am what I always Profess'd

P. Hodgkinson

Although several French ships, also bound to Canton, were immediately encountered in the Strait, Captain Green learned to his inexpressible satisfaction that they and the *Empress of China* apparently were the first China traders of the season to have arrived there. A few others may have preceded them by other routes to Canton, such as the Strait of Malacca, but, despite early fears to the contrary and the month-long delay caused by the ice in New York Harbor, they seemed to have reached a hungry market.

Yet another piece of good fortune befell the owners and the adventurers on board during the month of July, even though it would be weeks and months before they became aware of it. On the twelfth, forty-one French underwriters had pledged 438,500 Livres tournois to M. DelaVille of Nantes, who that day issued a policy of insurance on the one half share owned by Daniel Parker & Company. In translation, it read:

The Ship Empress of China, Captain John Green, &c. New York to Canton and Return to New York[4]
WE, THE UNDERWRITERS subscribed, promise & bind ourselves to you, *Monsieur A^d fr^s DeLaville* of this city, making & stipulating to insure & we do insure, each of us understanding the sum we have declared hereunder *for the account relative to the order of Messieurs D. Parker & Co. of New York, transmitted by Monsieur Holker, Jr. of Philadelphia and Messieurs LeCouteulx & Co. of Paris—Seven Hundred Thousand Eight Hundred Livres tournois on the half share of the value of the hull, rigging, gear, provisions, advances to the crew and supernumeraries of the American ship called Empress of China, Captain John Green, of the burthen of about four hundred tons, sheathed in copper, manned by 42 men and armed with 10 cannon of 9 [pounds] and 4 of 6 since her departure from New York and which we jointly estimate at Two Hundred Fifteen Thousand Six Hundred Livres tournois in value more or less: to run all risks since her departure from New York the twenty-second of February last to go to Canton in China and during all her voyage until her return to New York and the landing of her cargo—and Four Hundred Eighty Thousand Two Hundred Livres tournois on the half of the cargo of said ship, consisting of dollars, ginseng, cordage, and divers other articles going from New York to China and of the return in teas, silks, nankins, porcelains, and other articles which we jointly estimate to total Nine Hundred Sixty Thousand Four Hundred*

Livres tournois, which may fluctuate more or less; to take all the risks since the lading of the said cargo in New York until its arrival and discharge at Canton and on the merchandise which makes up the return [cargo] until its arrival and landing in good condition at New York—the whole conformable to the translation of the letter of authorization from Messieurs D. Parker & Co., signed by Monsieur Holker, Jr., dated at New York 10 March 1784, which we have read and has been initialed by one of us and which will be annexed to the present policy. The damages on the hull of the ship and the cargo will be adjusted separately as if the present insurance were made in two policies. We allow you to have insured your whole property as also the tenth which we take upon ourselves according to the inventory of the ship, her evaluation and that of the cargo, signed Dan. Parker & Co., amounting to Forty-Eight Thousand One Hundred Thirty-One Pounds Six Shillings Seven Pence Sterling. We approve the estimate here above of Two Hundred Fifteen Thousand Six Hundred Livres tournois assigned to the hull of the ship and that of Nine Hundred Sixty Thousand Four Hundred Livres tournois, given to the cargo, and we expressly promise in case of accidents to abide with the said evaluations without the ability to revoke them on any pretext whatever: as also in case of loss we covenant to reimburse you upon the presentation of the present policy, of the detailed invoice of the cargo and the bills of lading which we have read and have been initialed by one of us and which remains annexed to the present policy in the same manner as the ship's inventory and the letter of authorization, mentioned here above. We promise to require negotiation of other claims to the property or whatever, being under no pretext to reimburse you, in consequence, we renounce by word of honor all claims to the arrangements contrary to the several conditions of the present policy. We approve all the ports of call whatsoever that the said vessel is able to make during the course of the voyage described here above and which the captain believes proper for the good of the venture—

for which we take the burden of responsibility for good or bad news, waiving the mile and a half per hour; To know, on the ship since [leaving] *New York* and on the merchandise since the day and the hour that she has been or will be laden & embarked to be taken on board the said ship, & continuing, with regard to the ship, until she be arrived and discharged at the port of *as above* & having an estimated value *as above*, & as for the merchandise until it has been or will be taken and landed at *as it is said above* in good condition, without any damage; we bind ourselves to running the risks in barges, small craft, boats, dinghies, and other lighters used for its transport from shore on board at the time of embarkation and from on board to shore at the time of disembarkation. We agree that the said ship, making the said voyage, may

Le Navire Empress of China Capitaine Jean Green &c New York à Canton et à retour New York

NOUS, ASSUREURS foussignés, promettons & nous obligeons à vous, Monsieur *L. J.r Dehaville* de cette ville, faisant & stipulant pour *simple de qui il appartiendra, par ordre de Messieurs D. Parker & C.e de Newyork, transmis par monsieur* d'assurer & affurons, favoir, chacun de nous, la somme par nous ci-deſſous déclarée *toliès, fils de Philadelphie et messieurs le feu de ... & Deſpar...*

[several lines of handwritten text]

dont nous prenons les rifques à notre charge, fur bonnes ou mauvaifes nouvelles, renonçant à la fieue & demie par heure ; favoir, fur le Navire, depuis *New York* & fur les Marchandifes, depuis le jour & l'heure qu'elles ont été ou feront chargées & embarquées, pour mener à bord dudit Navire, & dureront, quant au Navire, jufqu'à ce qu'il foit arrivé & déchargé au Port de *comme deſſus* & l'avons eſtimé valoir *comme deſſus* & quant aux Marchandifes, jufqu'à ce qu'elles aient été ou foient amenées & déchargées à terre, à *comme deſſus* à bon fauvement, fans aucun dommage ; nous aſſujetiſſant à en courir les rifques dans les Gabarres, Barques, bateaux, Chaloupes, Canots, & autres Alleges fervant à leur tranſport de terre à bord, lors de l'embarquement, & de bord à terre, lors du débarquement. Accordons que ledit Navire, faifant ledit voyage, pourra naviguer avant & arriere, à dextre & à ſeneſtre ; nous foumettant de courir les rifques & périls de mer, de guerre, de feu, de vent, d'amis, d'ennemis, de repréfailles, de lettres de marque & contremarque, d'Arrêt & détention, des Rois, Reines, Républiques, Princes & Seigneurs quelconques, d'imprudence, d'abfence du Capitaine, lors de la perte de baraterie de Patron, Maître ou Mariniers, généralement de tous autres périls, fortune ou cas fortuits, qui pourroient avenir en quelque maniere que ce foit, prévus ou imprévus ; & fi, après la fortie du Vaiſſeau du port de fon départ, lefdites Marchandifes venoient, par néceſſité, ou dans la vue d'une plus grande fûreté, à être déchargées ou rechargées, en tout ou partie, à la mer ou en quelque Efcale, dans un autre ou d'autres Bâtiments, petits ou grands, ce qui pourra être fait fans attendre notre approbation ou notre confentement (parce que néanmoins ferez tenu de nous en inftruire auſſi-tôt que la nouvelle vous en fera parvenue, ou dans les trois jours fuivants au plus tard ;) nous courrons les rifques defdites Marchandifes fur les bâtiments, dans lefquels elles auront été renverfées, ainfi que nous les courrions auparavant ; nous mettant du tout en la place de *l'affuré* pour vous garantir & indemnifer de toutes pertes & dommages qui pourroient arriver. Et en cas de dommages, prife ou perte dudit Navire ou Marchandifes, (ce que Dieu ne veuille) promettons & nous obligeons de payer & rembourfer à vous, ou au Porteur de cette Police, toute la perte & dommage que vous aurez reçus, à proportion de la fomme que chacun de nous aura affurée, auſſi bien le dernier de nous comme le premier, & ce, dans mois après que nous ferons informés de la perte ou dommage arrivés audit Vaiſſeau & Marchandifes ou effets, & en tel cas, donnons, chacun de nous, pouvoir fpécial à vous, ledit *leur affuré* ou à votre Commis, de travailler ou de faire travailler, foit à notre perte ou profit, à la falvation, promettant, en tout événement, de payer les frais & dépens faits à ce fujet, foit qu'il y ait du recouvrement ou non, ajoutant entiere foi & crédit au compte & ferment de la perfonne ou des perfonnes qui auront fait lefdits frais ou dépens. Confeſſons être payés de la Prime d'aſſurance, par les mains de vous, M. *L. J.r Dehaville* à raifon de *huit* pour cent en vos billets, payables à *quatre* mois, après la connoiſſance de la ceſſation des rifques ; laquelle Prime nous eſt néanmoins acquife dès ce moment, & fera reçue en paiement de la fomme à payer en cas de perte ou d'avaries, fauf le rapport réciproque du plus ou du moins. Nous ne paierons point d'avaries, fimples ou groſſes, fi elles n'excedent *cinq* pour cent ; nous ne rembourferons que nonante & *Sept* pour cent, en cas de perte totale ou d'abandon. Nous vous permettons expreſſément de faire affurer tout votre capital. Il fera déduit pour cent, fur l'argent des Ifles, la Prime pour cent. Le tout fait de bonne foi, fans fraude, foit que le fufdit Navire ait une Commiſſion en guerre, ou non, fuivant l'Ordonnance de la Marine, fauf les cas dans lefquels nous y avons dérogé. Et en cas de conteſtation, nous conviendrons à l'amiable d'Arbitres-Négociants, pour juger nos différends. Et pour l'exécution du tout, nous obligeons tous nos biens, fpécialement de la part de l'Affuré, les chofes aſſurées, avec renonciation à toutes exceptions & tromperies contraires à ces préfentes. Convenu qu'en cas de guerre, hoftilités ou repréfailles, entre la France & quelques Puiſſances maritimes, la Prime ci-deſſus fera augmentée au cours de la place.

A Nantes, *ce 12 juillet 1784.*

5351

30. The insurance certificate, underwritten in Nantes, France, for the half-share of the *Empress of China* owned by Daniel Parker & Company.

sail forward and back, to starboard & to port; we submit to running all the risks & perils of the sea, of war, of fire, of wind, of friends, of enemies, of reprisals, of letters of marque and countermarque, of stoppage and detention, of kings, queens, republics, princes & lords whatever, of imprudence, the absence of the captain, at the time of loss by barratry [fraud against the owners] by the master, sailing master, or sailors, generally of all other perils, hazard or accident which in some manner may occur in the future, predictable or unpredictable; & if, after the sailing of the vessel from the port of her departure, the said merchandise comes, by necessity or with the regard for greater safety, to be discharged or reloaded, in full or part, at sea or in some port of call, in another or other vessels, small or large, which can be done without awaiting our approval or our consent (because, for all that, you will be held to inform us as soon as the news reaches you or within three days following) we shall run the risks of the said merchandise on the vessels to which it has been shifted in the same way that we ran them before, putting us in the position of the insured to guarantee you and indemnify against all losses & damages which might occur. And in case of damages, the capture, or loss of the said ship or merchandise (God forbid) we promise & bind ourselves to pay & reimburse you, or to the holder of this policy, all the loss and damage which you receive, in proportion to the sum that each of us will have underwritten, the last of us as well as the first &c, within a month after we shall be informed of the loss or damage happened to the said vessel or merchandise or effects, & in such a case, we each of us give special authority to you, the said *Gentlemen insured* or to your agent, to work or to make work, irrespective of our loss or profit, for ———, promising, in any event, to pay the costs & expenses involved, no matter whether it is recovered or not, attaching complete faith & credit to the account & oath of the person or persons who compile the said costs or expenses. We acknowledge being paid by you, M^r A^d f^s *deLaville*, the premium of insurance at the rate of *eight* percent with your bills, payable in four months after sight at the end of the risks, which premium is, nevertheless, acquired from this moment & will be received in payment of the payable sum in case of loss or of damage, except for mutual profit more or less. We will not pay for damages, simple or great, if they do not exceed *five* percent; we will not reimburse more than ninety and *seven* [97] percent in case of total loss or of abandonment. We expressly permit you to have insured your total property. There will be deducted ———percent, in money of the Isles [Paris and the five surrounding departments], the premium———. The whole done in good faith, without fraud, whether the said ship has a war commission or not, following the

Navy Regulations, except in cases contrary to custom. And in case of contestation, we agree to impartial arbitrator-merchants to settle our differences. And for the execution of the whole, we pledge all our property, especially on the part of the insurer, the things insured, renouncing all exceptions and deceptions contrary to these presents. It is agreed that in case of war, hostilities, or repraisals between France and other maritime powers that the premium here above will be augmented in conformity with the prevailing market.

At Nantes, *this 12 July 1784.*

Continuation of John Green's Journal

JULY 1784

Thursday, 1. Fresh breezes all through from SE quarter. Single-reefed topsails set. Split and unbent our middle staysail and bent a new one. Some hands overhauling our ground tier of water. Others repairing our old jib and some at the rigging. Made some trips to the NE and to the Southward as the wind would allow us to make most Easting.

Course made NE¼North, distance 72^m.
Difference of latitude 53.
Departure 49^m.
Latitude per account 6^{d}05^m.
Latitude per observation 6^{d}00.
Meridional distance 6,714^m.
Difference of longitude 49.
Longitude in 106^{d}08^m East.
Thermometer 83^d.

Our water on board 2,000 gallons.

Friday, 2. Fresh of wind from the SE quarter. Making sundry tacks this 24 hours to get to windward. The single-reefed topsails set. The people employed filling some casks in the hold with salt water. Heavy clouds and some light rain.

Course made SW¾W, distance 33.
Difference of latitude 20.
Departure 26.
Latitude per account 6^{d}20^m S.
Latitude per observation 6^{d}26^m S.
Meridional distance 6,688.
Difference of longitude 26^m.

Longitude in 105^{d}42^m East.
Thermometer 82^d.

N.B.—find a current setting to the South this 24 hours and imagine it goes to the Westward.

Saturday, 3. Blowing weather and uncertain heavy squalls and very heavy rains. Obliged to wear ship as the wind would favor our making most Southing. The wind from SbE to East, and some squalls brought the wind to ENE.

Course made good S¾W, distance 61^m.
Difference of latitude 60^m.
Departure 9.
Latitude per account 7^{d}26^m.
Latitude per observation 7^{d}27^m.
Meridional distance 6,679^m.
Difference of longitude 9^m.
Longitude in 105^{d}33^m East.
Thermometer 82^d.

Ship makes much water. A man named Bradey taken sick.

Sunday, 4. The fore and middle part, blowing fresh in squalls attended with dark, gloomy weather. The winds varying in the SE quarter. Wore ship several times as the wind would favor our making most to windward. The single-reefed topsails set. The staysails reefed. Jib and the spanker set at times.

Course made good S¾W, distance 24^m.
Difference of latitude 24^m.

Departure 3^m.
Latitude per account 7^d54^m.
Latitude per observation 7^d57^m S.
Meridional distance 6,676.
Difference of longitude 3^m.
Longitude in 105^d30^m.
Thermometer 81^d and 83^d.

Monday, 5. Winds this 24 hours from SEbE, EbS, North, and NNE. Single-reefed topsails set. The main-topsail tie gave way. Repaired ditto. Made several tacks to gain Southing as the wind would favor. Squally and some rain. The thermometer 82^d and 76^d. The weather as uncertain as they are in the West Indies before a hurricane comes on.

Course made SE, distance 28^m.
Difference of latitude 20^m.
Departure 20^m.
Latitude per account 8^d19^m S.
Meridional distance 6,696.
Difference of longitude 20^m.
Longitude in 105^d50^m E.

Tuesday, 6. Uncertain weather and variable winds. Hard squalls and violent rains. Mostly the single-reefed topsails set and they were obliged to be lowered 3 times in the watch. Latter part, mainsails hauled up. The winds SE, SEbE, and SSE. Made several tacks to get to the East.

Course made good NE¾E, distance 47^m.
Difference of latitude 28^m.
Departure 38.
Latitude per account 7^d52^m.
Meridional distance 6,734.
Difference of longitude 38^m.
Longitude in 106^d28^m.
Thermometer 77^d.

Wednesday, 7. Dark, cloudy, squally weather. No such thing as trusting much sail set, the weather looks so bad. At 6 P.M., reefed the three topsails. Handed the mainsail. Set the fore-staysail, main-, and mizzen-staysails with the foresail and three topsails. At 8, sounded. No ground 120 fathom. The hardest rain I ever saw. We catched in our water sail near 600 gallons of excellent water. The latter part, calm. All hands drying their clothes. Out all reefs to dry. Mend-

ing the main- and mizzen-topsails, which were blown from the foot-rope.

Course made good EbS½S, distance 38^m.
Difference of latitude 11^m.
Departure 36^m.
Latitude per account 8^d03.
Meridional distance 6,770.
Difference of longitude 36.
Longitude in 107^d4.

Thursday, 8. The fore part, squally. The middle and latter part, steady weather and calm. Hoisted out the yawl. Mr. S[haw] and R[andall] accompanied me in rowing round the ship to view her. The winds variable in the SE and ENE quarters. A-beating to windward.

Course made good South, distance 15^m.
Difference of latitude 15^m.
Departure 6.
Latitude per account 8^d13^m S.
Latitude per observation 8^d28^m S.
Meridional distance 6,770^m.
Difference of longitude 00.
Longitude in 107^d04^m E.
Thermometer 81^d.

A current we find has carried us 15m more Southerly than our course and distance will allow by the log made.

Friday, 9. Light winds, smooth water, and some heavy showers. The wind from ENE to NE. Stretching to the North mostly in order to get the benefit of the Northerly winds which we have in the night or towards morning. Got up the topgallant yards.

Course made NE¼E, distance 47^m.
Difference of latitude 35^m.
Departure 32^m.
Latitude per account 7^d53^m.
Latitude observed 7^d50^m South.
Meridional distance 6,802^m.
Difference of longitude 32^m.
Longitude in 107^d36^m East.
Thermometer 81^d.
Amplitude per sun setting 1^d47^m W.

Saturday, 10. Calms and light winds. Several schools of fish round the ship. Hoisted out the boat but could not catch any of the fish. Catched a shark alongside. The boat returned with 3 snakes and one booby which they caught. The snakes were 4 feet long, had two rows of teeth, and a sting in their mouths which they thrust out far as they had occasion. Winds SSE and NbW.

Course made NEbE¾E, distance 36^m.
Difference of latitude 15^m.
Departure 33.
Latitude observed 7^{d}35^m S.
Meridional distance 6,835.
Difference of longitude 33^m.
Longitude in 108^{d}09^m East.
Thermometer 83^d.

Sunday, 11. Light airs and calms. The water very smooth. The latter part, a fresh breeze at SE and some rain. The topgallant sails set.

Course made good NEbE, distance 34^m.
Difference of latitude 19^m.
Departure 28^m.
Latitude observed 7^{d}16^m S.
Meridional distance 6,863.
Difference of longitude 28^m.
Longitude 108^{d}37^m E.
Thermometer 82^d and 83^d.

Monday, 12. The fore part, light airs and variable. The middle and latter, squally. Single-reefed the topsails. Blows so strong in squalls obliged to clew down the topsails and haul up the mainsail. The winds from SE and E and ENE.

Course made SE¾E, distance 37^m.
Difference of latitude 23^m.
Departure 30^m.
Latitude per [   ] 7^{d}39^m.
Meridional distance 6,893.
Difference of longitude 30^m.
Longitude in 109^{d}07^m E.
Thermometer 76^d.

Tuesday, 13. Light winds and light squalls. Some rain and calms. People employed repairing the rigging. The winds from SE and ENE.

Course made good SbE¾E, distance 18.
Difference of latitude 17.
Departure 6^m.
Latitude observed 7^{d}55.
Meridional distance 6,899.
Difference of longitude 6^m.

Longitude in 109^{d}13^m E.
Thermometer 81^d.

Wednesday, 14. Steady winds and weather all this 24 hours. All sail set. Beating to windward as the wind would favor us most. The winds from East to ESE and ENE. The only pleasant 24 hours we have had for three weeks past.

Course made good SE¾E, distance 27^m.
Difference of latitude 22.
Departure 16.
Latitude per account 8^{d}17^m.
Latitude per observation 8^{d}20^m.
Meridional distance 6,915.
Difference of longitude 16^m.
Longitude in 109^{d}29^m East.
Thermometer 83^d.

Thursday, 15. Mostly moderate and pleasant weather. The water smooth. The winds from SE and ESE. The ship a-beating to windward as the winds would allow our gaining most Easting. Several waterspouts to the [   ] and some thunder and lightning.

Course NEbNorth, distance 42^m.
Difference of latitude 35.
Departure 23^m.
Latitude observed 7^{d}45^m.
Meridional distance 6,938.
Difference of longitude 23^m.
Longitude in 109^{d}52^m E.
Thermometer 81^d.

Friday, 16. Moderate weather and variable winds. The water smooth and some thunder and lightning. Made some tacks to gain Easting, as we imagine from yesterday's latitude we can't be far to the Eastward of Java Head, if as far East, though think from the thunder and waterspouts we can't be far from the land. The wind E and ESE.

Course made this 24 hours NEbE, distance 20^m.
Difference of latitude 11^m.
Departure 17^m.
Latitude observed 7^{d}34^m.
Meridional distance 6,955.
Difference of longitude 17^m.
Longitude in 110^{d}09^m E.
Thermometer 84^d.

31. Map of the Sunda Strait between the islands of Sumatra and Java,
through which the *Empress of China* passed en route to the South China Sea.

Saturday, 17. This 24 hours moderate and pleasant. At ½ past 3 P.M., the wind light from ESE, saw the island Java, bearing NEbNorth, and as we approached to 10 or a 11 leagues discovered the low land stretching to the Eastward of Java Head. The high land or mountain of the Head at the bearings NNE and NEbNorth make very high a hollow in the middle and gradually slopes to a low point, but when you get the distance of 8 or nine leagues from the above bearings you will observe the land from the high mountain of Java Head to grow more bluff and will soon see Princes Island which make in a high hammock and the land to the Eastward of the high mountain quite low, and at the distance of 5 or 6 leagues from the above bearings a ridge of mountains appear to the Eastward of the low land. Stood in for the land, and at 8 P.M. the wind came from the NNE. Lay off and on the remainder part of the night under easy sail. At daylight, made all sail. Stretched close in and bent our cables. Cleared our anchors. Saw the islands of Trowers and Claps. When the sun rose high the wind died away. At noon, the Friar Rocks bore NEbE, distance 4 miles, and the Carpenters Rocks at Princes Island NE½E, distance 6 miles, and Java Head bore SE½E, distance about nine

miles. Saw a ship under sail bearing NE, distance 4 or 5 leagues. Very sultry. Thermometer 84ᵈ.

Sunday, 18. At 2 P.M., a breeze sprang up from SE. Set all sail and at 4 some proas from Java came on board with fowls and fish which we purchased and soon opened out Mew Island. Saw a large French ship at anchor, and the ship we saw yesterday under sail was beating into the road. Stretched close by the wind and at 7 P.M. tacked and at 9 came to in Mew Road close by the French *ships whom showed us lights.* At dark, the first point of Java SWbS, the 2d of ditto ENE, and the extremes of Princes Island NNE and NWbW. At daylight, out boats to wood and water. Visited the French captain on board. At our departure he manned ship and gave us three cheers. Several Malay canoes came on board and purchased fowl and turtle from them. The watering place on Java, *in Mew Road South*, NW end of Mew Island West and the SE end of ditto SSW, the 2d point of Java NE when at anchor in 18 fathom water. Both boats made several trips for water and brought off some wood. Winds pleasant. Day sultry. Thermometer 86ᵈ.

32. William Haswell of the Boston bark *Lydia* in 1801-1802 sketched into his journal the appearance of Mew Bay, Java, just inside the Sunda Strait. From the streams pouring out of the jungle, the *Empress of China* refilled her depleted supplies of water.

Monday, 19. Winds ESE. The captain of the *Triton* and some of his officers came to visit us and offered their service in a polite manner. Invited Mr Shaw and Randall to dinner with them tomorrow in company. The boats made several trips a-watering and wooding. Several Malay proas came from Princes Island to dispose of fowls, turtle eggs, canes, shells, and fish. The boatswain and a gang overhauling the rigging, the carpenter on shore a cutting wood for knees to repair the ship's headrails. Thermometer 87ᵈ.

Tuesday, 20. At daylight, sent the boats wooding and watering. The carpenters repairing the head. The boatswain and a gang repairing the rigging. The latter part, scrubbed and cleaned the gross of ship's sides and bends. This day two Dutch ships came through the straits, showed their colors, and passed to the NE. Winds SE. Thermometer 86ᵈ. Latitude observed 6ᵈ45ᵐ South. Very sultry.

Wednesday, 21. The fore part, finished our wooding and got all our water on board. Peter Richard disobedient to command. Insults his officers. Drew his knife on Mr Hodgkinson. Swore he would murder every officer in the ship. In struggling to get the knife out of his hands, he cut Mr Fitch, the 2d mate's, finger. Ordered him in irons, hands and feet. The night moderate. At 3 A.M., hoisted in our boats, and soon after the *Triton* made signal for getting under way. Hove up in company. The winds ESE but in the offing and at noon NE a-beating to windward. Thermometer 85. Two men sick. Variation 51ᵐ West.

Thursday, 22. A strong current setting to the SW. The winds very light. At 4, the wind comes from South and some heavy rain. Find our ship to sail much faster than the *Triton*. At 10 P.M., light winds. Bent our stream cable and came to in 36 fathom water, muddy bottom, in Welcome Bay. The 3d point of Java bearing ENE, 10 or a 11 miles. At daylight, hove up and stretched to the NE, the winds at ESE. As the day advanced the wind died away. Saw several turtle, two of them a-cuteing [*sic* suiting(?)]. Out small

boat and sent after them and brought them on board. They weighed about 160 lb. At noon, a pleasant breeze at NNE. Sultry weather. Thermometer 85ᵈ.

Friday, 23. At 2 P.M., the wind comes to South and blows strong with some rain. The rain did not last long. When it cleared up saw the island of Serigny bearing E. Stood close in and came to in 7 and ½ fathom water, muddy bottom, the island of Serigny bearing SEbS about three miles distant. The 3d point of Java bearing SWbW, distance 3 leagues. The fourth point of Java NbE, 5 leagues distance, off of Java 3 miles at anchor. A Dutch proa came on board with several Malays and had a white man on board. He was a soldier belonging to the country, sent from Batavia to reside under the command of a sergeant stationed at the small town of Serigny laying about 7 miles to the North of the island of that name on the island Java. It is customary for those Dutchmen to go on board all ships which anchor in or on this coast to learn what nation, from whence they came, and wither bound, with the news and the commanders' names, all of which is sent to the Governor of Batavia. At daylight, out barge, and at nine o'clock Messrs Shaw, Randall, Hodgkinson, Swift, and Doctor Johnston all went on shore to see the place and purchase some necessaries. Cleaned ship's sides and tarred ditto. Thermometer 86ᵈ.

Saturday, 24. At 2 P.M., a light shower of rain and a fresh of wind from SSE. At 10 at night, the barge returned with the gentlemen whom went yesterday, all of them much fatigued. Their boat grounded, and they could not launch her before the water flowed. At 1 A.M., the *Triton's* boats returned, and at daylight hoisted in our boats and got under way in company with our consort. Several proas came on board, some having Dutch colors hoisted and a Dutch on board with several Javians in them, all having something for sale but sold everything much dearer than what we purchased at Mew Island. The wind died away. Obliged to come to an anchor with our stream anchor in 21 fathom. Java 4th point NEbNorth, distance 3 leagues, the island of Thorthway [Thwart-the-Way] NE-

½E about 4 leagues. Pulo Condang NWbW 4 or 5 leagues. Thermometer 84ᵈ.

Sunday, 25. Moderate. At anchor and a strong current setting to the SW at the rate of two knots per hour. The wind from NE. A Dutch and Swede with two French ships all at anchor. At daylight, hove up. The small air of wind from SE and at noon died away to a calm. Broke our viol [messenger] and obliged to get a new one. At noon, came to with the stream anchor and furled all our sails. Water 31 fathom. Island Thwartway [Thwart-the-Way] NbW, distance 5 leagues. The Cap NE½North, 4 leagues, and the Button NbE½E, 7 or 8 leagues. The 4 point of Java SbE, 4 miles distant. Sultry weather. Thermometer 85ᵈ.

Monday, 26. At 2 P.M., two proas came on board and had a white man in each of them, a Dutchman. At the same time, the Dutch proa wore a flag of Holland. Had for sale poultry and vegetables, all of which they sold high. They informed us we were the first ships that came through the straits this year for China. At 5 P.M., a small breeze at SE. Got under way and at 9 the wind died away. Came to with the stream anchor in 35 fathom. The weather sultry. Thermometer 86ᵈ.

Tuesday, 27. All this 24 hours at anchor. The current sets strong for 14 hours to the SW and runs at 2 and 2 and ½ knots per hour. The current which run to the NE don't run near so fast. The moon is ten days old this day; perhaps the current run stronger on the increase of the moon than when she is on the decline, and I have observed since my coming round the Cape of Good Hope the winds increase on the moon's increase. Thermometer 83ᵈ—86ᵈ. Winds mostly NE.

Wednesday, 28. The winds mostly at NE. At 5 P.M., a small breeze coming off the land. Hove up and sailed about 2 or 3 miles. The wind died away. Let go our stream anchor in 33 fathom water. People employed variously. Latitude observed 6ᵈ08ᵐ S. Thermometer 85 degrees. N.B.—opened 2 coils of cordage of the cargo for ship's use Nᵒ 1—Nᵒ 3.

Thursday, 29. Light winds and calms for the fore and middle part. At 5 A.M., sent Mr. Hodgkinson on board a Swede's ship which lay in Anger Road to get some news and purchase some tea and sugar for present use. At 6 A.M., a light breeze sprang up from SE. Got under way in company with the ship *Triton*, a Dutch ship from Holland bound to Batavia, and a French ship *Fabius*. At 8, Captain Hodgkinson returned [and] informed that the Swede ship's company was very sickly. She buried number of her hands in Batavia. The commander Claus Brailholtts. Ship's name *Concordia*, bound to Holland. At 11 A.M., the wind flat calm, and we were close in with Button Island. Out jolly boat and pulled the ship's head off the shore. At same time the *Triton* whom was to the NE and near the island Java had a fresh wind off the land which carried her fast to the NE whilst we lay becalmed. At noon, the wind came to the NE. In boat and pressed sail to windward. N.B.—out-sailed the Dutch ship very much. Thermometer 85ᵈ.

Friday, 30. Light winds inclining to calm. Let Peter Richards out of confinement. Soundings from 48 to 35 fathom. At 4 P.M., calm. Came to with our stream anchor in 35 fathom. The Button Island SEbS, 3 leagues. Ship *Triton* NEbNorth, 6 or 7 leagues. A strong current setting to the SW at 2½ knots. At 9 P.M., a fresh breeze from NW attended with hard rain. Hove short to get under way but when the anchor apeak fell calm. At 4 A.M., a pleasant breeze from WNW. Hove up. Set all sail. The wind varies. Set steeringsails. At noon, North Island SWbW. Point St Nicholas on Bantam Point SbE, distance off the Sumatra shore 8 or nine miles. When North Island bore NW had 14 and 15 fathom water. Thermometer 84ᵈ.

Saturday, 31. Pleasant breeze and clear weather. Winds SSE. At 4 P.M., saw the 2 Sisters bearing NNE, 7 or 8 leagues. The ship *Triton* NEbN, 6 or 7 miles, at anchor. Soundings 13 to 14-15 fathom, muddy bottom. At 6 P.M., the Sisters NE½E about 5 or 6 miles. At 8, anchored about a mile to the southward of the *Triton*. The Two Sisters NbW, distance 5 or 6 miles. At 5 A.M., got under way. At 8 A.M., the northernmost of the Sisters WbS; the Southernmost SWbW, about 3 leagues. The soundings very regular 11 to 13 fathom. At 11, the winds veers to the Eastward. Took in steering sails. At noon, the Sisters SbW, 6 or 7 leagues. Latitude at noon 4ᵈ57ᵐ South. Thermometer 84ᵈ.

Narrative by Samuel Shaw[5]
[From his Journal]

July 9th, Captain Hodgkinson, being out with the jolly-boat, endeavouring to take some small fishes, caught three snakes, which he struck with the grains. They were between three and four feet long, and had dark brown backs, yellowish sides and bellies, with black and white stripes or checks on the tail. As they had no fins, and on being opened had a kind of grass in their maw, we considered them as amphibious, and a corroboration of our being near land.

At sunrise on the 15th, we saw four water-spouts, to the eastward, very near. Where they appeared to touch the water, that element seemed to have a boiling motion, attended with smoke. They were visible more than an hour.

Friday, July 17th. Having, ever since the 25th ult., been beating to the eastward, and occasionally running in for the land, we had the good fortune, at half past three o'clock this afternoon, to discover it, and soon ascertained it to be Java Head. It bore N. E. by N. ten or twelve leagues. Having made up my reckoning to this time, we were, by account, in 7° 24′ south latitude, and 111° 13′ east longitude. Java Head, according to Moore, is in 6° 49′ south latitude, and 106° 55′ east longitude from London.

The next morning, between nine and ten o'clock, we opened the Straits of Sunda, and at noon saw a ship, distant between three and four leagues, sailing up the straits near the Java shore. At three o'clock we hoisted the American ensign, and at four saw a very large ship at anchor in the cove,—the first under sail for, and in half an hour coming to anchor by her, both of them having French ensigns hoisted.

At four o'clock, two canoes made towards us from the Java shore, one of which, with five natives, came on board, the other not being able to reach us: These people are middle-sized and well-made,—complexion similar to that of the North American savage, with regular features and a pleasing countenance, though their teeth are excessively black, owing to an herb they chew, which dyes their lips a claret, or rather, *pompadour* color. They wear a handkerchief about their heads, and a piece of calico or check round their waist, hanging as low as the knee. After selling us some fowls and cocoa-nuts, they went to Prince's island. Shortly after, another came on board, and for half a dollar gave us as many fish as would serve both cabins for supper. The boats, or canoes, are from fifteen to twenty feet long, and about two and a half wide; mast from ten to twelve feet long; canvass sail as long, and about four feet wide, extended on two pieces of reed, and crossing the mast diagonally; a piece of reed, six inches in diameter, fixed with outriggers from the side of the boat, to keep it by the wind, seven or eight feet distance from and two thirds the length of the boat. These boats are covered with pieces of reed, or bamboo, on which the occupants sit, and underneath keep their fish, fowls, &c.; they have oars, and steer with a paddle. The fish we had of them were the red spotted and common yellow-tailed snappers,—the former a most beautiful vermilion color. They, as well as the groper, a shorter and thicker fish, which we also had, are of the perch kind.

As soon as it was dark, we hung up two lanterns, which being answered by the ships, we came to anchor, at a quarter after eight o'clock, in nineteen fathoms of water,—our people all in good health, and no accident having happened since our departure from New York.

On the 18th, in the forenoon, the captain, Mr. Randall, and I, went on board the large ship, the captain of which, with his officers, received us very politely. She is called the *Triton*, a sixty-four, but armed *en flute*, with only sixteen light cannon, and one hundred and eighty-four men. She left Brest the 20th of March, and arrived here the day before yesterday; will sail for Canton, after watering and taking in wood to last thither and back to Europe. This is rendered necessary by the circumstance, that the season makes it unsafe to stop here on the return, and that at Canton wood is sold by weight, and none to be had at the Cape of Good Hope. Another ship of the same size is gone through the Straits of Malacca, and a third is daily expected here, all bound for Canton, and with their cargoes and money estimated at six million livres. There being no permanent East India company in France, the king has lent these ships to a company of merchants for the present expedition. The captain is a chevalier of St. Louis, appears to be a man of information, and has been repeatedly to China. He says, that, the day before he left Paris, the Marquis de la Fayette received the order of the American Society of the Cincinnati, and that the king had granted permission to such officers as were entitled to it to accept and be invested with it. He adds, that the French are much pleased with the honor done to their nation by the institution. On our leaving his ship, the sides and yards were manned, and we were saluted with thrice *vive le roi*, which we answered by three cheers.

The other ship is less than ours, called the *Fabius*, without guns, and carries thirty-six men. She arrived here yesterday, from the Cape of Good Hope, which she left the 15th of May, bound for Batavia, with cannon and stores for the Dutch government there. As no certain information had been received with respect to a definitive peace between England and Holland, it was politic to employ a French vessel. The captain was in the fleet under the Duc d'Orvilliers in the affair with Admiral Keppel, in July, 1778,—and in that under Count de Grasse, in the Chesapeake; at the surrender of the British army at Yorktown to the combined forces of America and France, in October, 1781; and afterwards in the memorable engagement between the unfortunate though gallant De Grasse and Rodney, on the 12th of April following. On leaving this ship, the same compliments passed as with the other, and in about two hours after, the captain returned our visit. The commanders of both ships are lieutenants in the royal navy, the first apparently sixty, and the other about forty years old.

We had many of the natives alongside this day. They are exceedingly fond of opium, and would put twelve or fourteen grains at once into their mouths without any bad effect. We bought of them turtle of fifty pounds' weight for half a dollar, and a dozen fowls for a dollar. They had monkeys, of which our sailors bought several, of the size of those we saw at St. Jago, but of a grayish dun color.

The captain of the *Triton*, M. d'Ordelin, and his second-captain, M. Cordeaz, returned our visit in the forenoon of the 19th. They examined our charts (Dunn's), which they said were good, and invited us to dine with them the next day. M. Cordeaz was with Count de Grasse's fleet in the Chesapeake, and in the action with Rodney. After dinner, the captain, Mr. Randall, Mr. Swift, and I, went ashore at Mew island, where the three ships get wood. Water is procured from the Java shore so conveniently, that casks are filled by a short hose without taking them from the boat; but it is dangerous going into the woods, as they abound with tigers and other wild animals.

In the forenoon of the 20th, a large Dutch ship passed up the straits. The same day, the captain, Mr. Randall, and I, dined on board the *Triton*. Dinner as elegantly served as if we had been at an entertainment on shore. There are twenty gentlemen every day at table,—exceedingly polite, and very glad at meeting us. The captain having acquainted us that he shall sail on Thursday, and expressed a wish to render us every service in his power, we concluded to go in company with him to Canton. He has been there eleven times, and is perfectly acquainted with the navigation in these seas. The principal supercargo, M. Trolliez, made us similar offers in his line. While we were at dinner, another Dutch ship passed up the straits. In the afternoon we went ashore at Mew Island, in company with the second captain, also M. Colombe (captain of the *Fabius*), and a captain of the French infantry, who obtained permission to make the voyage in the *Triton*, merely from motives of curiosity. This principle, combined with the cause of religion, and perhaps other considerations, has induced a young priest not only to undertake the voyage, but to bid his native country adieu for ever. He is to reside at Pekin, in quality of a missionary, where are many of his brethren, who have a large church, the free exercise of their religion, and a handsome establishment. He appears to be under thirty, is sensible and polite. The officers say he is a man of great science, is furnished with a complete apparatus for experimental philosophy, and is acquainted with the principles and construction of the air-balloon lately invented by M. de Montgolfier, at Paris. These, as well as his genteel deportment, will no doubt render him an acquisition to the Chinese, and to his brethren in that country. God speed him!—it is a great sacrifice he makes,—for, by the laws of China, no stranger, after having been allowed to reside in the imperial city, is ever suffered to return.

The next day, the captain of the *Triton* sent us his day and night signals. I wrote duplicate letters to Mr. Parker, in New York, and enclosed them separately to Messrs. John de la Neufville and Son, in Amsterdam. These letters I gave in the afternoon to the captain of the *Fabius*, on board the *Triton*, who promised to send one by the first opportunity from Batavia, and take charge of the other himself, if there should not be an earlier conveyance.

Mr. Swift, Captain Green, Mr. Randall, and I, in company with the second captain and two officers of the *Triton*, went ashore at Mew island, where, after planting Indian corn, oats, peas, beans, and potatoes, we drank a bottle of madeira, and another of champagne, to the success of our garden. This island, which is uninhabited, is called by the French Cantaya. In the creek that separates it from Java are plenty of fish, and in the neighbourhood a very large kind of bats, that take their flight about sunset. They appear to be as large as a full-grown fowl, and are said by the French to be excellent eating. At this place the captain of the *Triton* had a board nailed up, whereon were inscribed his name, that of the ship, and the day of her arrival and departure.

Thursday, July 22d, at sunrise, we came to sail, in company with the French ships. Anchored at ten o'clock at night. The next morning we weighed, and at noon lowered the jolly-boat and took two turtle. At four P.M., anchored off the island of Serigny. A sergeant from the shore visited the ship in his prow, with a printed paper containing queries,—"Where or by whom owned,—come from,—bound?" &c.,—to which the proper answers were annexed by the captain. Mr. Randall, the captain, and I, went on board the *Triton*. The officers commended the sailing of our ship highly. Tomorrow, should the weather be clear, they intend taking an observation to ascertain the longitude by the sun and moon. Four times during their voyage they have thus ascertained their longitude, on neither of which occasions, they say, were they out of their reckoning more than twenty miles. At sunset, the *Fabius* was scarcely visible astern. N. B.—Both the *Triton* and our ship are sheathed with copper.

After breakfast, on the 24th, Captain Hodgkinson, the doctor, Mr. Randall, Mr. Swift, and I, went ashore to the settlements of Serigny, on Java. A number of natives assembled, and, on our landing, an old man advanced and offered us his hand. From the beach, we went into the town, consisting of between four and five hundred huts, built of cane or bamboo reed, and covered with a thatch of leaves and straw,— apparently commodious and clean. When we were nearly in the middle of the settlement, we were met by the chief, attended by upwards of a hundred of his countrymen, some of whom were armed with spears, and all with knives. He received us with an open, smiling countenance, shook hands, and pronounced the words, "Me grandee Bantam"; and on our making signs to him and pointing to our ship, he replied, " 'Mericans," which information he must have had from the Dutchman on board of us the day before. After conducting us through the main street, he led us into a large yard, enclosed with a stone wall, and well shaded by large trees, his house being in the centre. He invited us to walk into the house, which we declining, he attended us to the gate, where we took leave, by shaking hands, and drinking a cup of our wine to his health. He was apparently about thirty years old, handsome, and clad in a rich chintz gown and underclothes, with a piece of fine chintz about his head for a turban, and a girdle, or rather sash, of blue, white, and red silk and gold, about his waist, in which was placed his poniard, in a sheath of yellow metal, highly polished; his feet and legs were bare. There was something noble and very pleasing in his looks, while his behaviour was altogether friendly and engaging.

From this settlement we walked to the other, about three miles farther,—not materially different from the first. Here we found the second captain, the surgeon, the captain of infantry, and three other gentlemen from the *Triton*, purchasing beef, turtle, fowls, &c.

The settlements lie on the seashore, and are surrounded by rice-fields, which the natives cultivate for their subsistence. They have also pine-apples, Indian corn, bananas, cucumbers, cocoa-nuts, besides all kinds of poultry in abundance, buffalo (which is their beef), and goats. The soil is rich, and from the place where we landed to the upper settlement the road is perfectly level, covered with a most beautiful verdure, and leading through a continued grove of cocoa-nut trees, whose shade afforded us a comfortable shelter from the scorching rays of the sun, and the milk of the nuts a most cooling and refreshing liquor.

The inhabitants of these places get a great part of their subsistence by fishing, there being not much short of two hundred boats, great and small, belonging to them. These are built and rigged in the manner already mentioned, and are of every size, from such as will carry only a single person, to those that will take thirty or forty. The larger kind have a shed over them, reaching from the stern to the middle of the boat, made of reeds and straw, to defend the crew from the weather. About seventy of the smaller sort went out at sunrise to fish, and at noon returned with their cargoes of small and large fish, having nets proper for each. The beach is very low for a considerable distance from the shore, over which the sea breaks a great length, and roars exceedingly, so that, if any boats were left there, they would soon be stove to pieces. To prevent this, and for the security of their small fleet, the inhabitants have dug canals from fifteen to twenty feet wide, leading to basins in the rear of their settlements, sufficient to contain the whole. Over these canals and basins, which in each settlement must be crossed in many places, are bridges, constructed of timbers laid from one bank to the other, and covered with strips of reed, interlaced in the manner of mats, well fastened, neatly wrought, and sufficiently strong. The people are numerous, and, from the great disproportion in favor of the children, the women must be exceedingly prolific. They are Mahometans, and in each settlement have a mosque. Both men and women are armed with knives, which they constantly carry about them, in a wooden scabbard hanging across the shoulder; notwithstanding which, they appear placid in their manners to each other, and courteous towards strangers. It is said, however, that they are not pleased with any attention paid by strangers to their women, who, for that reason, probably, are shy, and seldom make their appearance.

These places are dependent on Bantam and Batavia. That which we first visited has a Dutch sergeant and two privates as a garrison, with two small brass cannon, carrying a ball of about half a pound, and a Dutch flag, which is hoisted occasionally. The sergeant goes or sends to every vessel that passes, for answers to queries like those presented to us, and transmits them to Bantam, whence they are forwarded to Batavia. The carriers go along the seashore all the way, as it would be dangerous for them, on account of the natives, to go through the country. The sergeant showed a poisoned knife, and said many of the natives have them besides their spears, which are also poisoned;—he added, that, so virulent is this poison, that the smallest scratch with one of these weapons is quick and certain death.

Refreshments, in general, are nearly twice as dear here as we found them at the entrance of the straits. There are doves, paroquets, and a variety of other birds, both in respect to plumage and notes, to be bought here. After remaining till the tide made, we left the last of these places about nine o'clock, and returned on board ship by eleven, not a little fatigued with the adventures of the day.

On our concluding to sail in company with the *Triton*, M. d'Ordelin acquainted us that he intended not to go the common route, through the Straits of Banca, but to attempt one more to the eastward, between Banca and Biliton. He was informed of this passage by a French gentleman, M. Gaspar, who, in a Spanish vessel, made it with the utmost safety, in going to and returning from China, having from twelve to twenty-five fathoms soundings. Accordingly, having come to sail, on Sunday, July 25th, we proceeded as fast as the winds and currents would allow.

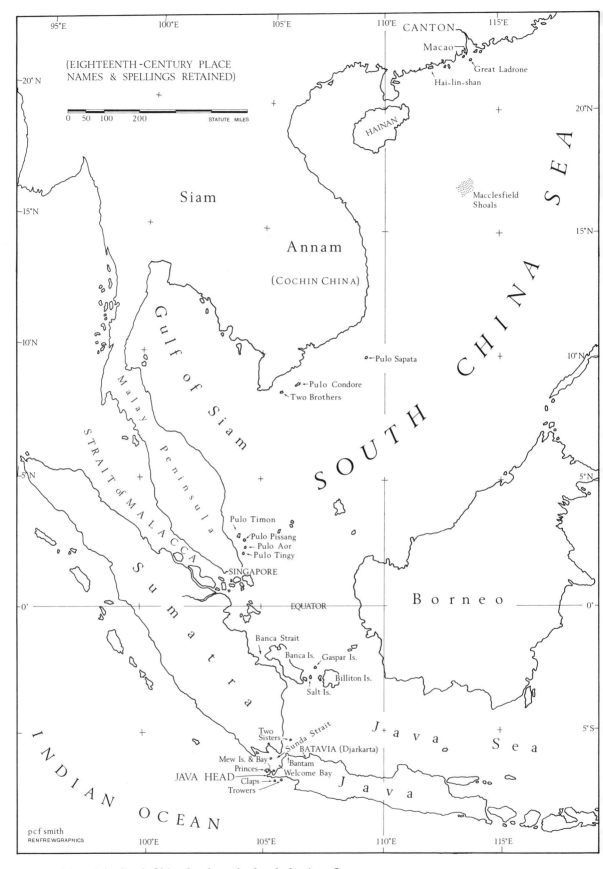

33. Map of the South China Sea from the Sunda Strait to Canton.

XI

Canton Cumshaw and Commerce

The distance from the mouth of the Chu-kiang, or Pearl, River to Canton is not dissimilar to that from Capes May and Henlopen up the Delaware to Philadelphia: one hundred miles, more or less, of winding rivers punctuated by natural and unnatural barriers throughout their lengths. On the Delaware, ocean-going navigation ends well upriver above Philadelphia, but on the Pearl River it ceased for the *Empress of China* and all other foreign shipping at Whampoa Reach, a dozen miles downstream from Canton itself.

Before entering the Pearl, however, ships were required to pause at the ancient Portuguese colony of Macao for the captain or the supercargo to row ashore and obtain a pass—known as a "chop"—and a pilot. The officer was well advised also to make himself known to the higher dignitaries of the Custom House, as well as to the Governor. "There is nothing to be gained by endeavoring to hurry these people into giving you a Pilot by loud talking," one American shipmaster would advise another in years to come, "coaxing & greasing the palms of hands being the only means of doing it."

John Green kept no journal from the day immediately following the departure from Macao until the ship sailed again from Whampoa for home four months later. Evidently, a ship's log was maintained during part of that time, but it has long since vanished from sight. Fortunately, Samuel Shaw's observations have survived, yet no one, including him, thought to describe the novel sights awaiting the Americans as their pilot and his three assistants guided the *Empress of China* upriver.[1] Other, later voyagers were kinder to

34. Shore profiles of land masses in the South China Sea. From lower left, clockwise, Camel Island, Pulo Saparta, St. Julian, Gaspar Island and the Gaspar Strait, and Java Head which "can be seen 18 miles of a clear night."

posterity, painting word images of scenes that scarcely changed throughout the first fifty years of the trade. One such picked up where John Green left off: riding to an anchor in plain view of the mountainous peaks of Lintin Island just above Macao and just below the river's mouth.

"Lintin," he wrote, "is a small, barren, ragged island, the ground composing various eminences, one of which is not less than seven hundred feet. The island is a mile and a quarter in diameter. . . .

"Some distance above Lintin, we passed an island called Lankeet, which means the Dragon's Den. A tongue of land runs out into the river on the opposite side, which bears the name of Chuen-pee, or the Bored Nose, from a single rock which forms its most striking feature, perforated through. . . .

"Tiger Island, which lies still higher up the river, has its name from the resemblance of its figure to that of a tiger in a reclining posture. On it is a battery of considerable size, and on the opposite bank another battery, called Anung Hoy, or the Lady's Shoe. Both these batteries are of granite, and one of them extends from the shore, up an inclined plane . . . the portlids are painted with figures of tigers and demons.

"The entrance to the river Tigris, called Bocca Tigris, a Portuguese name signifying the Mouth of Tigris, is between Anung Hoy and Tiger Island. The scenery here is more inviting, and we passed several plantations of bamboos, bananas, and rice. After passing the first and second bars"—to accomplish which the *Empress of China* was obliged to hire twenty-five tow boats—"we reached Whampoa, the anchoring ground for all foreign vessels trading with Canton."[2]

Here, the *Empress of China* arrived during the morning of August 28, 1784, one hundred and eighty-eight days and some 18,000 miles from New York, and with the United States salute of thirteen guns honored the shipping already riding within the Reach, which each vessel returned in kind. "The French ships," Shaw observed, "sent two boats, with anchors and cables, under an officer who assisted us in getting into a good berth, and staid on board till we were moored. The Danish sent an officer, to compliment; the Dutch a boat to assist; and the English an officer 'to welcome your flag to this part of the world'."[3] From Whampoa, small chop boats and lighters would whisk officers and cargo alike to and from the foreign compound— the "factories" or "hongs"—in Canton, to which all Westerners were restricted.

"We had a full view of a pagoda nine stories high," the word painter continued, while passing from Whampoa to Canton, "which is one of the largest in the vicinity of Canton. It is of great antiquity, and stands near groves of banana, orange, peach, and lichee trees, as well as plantations of rice and sugar-cane. Passing several forts called the Dutch and French 'Follies,' . . . is another ancient pagoda. The shores present many beautiful scenes along this portion of the river. The pagodas and joss houses, or idol temples, are numerous and conspicuous; while duck boats are drawn up in the rice fields, on the surface of which are seen thousands of ducks, under the care of their keepers.

". . . The surface of the river was thickly covered with vessels of different sizes, of singular forms and rigging, many of which were painted with gay and fantastical colors. Here were boats and small craft in great variety, with numerous junks of from four to five hundred tons burthen, covered with painted figures in glaring hues, of almost every device that ingenuity could invent, all containing men, women, and children, in grotesque garments, huddled together in great numbers, and actively engaged in different employments, while the crash of gongs, and the hum of business heard from every quarter, presented a scene full of life and hilarity.

"The city of Canton is situated on the north side of the river, known by the several names of the Choo-keang, or Pearl River, the Tigris, and Canton River. The foreign factories all stand in the south-western suburb, which, with the other suburbs, contains a population, as is said, about equal to that of the city proper. The latter is surrounded by a thick wall, built partly of stone and partly of brick, and divided by another wall, which crosses it from east to west. The northern of the two sections thus formed, is called the Old City, and the southern the New. The latter is the residence of the governor and of the *hoppo*, or officers of the customs. The foreign residents are required to confine their habitations to a narrow strip of land on the river's bank, without the walls, which might be very pleasant but for the crowds of dwell-

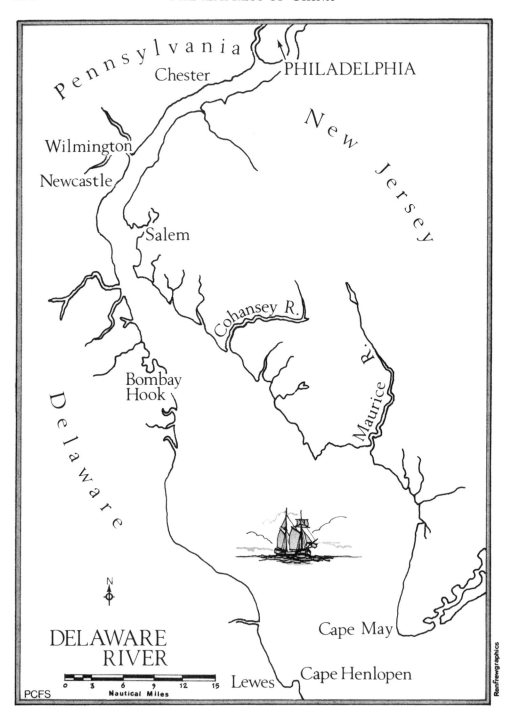

35. Drawn to the same scale, the Delaware River in North America and the Pearl River in China exhibit striking resemblances. Philadelphia and Canton, respectively, are nearly equidistant from the open sea.

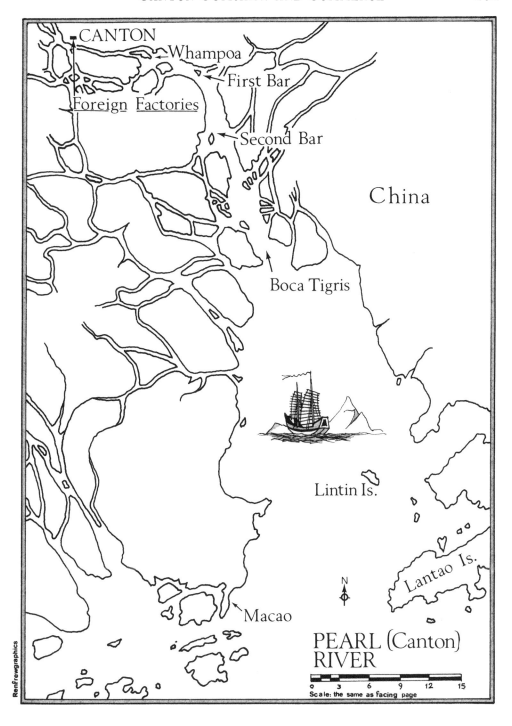

Foreign Factories

PEARL (Canton) RIVER

ing boats, which cover the surface of the water. Most of the inhabitants of these floating houses are said to have come from the south, who, being a despised people, were not permitted to land.

"The river at Canton is not more than one hundred and fifty yards wide. The shore is crowded with buildings, many of which encroach upon the water. The boats, always seen on the river for the distance of four or five miles, are said to amount to nearly forty or fifty thousand, and they may even exceed this estimate. The boats are of various sizes, forms and descriptions. Some are employed in fishing, some in rowing up and down the river with passengers, some as smugglers, and others come from the canal. There is another kind called dragon boats, seen at the annual celebration of a holiday in June. They are shaped somewhat like snakes, and are of great size. But the *tanka* boats are the greatest curiosities . . . the name is said to signify egg house, and if so, is certainly an appropriate one; for the form of the boat resembles that of an egg. Each of them is the habitation of a family, and though small, still affords as much space for their accommodation as many of the confined apartments in which the poor reside in our large cities."

During the season of 1784, thirty-four foreign ships engaged in trade with Canton: twenty-one English, four French, four Dutch, four Danish, and the *Empress of China*. The first to arrive had appeared on the fifth of July but had been obliged to wait for nearly a month until the beginning of August when the head of the Chinese customs, the Hoppo, and his assistant, had got around to measuring her to calculate the amount of duties.[4] Measurement of the *Empress of China* took place on September 14, 1784, as recorded in the sole surviving entry from her logbook:

> At 10 A.M., came on board the grand mandarin, with his attendants, and the principal merchants of Canton, to measure the ship. Saluted them with nine guns. At 11, they left the ship, in order to visit and measure the other ships,—after which we saluted them with nine guns, as did the other ships. P.M.—the grand mandarin sent on board, as a present to the ship, two bulls, eight bags of flour, and seven jars of country wine.[5]

The ritual of "Cumshaw and Measurement" was not fully understood by the Americans at their first appearance in the Canton marketplace. William C. Hunter, who spent many years from the age of thirteen in China during the second quarter of the nineteenth century, knew the drill intimately.

"When a ship had anchored at Whampoa," he wrote in his book, *The 'Fan*

Kwae' at Canton, "the pilot reported her arrival to the Hoppo through a branch Hoppo station at that place. This would be done, not by giving the name of the ship, but that of the captain. Two boats were made fast to her, to see that no smuggling was carried on; they were attached one on each quarter. Meanwhile the agent would select a Hong merchant to become 'security' for her and a Linguist to transact her business with the Hoppo's office, to send boats to bring her cargo to Canton, and to take to Whampoa her outward cargo, and these were all the 'official' duties that the agent had to attend to.

"Before she could open hatches, the formality of 'Cumshaw and Measurement' had to be gone through. The first word signifies 'present,' and was a payment made by the earliest foreign vessels for the privilege of entering the port; and the second is equivalent to tonnage duties. On a day of which notice was given to the agent, a specially appointed mandarin from the Hoppo's office was sent on board, attended by pursers and numerous servants. He was always received with some ceremony, and regaled with wine and biscuit. As with all the officials, they were men of a good deal of dignity and ease of manner. The captain would receive him at the gangway, while all hands were rigged out in their 'Sunday suits.' After the ordinary salutations, enquiries as to the passage out, &c., the measurement would be made by one of the attendants attaching the end of a measured tape to the forward part of the rudder head and running it to the after part of the foremast, then calling out the length, which others would note in writing; the breadth was then taken amidships close abaft the mainmast, between the plankshears, which being booked, a calculation was made of the dimensions for duty. . . .

"The 'Cumshaw and Measurement' having been duly disposed of, a permit was granted for 'opening hatches,' and the unloading went on uninterruptedly. . . ."[6]

Perhaps William Duer's information from Europe suggesting that the ginseng cargo would not prove to be as golden as had been expected was almost correct. This year, it seemed, everyone was bringing it to China. John White Swift had something to say on the subject as well as suggesting future considerations aspirant China traders should bear in mind.

"My dear Father," he wrote for the first time since Mew Bay. "If ever you receive this letter, it will acquaint you, that after a passage of 6 Months & 7 Days, we Came to Anchor at Wampoo, four leagues from this City, where all foreign Ships load & unload—we had no difficulty in comeing thro the China Seas, having fortunately met with Monsr. Dordelin Commr of the Ship *Triton* (bound to China) on entering the Streights of Sunda, with whom we kept Compy till we got our Pilot—the Chinese had never heard of us, but we introduced ourselves as a new Nation, gave them our history with a description of our Country, the importance and necessity of a trade here to the advantage of both, which they appear perfectly to understand and wish. Our Cargoe turn'd out but so so. We brought too much Ginsang, a little of the best kind will yield an immense profit but all the European Nations trading here bring this Article, & unfortunately this Year ten times as much arrived as ever did before. Old Doll[ar]s are 7 pr Ct better than new. A little Tar a little Ginsang a little Wine & a great many Dollars with some Tar &c makes the best Cargoe. I just mention this as a hint to Jacob, if he inclines to come here, which is my advice if he can get the Command of a Ship. Her burden out [ought] to be at least 700 or 800 tons, ours is much too small.

"I am now here purchasing my little matters, & we expect to sail in one Month, when perhaps, I wish it, Oh how I wish it! to see you in the month of May—but least I never shou'd I write by way of London to let you know that we had arrived in China—If we have a favorable passage, long before this reaches you, I shall be at home—

"I send you every best wish of a heart that loves you—make my most affectionate love to my Mother the Family & all our friends. . . ."[7]

Notwithstanding White's "so-so" assessment of the *Empress of China*'s cargo, she did not fare all that badly. It should come as no surprise to hear that the British East India Company was keeping a bright eye on the success or failure of its American cousins' first essay into the Canton market. Ultimately, the East India Company's Court of Directors received a report on the amounts realized by the *Empress of China*'s inward cargo. It was highly inaccurate, both as to specific items, quantities, and prices received. A picul was the equivalent of 133.3 pounds, and the tael equalled six shillings eight pence, or, in Spanish silver dollars, seventy-two cents.

	Taels
Cotton, 316 piculs, realized	3,160
Lead, 476 " "	1,904
Pepper, 26 " "	260
Camlets, 1,270 pieces	45,720
Skins (furs), 2,600 pieces, realized	5,000 estimated
Ginseng, 473 piculs, realized	80,410
	136,454[8]

By contrast, the *Empress of China*'s own records, headed "Sales in China," provides not only an accurate quantity count but also a more plausible set of figures when compared to Daniel Parker's "Estimate of Value" sent to LeCouteulx & Cie. in March for the making of insurance.

63,595 Pounds lead at 10 Ds pr Ct		6,000 Ds
97,445 lbs Cordage at 20 Cts		20,000
57,687 Do Ginsang $ 5 pr lb		240,000
4 Pipes Teneriffe wine	200	400
5 Do Madeira 400		2,000
1 Hhd Jamaica Spirits ⎱	250	500
1 Do Brandy ⎰		
2,395 Planks		100
437 Yds Cloth		2,000
20,000 Dollars in specie		20,000
		291,000[9]

A contemporaneous document, mentioned previously, states that the price of ginseng at the beginning of the 1784 season in Canton stood at $2,000 the picul, or $15 a pound, but by the time the Western ships carrying it had all arrived the bottom had fallen out of the market and a pound of the root was worth only $1.50 to $2.25.[10] At that rate, the *Empress of China* reached her market neither at the top nor at the bottom but somewhere two-thirds of the way through it. Nonetheless, the venture would still return a profit of between twenty-five and thirty per cent.

Continuation of John Green's Journal

AUGUST 1784

Sunday, 1. Commences light winds and sultry. At 3 P.M., sent the jolly boat on board the *Triton* with my second captain and Mr. Randall to make my compliments and thank him for his attention in waiting for me. The wind died away. Came to with stream anchor. We find in all these places a current setting to the SW, though it changes and sets to the NE. Nine, 10, 11, 12 fathom. At 11 P.M., hove up. Got under way. Steered NE. Winds ENE. Pleasant moonlight. At daylight, brought all our guns from forward aft to bring the ship by the stern and at 9 sent everything forward to find the trim of the ship, but the ship sails best at 2 feet 6 inches difference by the stern. Removed everything from forwards to aft. At noon, in latitude 40^{d}08^m South. Thermometer 84^d.

Monday, 2. Steady wind from SEbE. Course NE½North. 11 and 12 fathom water. The ship *Triton* about 4 miles ahead. She made signal for coming to. At 7 P.M., came to with the stream anchor in nine fathom. Hands all sails. At 5 A.M., hove up and made sail. The winds ESE. At ½ past 7, saw some breakers and small rocks to the ESE. About 2 miles on a bank which lay off the South part of Billiton. At 8, saw a small island bearing ENE, 2 leagues. At nine, saw more islands bearing North and NNE. At 10, saw land NNW. Our soundings 9, 10, 11, 13,

14 fathom. At noon, observed latitude 3ᵈ08ᵐ South. The *Triton* made signal for coming to. We brought to and let go a bower anchor in nine fathom. The islands NEbN. The land WbNorth. Thermometer 86ᵈ. Two of our men sick.

Tuesday, 3. A fresh breeze of wind. Went on board the *Triton* in company with Mr Shaw and offered my service in getting under way in the morning at 5 o'clock and stretching to NE where I made no doubt but the passage lay and from the appearance of his draughts and that of Mr Gaspars I was almost sure we lay at anchor off the south point of Salt Island; that the point of land which bore NNE must be the entrance of the passage, the land we saw to the Westward must be Banca SE point and the islands to the NEbN lay off Billiton. Mr d'Ordelin agreed that he thought as I did, but the depth of water which their lead gave was at times 4 and 5 fathom, and he was sure from what Mr. Gaspar had informed him of the passage this was not the place. I had no such soundings as he mentioned, and I was sure there must be some mistake; however, he hoisted out both his small boats. The largest he sent to the NNE to view the opening, which lay about 5 leagues from us. He promised he would send his second captain with me in the morning to reconnoitre the land and find out the passage in the ship and he would get under way and follow at 2 miles distance. He requested that when I thought I had the passage in sight and deepened our water to 13 fathom that I would hoist a white flag at the main-topgallant masthead and keep it there, but should we find less water than at present *which was unlikely we should* that I should hoist a blue flag and haul down the white. At 5 A.M., we got under way. His officers and a young gentleman, a volunteer, came on board. We steered to the NE, the wind SE, and when we opened the north point of Salt to bear NNW had 13, 14, 15, 17 fathom and in running from the place where the ship anchored to this spot had 9, and for 3 minutes 8 fathom, but there is a shoal lays off the south point of Salt and we was crossing that shoal to the East when we had that depth, but when the south point bore NWbN deepened immediately. This passage is

about 2 leagues wide. There is some rocks which lay above water and reefs to the Eastward of Salt about one mile off the shore, but you can see everything that will hurt you. Keep the Salt side in 16 fathom and there's no fear then. The depth of water when you bring the south point to bear West will be to the Eastward of you. There are two islands which lay to the east side; have very high rocks all along the shore and appear like houses. We gave those islands the name of Congress Islands, and when you come up with the north end of them there is a reef running off about 2 miles to the North. Between *they*, Salt, and the east point of Banca lay some islands but they lay to the West of Thay, Salt. When you discover the island of Gaspar it makes high and in fine day can be seen 8 or nine leagues. The east end of Banca appear high like an island, but as we advanced to the North observed the lowland joined. In the passage and about 3 leagues SWbS from the north end of Isle Gaspar we saw a rock at first sight from the masthead appearing like a sail and took it for such for a long time, but as we approached it saw a high tree on the top and one on the lower part which was all that grew there, the whole a rock in form of a sugar loaf. When you approach within 2 leagues you see a small rock about as large as a ship's longboat and distance of the large rock 50 or 100 yards. We gave this island the name of Parker's Island. Latitude observed 2ᵈ38ᵐ South. Thermometer 85ᵈ.

Wednesday, 4. When to SSW of Gaspar and steering for to find anchoring ground where we might bring to and send on shore to examine for fresh water in case we should want on our return from China. At ½ past 2 close in with the land. There is a rock which lay West of the north end of Gaspars. You may run outside or to the West of it in 17 fathom. Then you are ½ mile off, sandy bottom, but we discovered a reef and shoal water from the east side of this rock extending to a reef which almost run from the main island to the Westward. There's no passage between the rock and island which lay distant 2 miles of each other. Sent the yawl on shore to reconnoitre. Mr Shaw, Randall, Doctor Johnston and McCaver went in her. At 3 came to in 17 fathom, large brown sand, Gaspar Island SEbE 3 miles. The rock which lay to the West, Mr Shaw named Smasham Rock from the great quantity of birds eggs they broke whilst they were on it. Bore SbE one mile and a half distance. The boat returned at sunset but found no water, or if there was water its a bad road to stop in when the westerly monsoons blow. At 5, got under way. Steered NbW and run distance 4 leagues off when we discovered some rocks and breakers bearing NNE 3 miles. At noon, in latitude 1ᵈ40ᵐ S. Made course from the anchoring place NNW distance [   ] 45ᵐ. Thermometer 85. The water smooth and the weather pleasant. Winds SE. Steering sails set alow and aloft. Got out fore topsail yard.

Thursday, 5. Fresh breezes. All sail set at day. At night shortened sail, our consort at distance of 1 mile astern. People all employed. Some making spunyarn, others cleansing their berths, and the remainder overhauling the rigging. The winds SE and SSE.

Course steered this 24 hours NbW¾W, distance 160ᵐ.
Departure 54ᵐ W.
Latitude observed 00—49ᵐ North.
Thermometer 85ᵈ.

Friday, 6. Clear weather until at 11 at night when it began to thunder, lightning, and rain hard for 3/4 of an hour. The fore part of the day and latter, the winds at SSE. The middle, at WSW. Course steered until we saw Pulo Aor, which was at 10 A.M., NWbW, distance 73ᵐ. Then we were about 8 or 9 [?] leagues distant from the land. After making the island Pulo Aor, we steered NNW until noon and run distance 16 miles per log. At noon the island bore NWbN½North, distance 4 or 5 leagues. Course made good from Gaspar to Pulo Aor NNW½W, distance 297 miles. When the south part of the island bore NW, distance 3 leagues, our logline marked 47 feet and the glass 28 seconds. Latitude observed 2ᵈ07ᵐ North. Thermometer 85ᵈ. Painting our longboat and overhauling rigging.

Saturday, 7. Commences with some rain. At 6 P.M., Pulo Timon bore WbN, distance 6 or 7 leagues. Light winds and pleasant weather. The winds SSE. All sail set. The water remarkable

smooth. Not a fowl or fish to be seen but when off Pulo Pisang much fish spawn and scum on the surface of the water. Steering to the NbE. Pulo Tingy SWbW, 7 leagues. Steered from the bearings of Pulo Timon's south ends bearing WbNorth, 7 leagues to noon NbE¼E. Run distance 87ᵐ per the log. Latitude observed in at noon 4ᵈ33ᵐ North. Thermometer 84ᵈ. The next land to run for is the 2 Brothers.

Sunday, 8. Pleasant weather and smooth water. The winds SbW and SWbS. Steered all this 24 hours NbE and run distance 126ᵐ per log. At noon sounded in 29 fathom water, muddy bottom. All sail set alow and aloft. Latitude observed 6ᵈ51ᵐ North. Thermometer 85ᵈ. *Triton* in company.

Monday, 9. Pleasant weather. The winds for the fore and middle part, SSE. The latter part, at SW and some squalls and light rain. Smooth water and many sea fowl after small fish hovering near the ship. Midnight, sounded in 20 fathom. At ½ past 7 A.M., sounded in 19 fathom. At 9 A.M., saw the 2 Brothers bearing NEbN, 6 or 7 leagues. Hauled the ship to the NEbE and run until noon when the Brothers bore NbW, distance 3 leagues. At same time saw Pulo Condore ENE distance 7 or 8 leagues. Latitude observed 8ᵈ25ᵐ. Thermometer 84ᵈ. N.B.—the course made from our departure of Pulo Timon to making the Brothers is NbE¼E, distance 292 miles per log, and from our first seeing them until they bore NbW we run distance 16 miles NE½E. Steering for the Pulo Sapata.

Tuesday, 10. Commences moderate and continues pleasant all this 24 hours. Winds SSW and SWbW. At 6 P.M., the W end of Pulo Condore WNW 5 leagues, the body of the land NW, distance 3 leagues. All sail set a-steering for Pulo Sapata. Run distance from the above bearings 70ᵐ NEbE¼E course. Latitude observed 9ᵈ04ᵐ North. Thermometer 84ᵈ. Sea smooth and winds light.

Wednesday, 11. Moderate and pleasant. The winds from WSW to SW. Course steered from noon until 12 at night NEbE and run distance

53 miles. At midnight, took in all our small sails and hauled the ship by the wind under her 3 topsails to the SSE until 2 A.M. and run distance 4 miles. At 2, hove to the fore-topsail to the mast and at 3 A.M. saw Pulo Sapata bearing NEbN 2 or three leagues. Made signal to the *Triton* for seeing the land. At 5 A.M., bore away to the eastward. Saw two small rocks to the NW of Pulo Sapata about 3 miles distance. Sounded in 75 fathom before we saw the land but got no ground. Our course made from the departure of Pulo Condore until Pulo Sapata bore North 2 leagues ENE distance 45 leagues. Latitude observed at noon 10ᵈ07ᵐ N. Thermometer 85ᵈ. At 10 A.M., Pulo Sapata bore WSW, 7 or 8 leagues distant. A-steering for the Macclesfield Shoal. Run distance from 10 until noon 10 miles NE by the compass. Current setting to the NW.

Thursday, 12. Fine weather, smooth water, and a crowd of sail alow and aloft.

Course steered all this 24 hours NE½North, distance 135ᵐ.
Difference of latitude 135.
Latitude observed 12ᵈ22ᵐ North.
Winds SW.
Thermometer 85ᵈ.

Friday, 13. Pleasant weather and smooth sea. All sail set alow and loft. Winds from SW and SSE.

Course made good NE¼North, distance per log 123ᵐ.
All hands employed.
Latitude observed 14ᵈ01ᵐ North.
Thermometer 84ᵈ.

Saturday, 14. Pleasant weather and steady breeze. All sail set alow and aloft. Winds from SW. Steering to the NE until 9 A.M. when the *Triton* hove to and sounded and got no ground. He then hauled up EbN.

Latitude at noon 15ᵈ45ᵐ North.
Course made good this 24 hours NE½E, distance 153ᵐ.
Difference of latitude 104ᵐ.
Latitude observed 15ᵈ45ᵐ North.
Thermometer 86ᵈ.

Sounded at noon in 90 fathom. No ground and imagine we must be to the Eastward of Macclesfield Shoal. Lost our line and lead, the line being rotten.

Sunday, 15. Pleasant breeze and smooth sea. Winds SW and SSW. Steered from noon until 5 P.M. E½S, distance 26 miles, and from 5 until midday North, distance 91ᵐ. Sounded but got no ground. All sail set fore and aft.

Latitude observed 17ᵈ06ᵐ.
Thermometer 84ᵈ.

Monday, 16. Fresh breeze of wind from SW. All sail set. Course made good NWbNorth, distance 98ᵐ. People all employed. The sea smooth and the weather pleasant.

Variation per amplitude sunrise 2ᵈ30ᵐ West.
Latitude observed 18ᵈ19ᵐ North.
Thermometer 86ᵈ.

Tuesday, 17. Light winds and sultry. All sail set, low and loft. Winds from SSW. The *Triton* at noon about 4 miles ahead.

Course made NW, distance 75ᵐ.
Latitude observed 19ᵈ28ᵐ.
Thermometer 85ᵈ.

All hands employed. Occasionally observe our rudder work very much in the irons.

Wednesday, 18. Light winds and variable from SE to SW. At 6 A.M., the *Triton* a long way ahead. She hove to for us to come up, and at 9 she made sail. Three men in the doctor's list, two of them lamed, the 3d a light fever.

Course made good NW½North, distance 70ᵐ.
Latitude 20ᵈ36ᵐ.
Thermometer 86ᵈ.
In the sun the thermometer rose 130ᵈ.

Thursday, 19. The fore part moderate and pleasant. At 2, sounded in 45 fathom, coarse shells and sand. At 4, the *Triton* sent her boat and an officer on board to observe our position on the chart. Hers per account was at noon 15 miles to the West of the Grand [Great] Ladrone; ours 13 leagues. Stood in for the land, the [course] NEbE and light. At 5, our super-cargoes intimated they had some business with the supercargoes of the *Triton*. Lowered down our jolly boat and sent the first mate on board to attend them. At 6, they returned. Saw the land bearing NNW, which we took for Hai-lin-shan, about 12 leagues distance. At 10 at night, tacked and stood to the SE until 4 A.M. Tacked and stood to the NNW close by the wind. At daylight, made the land *of Hai-lin-shan, San-ciam Falso, and St Johns*. Stood in and at 10 saw some boats stretching off. We tacked to the SEbE. Latitude observed at noon 21d15m. Thermometer 85d. N.B.—our course from Sapata to Macclesfield Shoal [   ] distance [   ] and from that part to making the land [   ].

Friday, 20. Fresh breeze of wind from ENE and NEbE. At 6 P.M., the island of Sanciam Falso bore North, distance 10 leagues. Reefed main-topsail a-beating to the windward. Hands topgallant sails. At noon, the island St Johns bore North NE, 7 or 8 leagues. Latitude 21d-24m North. Thermometer 84d.

Saturday, 21. Fresh breezes and dark cloudy weather. The island of St Johns NNE, extremes of the land WNW. At 6 P.M., sounded in 21 fathom. We were then off the high hill on Sanciam Falso, it bearing North, distance 5 leagues. This hill makes on the west end and appears in a saddle at top. The winds all this 24 hours NEbN to the ENE. Mostly a-standing to the SE under single-reefed topsails. Some heavy squalls and hard rains. At noon, overhauled our water in the hold and find about one thousand gallons on board. 3 men in the doctor's list. Latitude observed 20d42m North. Thermometer 80d and 82. The sky much troubled with sharp lightning to the NE.

Sunday, 22. All this 24 hours heavy squalls, hard rains, and short cross sea. Mostly beating to the NE as the winds would best answer. At 5 P.M., thought we saw the looming of the land. Sounded ground 32 fathom, soft mud. At 4 A.M., sounded in 36 fathom, muddy bottom. 2 men sick. No observation. Grand [Great] Ladrone per at NNE, 13 leagues.

Monday, 23. The fore part fresh breezes and a tumbling swell from the NE. In company with ship *Triton*. The first part this day, winds SSE and some rain. Steering to the NE. At 9 P.M., the wind ESE. A-steering to SW until midnight. Steered to the NE. At 6 A.M., stood to the NWbNorth. Made all sail and at 9 A.M. the Grand [Great] Ladrone bore NbE, distance 3 or 4 leagues. At same time the islands to leeward which we took for St John's NWbW, 7 or 8 leagues and the islands we saw to windward of the G[reat] Ladrone ENE, 4 or 5 leagues distance. At ½ past ten, got a fisherman whom came on board to carry us to Macao Road for ten dollars. All agreed but the fishermen asked 25 on coming on board. At noon Grand [Great] Ladrone EbNorth, 4 or 5 miles. Cleared anchors for coming to.

Tuesday, 24. At 4 P.M., light winds from Eastward. Came to anchor with our best bower anchor in Macao Road in 5 fathom, the town of Macao bearing WNW, 3 miles. Saluted the town with 7 guns, which was returned by the fort. Mr S. Shaw, our supercargo, accompanied by Mr Swift, Purser, had the honor of hoisting the first Continental flag ever seen or made use of in those seas. Hoist out our pinnace and accompanied by Messrs Shaw and Randall waited on Mr d'Ordelin, our worthy *Commodore*, to return that good man our thanks for his polite attention to us through the China Seas. At 6 o'clock, returned. Our pilot paid and left us. Mr d'Ordelin promising to send for a Canton pilot for taking us to Whampoa. At 4 A.M., several of the greatest quantities of Chinese boats I ever beheld were out a-fishing. At 5, a Chinese boat came on board, took down the ship's name, master's name, quantity of men and guns on board, where from, and of what nation; then left us. Soon after came several boats with eggs, sugar, breadfruit, and shoes with sundry other articles for sale. At 8 o'clock, a boat came alongside with several gentlemen. Amongst the number was a good and an agreeable acquaintance whom I knew in France in 1780. We lived together for 6 weeks. This is Mr William Chalmers of Göteborg, now 3d of the Swedish Consul and supercargo. Last evening he heard of the pilot my name, and he was unhappy until

36. Macao's two shorelines are strikingly depicted in this mid-nineteenth-century view of the Portuguese colony. The famous Praya Grande is the crescent-shaped beach at the right. Western vessels trading with China always stopped at Macao coming and going to obtain

he came to see me in this country and render me every civility. He brought Messrs Sibears 2 French gentlemen, the elder I had the honor to see in Nantes some years back. He also brought Mr. Vieillard, the French Consul, all to welcome and offer their service. They stayed breakfast. I introduced my supercargoes to the friendship of my good friends Chalmers and Sibear. They pressed me much to go on shore, but as I had a prior engagement to dine begged excuse. Mr Shaw accompanied them. We gave them

three cheers at parting and saluted with 7 guns. I promised to attend them on shore after dinner. About 10, Mr George, son of Mr Paul George of Lisbon, accompanied with a Portuguese gentleman, came also on board to offer me their civilities and requested my company on shore. Those gentlemen not liking the looks of the weather, which began to look for more wind, left us and offered us their service. At noon, hard rain and strong wind from ENE.

passes. During the off-season at Canton, when foreign merchants were not permitted to remain there, they set up residence in Macao. Resident Western ladies, who were never permitted in Canton by the Chinese, made Macao their year-round home.

Wednesday, 25. At one o'clock, much rain and a fresh of wind. Mr Randall asked the longboat to go on shore and as I declined going on shore took with him some French gentlemen belonging to the *Triton* which dined on board, Mr Hodgkinson, and my son. At 3 o'clock the wind freshened. Obliged to give the ship more cable. Cleared our bower anchor and cable for running and pointed the yards to the wind and sent down topgallant yards. At midnight, less wind, fair weather. Shortened in our cable to proper

service. At daylight, all hands employed drying sails and swaying up topgallant masts [and] yards. At 10, the longboat returned with Mr Shaw and R[andall] with our chief mate and some French gentlemen belonging to the ship *Triton*. Soon after a pilot came on board. Winds ENE. N.B.—St Louis' birthday. Fired at sunrising and at noon 13 guns each time.

Thursday, 26. At one, got under way. The wind ESE and pleasant. At passing the *Triton* I saluted this good man as he lay at anchor with nine guns, which he returned. At 4, Lintao the body EbNorth, 2 leagues, and Lintin Hill NEbN 3 leagues. At 7 calm. Came to in 5 fathom. Hands all sails. Condemned half barrel of beef rotten and hove it overboard. At 6 A.M. hove up. Light air at SE. At nine, calm. Let go stream anchor. The latter part winds West and a strong ebb tide. Laying at anchor.

Friday, 27. [No entries]

Narrative by Samuel Shaw[11]
[From his Journal]

Accordingly, having come to sail, on Sunday, July 25th, we proceeded as fast as the winds and current would allow, till the 2d of August, when the two ships came to anchor, and the *Triton* sent out her boat to explore the passage. On visiting M. d'Ordelin, he informed Captain Green and me that his coming to so early was owing to an apprehension either that the land we saw could not be that through which the passage would be found, or that his information respecting it must have been wrong, as, on sounding, he found only five and a half, where he expected twelve fathoms. His charts seeming to confirm the latter opinion, he sent out an officer in a boat to make further discovery,—and we agreed, that, if the wind should not permit the boat to return during the night, we would, in our ship, taking one or two of his officers with us, stand in towards the shore at daylight, under easy sail, and make him signals. He gave us one of his charts, and the next morning, when M. Cordeaz with another officer came on board, we had the satisfaction to learn that their boat had just returned, after finding the passage, with the soundings as marked in the chart; and that the apprehension they had been under arose from a mistake of the man who gave the soundings at noon, in calling the *eleven* mark *five*. Making sail, at five o'clock in the morning, we led the way through the straits, having regular soundings, and came to anchor at three o'clock, P.M., the body of Gaspar isle bearing from our ship S. E. by E., two miles distant. Mr. McCaver, Mr. Randall, the surgeon, and I, went on shore. On the rock off Gaspar we found many eggs and young birds. There is only a boat-passage between it and Gaspar, and on the other side of the island there are shoals which render it imprudent to go nearer than we did. We had not time to ascertain whether there was water on the island, but, from its verdure, the croaking of frogs, and the flocks of white pigeons, that article is no doubt to be found there.

Leaving Gaspar island, on the morning of the 4th of August, the two ships proceeded in company; and having, on the 23d, in the forenoon, got pilots from Macao, they anchored in the roads at four P.M., and saluted the town.

On the 24th, in the morning, the French consul, with several gentlemen from Macao, visited us, and, on leaving the ship, were saluted with nine guns. These gentlemen having invited me to pass the day with them at Macao, I accompanied them in their boat. The consul went with me to present me to the Portuguese governor, but his Excellency not being at home, he left a written report of our visit.

37. The Bogue Forts guarding the Boca Tigris (Tiger's Mouth) were located about two-thirds of the way up the Pearl River between Macao and the Whampoa anchorage.

I dined at this gentleman's house, in company with the French, Swedish, and Imperial supercargoes, and some gentlemen from the *Triton*. In the afternoon, Mr. Randall, Captain Hodgkinson, the doctor, Mr. Swift, and Mr. Green, with some gentlemen of the *Triton*, who had dined on board our ship, came on shore. The doctor, Captain Hodgkinson, and I passed the evening and lodged with the Swedish consul; Mr. Randall and the other gentlemen did the same with the French consul. Having given these gentlemen copies of the treaties between America and the European powers in amity with her, we took leave of them the next morning, and returned on board.

This day (25th) being the anniversary of St. Louis, the same was announced by twenty-one guns from the *Triton*, at sunrise, which were answered by thirteen from our ship. These salutes were repeated at noon. At two P.M., having our pilot on board, we came to sail, and, in passing M. d'Ordelin, saluted him with nine guns, which he returned with an equal number.

"The city of Macao," says the writer of Anson's Voyage, "is a Portuguese settle-

38. The only known contemporary likeness of the *Empress of China* appears on this Chinese painted fan made during her 1784-1785 voyage. She is shown at the far left, anchored at Whampoa, the limit of ocean-going navigation for foreign ships on the Pearl River. Astern lie

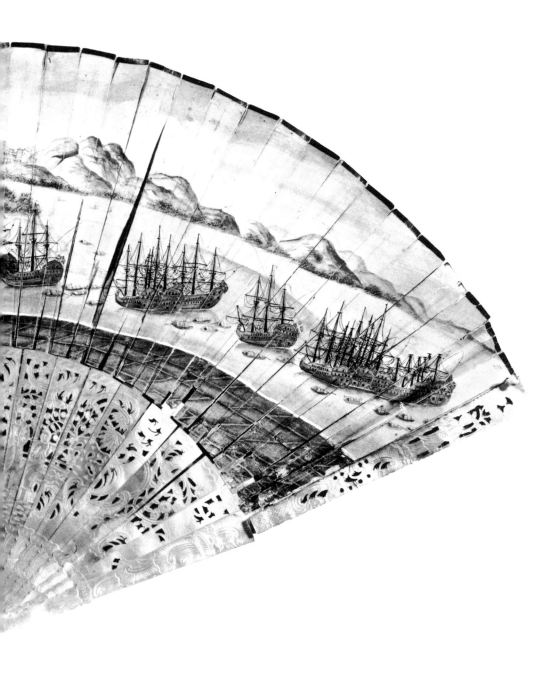

East Indiamen from Denmark, France, Holland, and Great Britain. Small "chop boats" lighter merchandise to and from the foreign factories upriver. The Chinese artist unfortunately took numerous liberties in his depiction of the little American ship.

39. Whampoa Reach, *circa* 1800. Trading ships moored here during their stay in China while their supercargoes conducted business in Canton. The small Chinese craft lying alongside each ship were stationed there by the Hoppo, the chief of Chinese customs, to discourage smuggling. The landmarks are identified in Figure 55. The nine-story pagoda on Whampoa Island was one of the river's wonders.

ment, situated in an island at the entrance of the river of Canton. It was formerly very rich and populous, and capable of defending itself against the power of the adjacent Chinese governors; but at present it is much fallen from its ancient splendor; for, though it is inhabited by Portuguese, and hath a governor nominated by the king of Portugal, yet it subsists merely by the sufferance of the Chinese, who can starve the place and dispossess the Portuguese whenever they please. This obliges the governor of Macao to behave with great circumspection, and carefully to avoid every circumstance that may give offence to the Chinese."

The situation of Macao is very pleasant, and the gentlemen belonging to the European nations trading at Canton are well accommodated there. As soon as their ships leave Canton, and the factors have settled their accounts with the Chinese, they return to Macao, where they must reside till the ships of the next season arrive. The Dutch, Danes, and English had gone to Canton a few days before our arrival.

From Macao we proceeded towards Canton, and on the morning of the 28th, on opening the shipping at Whampoa, we saluted them with thirteen guns, which were returned by the vessels of each nation. At eight o'clock we came to anchor, and again complimented the shipping with thirteen guns.

Previously to our coming to anchor, the French ships sent two boats, with anchors and cables, under an officer, who assisted us in getting into a good berth, and staid on board, till we were moored. The Danish sent an officer, to compliment; the Dutch a boat to assist; and the English an officer "to welcome your flag to this part of the world."

In the afternoon, the captain, Mr. Randall, and I, with Mr. Green, returned the several visits in the following order:—to the two French ships, a British, a Danish, a Dutch, a Danish, three British; all of which, excepting two of the last, saluted us, on taking leave,—the French commodore with seven, and the others with nine guns, our ship returning each time an equal number. Those that did not fire were two country ships from Bengal, the guns of one being dismounted; those of the other were loaded, but, it being sunset before our visit was finished, it was contrary to custom to fire. The officers of both made suitable apologies, and gave us three cheers on leaving their ships, which we returned.

The behaviour of the gentlemen on board the respective ships was perfectly polite and agreeable. On board the English it was impossible to avoid speaking of the late war. They allowed it to have been a great mistake on the part of their nation,— were happy it was over,—glad to see us in this part of the world,—hoped all prejudices would be laid aside,—and added, that, let England and America be united, they might bid defiance to all the world. None of the captains were on board; the Dutch and Danish were at their banksalls, the French had gone to meet M. d'Ordelin, and the English were at Canton.*

---

* I cannot close my journal of our voyage to China, without expressing the great obligations we are under to M. d'Ordelin for the politeness and attention shown us by himself and his officers, and for his constant advice and assistance, since we met in the Strait of Sunda. On the 4th instant, after having cleared the Gaspar passage, he wrote us a letter, whereof the following is a copy:—

"J'ai l'honneur de souhaiter le bon soir à Monsieur Green, et de le remercier de nous avoir constamment manifesté le bon fond dans ce passage de Gaspar. Nous l'avons passé bien promptement et heureusement. Nous n'avons pas pu reconnaitre toutes les îles qui bordent l'île de Sel dans l'est. Nous trouvons une grande faute dans la position de l'île Gaspar, et la pointe de l'est de Banca, que les cartes placent E. et O. Enfin nous en voilà dehors, et bien convaincus que sans l'étourderie de notre second pilote, qui sondait hier matin, nous aurions passé dès hier sans la moindre inquiétude.

"Comme des cartes marquent un banc de roche droit au nord, quatre lieues de l'île Gaspar, nous n'appareillerons que de jour,—je dis à six heures, pour le pouvoir voir, en cas qu'il ne fût pas bien placé. Après, nous fairons valoir la route à N.N. O. jusqu'à la ligne, et peut être aux deux bancs nommés Doggers. Après, le N. O. ¼ N. et N. O. suivant la sonde, pour ne pas manquer l'île de Pulo Timon. Les courans qui sortent des détroits de Malacca, et autres voisins, portent ordinairement au N.E.

"Nous aurons, au reste, le plaisir de nous parler,—et ce qui en sera toujours un pour moi, ce sera de vous pouvoir assurer et prouver que je suis, avec un véritable attachement,

"Monsieur,
"Votre très-humble serviteur,
"D'ORDELIN.

"Bien des amitiés à tous vos messieurs. Notre canot est allé voir s'il y a de l'eau sur l'île de Gaspar, et s'il est facile de la faire."

On the arrival of the *Triton* at Whampoa, the

41. The approaches to Canton, *circa* 1760, the second
of the panoramic views.

43. The fourth panoramic view along the Pearl River, *circa* 1760, showing the Foreign Factories
(Hongs) as they appeared prior to the entry of the Americans into the China trade. The flags flying
before the buildings signify the nationalities trading within. From left: Danish, French, Imperial
(Austrians operating from Ostende, in modern Belgium), Swedish, British, and Dutch.

40. The approaches to Canton, *circa* 1760. This gouache painting by a Chinese artist, together with the following three illustrations, provide an impressive panoramic tour of the Pearl River between Dutch Folly Fort (extreme right) and the Foreign Factories at Canton. Each should be viewed from right to left.

42. The approaches to Canton, *circa* 1760, the third of four panoramic views proceeding upriver.

The other two French ships that left Europe in company with the *Triton* being arrived, and the supercargoes provided with a factory, M. Trolliez gave Mr. Randall and me an invitation to stay with them till our own domestic arrangements should be completed. We accordingly went to Canton, the 30th of August, with M. Trolliez, and other French gentlemen and remained with them till the 6th of September, when, our factory being ready, we took possession of it, after thanking him and his friends, Messrs. Rose and Timothée, for the attention they had shown us. They assured us that they were very happy in forming an acquaintance with us, and would consider themselves much obliged for any opportunities we should afford them of being useful to us. M. Desmoulins, to whom we had a letter from Mr. Mallet, of Philadelphia, was very friendly to us on all occasions, and assisted us particularly in procuring a factory and getting ourselves settled.

On the day of our arrival, we were visited by the principal Chinese merchants, and by the chiefs and gentlemen of the Danish and Dutch factories; the next day, by several English gentlemen; and the morning following, by the chief (Mr. [William Henry] Pigou) and six gentlemen of the English factory. They apologized for deferring their visit till then, on account of their house having been entertained the day before by one of the Chinese merchants, at his residence, on the opposite side of the river.

We returned these visits in the order they had been made, and received invitations from the chiefs of the several factories, who, each in rotation, gave us a national dinner and supper, and desired we would call upon them in future without ceremony. On leaving the English factory, Mr. Pigou, after thanking us for our company, expressed himself nearly in these terms:—"This, gentlemen, has been a day of ceremony. We shall be glad, if you will call upon us often, in a social way,—and if we can be of any service to you, it will afford us a real pleasure." Mr. A. Roebuck, the second in the factory, would not part with us so soon; but, though past eleven,

---

29th, we visited M. d'Ordelin, and Captain Green delivered him a letter of thanks which I had written in his name, whereof the following is a copy:—

"MONSIEUR D'ORDELIN;

"Dans le moment que nous y sommes heureusement arrivés, c'est pour moi un devoir, autant que c'est un plaisir le plus sincère, de vous témoigner ma reconnaissance pour l'intérêt que vous avez pris dans toutes les choses qui m'intéressent, et de vous en faire mes remercîmens. L'assistance que vous m'avez donnée, dans ce premier voyage qui a été entrepris par les enfans de l'Amérique, et la politesse avec laquelle vous et vos messieurs ont démontré leur amitié et bonne volonté envers moi et aux miens,

ne seront jamais effacées. C'est un bonheur pour nous que, dans une traversée aussi longue qu'a été la nôtre, nous ayons rencontré les amis de notre pays; et que dans une région aussi éloignée, les premiers et les seuls bienfaits que nous ayons reçus ont été accordés par ceux dont la nation a été le soutien et l'ami magnanime de la nôtre. Que cette alliance entre les deux nations, si bien commencée, et cimentée par plusieurs bons offices de la part de la vôtre, soit perpétuelle, et que vous et tous vos messieurs soient toujours bien heureux, c'est ce qui est sincèrement souhaité par,

"Mon cher monsieur,
"Votre très-obligé
et très-obéissant serviteur,
"J GREEN."

insisted we should adjourn to his room, where, with several gentlemen of the factory and officers of their ships, we passed a couple of hours very agreeably.

After being settled in our factory, we occasionally returned the national dinner and supper to the Europeans, respectively, beginning with the French. To the Swedes and Imperialists, who arrived after us at Canton, and showed us the same civilities as the others had done, we made the like return.

XII

Learning to Trade with the Hong Merchants

The British East India Company's report of the *Empress of China*'s outward cargo was just as inaccurate as that of her inward one. Why it was so far removed from fact is odd; the Americans may not have gone out of their way to inform their English colleagues of their every move, but they were not being purposely secretive, either. As a matter of fact, throughout the first three-quarters of their stay in Canton, most of the Chinese had supposed that the Americans—whom they called the "Flowery Flag Devils"—were some kind of different Englishmen ("Red-Haired Devils") hailing from India, a misunderstanding not helped by the striking similarities of the United States' flag and that of the British East India Company. This ploy, adopted by the Chinese merchant who represented the *Empress of China*'s interests, had been calculated to avoid the necessity of giving the Hoppo elaborate presents as an initiation tribute from a new nation entering the trade. It had been a useful deception up to a point but became a burden shortly before the ship left Whampoa and had to be corrected.

According to the East India Company's report, *Empress of China*'s outward cargo consisted of:[1]

				Taels
Tea, black,	2460	piculs, cost		49,240
" , green	562	"		16,860
Nankeens,	24	" (864 pieces)		362
Chinaware,	962	"	cost	2,500

Woven silk	490	pieces	"	2,500
Cassia	21	piculs	"	305
				71,767

Measurage for ship	2,550	
Disbursements for ship & factory	5,000	estimated
	79,317	

The equivalent enumeration, compiled for the ship's owners, bears not the slightest resemblance to the above, even after translating piculs into pounds and taels into dollars:[2]

700 Chests Bohea tea, 360 lbs each	
at 60 Dollars pr Chest	42,000 Ds
100 Do Hyson 320 lbs at 300	30,000 Ds
20,000 pr Nankins at ½ Ds	10,000 Ds
[amount obliterated] Porcelains	25,000 ds
	107,000
Gold & Silks	169,000
Dollars	276,000
Duties &c	15
	291,000

Another copy of the same accounting puts the value of "Silks and other Valuable Goods" at $193,000 for a total purchase value of $300,000.[3]

Bohea is a black tea, made by fermenting the leaves for about twenty-four hours, and derived its name from the Woo-E Hills of Fuh-keen. *Hyson* tea is green and means "opening of spring," as opposed to *Young Hyson* ("before the rains") and *Hyson Skin*, the last pickings of the season. Small quantities of *Gunpowder*, a green tea made into small "pearls" or pellets, *Imperial* ("large pearls"), *Souchong* ("small seeds"), another black tea, and *Padre Souchong*, the choicest of all, grown by priests in a monastery, also found their way back to America in the *Empress of China* even if not into the general listings of her principal cargo.

The selling and buying of merchandise in Canton was accomplished through the intermediary functions of the hong merchants, one of whom "sponsored" each arriving vessel. "For infractions of 'regulations' by a ship or by her agents they were liable," William C. Hunter explained. "It was assumed that they could, or should, control foreigners residing in the Factories as well as the vessels anchored at Whampoa. In both cases they were required to 'secure' due 'obedience.' Every resident therefore had his 'sponsor' from the moment of landing, as every ship had hers, and hence the Hong merchants became 'security merchants.' "⁴

Theoretically thirteen in number, but frequently less, the co-hong had been established by imperial edict in 1720 as a device to control all aspects of foreign trade and traders. The position was obtained by payment of a staggering sum of money to the Emperor and could be relinquished only by doing the same or, in the case of the occasional bankruptcy, by lifelong banishment to the mountainous wastelands of northwestern Sinkiang province. Each member of the co-hong was directly answerable to the Hoppo, the chief of Customs, who was an appointee of the Emperor. Otherwise, the hong merchants were laws unto themselves; free to make personal fortunes; suffer individual losses; control the Fan Kwae with an iron, although usually benevolent, hand; and also contribute generously to imperial squeezes and sweeteners to officialdom. Wrote Hunter of them: "As a body of merchants, we found them honourable and reliable in all their dealings, faithful to their contracts, and large-minded. Their private residences, of which we visited several, were on a vast scale, comprising curiously laid-out gardens, with grottoes and lakes, crossed by carved stone bridges, pathways neatly paved with small stones of various colours forming designs of birds, or fish, or flowers."

Dissolved as a body in 1771, the co-hong had been reinstated in 1782, two years before the arrival of the *Empress of China*. As a consequence, out of seven current members of the co-hong, three—Geowqua, Pinqua, and Sinqua—had been newly appointed in August 1782. The other four—Chowqua, Munqua, Shy Kinqua, and Puankhequa—had been around the foreign compound for a long time. Chowqua was old and doing less and less business each year, but Munqua and Shy Kinqua continued to be active. Puankhequa was held in the highest esteem of them all. "His abilities and interest with the Mandareens," the East India Company believed, "makes him the most useful in this place, and with a little management, he is a Merchant the most to be depended on."⁵

It was this last, Puankhequa (spelled "Pankekoa" by Samuel Shaw and pronounced "Pan-kéy-kwah"), who became the *Empress of China*'s fiadore or security merchant and who had conveniently omitted to clarify to the Hoppo the difference between Englishmen and Americans. In addition to the American vessel this year, Puankhequa also represented several of the European ships and the East India Company's *Earl of Sandwich*, a hangover from the 1783 season, and the *Foulis*, Captain Blatchford, London to Canton via Madras.⁶

44. Dutch Folly Fort below the Foreign Factories. Painting
by nineteenth-century Chinese artist Sunqua.

All business with the security merchants was transacted in one of the
"hongs" or "Factories" leased for the purpose. Old China hands used the
terms interchangeably even though they were not precisely synonymous. A
factory implied a structure in which living quarters and office space were
combined; a hong was that, too, but included working areas for servants and
warehousing facilities capable of storing an entire ship's cargo. The foreign
factories were located outside the city walls adjacent to the riverbank and
stretched from east to west about 1,000 feet, facing Honam Island to the
south. Before each one stood a flagstaff upon which flew the national colors
of the traders.

"The Factories were the individual property of the Hong merchants,"
Hunter wrote, "and were hired of them. By law, no women were permitted
to enter them, nor were guns, muskets, powder, or military weapons allowed
to be brought within the gates. Entrance to the rear Factories was by arched
passages running through those in front. The lower floors were occupied by
counting-rooms, go-downs, and store-rooms, by the rooms of the Compradore, his assistants, servants and coolies, as well as by a massively built
treasury of granite, with iron doors, an essential feature, there being no banks
in existence. In front of each treasury was a well-paved open space, with
tables for scales and weights, the indispensible adjuncts of all money transactions, as receipts and payments were made by weight only, except in some

peculiar cases. The second floor was devoted to dining and sitting rooms, the third to bedrooms. As almost all were provided with broad verandahs and the buildings put up with care, they were quite comfortable, although in every respect devoid of ornamental work. In front of the middle Factories between Old China Street and Hog Lane ran a broad stone pavement, and this bordered an open space running down the banks of the river, a distance of about 300 feet. . . ."[7]

Narrative by Samuel Shaw[8]
[From his Journal]

In a country where the jealousy of the government confines all intercourse between its subjects and the foreigners who visit it to very narrow limits, in the suburbs of a single city, the opportunities of gaining information respecting its constitution, or the manners and customs generally of its inhabitants, can neither be frequent nor extensive. Therefore, the few observations to be made at Canton cannot furnish us with sufficient data from which to form an accurate judgment upon either of these points. The accounts given in the writings of the missionaries are enveloped in much mystery, and, in many instances, border not a little upon the marvellous. All we know with certainty respecting the empire of China is, that it has long existed a striking evidence of the wisdom of its government, and still continues the admiration of the world.

The following remarks relate only to the manner in which the commerce of the European nations and Americans with this singular people is conducted, and contains a few scattering particulars, which somewhat less than a four months' residence enabled the writer of them to collect.

To begin with commerce,—which here appears to be as little embarrassed, and is, perhaps, as simple, as any in the known world. The Danes, Imperialists, Swedes, English, and Dutch, have regular establishments, and trade by companies. The French have no company. Last year, their king made an expedition on his own account, and this year he lent his ships to the merchants. The Spanish trade by private supercargoes from South America, by the way of Manila. They had last year four ships, but have none this. The Portuguese, although they are in possession of Macao, do not, in the manner of other nations, keep a public establishment for this trade, but carry it on by agents sent from Europe, who also return in the ships. As the business is, by particular indulgence, transacted at Macao, a considerable savings thence accrues on the duties which other nations are obliged to pay.

The English ships bring out from Europe lead and large quantities of cloth; which latter the company are obliged by their character to export annually to China, for the encouragement of their home woollen manufacture. Some of their ships go first to the peninsula of India, part of their cargoes consisting of supplies for the company's establishments, and such other commodities as will answer the markets in that quarter. After having disposed of these, they take on board cotton, with which, their lead, and cloth, they proceed to China. The English derive considerable advantages from the permission granted to private ships, owned by their subjects in India, to trade with China. These vessels, besides the cotton, sandal-wood, putchock-root, ebony, opium, sharkfins, and birdsnests they bring from the coast, carrying on a smuggling trade with the Dutch settlements, in and about Malacca, and with the natives, whom they supply with opium, clothing, fire-arms, &c., in return for which they receive pepper, block-tin, and spices. The proceeds of these, with the silver and other articles they bring from India, are, to the amount of about one third, carried back in such merchandise as will suit the India markets; and the remainder, either in cash or transfers from the Chinese merchants, is paid into the company's treasury, for which they receive bills on the company in England, at the exchange of five shillings and sixpence sterling the dollar, payable three hundred and sixty-five days after sight. This fund has for a number of years rendered it unnecessary for the company to export from Europe any specie for carrying on their commerce with the Chinese.

The Dutch, by their resources from their settlements on Java, Sumatra, Malacca, and other possessions in India, are enabled to manage their trade with China under equal, if not superior, advantages to any other people.

The other companies depend principally upon their lead and silver brought from Europe; though sometimes the English captains from the coasts of India furnish them with the latter, in return for which they take bills. This exchange is forbidden by the English company, and any person detected in it forfeits his privilege, and may be sent prisoner to England. However, this penalty, as it is seldom if ever inflicted, is but little regarded. British subjects in India, who wish to remit their property to Europe, will find means of doing it through other channels than that of the company's treasury. They get a penny, and sometimes twopence, more on a dollar, and bills at a shorter sight. Besides, the credit of the English company is not now so good with their subjects in India as formerly. One of their captains informed me that his orders were, to offer his money first to the Swedes, afterwards to the Danes and the Dutch, and last to the English.

The French had formerly a company here, but its affairs going behindhand, it was dissolved. Last year, as has been observed, the king sent four ships to Canton on his own account, and this year he has lent three ships of the line to a company of merchants, whose stock was divided into shares, and a certain number sold to such individuals as chose to become adventurers. The capital is six millions of livres, whereof about one half is in specie; the expense of the expedition, a quantity of woollen cloths, looking-glasses, coral, and other merchandise, employing the remainder. A consul of France, part of the former establishment, is still retained. He has a house and table found him by the king, with a salary of six thousand livres per annum. Should any disputes arise among the subjects of France, his decision,

45. Ginseng, the major commodity shipped to Canton in the *Empress of China*, was not only chewed by its advocates—much as New England fishermen of the day chewed chunks of uncooked salt cod— but also was used in the manufacture of medicines such as those sold in this Cantonese medicine shop of about 1830.

in a court of chancery, where he presides, is final, unless an appeal be made to the king and council.

The commerce of the Imperialists is drawing to a close. The German dominions are not well situated for prosecuting it. The company are very much in debt. They have no ships this year, nor will they, it is thought, have any the next. Their chief (Mr. Reid, a Scotch gentleman) informed me that he expected to receive orders to settle his accounts with the Chinese, and return to Europe.

The establishments of the Swedes and Danes are principally supported by the smuggling trade they carry on in the Channel and upon the coasts of Britain. Would the British parliament repeal the acts laying a duty on teas, the prosecution of this commerce would probably not be an object for either of those powers, and the trade with China would be conducted by the nations who are the greatest consumers of its produce. This is the idea of all the Europeans at Canton. Mr. Pigou told me that the annual consumption of teas in Great Britain and its dependencies amounted to fourteen million pounds' weight, while the company's sales did not exceed six.

"Would our legislature," said he, "but commute the duty on teas for some other tax, there would be no inducement to smuggling; nor would the Swedes, Danes, and French find their account in this commerce. It would then naturally fall into the hands of the consumers, who are the Dutch, yourselves, and us. We could employ twenty ships, and the trade still be sufficient for us all."

Besides the Europeans, the Armenians and Moors drive a considerable trade with China, in pearls, precious stones, and other merchandise, which they freight, in Portuguese and English bottoms, from the Red Sea, the Persian Gulf, and the peninsula of India.

Such are the outlines of the commerce carried on by the Europeans with China. The national establishments are on a liberal footing. The supercargoes are provided with elegant factories, and every accommodation they can wish. All expenses are paid, and a commission allowed them for transacting the business, which is divided among them according to seniority. In the English factory, a young gentleman, whose father, perhaps, or other near relation, is one of the company, comes out at fourteen or fifteen years of age, as a writer, with all expenses paid and one hundred pounds sterling per annum. At the expiration of five years he commences supercargo, when his salary ceases, and he is included for part of the commission. The amount of this will depend on the number of ships. The present chief has been in the factory fourteen years, and his commission this year is reckoned at upwards of seven thousand pounds sterling. That of the second, as Mr. Roebuck himself informed me, is something more than four thousand, and the others receive in proportion. No person is allowed to hold the office of chief more than three years.

The English captains in the company's service, and all the officers, are allowed the privilege of private trade; on which account, as soon as their ships are moored at Whampoa, the captains take each his own factory at Canton. Their adventures consist chiefly of clockwork of all kinds, of which the Chinese are extremely fond, cutlery, glass, furs, dollars, and some ginseng, besides articles from the coast of India. The captain's privilege in the ship is about sixty tons measurement. This he commonly fills up with fine teas, cassia, Nankin cloths, porcelain, &c., a considerable part of which, on his entering the English Channel, is disposed of to smugglers, between whom and the custom-house officers there is always a clear understanding. The ships are built and equipped by private merchants, who charter them to the company at a certain tonnage. They are generally from six to eight hundred tons, and no ship, in common cases, is suffered to perform more than four voyages. A captain must have great interest to get one of these ships, or pay from five to seven thousand pounds for the command. In this case, he may sell again, and, if he should die during the voyage, the privilege is filled up for the benefit of his heirs or assigns. The latter part of this arrangement extends to the subordinate officers. The country captains also take factories at Canton, and for privileges make the best bargain they can with their employers.

Other nations, instead of privilege of private trade to their officers, allow gratuity money, to each according to his rank. And as the ships are the property of the company, every captain has an apartment in the factory, and a place at the table, where there is also a plate and accommodation for any other officer who may come to Canton.

No Europeans are suffered to remain at Canton throughout the year. After their ships are gone, and they have settled their accounts with the Chinese, they repair to Macao, where each nation has its separate establishment. There they continue till the arrival of their ships the next season, when they return to Canton.

As soon as a ship, whether public or private, arrives at Whampoa, a *fiador*, or surety, must be engaged, before she can discharge any part of her cargo. This person is one of the principal merchants, and generally the one with whom the business is transacted, though this circumstance does not prevent dealing with others. He is answerable to the custom-house for payment of the emperor's customs of entrance, which, on an average, amount to somewhat more than four thousand dollars a ship. Besides this tax, there are duties on every article, whether of import or export, imported specie excepted; but with these there is no trouble, it being understood in all bargains with the Chinese, whether buying or selling, that they pay them.

The trade on the part of the Chinese is conducted by a set of merchants who style themselves the *co-hoang*, a word expressing our idea of a trading company. This co-hoang consists of ten or twelve merchants, who have the exclusive privilege of the European and country trade, for which they pay a considerable sum to government; and no other dealers, if we except the petty shopkeepers, who are also licensed by government, can be concerned in it but by their permission. The co-hoang assemble as often as is necessary, communicate the information each has obtained respecting the commodities at market, agree on the prices at which they will purchase, and fix those of their own goods in return. When it happens that a ship has but a small cargo, an individual of the co-hoang is unwilling to be its fiador, as perhaps his profits will not pay the duties. In this case, a fiador is nominated in the co-hoang, and the vessel's business done on their joint account. There is generally no material variation from the prices fixed by the co-hoang.

Each ship and factory must also have a *comprador*; this is a person who furnishes provisions and other necessaries, for which he contracts at certain prices. There is much imposition in these articles, and if the ship is small, the comprador, besides being paid for all supplies, will have a douceur of a hundred or a hundred and fifty taels. This must be submitted to, as the government derives a stated revenue from every ship, of whatever size, which the comprador has permission to supply.

All company ships, on coming to Whampoa, have each a banksall on shore, for the reception of their water-casks, spars, sails, and all the lumber of the ship, and containing, besides, apartments for the sick. The French have theirs, separate from the other Europeans, on an island, thence called French island; the others are on the opposite side, and confined to the ground they occupy,—for the remainder being rice-fields, and constantly watered, renders it impossible to go beyond the limits of the banksall; whereas French island is a delightful situation, and the resort of the gentlemen generally, of all nations, who go on and off at pleasure. Except those of the French and Americans, no common sailors are allowed to go there. For the exclusive privilege of this island, every French ship adds one hundred taels extra to the *hoppo*'s present. The banksalls are large buildings, framed with bamboo reeds, and covered with mats and straw. They are erected by the Chinese, who pull them down immediately on their being left, in order that they may have the advantage of setting up new ones. The price of a banksall is about two hundred dollars. As our ship was small, the French gentlemen advised us not to have a banksall and offered us as much room in theirs as we should want. The Chinese mandarins, of whom there are four on the island, before they would permit us quietly to send any thing ashore, demanded a douceur to the amount of the price of a banksall,—alleging that it was the same thing to them, whether we had one of our own, or made use of another. After altercating with them for several days, till our ship's provisions were stopped, I found it necessary to compromise for thirty dollars a month.

Besides a fiador and comprador, each ship must also have a linguist, at an expense of about a hundred and twenty taels. This person is absolutely necessary, as he is employed in transacting all business with the custom-house,—which is in the city, where no stranger can be admitted,—provides sampans for unloading and loading, and is always at call.

46. Sea otters frolic on the rocks of the Northwest Coast. Within a few years of the *Empress of China*'s pioneering voyage, sea otters for the Chinese market were killed in devastating numbers. Engraving from Cassell's *Popular Natural History* (London and New York, n.d.).

When the hoppo goes to measure the shipping at Whampoa, which he does as often as there are three or four that have not been visited, he is attended by the co-hoang. On these occasions, the captains produce their clock-work and other curiosities, of which the hoppo lays by such as he likes, and the fiador for the ship is obliged to send them to him. Some time after, the hoppo demands the price,—for he will not receive them as a present. The merchant, who understands matters perfectly, tells him about one twentieth part, or less, of their value, and takes the money. On our ship being measured, the hoppo inquired if we had any *sing-songs*,—the name they give to this sort of articles,—and, on being answered in the negative, seemed rather displeased. However, when we told him that we were from a new country, for the first time, and did not know that it was customary to bring such things, he appeared satisfied, but did not forget to enjoin it upon us to bring some when we should come again.

As soon as the ship is measured, the fiador takes out a permit for unloading, and the linguist provides two sampans to receive the goods, which are hoisted out of the ships in presence of two mandarins, who live in their sampan alongside. When the goods arrive at Canton, one of the principal mandarins, with his assistants, attends to weigh, measure, and take account of every thing, after which liberty is granted to sell. Such articles as the fiador or the co-hoang do not want may be disposed of to any other person, from whom the linguist receives the duty, and settles with the fiador. When the return cargo is to be sent on board, the mandarins

47. Hawking his wares from corner to corner, this Chinese fur peddler exhibits a variety of lush pelts for sale.

attend, as before, and each package must have the seller's *chop* upon it, in order that the linguist may know where to apply for the duty; otherwise, the purchaser is himself obliged to pay it. No fees are paid to these officers, either by the buyer or seller, their salaries being fixed by the emperor. The expense of unloading is paid by the Europeans, and the Chinese deliver the return cargo alongside the ship, free of all duties and charges whatever. All merchandise must be unloaded and loaded by Chinese sampans.

In the customs of Canton, as of other parts of the world, instances of knavery sometimes occur. The duty on silks may be compromised with the mandarin, who will accept a present of about half the amount of the duty for letting them go free. In these cases, the ship's boat, carrying the flag of its nation, attends at the time appointed, and takes in the goods, for which the mandarin's chop is produced, and the boat passes without further examination. All boats are searched, on coming to or going from Canton, and must have a chop; besides which, they must, unless carrying the national flag, stop and be searched at three different chop-houses on the river.

The factories at Canton, occupying less than a quarter of a mile in front, are situated on the bank of the river. The quay is enclosed by a rail-fence, which has stairs and a gate opening from the water to each factory, where all merchandise is received and sent away. The limits of the Europeans are extremely confined; there being, besides the quay, only a few streets in the suburbs, occupied by the trading people, which they are allowed to frequent. Europeans, after a dozen years' residence, have not seen more than what the first month presented to view. They are sometimes invited to dine with the Chinese merchants, who have houses and gardens on the opposite side of the river; but even then no new information is obtained. Every thing of a domestic concern is strictly concealed, and though their wives, mistresses, and daughters are commonly there, none of them are ever visible. We dined with four of the co-hoang, at separate times, two of whom entertained the French gentlemen and us at their country-houses. On these occasions, the guests generally contribute largely to the bill of fare. Both at Chowqua's and Pankekoa's, the French supplied the table furniture, wine, and a large portion of the victuals. The gardens belonging to Chowqua are extensive; much art and labor are used to give them a rural appearance, and in some instances nature is not badly imitated. Forests, artificial rocks, mountains, and cascades, are judiciously executed, and have a pleasing effect in diversifying the scene. The Chinese, however, discover a vitiated taste in their fondness for water. Every garden must have abundance of this element, and where it does not flow naturally, large, stagnant ponds, in the middle of which are summerhouses, supply the deficiency. Chowqua says that his house and gardens cost him upwards of one hundred thousand taels.

The Europeans at Canton do not associate together so freely as might be expected,—the gentlemen of the respective factories keeping much by themselves, and excepting in a few instances, observing a very ceremonious and reserved behaviour.

At the Danish factory, there is, every Sunday evening, a concert of instrumental music, by gentlemen of the several nations, which every body who pleases may attend. This is the only occasion when there appears to be any thing like a general intercourse. On the whole, the situation of the Europeans is not enviable; and, considering the length of time they reside in this country, the restrictions to which they must submit, the great distance they are at from their connections, the want of society, and of almost every amusement, it must be allowed that they dearly earn their money.

When any European dies at Canton, the chief of the nation to which he belonged sends and acquaints the different factories with the event. The flags are dropped, and remain at half-mast till the corpse is sent off to Whampoa, when they are hoisted up; the friends of the deceased, in the meanwhile, receiving visits of condolence from the other Europeans. The ships observe the same ceremony, and when the corpse appears in sight, the commodore of the nation to which it belongs begins to fire minute-guns, which are repeated by the other ships in port, and continued till the corpse is interred, on French island, when the flags are again hoisted as usual. Next day, the chief, with one or two gentlemen of his nation, returns the visits of the other Europeans, and thanks them for their attention on the occasion.

About ten days previous to our leaving Canton, Mr. Randall and I visited the respective chiefs (a ceremony not to be omitted), thanked them for their civilities, and informed them of our intended departure. Invitations from every nation followed, and we were obliged to receive from each another public dinner and supper, the consul of France insisting also upon paying us this honor in his separate right. The attention paid us at all times by the Europeans, both in a national and personal respect, has been highly flattering. From the French it was peculiarly friendly. They aided us in mooring our ship, insisted on our making ourselves at home in their factory, and accommodated us with part of their banksall, for the use of which they would not suffer us to make them any remuneration. "If," said they, "we have in any instance been serviceable to you, we are happy,—and we desire nothing more than further opportunities to convince you of our affection."

The Swedes, the Danes, the Dutch, and the Imperialists paid us every proper attention; nor were the English behindhand with them. Besides the gentlemen of the factory, many of their captains visited us, gave invitations, and accepted ours in return. During this intercourse, it was not difficult to discover their jealousy of the French; nor could they conceal their dislike of the good understanding we kept up with them, which would sometimes appear, in spite of their breeding. One evening, in particular, at the English factory, after the company had risen from table, the chief asked us if we could not take a sociable bottle together. This was a proposition to which we were not disposed to object, as he had always been particularly civil to us. In the course of our *téte-à-téte*, after professing much regard for us, and hoping that our nation and theirs would ever maintain a friendly correspondence, he observed, that there had been a small mistake in the *mode* of our reception, with respect to which he wished to set us right. "As soon as it was known," said he, "that your ship was arrived, we determined to show you every national attention; and when, in company with the French gentlemen, you returned our visit, it was our intention that *you* should dine with us the next day, and the *French* the day after. We were, therefore, not a little disappointed at your coming together, and you may remember we then told you there had been a mistake on your part, for which we were exceedingly sorry; for, trust me, gentlemen," added he, with a smile, "that *we* would not designedly have put you in such company."

Exclusive of the country ships returning to India, there sailed last year from Canton and Macao forty-five ships for Europe, sixteen of which were English. The present season the numbers were as follows (Dec. 27):—

English, 9,*—French, 4,†—Dutch, 5,
Danish, 3,—Portuguese, 4,   } 25 for Europe.

American, ...   1 for America.

English country ships, 8,‡ .....
Danish Snow, 1, ...   } 9

In all, 35

*Sulivan, ...Captain Williams.	‡Biram Gore, ...Captain Maughan.
Calcutta,...... " Thompson.	Bellona, ... " Jas. Richardson.
Hawke,....... " Rivington.	Pallas, ... " O'Donnell.
Ponsborne, ... " Hemmet.	General Elliott, " McClew.
Middlesex, ... " Rogers.	Le Neckar, ... " Woolmore.
Contractor,.... " McIntosh.	Triumph, ... " Wm. Richardson.
Foulis, ... " Blatchford.	Lady Hughes, " Williams.
Latham, ... " Robertson.	Nonsuch, ... " Stevenson.
Nassau, ... " Gore.	

†Triton,   Captain, M. D'Ordelin, 64 }
Provence,   " M. Mancel, 64 } armed *en flute.*
Sagittaire,   " M. Morin,   50 }
Pondicherry,   " M. Beaulieu, chartered at the Isle of France.

The Swedes lost their passage; and the Imperialists and Spaniards, as has been remarked, had no ships here.

Our being the first American ship that had ever visited China, it was some time before the Chinese could fully comprehend the distinction between Englishmen and us. They styled us the *New People*, and when, by the map, we conveyed to them an idea of the extent of our country, with its present and increasing population, they were not a little pleased at the prospect of so considerable a market for the productions of their own empire.

The knavery of the Chinese, particularly those of the trading class, has become proverbial. There is, however, no general rule without exceptions; and though it is allowed that the small dealers, almost universally, are rogues, and require to be narrowly watched, it must at the same time be admitted that the merchants of the co-hoang are as respectable a set of men as are commonly found in other parts of the world. It was with them, principally, that we transacted our business. They are intelligent, exact accountants, punctual to their engagements, and though not the worse for being well looked after, value themselves much upon maintaining a fair character. The concurrent testimony of all the Europeans justifies this remark.

Notwithstanding the encomiums which are generally bestowed on the excellence of the Chinese government, it may, perhaps, be questioned, whether there is a more oppressive one to be found in any civilized nation upon earth. All offices in the provinces are bestowed upon such as can make most interest for them with the great mandarins at court, in consequence of which the subject undergoes every species of oppression. He is squeezed by the petty mandarins,—these, again, by the higher, —they, in their turn, by their superiors, the governors and viceroys,—and these last are sometimes, themselves, under pretence of maladministration, stripped of every thing by the emperor, and doomed to end their days in banishment in Siberia. Two instances, which came to my knowledge, may serve to convey some idea of the despotic nature of the government.

A few years since, Shykinkoa, one of the most respectable merchants of the co-hoang, having failed in an engagement to send some teas to the English ships, assigned as a reason for it, that he had been disappointed of seeing the hoppo, who, he said, was drunk when he called at his house to take out the chop. Shortly after, another of the co-hoang coming to the English factory, the chief casually mentioned the disappointment, and the reason given for it by Shykinkoa. This man, who was Shykinkoa's enemy, reported the matter to the hoppo, and Shykinkoa was forced to make his peace by a present of thirty thousand taels! This account I had from Mr. Pigou. Such has been Shykinkoa's dread of all hoppos, ever since, that he never dares make application to them personally, and submits to the payment of an annual sum for an exemption from attending the hoppo with other merchants, when he measures the shipping.

The other instance is that of our comprador. Every Chinese, excepting the co-hoang and persons in office, is obliged to have a chop for visiting the factories, which is renewed every month, and for which servants, and even *coolies*, hired at three dollars a month, must pay half a dollar. Our comprador was met one day by the second officer of the customs, who demanded to see his chop. He had left it at home, and, on being questioned, answered that he was such a man's purser; well knowing, that, should he own himself a comprador, the officer would extort money from him. Unluckily, one of the merchant's people, known to the officer, was passing at the instant. The poor comprador was detected, and immediately sent to prison in the city, where he remained a week, with a board, like the yoke of a pillory, fastened about his neck. He offered a thousand dollars for his release, which the officer refused; and there is no knowing what would have been the price of his liberty, had not accident procured it by other means.

48. While coolies stomp tea leaves down into large chests or carry it outside to an awaiting chop boat, Western merchants transact their business with the Chinese tea merchants and their clerks.

The Europeans, as has been noticed, are exceedingly straitened in their limits, and the Chinese let slip no opportunities of laying new impositions. The mandarins on the quay are very vigilant, and every servant in the factories is a spy. A house had been lately set up on the part of the quay where the strangers commonly walk, and was intended for the residence of another mandarin, who would be an additional spy. This, with several other matters considered grievances, induced the Europeans to join in an application to the hoppo, the next time he visited the shipping. A deputation from every nation, in which I was desired to represent ours, met the hoppo, on board an English ship, and he promised redress. The house was shortly after pulled down, the comprador, whose case was particularly mentioned, released, and most of the causes of complaint removed. Though applications have been repeatedly made, this was the only instance in which the Europeans ever acted in concert. The comprador went round to all the gentlemen, and thanked them for their good offices in his favor; but, though the hoppo promised he should be released without expense, the poor fellow found it necessary to make a present to the officer who had confined him. . . .

There are many painters in Canton, but I was informed that not one of them possesses a genius for design. I wished to have something emblematic of the institution of the order of the Cincinnati executed upon a set of porcelain. My idea was to have the American Cincinnatus, under the conduct of Minerva, regarding Fame, who, having received from them the emblems of the order, was proclaiming it to the world. For this purpose I procured two separate engravings of the goddesses, an elegant figure of a military man, and furnished the painter with a copy of the emblems, which I had in my possession. He was allowed to be the most eminent of his profession, but, after repeated trials, was unable to combine the figures with the least propriety; though there was not one of them which singly he could not copy with the greatest exactness. I could therefore have my wishes gratified only in part. The best of his essays I preserved, as a specimen of Chinese excellence in design, and it is difficult to regard it without smiling. It is a general remark, that the Chinese, though they can imitate most of the fine arts, do not possess any large portion of original genius.

The Chinese traders are in their manners open and free. They have great command of their own temper, and watch narrowly that of others, I had sufficient information on this head, and was always upon my guard; though a person's patience is often put to severe trial, especially by the smaller traders. They will not scruple to offer one third of what is demanded for merchandise, and, though told that nothing will be abated, they will repeat the same offer every day for a week together. One of them offered me for an article less than one half the price at which I valued it, and would come day after day and make the same offer. I treated him politely every time, and adhered to my first demand, with which he finally complied. After the bargain was settled,—"You are not Englishman?" said he. "No." "But you speak English word, and when you first come, I no can tell difference; but now I understand very well. When I speak Englishman his price, he say, 'So much,—take it,—let alone.' I tell him, 'No, my friend, I give you so much.' He look at me,—'Go to hell, you damned rascal; what! you come here,—set a price my goods?' Truly, Massa Typan, I see very well you no hap Englishman. All China-man very much love your country." Thus far, it may be supposed, the fellow's remarks pleased me. Justice obliges me to add his conclusion:—"All men come first time China very good gentlemen, all same you. I think two three time more you come Canton, you make all same Englishman too."

XIII

Chinese Justice

At Canton, Daniel Parker's perfidious behavior the past February—the with-holding of specie without amending the bills of lading—became general knowledge. Samuel Shaw, the one person aware of Parker's actions at the time, had endured many a tortured thought during the passage out and eventually had relieved his mind by telling all to his good friend Thomas Randall. Perhaps they hoped that when the boxes were opened and the coins counted they would discover that Parker had made up the deficiency at the last moment after all. Alas! The first box was cracked by John Green in September; the remaining six were opened on the twenty-fourth and the twenty-fifth of November 1784, when the contents were required to pay for the goods daily coming on board. The dreaded $2,300 shortage was not a nightmare. It was true.

The affair was so serious that Randall and Shaw felt compelled to swear a deposition to the facts as they knew them and to have officials of both the Imperial and the French factories witness the resulting document. Coming as it did, immediately on top of a discrepancy through leakage found in the contents of ten pipes of wine shipped from New York, they had no other realistic alternative.[1]

"Canton in China
November 24th 1784 This day six boxes of money came from the ship, under the care of Mr McKaver, the second mate, and Mr Swift the purser, who never left them until they were delivered to me in good order, as when shipped—The Man-

darins insisted on opening one of them which was done, in order to satisfy them that it was only money, This box was immediately carried into my room, and there counted by Captain Green, Mr Swift, Mr Randall and myself, and found to contain (2900) Twenty nine hundred dollars—

This day the 25th Mr Randall and myself opened and counted the remaining five boxes of money, in company with M Desmoulins, to whom we paid them, and found therein only (13999) Thirteen thousand nine hundred ninety nine dollars, as per his receipt for the same—

The remaining box was opened on board Ship, in September last, by Capt Green, and contained only (801) Eight hundred and one dollars, as per certificate given him by Messrs Swift and Randall—

The whole sum contained in the aforesaid seven boxes amounts to (17700) Seventeen thousand seven hundred, Spanish dollars, and no more.

(signed)   S. Shaw

Tho: Randall[2]

49. Large tubs of porcelain are transported downstream from the inland kilns for delivery in Canton. The porcelain was tightly packed in containers filled out with sago. An alternative method was to add large quantities of beans around the porcelain, fill the tub with water and secure the head. The beansprouts which subsequently grew inside formed their own, naturally unique packing material.

50. A retail porcelain shop in Canton stocks everything from tea sets to jardinieres. Most of such shops frequented by Westerners for their "souvenir" purchases were located along Thirteen Factory Street, which paralleled the river behind the hongs, or along alleys such as Hog Lane and Old China Street cutting through the factory buildings towards the open public square in front.

"As every man is at all times liable to accident, it will not be improper in this place that I commit to writing the substance of what passed between me and Daniel Parker Esq respecting the abovementioned money," Shaw went on. "Mr Parker, a few days previous to the sailing of the ship from New York, in February last, informed me that he was obliged to put (20,000) Twenty thousand dollars on board for the Account of the owners, and had accordingly charged that amount in the invoice and should take bills of lading for the same, as is customary—but that in fact he had only and could put on board no more than (18000) Eighteen thousand dollars, though he had charged and should take receipts for (20,000) Twenty thousand—On my remark to him that there would be difficulty in the matter, he answered, That he was under an absolute necessity of doing it, as he had been disappointed by the non payment of monies due to him, and his credit required the detention of that sum to answer demands that were made on him, that it was expedient the affair should be kept a secret from every body, excepting Mr Randall, my friend and partner, and that he would never suffer me to sustain any injury from it. And further he told me, that, as it was probable our ship would not be able to invest the whole of her cargo from America in China goods, but must bring back part of it in money, the Accounts should be made out in the same manner as if there were, *bona fide*, on board Twenty thousand dollars, and that on her return he would make up to me the deficiency together with the profits which should have been made thereon, in order that the accounts should be equitably and properly adjusted—Singular as the proposition was, I had nevertheless so much reliance on the Personal honor of Mr Parker as to accede to it, and the many proofs I had experienced of his friendship towards me, as well as the most unshaken confidence in his integrity, induced me to do it without insisting on any written voucher from him for the transaction. It is not that this my reliance and confidence in the honor and integrity of Mr Parker is the least abated that I now commit the affair to writing, but I do it from a conviction of the uncertainty of human life and that, in case either of us might be called to another world before the return of the ship, my conduct should be acknowledged upright, though it must be allowed exceedingly imprudent, in a transaction that otherwise would appear very mysterious and unwarrantable. On the same principal it is that I shall confirm the truth of what I have now written by the sanction and solemnity of an oath. Could I harbour the least suspicion that this process would be necessary, if it were *certain* Mr Parker and I should meet again it would have been easy for me to secure myself from the smallest imputation against my character by calling on Captain Green and the Officers of the ship to see the money opened and counted to me, and to have taken their joint certificate of the sum as I should receive it. Indeed, it required some dexterity in me to conceal the matter from Captain Green, who has several times expressed a surprise that Twenty thousand dollars could be contained in seven boxes of no larger dimension.

"Done at Canton in China

"this 25th November 1784"[3]

Thomas Randall was moved to make a statement of his own, which he penned at the same time. "The same principals," he wrote, "which have induced my friend Mr Shaw to make and sign the aforegoing declaration influence me to declare that during our voyage from America to China he mentioned the transaction between Mr Parker and himself to me, and several times while on board the vessel, and since his arrival here he expressed to me the greatest uneasiness for having taken no voucher for the transaction which the intervention of many accidents might render difficult if not impossible to be satisfactorily accounted for—and I do therefore declare upon honor that the whole sum of money received from the ship in six boxes in

51. Workers prepare skeins of silk while a woman busies herself at a loom. Paintings such as this, one of a series illustrating the process of silk manufacture, became popular with the "Fan Kwae." They were the Chinese picture postcards of the day.

good order and which I myself saw opened and assisted in the counting of amounted to no more than (2900) Twenty nine hundred dollars now in the hands of Mr Shaw, and thirteen thousand nine hundred ninety nine dollars (13999) counted and delivered to Mr Desmoulins this day, agreeably to his receipt this day, which together with one box opened by Capt Green, containing (801) eight hundred and one dollars still in his hands to be accounted for, make up the just sum of Seventeen thousand Seven hundred dollars (17700) and no more—notwithstanding which Mr Shaw as supercargo gives up to Captain Green the bills of Lading signed by him for Twenty thousand dollars, still keeping the affair secret from him, in compliance with the injunctions of his and my friend Mr Parker."[4]

The document, however, did not stop there, continuing;

We the undersigned S. Shaw and T. Randall do hereby make oath, that all and every the things in the within Paper by us written and subscribed, are true, So help us God.

(signed)   S. Shaw
Tho: Randall

Canton 22nd Decr 1784
Sworn before me
  Jno Reid
His Impl Majestys Consul

True Copy
Canton in China, November 24 1784—We hereby certify on honor, that we this day opened and counted one box of dollars, no mark or number, in company with Mr Shaw and Mr Randall, at their house, as it came from the Ship *Empress of China* this day in good order, and that it contained the just sum of two thousand nine hundred dollars and no more

Copy		(signed)	Jno Green
Old dollars	188		John White Swift
New	2712		
	2900		

Canton 26 Novem. 1784—We the Subscribers do certify upon honor that Capt Green did by the desire of Mr Randall open on board the Ship *Empress of China*, a box of money the 29th Septemr 1784, and found therein, but one bag sealed, which he opened and we counted and found contained therein only Eight hundred and one dollars

(signed)   Tho: Randall
John White Swift

Copy
Compte de L'argent du V[aisse]au *Imperatrice de la Chine*

No 5	3000 Piastres		
2	2999	do	532 Vielle Piastres
4	3000	do	Recu treize mille neuf cent quatre
3	3000	do	vingt dix neuf piastres a Canton le 25
7	2000	do	9bre 1784—souque desMoulin & F. Terrier
Total	13999		

Copy
Canton 25 Dec. 1784
A true copy from the originals

(signed)   S. Shaw
Tho: Randall

On the same day that the six money boxes were removed from the *Empress of China* and carried upriver to the American factory in Canton, an international incident was taking place at Whampoa Reach.

One of the vessels anchored there, awaiting a lading, was the British ship *Lady Hughes*, Captain W. Williams. Known as a "country ship" because she came to the China coast from India (Bombay) rather than from the British Isles, she had arrived at Whampoa on the seventh of September.[5] On November 24, Captain Williams invited several gentlemen of the foreign community to dine with him. As they took their leave over the side, they were accorded a parting salute, when "A Chop Boat which was lying alongside, being unfortunately in the way of one of the guns while fired in Saluting, received very considerable damage, three Chinese belonging to her were so much hurt that their lives were in danger, & one in particular despaired of; on the following day we were informed that he was dead, & that the Gunner tho innocent of any criminal intention had from apprehension of the undiscriminating Severity of the Chinese Government absconded."[6] Fresh in everyone's mind was the fate of a Frenchman who, four years previously, had in self-defense killed a Portuguese. He had been spirited away by the Chinese authorities and strangled.[7]

In the *Lady Hughes* affair, the chief of the British East India Company's factory, W. H. Pigou, was visited by the Weyyen, the Hoppo's principal secretary, and all the hong merchants, who insisted that the gunner be given up to the Chinese, because "some form of public examination was necessary to satisfy the Laws of the Country." Pigou pointed out that he had no jurisdiction over country ships and, in any event, the gunner had taken to his heels and was nowhere to be found. Two days passed in debate, when it was learned that another of the wounded men had died. The same officials as before, including Puankhequa, returned to the factory and again demanded the unfortunate gunner, or a substitute to stand in during the formalities of a hearing.

Pigou once more said he had no authority in the case; that the supercargo of the *Lady Hughes*, George Smith, would be better qualified to arrange satisfaction. Smith, who had been in Canton at the time of the accident, already had pledged to the Chinese that he would not leave Canton for three or four days until the matter had been resolved. It came as a tremendous shock and filled the Europeans with alarm when, on the morning of November 27, the Chinese decoyed Smith "from his Factory by a pretended message from Puankhequa, seized and conveyed him into the City under a Guard of Soldiers with drawn Swords."[8]

52. Another incident similar to the *Lady Hughes* affair of 1784, which involved the death or wounding of several Chinese by British seamen, took place in 1807. The Court of Justice inquiring into the *Neptune* affair was painted on the spot by a Chinese artist, possibly Spoilum.

It was during the tensions of these first few days that Samuel Shaw and Thomas Randall acknowledged the uncertainties of Fate and life and decided, lest something should happen to them, that the events surrounding the shortfall of specie should be committed to paper.

George Smith's abduction brought all business to a halt. The Chinese merchants withdrew into the city; the compradores, linguists, and servants all deserted the hongs; communication with Whampoa was forbidden to the foreigners, leaving them all in a state of acute uneasiness and cut off from escape by barricades patrolled by soldiers. Two ships' boats, however, succeeded in getting through to Whampoa with written orders for all ships immediately to dispatch up to Canton their pinnaces manned and armed. En route, the boats took gunfire from one of the forts but held their own. By late evening of the twenty-seventh, the factories—where weapons ordinarily were explicitly prohibited, had become an armed compound, the Europeans unanimously agreed to treat the situation as a common cause. Pigou requested American cooperation and got it.

That same night, the Fuyuen (Governor) of Canton caused a copy of his mandate to be sent to the foreign compound.

A Native of this Country having been killed by a Gun fired from the Ship of Captain Williams, whether by accident or design it is necessary that this man [the man implicated] should appear before me for examination that he may be tried conformably to our Laws: Three days are now elapsed, & you have not sent me this Gunner that he may appear before our Tribunal & I can return Mr. Smith to you as soon as this Gunner shall arrive; I exhort you therefore to remain quiet & conform yourselves to my Mandate, & shew no token of resistance for if you refuse to submit, I the Fouyuen shall range my Troops with Musquets & Artillery even to the Bogue [Boca Tigris] to cut off your retreat from place to place along the course of the River, & will subject you and treat you agreeably to the Laws: Reflect therefore & see what is your force and your ability, if you dare in our Country to disobey and infringe our Laws, consider well that you may not repent when it is too late.[9]

The following morning, the foreigners replied, objecting most strenuously to Smith's detention. The fact of the matter was that he was being held hostage pending production of the offending gunner.

About two o'clock [Samuel Shaw observed], M. Vieilliard, the French consul, came and informed me that he had, with M. Galbert, the king's interpreter, been with a mandarin at the pagoda, who informed him that chops would be granted to such of the strangers as would apply for them, the English excepted, to send back their boats whenever they pleased; and that, as the Danes, French, and Dutch were determined not to make war for the English, he advised me to apply for one and send away our boat immediately. After thanking him for his advice I answered, that I considered the rights of humanity deeply interested in the present business, to support which I had, at the request of the English chief, ordered the American boat to Canton;—that when the English chief assured me that the purposes for which she had been required were answered, I would send her back, and not until then.

Towards evening, two mandarins, attended by linguists, came out and requested that a representative from each nation, the English excepted, should meet the Fuen, who was then in his tribunal ready to receive us. After communicating with the English gentlemen, it was agreed that we should represent to the Fuen, that the seizing of Mr. Smith was considered, not as a matter affecting the English only, but as nearly concerning every foreign trader in Canton, whose property or person could now no longer be considered secure.

On coming before the Fuen, who held his tribunal at a pagoda in a part of the suburbs not frequented by the Europeans, we were received by a mandarin of war, who led us through two ranks of soldiers armed with long scymitars, and presenting himself on his knee, announced us. The Fuen said that he regarded it as a mark of our good disposition that we came to him, and that we need be under no apprehension for Mr. Smith, who should not receive any injury, but be restored on the gunner being given up. On being told that the gunner had absconded, he answered, "No matter, he must be produced"; and when M. Galbert attempted to explain the cause of the boats being ordered, and to vindicate the English, he commanded him to be silent, and declared that it was only in consideration of the other nations that the English were not on this occasion a lost people. After offering us tea, which we declined, the Fuen presented each gentleman with two pieces of silk, in token of amity, and then dismissed us.[10]

George Smith, meanwhile, had written a letter to Captain Williams of the *Lady Hughes* to produce the gunner. This was sent down in the English boat, a Chinese standing at the bow with a red flag, a signal of safe conduct through the nearly forty Chinese gunboats ranged before the factories. When he approached Whampoa and saw all the foreign ships with their gunports open, cannon run out, and in every way prepared for immediate action, the linguist bearing the message lost courage and returned to Canton.

Captain McIntosh of the East India Company ship *Contractor* was then sent down with the linguist as security for his safe return. Captain Williams of the *Lady Hughes* was ordered to find and produce the gunner, while McIntosh was under instructions to prevent "by such methods as you judge proper" any attempt by Williams to sail before agreeing to Chinese demands.

On November 30, five more boats from the English ships, under flags of safe conduct, left the factories for Whampoa. At sunset, McIntosh returned with the gunner, who bore a note from Williams to the hostage supercargo: "I now send this Chit by the poor Gunner, I hope you will leave a maintenance if he is detained; pray Dear Smith take care of the old Man, you had better leave something with Munqua for the old Man's maintenance, I hope the Chinese will not do harm to the poor old Man as it was only a misfortune."[11]

A few minutes after his arrival at the English factory, the gunner was taken to the pagoda, where the mandarins awaited him. They 'desired the Gentlemen present not to be uneasy respecting his fate, that nothing should be done till the Emperors pleasure shall be known, & . . . he had no doubt that in about 60 days he would be sent back again." An hour later, George Smith was released and returned to the factories.

At almost the same time, Samuel Shaw was advised by the linguist that the *Empress of China*'s chop (permit) to ship merchandise from the factory to Whampoa had not been reissued. Inquiry brought to light the fact that

53. Spanish dollars were essential to the early China trade. At each transaction, the Chinese "shroff" certified the goodness and correct weight of each coin by stamping his mark on it. After many "shroffings," the coins fell apart and became known as "chopped dollars."

Puankhequa, the ship's security merchant, "had caused our vessel to be registered in the hoppo's books as an English country ship." The ruse may have been helpful in avoiding the payment of bribes by a new nation entering the trade, but now it was a hindrance that could not be allowed to go uncorrected. Shaw and Randall memorialized the French Consul for assistance in setting the record straight:

Sir—

The undersigned, supercargoes for the American commerce in China, beg leave to acquaint you that they have undoubted reason to believe, that, through the misrepresentation of Pankekoa, they have been reported to the hoppo as being Englishmen, and the ship in which they arrived at this place as an English country ship, and consequently that they should be considered subjects of Great Britain.

To take off from this misrepresentation, and to announce to the Chinese that we are the subjects of a free, independent, and sovereign power, is the reason of our present application. And we request, in the name of the United States of America, the allies and good friends of his Most Christian Majesty, that you will cause to be made known to the Chinese, by means of M. Galbert, the king's interpreter, that we are AMERICANS, a free, independent, and sovereign nation, not connected with Great Britain, nor owing allegiance to her, or any other power on earth, but to the authority of the United States alone; and that we pray the Chinese to consider us in that view, and grant our passports accordingly,

Done at Canton, in China, this 30th of November, 1784.

(signed) S. Shaw,
Tho: Randall.[12]

It was taken care of the next day:

Les représentations contenues dans votre mémoire en date du trente novembre, 1784, étant, Messieurs, de toute justice et équité, j'ai donné ordre à M. Galbert premier interprète du roi en langue Chinoise de l'être aux vôtres, et de représenter au gouvernement que c'est par erreur que le nommé Pankékoa fiador de votre vaisseau l'a fait inscrire sur les regîtres du hopou comme vaisseau Anglais de côte, que vous êtes Américain, que votre nation est reconnue comme nation indépendante, souveraine et aussi étrangère à la Grande-Bretagne que la nation Française, ou tout autre commerçante à la Chine. J'aurais soin, Messieurs, lors de l'arrivée de vos vaisseaux de les avertir de cet incident, et de leur fournir les moyens de se mettre à l'abri des inconvéniens qu'une non distinction entre la nation Américaine et la nation Anglaise peut occasioner dans ce pays, où le défaut de connaissances géographiques et une séperation entière des autres nations du globe occasionera toujours la même erreur, toutes les fois qu'une nation nouvelle entreprenda de former des liaisons du commerce avec les Chinois.

Donné à Canton, en notre hôtel, le premier décembre, 1784.

(signed) Vieillard.[13]

Shy Kingqua did the honors and explained to the Hoppo the difference between Americans and Englishmen.

The embargo on trade was lifted on December 6, 1784 as relations returned to normal. The *Lady Hughes* sailed for Bombay the next day, preceding the *Empress of China* to sea by three weeks.

On January 8, 1785, eleven days after the *Empress of China* left Whampoa Reach for home, those Westerners still remaining in the factories in Canton learned the fate of the *Lady Hughes*'s starcrossed gunner. The Chinese had quietly strangled him, too.[14]

XIV

Bound for Home

Hopefully some day, somewhere, Captain John Green's Journal of the *Empress of China*'s return passage to the United States will be located and identified. As it is, we now have only his remarks from December 28, 1784, when the ship unmoored at Whampoa for her departure from the Pearl River, until January 12, 1785, ten days before she again raised the Sunda Strait between Java and Sumatra. For the rest, we still must rely on Samuel Shaw.

Thomas Randall did not return in the *Empress of China*. "I should endeavour to give some idea of this country and my prospects in it," he wrote from Canton to Major General Henry Knox, "but as my friend Mr. Shaw will personally deliver this letter his account will be more full and expressive than any I could convey . . ."[1] Randall was remaining behind long enough to oversee the outfitting and lading of the ship *Pallas*, which the two supercargoes had chartered to bring to the United States additional quantities of Oriental produce and manufactures.

A ship's departure from Whampoa began with the issuance by the Hoppo of a "Grand Chop," a form printed from wood blocks and completed by hand. It attested to the fact that all formalities had been complied with and that the requisite duties had been collected, specifying also the vessel (identified only by the name of the captain), where she was bound, the number of sailors and guns on board, and the amounts of shot, swords, muskets, and "fire-physic" (gunpowder) carried. The typical Grand Chop, of which very few examples have survived, translated in terms similar to the following:

[*Name of person*], filling the office of Hoppo by Imperial appointment, issues this in obedience to his will. When Western Ocean ships have been measured, paid their duties, and departed, should bad winds and water drive them to the shores of another province (not being within the accorded limits of trading), if it is found that they possess this sealed discharge they must be allowed to continue their voyage without delay or opposition. Which is on record.

Now the foreign merchant ship [*name of captain*] having loaded with merchandise, goes to the Hwa-Ke ['Flowery Flag,' i.e. United States of America] country, there to manage her business. She has been measured, and duties incurred by her have all been settled, as customary. As she is now departing, this is given as a clearance into the hands of the said merchant to grasp and hold fast, so that, should he meet with any other custom-house, he must not be detained. Military stations to which it may be shown must also let the said vessel pass without interruption, and not induce her to remain and trade that they may be benefited by any charges or duties. Should they act otherwise, it will give rise to trouble and confusion.

According to old regulations, the guns and ammunition and other arms she carries for her defence are herein enumerated. An unnecessary quantity is not allowed, nor has she dared to receive on board any contraband articles. Should it have been discovered that these rules were broken by her, this permission to sail would assuredly not have been granted.

Respectfully examine this *and depart*

(Hoppo's seal)[2]

"The grand chop having been received from the Hoppo," one old China hand remarked, "the pilot was obtained at Whampoa. As the ship got under way, the Compradore's 'cumshaws,' according to 'olo custom,' were brought on board. They consisted of dried lychee, Nankin dates (the 'latest dates,' as they were christened), baskets of oranges, and preserved ginger; then, amidst a firing off of crackers attached to the end of a long pole from the Compradore's boat—'to awaken the gods to the vessel's departure,' that they might vouchsafe to her 'good wind and good water'—she departed. As in entering the river, she hove to off Anonghoy Fort at the Bogue, that the pilot could exhibit his pass. Sailing by Macao, this individual was cast off, and soon outside, she was rolling down the China Sea—homeward bound!"[3]

The homeward passage of the *Empress of China* took her back through the Sunda Strait, which she passed on January 25 or 26, 1785. During the

---

Facing page: 54. Once a vessel was ready to sail for home and had complied with all formalities, she was given a final exit pass, or "Grand Chop." This one, issued from the Macao Custom House in 1831 to Captain Charles Roundy of the Salem, Massachusetts, ship *Sumatra*, is one of the few to have survived. Roundy's name in the document transliterates from the Chinese as "Don-lee."

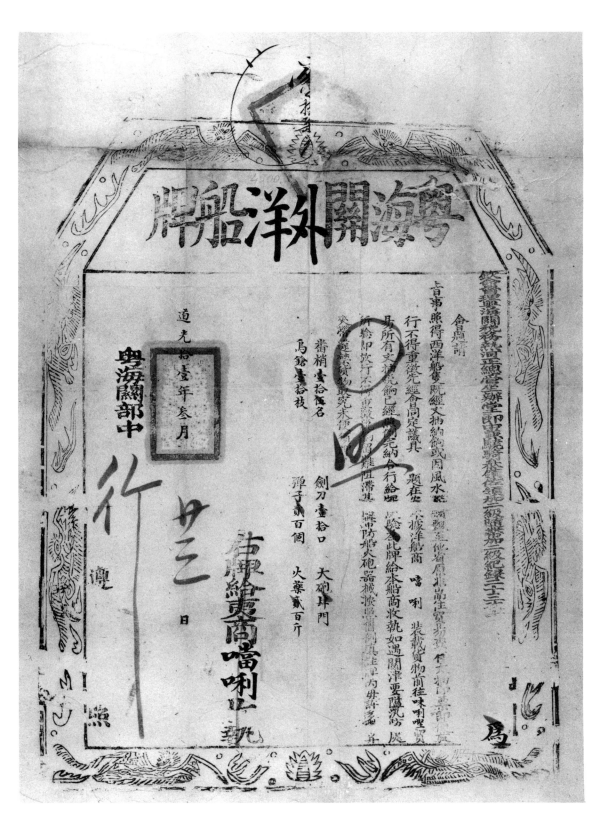

粵海關洋船牌

欽命督理粵海關稅務兼巡視河工總督辦堂加四品御軍功紀錄二級隨帶加一級紀錄十二次

會奸司

旨事照得西洋船隻凡經夷人抵泊或因風水等
事頒發至他省者屢不常主貿易故自本關起程往他省貿易
行不得重徵兔餉經全局定議具
題在案今撥洋船商　噹喇　裝載貨物前往味利喫貿
易所有文移兔餉已經物業約合行給賜
驗即依行定數給夷人夷船其停泊難以滯其
茶常蜜慈等貨物究未便

驗今此牌給本船商收執如遇關津要隘沈防展
攜帶防船火砲器械煖照禮例開具主印為憑許多夷
番梢壹拾伍名
鳥銃壹拾枝
劍刀壹拾口　大砲肆門
彈子貳百個　火藥貳百斤

粵海關部中

道光拾壹年叁月　廿三日

給牌紅夷商噹喇收執

first week in March, she doubled the Cape of Good Hope and on the ninth anchored off Cape Town in Table Bay, where she remained until the fourteenth.

There, John Green found another American vessel riding to an anchor: the former privateer ship *Grand Turk*, owned in Salem, Massachusetts, by Elias Hasket Derby, that burgeoning and resourceful merchant prince of one blue eye and one brown, whose ships soon would be roving the world from the Baltic wastes to the China coast and beyond to the uncharted, reef-strewn waters of the South Pacific. Green's conversations with the *Grand Turk*'s Captain Jonathan Ingersoll had much to do with Salem's rise as a town famed

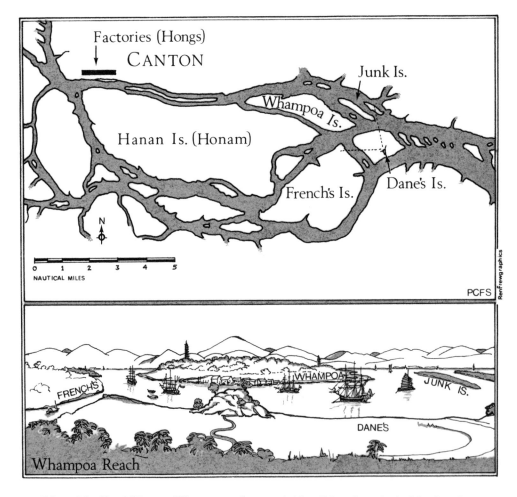

55. Map of the Pearl River at Whampoa and a sketch identifying the principal landmarks most often seen in Chinese paintings of the anchorage.

56. Cape Town, where the *Empress of China* paused on her return passage to New York, is dwarfed by Table Mountain in the background. At this port, East Indiamen to or from Europe often stopped to replenish stores and water. From the sea journal of the ship *Potomac*, 1825-1826.

for its exotic trade with the East Indies. The *Grand Turk* had come to the Cape to investigate the commercial success enjoyed the year before by the sloop *Harriet*, Captain Hallet, and the sales of Colonel Sears's ginseng for double its weight in China tea to alarmed officers of the East India Company's China traders. The sloop had returned under Captain Sturges, Hallet's former mate, in order to try her luck yet again, but both Captains Ingersoll and Sturges were discovering that the *Harriet*'s first triumph had been merely a fluke.

"This port," Ingersoll advised his Salem owner, "is Calculated only to Suppli Ships bound Too and from India and not purchases of Cargos as the port receives all Supplis by the Company from Europ and Batave, and exports nothing but bad Wines not fit for any market but this. . . ."[4] When Captain Ingersoll returned to Salem, he recounted to Derby in detail all he had heard from Captain John Green of Philadelphia about the *Empress of China*'s trailblazing accomplishment. Eighteen months following the encounter at Cape Town, Green, in command of the *Empress of China*'s second voyage to Canton, met the *Grand Turk* again; this time at Whampoa Reach.

From Cape Town, the *Empress of China* sailed northwestward into the Caribbean Sea, where quartering winds caught in her sails and pushed her northeastward along the rim of the North American continent.

57. Captain Jonathan Ingersoll of Salem, Massachusetts, was captain of the ex-privateer *Grand Turk* when she met the *Empress of China* at Cape Town. The information Ingersoll gleaned from this chance meeting was largely responsible for Salem's storied entry into the China trade.

On May 11, 1785, America's first China trader sailed triumphantly through the Narrows, saluted the City of New York with thirteen guns, and came to anchor in the East River where it had all begun nearly fifteen months before.

Loudon's *New York Packet* was the first of the local newspapers to report her return, but it was left to the *Independent Journal, or the General Advertiser* to provide the fullest accounts published at the time. It erred in a number of details, including the date of departure from New York and the report that Shaw, rather than only Randall, had remained behind, but, generally speaking, it echoed the sentiments of tremendous satisfaction that so potentially fragile a venture could have been concluded so well:[5]

Last Wed. arrived safe in this harbour, the ship *Empress of China*, Capt. John Green, who sailed from hence on the 24th of Feb. 1784, arrived at Port Whampoa, in the River Canton, August 28th, no gales but a little blowing weather on leaving this coast; the crew was remarkably healthy, only one man, [John Morgan] the carpenter, a person long invalided died on the 15th ult after crossing the line. On his arrival at Whampoa the British commodore (Capt. Williams) show Mr. Green much civility; after saluting the ship, he sent an officer on board with expressions of a cordial welcome, and offers of any services in his power. On his return and touching at the

58. Elias Hasket Derby (1739-1799), of Salem, Massachusetts, was the owner of the *Grand Turk* as well as another, much larger vessel of the same name he had built for the China trade in 1791. He is reputed to have become the first millionaire in the United States for his far-flung shipping enterprises.

Cape of Good Hope (which he left about two months ago) he was informed that the ship *United States*, Capt. Bell, from Philadelphia, having missed his passage, had got safe into Pondicherry; the *Grand Turk* from Boston [Salem], was arrived at the Cape, from whence Capt. Green has brought some sheep of that country. The *Empress of China*, highly to the credit of her commander and his officers effected the voyage out and home in fourteen months and 24 days; Capt. Green left two gentlemen, Messrs. Shaw and Randall at Canton, to superintend the interest of the several gentlemen concerned in this judicious, eminently distinguished, and very prosperous achievement.

Amongst many articles sent from our port to China in this Ship was a considerable quantity of root ginseng, which used to be in such high estimation with the inhabitants of that country, that they never found it too dear. The gov't of China sends out 10,000 Tartar soldiers every year to gather this plant, and each is obliged to bring home two ounces of the best ginseng gratis, and for the rest they are paid its weight in silver. Private persons are not allowed to gather it but this odious prohibition does not prevent them. If they did not break this unjust law, they would not be able to pay for the commodities they buy in the Empire, and consequently must submit to the want of them. From the ill behavior of the first Europeans, visiting this country, they are now suffered to put into and trade [only] at the port of Whampon [*sic*], in the River of Canton. There were four British ships in Canton River. The Commanders were Capts. Thomson, Gore, and Blatchford.[6]

A Journal from Canton in China to New York
[Continuation of John Green's Journal]

DECEMBER 1784

Tuesday, 28. At 11 A.M. sent pinnace on board *Sagittaire* requesting the use of boats and men to help down clear of the shipping. On the flood's setting began to unmoor and at 2 o'clock abreast of the French Commodore. Mr Desmoulin and Randall took their leave of us. We saluted them with three cheers and nine guns. Soon after some of the ships saluted and when we got below of the shipping at Whampoa we saluted all the shipping when the Dutch Commodore returned our salute. Winds SSW and very light. At 8 P.M., came to anchor the tide being done and the *Latham*'s longboat by desire of her 2d mate, Mr Pervis, was ordered to assist us.

Wednesday, 29. At 2 A.M., light wind. The pilot desired some tow boats to tow the ship to 2d bar and insisted on 20 which was granted. We hove up and got the boats ahead. At 9 A.M., came to the tide being expended about one mile above 2d bar. At 3, got the boats ahead the ebb commencing and towed about 3 miles below the bar. On passing the shipping at 2d bar Mr Shaw and my son went on board Mr d'Ordelin accompanied with Mr Mollineux to deliver a letter for Mr J. Nesbitt of Lorient and to return my sincere thanks to this good and generous commander for his polite and civil attention to me and our colors since I had the honor of meeting him at Isle of Cantey to this day. We towed about 3 or 4 miles below Second Bar, sent a letter of thanks to Captain Robinson and Mr Pervis for the use of their boat and people. We came to anchor.

Thursday, 30. At 3 A.M., light air from NE. Got the towboats ahead and on 6 A.M. abreast of the Bogue of Tigress [Boca Tigris]. The wind freshening up the towboats all left us. Continued to sail down the river, and at 10 A.M. saw the ship *General de Klerk*, commanded by Mr Banks in service of the East India Company of Holland about 6 miles to the Southward. When abreast of Macao the Canton pilot desired his discharge. He said they never went further than this. I desired him to get me a fisherman to carry me out as far as the island Potoe, to bring that island to bear East. The winds very light.

Friday, 31. Light winds. The pilot left us at 5 past Meridian, first furnishing a fisherman to carry us as far as Grand [Great] Ladrone, for which I engaged him 5 dollars. When abreast of Caperita point it bearing WSW 5 and ½ fathom, about 2 miles off, we steered SbW. Winds EbS. And at 8 at night it fell calm. Came to anchor and furled all sails. 5 fathom water.

JANUARY 1785

Saturday, 1. At 3 A.M., light air from NW. Hove up being then abreast or rather Isle Potoe bearing E¾S, distance 2 miles, and at 4 A.M. the fisherman was paid his 5 dollars and he left us, the Grand [Great] Ladrone bearing SEbE 6 miles. Set the main-topsails. Steered SbW 3 miles and then hauled up SbE and at 8 A.M. the body of Grand [Great] Ladrone bore NNE 5 leagues. N.B.—from Point Caperita steered SbW 5 and ½ to 5 fathom to Isle Potoe and from our leaving Isle Potoe steered as above. Moonlight night and pleasant. At noon latitude observed 21ᵈ28ᵐ. Run distance from the above bearings G. Ladrone 14ᵐ.

Course SbE.
Meridional distance 4ᵐ E.
Difference of longitude 4.
Longitude in 113ᵈ50ᵐ E.

Sunday, 2. The fore part, fine pleasant weather and smooth sea. All sails set. Winds NNE. Saw the *General de Klerk* and at 5 P.M. spoke him and he invited me to dine on board tomorrow, which I begged excuse but promised him to dine with him when we came further to the

Southward and when we might probably have better weather than we could expect here at this season. Handed all our sails but the 3 topsails and fore-staysails and the topsails on the cap to keep astern of this European Indiaman. At noon, a fresh of wind.

Course made good SbE, distance per log 104^m.
Latitude per observation 19^{d}40^m.

The fore- and main-topsail single-reefed. All other sails handed. A fresh breeze and tumbling sea. Our consort on our lee quarter with all the sail his ship could bear, such as courses, topsails, staysails and all his topgallant sails and spritsail. Our officers recruiting. 2 able for duty. The men something recovered. Latitude Macao 22^{d}13^m N and longitude from London 113^{d}46^m E.

Course made good SbE, distance 100^m.
Difference of latitude 98.
Departure 20.
Latitude observed 19^{d}40^m N.
Meridional distance 24^m.
Difference of longitude 21.
Longitude in 114^{d}11^m E from London.

Monday, 3. Strong winds and the latter part attended with drizzling rain and foggy weather. At 4 P.M., the ship *General de Klerk* carrying a press of sail. Imagine he carried some shrouds or something away. He clewed up his topgallant sail, topsails, and hauled down all staysails, wore ship to the NW and lay to for some time, when he wore, made sail, and continued his course. We generally carrying reefed fore- and main-topsails and sometimes the fore-staysail. At 8 A.M., the main-topsail tie gave way. The watch employed fitting a new one. No observation. The winds from NE and a tumbling swell.

Course made good SbE, distance 149^m.
Difference of latitude in 146^m.
Departure 29^m.
Latitude per account 17^{d}14^m N.
Meridional distance 53^m.
Difference of longitude 30^m.
Longitude in 114^{d}41^m E.

N.B.—the 2d and 3d mate able to do duty. The chief mate still lame but a-mending. N.B.—in viewing the journal of the *Royal Henry*, she made SbE¼E course to Macclesfield and run

distance 118 leagues. She got aground in latitude 15^{d}50^m North at 45 fathom water, some shells and white sand. She run after her getting ground on the Macclesfield 18^m South and then hove and had no ground in 50 fathom.

Tuesday, 4. Commences squally and some flying showers. The ship *General de Klerk* shortened sail. We were too close. Reefed main-topsails and lay him aback with the reefed fore-topsail on the cap to keep alongside her. The wind NE. Steering to the SbE. The night very dark. At 12, hove to. Sounded in 20 fathom rocky bottom and some red coral rocks. Steered from yesterday noon SbE. Run the distance 82^m. When we sounded and had ground made us in latitude per account 15^{d}58^m and longitude from Macao in 114^{d}57^m E.

Meridional distance 69^m East.
Course run and distance made until bore away to the SWbS—SbE and run distance 111^m and at 7 A.M. steered SWbS.
Run distance 24^m per log.
At noon latitude in 15^{d}05^m North.
Longitude 08^m.
Meridional distance 61^m.
Longitude in 114^{d}33^m E.

A steering to SWbS. Winds NE. *General de Klerk* in company.

Wednesday, 5. A fresh of wind all this 24 hours and a short, cross sea. Find the ship is very slight in her upper works and work much. Generally the reefed fore-topsail on the cap to keep way with the *General de Klerk* whom has foresail and fore- and main-topsails single-reefed with spritsail set. The winds are not violent but we might carry our single-reefed topsails, topgallant sails, foresails, and other sails but wish to keep company as I am an entire stranger through the Straits of Banca and the commander of the *General de Klerk* well informed of all the passages.

Course made good this 24 hours SWbS, distance 139^m.
Difference of latitude 116^m.
Departure 77^m.
Latitude per account 13^{d}09^m North.
Meridional distance 16^m West.
Difference of longitude 79^m.
Longitude in 113^{d}04^m E.

Carried away one lanyard larboard main shrouds; also, the sheave in wheel rope chock split. Repaired all damage. All hands in health, chief mate excepted, whom is very lame and sick.

Thursday, 6. Commences fine steady wind from NEbNorth and NNE. Fleeted main-topmast backstays and set ditto up under the reefed fore-topsail on the cap. At or [on] the 3d watch from 12 to four commanded by the 3d officer lost sight of the Commodore from ½ after one A.M. to 4 ditto when we discovered him about 2 miles bearing SWbW. After making more sail the officer inattentive to duty and at times in liquor. At 7 A.M. winds from North. Set 3d reef main-topsail, mizzen-staysail and fore ditto.

Course made good SWbS, distance 127^m.
Difference of latitude 106.
Departure 71.
Latitude 11^{d}23^m.
Meridional distance 87^m W.
Difference of longitude 72.
Longitude in 111^{d}52^m E.

Friday, 7. Commences fine weather and steady breeze. At 3 P.M., in latitude 11^{d}10^m. Imagined we could not be far to the North of an island which lay in latitude 11^{d}7^m and longitude 111^{d}31^m E. Made sail and soon run ahead of our comrade in order to make this land before dark, but we soon run the Dutch ship's hull in the water. Saw no sign of land. At 4, shortened sail. Hands courses, staysails. Wore ship and joined our companion. At 5, sounded in 80 fathom but no ground. At sundown, handed all sail. The winds NNE. Our course steered SWbS. Our companion under his fore-topsail. We under the poles and a hard match to keep astern all night. We find a strong current setting to the Southward. Course steered SWbSouth, run distance per log this 24 hours 118^m, but find by observation to make 128^m difference of latitude on a SWbS course. Latitude observed 9^{d}15^m North. That with current think the ship to have made a South course if not to the Eastward. Longitude in 11^{d}52^m. Meridional distance from Macao 87^m. Our consort got up his topgallant yards and makes more sails, steering at noon to the WbSouth.

Saturday, 8. Former part, fresh of wind and a tumbling sea with close dark weather. At 4 P.M., hove to and sounded. Got ground in 60 fathom, dark brown sand and small shells. The wind from NNE and NE. A steering WbS. At nine P.M., hands all sails but the reefed fore-topsail which we carried on the cap. The water something smooth. At ½ past 8 A.M., made Pulo Condore bearing NWbNorth 4 leagues and at 10 the land bore NbE about 3 leagues. Steered SSW½W until noon and run distance 129^m per log. In latitude per [   ] 8^{d}35^m. Thermometer at noon 76^d. From yesterday noon we steered WbS and run distance per log 129^m before the North end of Pulo Condore bore NorthbE distance as mentioned. Run distance on a SSW½W course from the bearings Pulo Condore until noon. 29^m in latitude at noon per account 8^{d}35^m North. Thermometer 77^d.

Sunday, 9. Steady wind from NNE. Our consort carrying all sail; we all sail handed excepting the reefed fore- and main-topsails. Mostly a half mile on his larboard quarter. Course made this 24 hours SSW¼W distance per log 155 miles. Mr Shaw taken sick this day. Our chief mate continues [with] lame hand and a small touch of the gout. Close dark weather. The evenings and mornings quite cold. Thermometer at noon 76^d. No observation this day.

Monday, 10. Close weather all through and a fresh breeze attended with some rain. The winds mostly at NNE. The latter part out all reefs, fore- and main-topmasts, and spoke Captain Banks. At same time went ahead to make the land or island Pulo Timon. Shifted the starboard cable end for end and got the stream cable clear for bending. This day stopped giving wreck [?] to the seamen. Course made good SSW¼W, distance 135^m. Latitude observed in 3^{d}30^m North. The *General de Klerk* about 5 miles astern. Mr Shaw, the chief mate, and carpenter all sick and taking medicines.

Tuesday, 11. At ½ past two, made the island Pulo Timon bearing SbW, distance 3 leagues. Our consort a long way astern. Winds NE. Made the signal for seeing the land by hoisting our ensign. Soon after he answered by hoisting his; we continued bowling to the SE in order to go to the Eastward of the island, but our consort continue his course to the SSW¼W. As he was more in those seas than I was I followed him thinking he meant to come to anchor under Pulo Timon for the night, but he carried a press of sail to the Westward of Pulo Timon. That convinced me this was not his intentions and the sun going down I shot up spoke him and asked him what passage he intended going. It then blowing fresh and a swell from the North. He informed me he did not well know the land and would come to at 8 o'clock and lay all night; that when he came to he would show 2 fires or lights. We came to in 19 fathom with a bower anchor. Furled sails. At daylight, began to heave up and when the anchor apeak, the ship pitching heavy, tore away the larboard "S" cheek of the windlass, overset the pawls, and the windlass having nothing to support it run round. We were obliged to cut the cable or lose all of what remained on board, and by cutting we lost the anchor and about 20 fathom cable. Stood off and on all day. At noon observed in latitude 2^{d}58^m. Pulo Timon bearing ENE, distance 4 or 5 leagues. The *General de Klerk* got under way. I spoke him. He informed me his charts were bad and desired me keeping ahead of him through the passage, which I did. Repaired the windlass. Carpenter unfit for duty. 2d and 3d mate and some seamen at work for the purpose of fitting w[indlass].

Wednesday, 12. Commences fine weather. Run ahead of the *General de Klerk*, the passage large and the wind North. When the islands which lay to the NW of Pulo Timon bore NE we kept SEbE and run about 5 miles to the Westward of these islands. Several islands on our starboard hand but I run directly for Pulo Timon middle of the island, and on running down for the SW end saw the rock which lay off the south end raising out of the water. Also Pulo Pisang and a small rock which had not a tree on it, bearing from the SW end of the island Pulo Timon SWbS, distance 2 leagues. The night coming on dark, came to in 26 fathom clay and good bottom, but we saw in the morning the best anchoring ground is near the SW end and appears a fine bay and good shelter from the NE and North winds. The land high, the beach sandy, and the land covered with weed and large trees. Imagine this the best island for wooding and watering by ships from China bound for Europe. At daylight, got under way and run ahead of our consort. Winds light, but as the day came on the winds increased. Steered from our place where we anchored SEbE. At 10, Pulo Pisang ENE distance 4 leagues. At noon, Pulo Aor NEbE, distance 5 or 6 miles. Our consort a long way astern or hull down. Took in all sail and brought to under the main-topsail to the mast. Latitude observed 2^{d}29^m. Mr Shaw recovered. The first mate better. The carpenter and one seaman very sick. Sounded ground 28 fathom.

Narrative by Samuel Shaw[7]
[From his Journal]

Mr. Randall and I having settled all our affairs, and the ship being ready to sail, we, on the 26th day of December, made our visits of leave to the chiefs and gentlemen of the respective nations, again thanked them for their attentions, and received their good wishes for our prosperity. The next day I went on board, and the day after the ship came to sail, on her return to America.

It having been understood, at the time Mr. Randall engaged to go the voyage with me, that, if any opportunity offered to his advantage when in China, he should not be obliged to return in the ship, but might remain in China, or go where he judged it most conducive to his interest, he accordingly availed himself of an opportunity which seemed to promise something advantageous to him, and did not return in the ship. In consequence of this permission, the owners had the benefit of his services, without adding any thing to the allowance they first offered to me, besides the advantage of a double security for their property; as their instructions to me were, in case of my death, directed to and binding on him.

On the 28th of December, 1784, we came to sail at Whampoa, and in passing the shipping, at four o'clock, P.M., saluted them with nine guns, which were returned by the respective commodores. On the 30th, while passing Second Bar, I went on board the *Triton* and took leave of M. d'Ordelin and his officers, whose politeness and attention to us on all occasions merited our sincerest acknowledgments. On the 31st, at sunset, being clear of Macao, the pilot left us.

The Dutch ship *General de Klerk* having sailed a day before us from Second Bar, and it having been agreed, before we left Canton, that we would keep company through the Chinese seas, we spoke the next day, and proceeded together towards North island, where we anchored at noon on Wednesday, the 19th of January, in fourteen fathoms, the island bearing from our ship N. by E. ½ E. two miles, and the Watering Place, on Sumatra, S. W. the same distance. Here we found at anchor one Dutch, two English, and two Portuguese ships, bound for Europe. The English ships, the *Ponsborne* and *Hawke*, sailed from Second Bar three days after us, and, going through the Gaspar passage, arrived at North island one day before us. Our keeping company with Captain Banks was with the view of availing ourselves of his experience, as we did not go through the Straits of Banca on our way to Canton. All the time we were with him we were constantly obliged to shorten sail, and it was no small mortification to us, on arriving at the island, to find that he was equally a stranger in those seas with ourselves, it being his first voyage to China; nor did it console us for the loss of an anchor, in weighing from Pulo Timon on the 11th of January, on which occasion he lost one too.

On coming to anchor, the captain, Mr. Swift, and I, went on board the *General de Klerk*, and dined with Commodore Banks and Mr. Benthem, one of the Dutch supercargoes from Canton. It is the custom of the Dutch residents to send annually a supercargo to Holland, to report to the directors the state of their affairs and to bring back their orders. The Swedes and Danes send out supercargoes, who assist their residents at Canton and return with the ships.

After dinner, Captain Banks and Mr. Benthem went with us on board the other Dutch ship. She was called the *Hoorn*, commanded by Captain Terence, and bound from Batavia to Holland. The captain had his wife on board, whom he married at Batavia. Her dress was singular, and differed from any thing I had before seen. It was composed of a long, loose, calico gown, which covered her neck and reached to the floor,—the sleeves wide down to the wrist, where they buttoned close upon the hand. Under this garment was another of calico, which served as a petticoat and bodice. These articles, I believe, composed the whole of her dress, except a pair of slippers,—her feet being without stockings. Her hair, without any ornament, was put up behind with a comb. After drinking a glass of wine, and engaging the captain

59. Chinese export porcelain Hong bowl, *circa* 1785, showing the Foreign Factories. The ship depicted inside may be intended to represent the *Empress of China* inasmuch as the family tradition associated with the bowl suggests it was brought to America in her. The presence of the American flag between those of the British and Dutch implies that it may have returned with Captain Green on his second voyage even though his accounts for the first specify "4 Factory painted Bowles."

and his lady to dine with us the next day, he accompanied us ashore on the island of Sumatra, where we found a convenient place for wooding and watering. Again going aboard the *General de Klerk*, we found Captain Rivington, of the English ship *Hawke*, who passed the evening with us, and at ten o'clock we returned to our ship.

The next day, Captain Banks, Mr. Benthem, and another gentleman from their ship, Captain Terence, his lady, and their doctor, together with Senhores Jorge and Soarez, supercargoes of the Portuguese, dined on board. The lady was dressed as yesterday, except in finer calico, and with the addition of stockings and shoes. She appeared to be upwards of thirty, easy in her manners, sociable, and expressed much satisfaction at her entertainment, especially as it was on board the first American ship that had visited these seas.

After dinner, several gentlemen from the Portuguese ships visited us, among whom was one returning as a prisoner to Lisbon. Being by profession a painter, he had, in company with a clergyman, gone to China, with the view of spending his days at Peking. On his arrival at Canton, the idea of bidding adieu for ever to his country and friends operated so powerfully on his mind, that he refused to go any farther. This determination embarrassed the mandarins at Canton, who, in their despatches to the court of Peking, had mentioned both him and the clergyman. On being told that he must assign a reason for his refusal, he said, that, since his departure from Europe, his father had died, and that he had received letters from his mother, conjuring him to return and take care of her and the children. The mandarins said it was a good reason, but, as it would not be judged sufficient by the court, they would in their next despatch say he was sick, and afterwards report him dead, which would settle the matter. The clergyman, dignified with the rank of bishop in China, set out for Peking, where he must end his days, without a hope of ever seeing those friends and that country of which he had taken a final leave,—while the painter, though a prisoner, in my opinion more happy, was returning to both.

Senhor Jorge informed us that the ship on board which he was passenger was built forty-eight years ago, in Brazil, and that it was upwards of two years since she had used either of her pumps. On the passage from Europe, they tried them, but could get no water; and he observed that he had no doubt she would be a safe ship forty-eight years longer.

Having finished wooding and watering, we left North island on the 22d, and the next day anchored at Krokatoa, where we remained two days. At both of these places the Malays supply ships with fruit, yams, poultry, turtle, and sometimes with buffaloes. Leaving Krokatoa, and clearing the Straits of Sunda, we, on the 26th, at noon, had Java Head bearing east ten leagues distant.

From Java Head we proceeded towards the Cape of Good Hope. On the 4th of March, at nine, A.M., we made the land, bearing N. by E. eleven or twelve leagues. At eleven, had no ground, with one hundred and thirty fathoms of line. At noon, by observation, in 34° 35' south latitude, and, by my reckoning, in 25° 44' east longitude from London. Thence, keeping the coast aboard a considerable part of the time, we doubled the cape, and anchored in Table Bay on the 9th, at five P.M., having saluted the Dutch commodore with seven guns, for which he returned a like number. We found there several ships, Dutch, Swedish, Danish, French, and American. On our coming to anchor, a gentleman from the shore came on board, who, after inquiring whence we came and where bound, the number and condition of our crew, which he took down in writing, gave the captain the rules of the port, and took leave. The captain of the Swedish ship (Peter Aferdson) visited us, and we sent our boat on board the American ship, which returned, bringing Captain Ingersoll and Doctor Leavitt, who were on shore when we cast anchor. The ship was called the *Grand Turk*, from Salem, owned by E. H. Derby, Esq., of that place. These gentlemen passed the evening with us; and the next morning Captain Green, the doctor, and I, went ashore, and took lodgings at the same house with them. There we remained till Sunday evening, when, having taken in water and procured the necessary refreshments, we went on board, and the next day (14th) at three P.M., we came to sail.

"The Cape of Good Hope," says the writer of Anson's Voyage, "is situated in a temperate climate, where the excesses of heat and cold are rarely known; and the Dutch inhabitants, who are numerous, and who, here retain their native industry, have stocked it with prodigious plenty of all sorts of fruits and provisions; most of which, either from the equality of the seasons or the peculiarity of the soil, are more delicious in their kind than can be met with elsewhere; so that by these, and by the excellent water which abounds there, this settlement is the best provided of any in the known world for the refreshment of seamen after long voyages."

There is no doubt but that the foregoing description is very just, though, from what we observed, there must have been great improvements since that period. The town is laid out in squares, with wide and commodious streets. Besides two churches (Lutheran and Calvinist), a state-house, library, hospitals, and other public buildings, there may be about eight hundred dwelling-houses, many of which are elegant, besides gentlemen's seats and gardens towards the country. The Dutch East India Company are proprietors of the soil, and let it out to the settlers, whom they are obliged to supply with every necessary of life, at moderate prices; for which purpose they have public magazines, and no commerce is carried on but by their permission. The governor, fiscal, and other officers, are under their orders. The company's garden is extensive, open at all times, and on Sundays is the resort of persons of every condition. There are to be seen several sorts of wild animals, particularly a hedgehog, a wild boar, baboons, antelopes, goats, rabbits, &c; also, ostriches, hawks, eagles, peacocks, owls, and other birds. The collection does not consist of so great a variety as formerly, there being at present no lions, leopards, zebras, or the like, though the skins of such beasts are to be purchased in plenty at any of the tanners' shops.

The inhabitants, most of whom are in the company's service, add considerably to their income by subsisting the Europeans, and supplying such ships as touch there for refreshments, on their way to India. The bay is protected by lines and forts, to which great additions have been made since Governor Johnstone's visit, during the war, to Saldanha bay, where he took five sail of their Indiamen. The garrison is amply furnished with ordnance and every military apparatus, and consists of about a thousand Dutch, and as many Swiss troops, hired by the republic. These make a good appearance, and with the inhabitants, who are all enrolled as militia, would, in case of an invasion, form a very respectable force. They are subject to the governor, as commander-in-chief, who is himself a colonel in the Dutch service. On going ashore, Captain Green and I made him a visit of ceremony. He spoke French and English, appeared to be well informed, as well respecting America as Europe, and politely proffered us his assistance in any matters where we might find occasion for it.

Perhaps at no place in the world do ships more easily obtain fresh water. There is a large wooden pier, where the boats come and take in that valuable element,

60. Side view of a Chinese porcelain bowl, 15½″ in diameter,
circa 1784, brought to the United States by John Green.

which is conveyed through pipes from the town, and by means of hose into the
casks, without removing them from the boats. Ships may be watered either by their
own boats, or by boats hired of the company, which are always in readiness.

Back of the town is the Table mountain, and other high grounds. From Table
mountain is an extensive view of the neighbouring country, bays, and inlets. To
gratify our curiosity, Doctor Leavitt, Mr. Green, and I, the day after our arrival,
ascended this mountain. When we set out it was perfectly clear,—in a short time it
was clouded over, and again clear. After three hours and a half of hard travelling
we gained its summit, when, to our great mortification, we were entirely disappointed of our object. The top of the mountain remained enveloped in clouds, the
fog thickened,—it began to rain, and we returned through a continual shower. Just
after setting out upon this jaunt, an invitation came for Captain Green and me to
dine with the governor. The captain went, but my excursion to the mountain
deprived me of that pleasure.

The ladies at the Cape are fond of dress, well-bred, conversable, and not unin-
teresting. The residence of the military among them, particularly the French and
Swiss, has not a little conduced to this disposition, and has rendered the French
language very familiar to most of them. At a ball given a few days before our arrival,
by the governor, in honor of the Prince of Orange's birthday, there were present

upwards of eighty ladies, quite in the European style. The gentlemen do not appear to equal advantage; and it is a general remark among the Europeans there, that few of the natives ever turn out good for much. To what this may be owing, or how far the observation is just, it is difficult to determine; but it seems to be corroborated by an author of no small reputation, who has critically examined human nature. In the Sketches of the History of Man, he says:—"Instances are without number of men degenerating in a climate to which they are not fitted by nature; and I know not of a single instance where, in such a climate, people have retained their original vigor. Several European colonies have subsisted in the torrid zone of America more than two centuries; and yet even that length of time has not familiarized them to the climate: they cannot bear heat, like the original inhabitants, nor like negroes transplanted from a country equally hot; they are far from equalling, in vigor of mind or body, the nations from which they sprung. The Spanish inhabitants of

61. Top view of the same bowl, illustrating the ship decoration surmounted by a streamer bearing the words: "John Green EMPRESS OF CHINA Commander". The ship was copied by the Chinese artist from the engraved frontispiece of William Hutchinson's *Treatise on Naval Architecture* (London, 1777), other examples of which include the punchbowls of the *Grand Turk* (Peabody Museum of Salem) and of Richard Dale (Philadelphia Maritime Museum).

Carthagena, in South America, lose their vigor and color in a few months. Their motions are languid; and their words are pronounced in a low voice, and with long and frequent intervals. The offspring of Europeans born in Batavia soon degenerate. Scarce one of them has talents sufficient to bear a part in the administration. There is not an office of trust but must be filled with native Europeans. Some Portuguese, who have been for ages settled on the seacoast of Congo, retain scarce the appearance of men."

The fertility of the country about the Cape, and the provision made by the Dutch for supplying the inhabitants with every foreign commodity, render the settlement very independent of the rest of the world. Captain Ingersoll's object was to sell rum, cheese, salt provisions, chocolate, loaf-sugar, butter, &c., the proceeds of which in money, with a quantity of ginseng, and some cash brought with him, he intended to invest in Bohea tea. But as the ships bound to Europe are not allowed to break bulk by the way, he was disappointed in his expectation of purchasing that article, and sold his ginseng for two thirds of a Spanish dollar a pound, which is twenty per cent better than the silver money of the Cape. He intended remaining a short time to purchase fine teas, in the private trade allowed the officers on board India ships, and then sail to the coast of Guinea, to dispose of his rum, &c., for ivory and gold dust; thence, without taking a single slave, proceed to the West Indies and purchase sugar and cotton, with which he should return to Salem. Notwithstanding the disappointment in the principal object of the voyage, and the consequent determination to go to the coast of Guinea, his resolution not to endeavour to retrieve it by purchasing slaves did the captain great honor, and reflected equal credit upon his owner, who, he assured me, would rather sink the whole capital employed, than, directly or indirectly, be concerned in so infamous a traffic.

Besides the American vessel, there were eighteen others in the bay, under French, Danish, and Dutch colors; the latter from Batavia, waiting for their China ships to sail in company with them to Europe; the others from the coast of India. The day before we left the Cape, a sloop of war arrived from England, in eleven weeks, bound to Madras.

How precarious is all earthly happiness! And how liable are we to be disappointed, even in our fondest and most virtuous expectations! The American papers brought by Captain Ingersoll announced to me the death of the best of fathers, and destroyed the pleasing hope I had entertained of meeting that dear relation, and cheering his declining age with the society of a beloved son.

Leaving the Cape of Good Hope, on the 14th of March, we proceeded towards America, without any extraordinary occurrence,—excepting the death of our carpenter, John Morgan, whose body was committed to the deep at noon, the 15th of April, in latitude 5° 2′ north, and 27° 23′ west longitude from London,—till the 25th of April, at daybreak, when we unexpectedly saw the land, being the island of St. Bartholomew, in the West Indies. At ten, the same day, we spoke the brig *Rebecca*, John Carson, from Baltimore, bound to St. Eustatia. At noon, made the island of St. Martin, S. W. ½ W. distant six leagues. This island lies in 18° 5′ north latitude, and 62° 30′ west longitude from London. Our observation that day was 18° 8′ north latitude, and my reckoning 52° 49′ west longitude, which will account for the expression "unexpectedly," on making the land, especially as it was equally unexpected to every body on board. The captain, the day before only, having asked me my longitude, expressed surprise at my being so far to the westward, as my reckoning was ahead of every other in the ship, and jocosely accounted for it by my hurry to get home. We were at a loss how to account for the difference, especially as we were all equally in a "hurry to get home," and had accordingly made our allowances westerly. A discovery, on the 27th, helped to solve the difficulty; our glass, which should run fourteen seconds, was found to be only twelve and a half, and the twenty-eight but little more than twenty-five. A new glass was adjusted to fourteen seconds, and the knot of our logline to forty-five feet. Taking a fresh departure from St. Martin's, we shaped our course for New York, and on the 10th of May, at six P.M., saw the Neversink. During that night we stood off and on, and at nine the next morning got a pilot on board, who at noon brought us to anchor in the East River at New York, when we saluted the city with thirteen guns, and finished our voyage.

X V

Sales and Selling Out

William Duer, for one, was mighty relieved to see the *Empress of China* back in the East River, because for months he had worried about what mischief Daniel Parker might concoct from his place of exile in Europe. During December 1784, when John Holker expressed his belief that Parker might soon return to the United States, Duer revealed his worst fears: "Don't, my Friend," he wrote, "be deceived by the Artifices of bold and designing Men; he will go from Amsterdam to the Cape of Good Hope, where he has a fair prospect of falling in with the *Empress*; the Reason of Endeavouring to Impress you and Myself with the Belief [of his return to America] is to prevent our sending a Vessel in the Course of this Month to Intercept Green and defeat the Plan. . . ."[1] Just what he supposed the plan might be Duer did not say; presumably, he was convinced that pirate Parker would hijack the *Empress of China*, run her ashore in some deserted cove, and make off with the booty. Duer always verged on the melodramatic. Fortunately, in the present case, it was nothing more than a fertile imagination.

Holker was much more concerned about the extraordinarily embarrassed state of his finances than he was about hair-brained schemes Parker may or may not have cooked up. "I am not so very much alarmed about Parker's views or attempts," he told Duer. "The Captn Cannot vary from his Instructions . . . However I am selling out of the *Empress* as fast as I can, some have purchased in at Prime Cost. . . ."[2]

The "selling out" had begun, in fact, as far back as the discovery of Daniel

Parker's creative business methods; possibly even before. The raising of funds or causing insurance to be made by using the hull or fractions of the cargo as collateral was the true beginning; Holker had authorized his Parisian bankers, LeCouteulx & Cie., to sell all or part of his shares in the cargo and ship should that be in his best interest, and he had provided a power of attorney to enable them to do it. But, by the end of December 1784, no word on that subject had been received from France. Funds were still almost impossible to acquire from any source, and Holker was becoming thoroughly irritated by Duer who was yammering opposition to his selling out but had not come forward with funds to provide an option to do otherwise.

"I am sorry you do not approve," he snapped at Duer toward the end of January 1785, "that the Property of the Company—in the *Empress of China*, should be given up in order to take up the engagements of the Company, & my Bills drawn in Consequence thereof: if the *Empress of China* had sold in Europe at twenty percent under the nominal amount of the Bills, should we not be where we are? If we sell out of her in part to save the damages of Returned Bills is it not a great Saving? But if money is due, is it not to be paid with the Property of the Company? But if the *Empress* is not to be sold here because unsold in France, why do you not Come forward to take up your share of the engagements of the Company? Messrs Ellis & Cockle would not take the whole debt in the *Empress* which I offered, & they are willing to Release £1800 sterling . . . the payment of the 1800 sterling on her Return, either By yourself or your friends—& then one half only of the duty will be done, since I am bound for 1800 more, for which I have mortgaged my personal Estate: & all these misfortunes happen me through your introducing to me D:P: as a worthy Caracter . . . & in this situation you'll talk of engagements of honour, when I am honorably pledging every farthing in the world for the Company's debts, which I did not Contract, at the very time that you are so very largely in debt to me Personaly, for heavy sums, Besides the Company's debts, & will not come forward to give me security either for the Present or a future period: However whether you assent or not Mr Fitzimmons with the Property of the Company must take up, the Engagements of the Company, without you'll step forward, and with me supply the necessary funds: & if the ship should return and make a loosing voyage, to whom shall I look for the defficiency?—from Parker, who has acted such a Role or part:—Pardon me, my friend, I will go no further, But call upon you to Ratify what I have been doing for the Common interest, honour and advantage; & if you do not, it will hereafter lay with you to make good your claims whatever In the mean time, I call upon you to Come & settle the account, Personal to ourselves—& I hope that th[   ] claim I have on your Honour in this respect, w[   ] dictate to you the Propriety thereof, & the necessity, if you sincerely wish to have any claim to my Esteem or friendship . . . [PS] I have just received your letter of the 18th Inst. I fear no Consequences Respecting my Conduct in the *Empress*. I wish you would please to inform me soon, to what share you Pretend in the *Empress of China*: is it in ye half-share, of the Company, or 1/6th this ought to have been fixed Long ago, & it is not yet too late before the adventure is Run out."[3]

On January 25, 1785, Thomas Fitzsimons, that influential Philadelphian who had been recruited to act as the Trustee of Daniel Parker & Company's affairs, penned similar thoughts to Duer:

". . . I take for granted you Intended to get my opinion upon the propriety of his [Holker's] sales of Shares in the *Empress of China*—I have no hesitation in Giving it Explicitly in favor of that measure tho Mr Holker made these sales without any previous Concert with me—I found my opinion first on the Agreement of DP & Co that the whole or any part of the property should be disposed of in Europe if possible & Secondly the Impossibility of taking up or Compromising their Engagements without a sale there or here. The

62. Before John Morgan, the ship's carpenter from Groton, Connecticut, died on the return passage, he asked his friend Thomas Blake, the ship's gunner and steward, to see that his possessions were delivered to his father. This cream pitcher was one of Morgan's private purchases in Canton.

63. Another of John Morgan's purchases was this nine-inch-diameter
bowl with exterior decorations depicting a Swedish East Indiaman.

sale here is Conditional—that in Case it is made in Europe then this is to
be void so that in all Events the Co are exactly on the footing they wd be if
the Agreement they made together had been fulfilled—but there are other
reasons—Mr Holker must have given Security of some kind & could it be
expected that he would pledge his private fortune upon the Event of a
Voy[ag]e which if unfortunate he must abide the Intire loss of and if prof-
ittable he would Receive but a part of that profitt—Surely this cannot be
Right—You will understand what I mean by his abiding the whole loss—
the Co has no funds from whence the loss could be borne. Mr Parker has
none evidently, of yrs I do not pretend to Judge but at all events you should
produce them to make good your proportion of the loss if You expect to
derive advantage from the Event. There is yet an Alternative which you have
Intirely in Your power—and which I beg you to keep in Remembrance—if
you do not avail yourself of it that is three of the partys who have taken the
assignments on shares of the *Empress*—say Ellis [&] Cockle & [Mordecai]
Lewis & Co will at this Moment Resign all claim to profitts if they are
Secured—the principle sum with Interest to be paid on the Arrival of the

ship—this puts the business beyond all dispute & if you Chuse to abide the event of the voyage You have only to produce the Security & the business will be done. You will excuse my being Explicit in this business. All partys are Equal to me in the Part I am to act & when called upon for an opinion I think it my duty to give it without reserve . . . I will at all Events go to N York & see what can be done as to Parker. I suspect very much he will not come back."[4]

The return of the *Empress of China* caused immediate and approving editorial fanfare in the New York press, much of it being picked up and repeated in Philadelphia and elsewhere along the coast. Few readers, however; indeed, no one on board the vessel herself, was aware of its truly precarious financial footing and the extent of the bickering that had gone on in the background long before she even sailed. For almost everyone, her safe arrival was an omen of bright commercial days ahead, a fact relished by the *New York News Dispatch* the day after her return.

As the ship has returned with a full cargo, and of such articles as we generally import from Europe, a correspondent observes, that it presages a future happy period

64. John Morgan also acquired in Canton this 11³⁄₁₆″ diameter bowl containing a Chinese version of an English hunting scene.

in our being able to dispense with that burdensome and unnecessary traffick, which hitherto we have carried on with Europe—to the great prejudice of our rising empire, and future happy prospects of solid greatness; And that whether or not, the ship's cargo be productive of those advantages to the owners, which their merits for the undertaking deserve, he conceives it will promote the welfare of the United States in general, by inspiring their citizens with emulation to equal, if not excel their mercantile rivals.

Some years ago, when the advantages of trade and navigation were better studied and more valued than they are now, the arrival of a vessel after so prosperous a voyage, from so distant a part of our globe, would be announced by public thanksgiving and ringing of bells!—Should not this be our practice now, since Providence is countenancing our navigation to this new world? We hope in our next, to be able to give our readers a more perfect detail of this important voyage.[5]

For Samuel Shaw, the return to New York meant seeking out corroborative evidence that it had been Parker, not he, who had caused the shortage of specie. Two days after the ship docked, he buttonholed Seth Johnson, Parker's former counting-house clerk. Johnson agreed that the sum put aboard had not been the twenty thousand dollars claimed on the bill of lading but,

65. Another view of the Morgan bowl illustrated in Figure 64.

by his own count, seventeen thousand eight hundred.[6] The figures still didn't add up or match.

For Shaw, too, the return also resulted for him in an unexpected seat center stage in a heated controversy. He and Randall inadvertently had created it. It began as soon as the ship arrived and explanations were given about Randall's reasons for remaining in China. When it was learned that the two supercargoes had made arrangements for the ship *Pallas* to carry home an additional $50,000 in teas and other merchandise and that Randall would be returning with her, the shock waves among the *Empress of China*'s owners were severe. The very persons they had employed to trade in their best interests had undercut the limited North American markets for Oriental produce by bringing even more aboard a vessel of their own!

The affair was considered so serious to the commercial success of the original voyage that Robert Morris, on behalf of his half interest, and Thomas Fitzsimons, representing the stake of Daniel Parker & Company, travelled all the way to Elizabethtown, New Jersey, as a place of common convenience, to meet with Shaw. "Upon enquiring into the circumstances of the 2d Ship," Fitzsimons apprised Holker upon his return to Philadelphia, "it appears that Parker had not only authorized a speculation of that kind, but had even recommended the making [of] an establishment in China, in conjunction with him. Mr Shaw however appeared to agree to any reasonable terms, & it was finally agreed that the expected Cargo should be put under the direction of the owners of the *Empress of China* to prevent any interference in the Sale, that they should be interested 2/5 Shaw & Randall 2/5 & a Gent in China 1/5 in the Cargo, their agreement respecting it, is to pay for it by Bills on Europe at 6 Mos Sight to be remitted in one month after the Ships arrival, for each Dollar value, to allow 5/6 St[erlin]g together with 10 p Ct for Respondent and they have given 1/5 for the Freight the whole Amt will be abt 50,000 dollars. Mr Shaw in making this agreement stipulated that he should have the Sale of such part of the Cargo as might be sent to Boston, & that in calculating the Profits in the *Empress* Voyage the Money actually sent should only be admitted He indeavored to stipulate an indemnity for the 2300 dollars [the missing specie] but this I absolutely refused, the other propositions I thot reasonable & agreed to but I did not think myself warranted in agreeing to take an Interest for DP & Co in the 2d Cargo till I had consulted you, & it remains for you to decide whether that shall be done or not.

"Having not yet seen one of the papers whereon to form any calculation, I cannot venture to give an opinion upon this subject, I suppose there will

66. Gouverneur Morris (left) and Robert Morris were unrelated but were close friends, confidants, and business associates. Portrait by Charles Willson Peale (1741-1827), 1783.

be profit on the Voyage but that it will take a long time to wind up, the stipulation for payment cannot be complied with out of the Sales of the Goods, but an allowance of Interest, will I apprehend be satisfactory on that head.

"You will please to observe that Mr Morris thot it of so much consequence to the sale of the present Cargo to secure the direction of the other Ship that he compleated the agreement with Shaw in his own name, reserving to the other owners of the *Empress*, the right of holding an equal concern in it, I wish you to consider the matter & give me your directions, in the mean time I will endeavour to form some calculations for your Government. . . ."[7]

Parker's willful and unilateral authorization for Shaw and Randall to engage in private speculations on their joint accounts entirely changed the marketing strategy for the *Empress of China*'s cargo. Originally planned to be sold at public sale, the new circumstances suggested the prudence of selling it privately, instead. Much less of the cargo than anticipated could be transshipped from New York to Philadelphia if the *Pallas* were bound up the Delaware River, as was generally the belief.

On May 19, 1785, the *New York News Dispatch* observed that: "A report has prevailed for some days past, that the *Empress of China* was to deliver her cargo at Philadelphia—From certain information, we can assure the citizens that she is to unload her rich cargo of Teas, Silks, China, Nankins, &c. here; by which the city and country will be supplied with those articles on moderate terms."[8]

The mercantile house engaged to sell the cargo was that of Constable, Rucker & Company of New York, consisting of William Constable, John Rucker, Robert Morris, and the latter's close friend and associate, Gouverneur Morris, of New York. The partnership had been formed on June 10, 1784, under the name of "William Constable & Company," each of the three original partners—Constable and the two Morrises—putting up a working capital of £5,000 Pennsylvania currency for a term of seven years.[9] Dublin-born William Constable had been raised in Schenectady, New York, and was educated in Ireland, only to return during the first months of the Revolutionary War and engage in mercantile pursuits in Philadelphia. After a term of service in the Continental Army, during part of which he was the aide-de-camp of the young Marquis de Lafayette, Constable returned to Philadelphia as a partner in the house of Seagrove & Constable. Upon its dissolution in 1783, Constable removed his base of operations to New York City.[10]

Advertisements for the "India Goods" imported in the *Empress of China* began in the New York newspapers on May 23, 1785 and continued in strength into July, many of the same being repeated again and again. Numerous merchants became involved, and among those who advertised were:

Constable, Rucker & Company, No. 39 Great Dock Street: Gunpowder, Hyson, Souchong, Singlo, and Bohea teas, chinaware, silks, muslins, and nankeens.

Robert C. Livingston, No. 13 Great Dock Street: silks, padufoys, satins, lutestrings, "Taffities," etc.

Josiah Shippey & Company, No. 43 Little Dock Street, corner of Coenties Slip: "A few chests of Hyson Tea of the best quality, by the chest," breakfast and tea china, china bowls, salad dishes "in small packages, which will be sold by the package. A few pieces of Silks, India Silk Handkerchiefs, Sattin Vests and Breeches." In another ad: India silks, India handkerchiefs, embroidered Nankeens, readymade vests and breeches, bamboo and wangee walking sticks, Hyson tea by the chest, sago, Batavia arrack.

67. William Constable (1752-1803) was born and educated in Ireland but was raised in the colony of New York. He became a Philadelphia merchant, yet at the end of the American Revolution he transferred his place of business to New York City. There, he entered into partnership with Gouverneur Morris, Robert Morris, and John Rucker. The firm of Constable, Rucker & Company was given the charge of selling the *Empress of China*'s cargo and ultimately bought the vessel herself for a second China voyage.

Craigie, Wainwright & Company, No. 37 in Wall Street and Corner of Hanover Square: Gunpowder and Hyson tea, sold wholesale and retail.

Barnes & Livingston, No. 2 Crugar's Wharf: "Elegant assortments of fine Tea Table China in setts; The very best of Nankeens by the piece or dozen; Elegant Silk Waistcoat Patterns, embroidered; Silk Handkerchiefs, Taffeties; Lute Strings, Muslins, fans &c; Padre Souchong, Padre Sougey, Padre Peco, Hyson, Souchong, Fine Gunpowder, and Bohea Teas, of the first quality. N.B. Reasonable allowance made to those who purchase to sell again."

Maria S. Morton: complete table and tea sets, blue and white and enamelled half pint basins and saucers; blue and white breakfast and common cups and saucers; blue and white bowls of different sizes; Best Gunpowder, Hyson, and Souchong teas "by the chest, half doz or smaller quantities, Two very curious small Tea Chests, All of which will be sold low. Jersey currency taken as payment."

Smith Richards, 28 Corner Old Slip and Little Dock Street: Fine Hyson, Souchong, Congo, and Bohea teas.

Fears that Thomas Randall and his East India goods would arrive in the *Pallas* within a matter of a few weeks prompted several early shipments of goods from the *Empress of China* to the Philaldelphia market. As it turned out, the *Pallas*, Captain John O'Donnell, manned by natives of China and Bengal, arrived on August 9, 1785—neither at Philadelphia nor at New York but, rather, at Baltimore. Sale of the cargo would not take place until the beginning of October and then only at Baltimore and by "public vendue."[11] But no one knew that in late May and early June.

Purser John White Swift seems to have been possessed of a pessimistic nature. In Canton, he had considered the ginseng sales only "so-so"; now, in New York, their tea was a "dull sale."

> Dear Papa—
>
> I write to you by Capt Green who goes to Philada. We are not yet unloaded owing to one or other delay, & of Course I am not discharged—Next Week & not before shall I have the pleasure of seeing you. Company almost distracts us, the Novelty of an India man has brought the City to see us.
>
> Our Tea is but dull sale. We have ship'd some to Philada by the Vessel I have sent some very fine to Andw Bunner to sell for me, some I have sold here at only 10/Pct, and my remainder I intend sending a little at a time to Philada . . . however anxious I am, but I must arrange all my business first—Give my love to Molly— The piece of Silk I have brought her, my Mother & Sister admires. . . .[12]

Within two weeks, Swift was finished with the ship's business and ready to go home. Again, writing to his father:

I recd your letter informing me of the safe arrival of my Mother. I had previous to it, sent my trunk via Burlington, I hope it has arrived. Mr Green Jr will send this to you. I have ship'd in the *New York Packett* Capt Wade a Cask of Arrack & some Tea China &c for the Farm, & a Trunk of Cloths, sugar Candy, sweet meats &c. John Green has the Accts and will send them with his fathers things to Bensalem, as soon as they arrive at Philadelphia. I am at last clear of the Ship, & will make the best of my way to see you, as soon as I arrange a few matters of my own. Tea is very dull sale, I brought none but the first quality . . . I propose leaving New York a friday Evening with Mrs Green.[13]

The first part of the *Empress of China*'s cargo arrived in Philadelphia on the eighth of June and was received by Peter Whiteside & Company. Everyone had agreed that no matter who sold what, the proceeds would go into a General Account for later division in order that no one owner could be accused of taking advantage of another.[14] Other shipments followed in the sloops *Experiment*, *Polly Bird*, *Sally*, and the *New York Packet*, which together conveyed from New York to Philadelphia over 1,000 chests of tea, twelve of cottons, eight chests and three bales of Nankeens, four bales of muslins, and fifty-two chests of porcelain. Five further bales of Nankeens jostled their way southward via the stagecoach line.[15]

John Holker, his personal honor and financial credibility at stake, owing to the debts of Daniel Parker & Company, informed Thomas Fitzsimons, as its Trustee, at the end of June that he intended to settle accounts by turning over portions of the company's share of the cargo. "You'll be so kind," he cautioned, "as to take my bills from them when you deliver up the goods in Payment & also to take a discharge from all claims against me. . . ."[16]

Wrote Fitzsimons in a memorandum to himself: "I was very soon after applyd to by some of the Creditors, to whom I read or shewed this letter— on the 6th of July some of the Creditors met together . . . on the 7 July . . . Kuhn & Risberg who were Creditors applyd & Received a part of the Goods— on the 11th July Adam Zantzinger Received his part of the 12 Kaign & Altmore Recd theirs & on the 13 Mordecai Lewis Recd a part as Creditors. . . ."[17]

The case of Mordecai Lewis & Company seems to have been fairly typical. Essentially, being heavy creditors for the *Empress of China* venture, it could claim a lien on a fraction of the ship and cargo: the company, therefore, had become a shareholder. It was not alone; most of the other significant creditors had, too. Mordecai Lewis & Company's nearly final tally with John Holker went as follows:

```
                    Amot of our Share in the Ship Empress
                    of China & Cargo                    £2125.
                    Our proportion of Profit             179.13 [torn]
                                                        2304.13.8
1785
July  13    Recd 9 Chests Bohea Tea Amot                 418.10.
      15        200 ps Nankeens        9/                 90.
      22        410 ps   ditto          "               184.10
Augt  4         390 ps   ditto          "               175.10
Octr  17         10 Chests Bohea Tea                     465.
      22         20       ditto                          934.1  [torn]
                 10       ditto at New York              455.   [torn]

                 28 Chests 1st Hyson Tea                1190.
                 12   do     2nd    do                   398.2
                 deduct our Interest therein            4311.16. 8
                 as above Sates                         2304.13. 8
                 Remains to be carried to the Credit
                 of Mr Holkers general Accot 22d Octr 1785  2007. 3.
Decr  15    Recd 17 Chests 1st Hyson Tea    711.0.10
                  8  do    2d    ditto      265.8. 0      976. 8.10
                                                        £2983.11. [torn]
                    Errors Excepted
June 1. 1788        Mordecai Lewis & Co 18
```

Very soon, the merchandise arriving from New York began to go on sale.
One such place was to be found in the vicinity of Elfreth's Alley, Philadelphia:

> CHINA WARE, of the newest Festoon Patterns,
> Equally useful as ornamental, and lately imported
> in the Ship *Empress of China*, from Canton. Now
> opening for SALE on the west side of Front-Street,
> between Arch and Race-Streets, A few blue and
> white long Dining Table Sets; Tea Table sets, Cof-
> fee ditto ditto, of the best enamell'd China; some
> half dozens of Cups and Saucers of pencil'd and
> enamell'd common China, and a few nests of blue
> and white Nankeen or Stone China Bowls, on very
> reasonable terms, for cash only.
> July 16, 1785.19

From the very beginning of the China scheme, it had always been the
intention of the shareholders to sell not only the cargo but also the *Empress
of China* herself immediately after her return to the United States, provided
she had not already been disposed of through LeCouteulx & Cie. in Paris.
Despite the shifting ranks of proprietors, the Parker fiasco, the debts, the

68. Philadelphia's Arch Street Ferry was one of the city's busiest waterfront areas. To such docks as this came the Oriental goods from the *Empress of China*, transshipped from New York for the local market. Engraving by William and Thomas Birch, 1800.

risks, and the pervasive growth of ill-disguised animosities between personalities involved, the venture did clear the profit of between twenty-five and thirty percent already mentioned. All the same, too much had happened for the same combination of men to entertain thoughts about working in concert again to send the ship back to the China coast. Those who had the inclination to dabble in the trade again preferred to go it alone or to ally themselves with other persons. As a result, and in accordance with their first plan, the *Empress of China* was prepared for sale.

> The Ship *Empress of China* as she arrived from Canton will be SOLD at the Coffee-House on Saturday, the second of July. She is copper-bottomed, scarcely two years old, built by the celebrated Peck of Boston and so well found, that she may be fitted for a voyage to India with small expense. The remarkable short passage that she made from China

& the good order in which she delivered her cargo prove the superior excellency of her sailing and construction.

N.B. A reasonable credit will be given on good security. Her inventory to be seen at Constable, Rucker & Co., New York, June 11, 1785.[20]

The purchaser in the end was Constable, Rucker & Company itself. During the next six months, as starry-eyed merchants in New York and elsewhere began to lay their own grand plans for entry into the glorious China trade, the *Empress of China* was repaired, refitted, and reprovisioned for a second voyage to Canton. On February 1, 1786, she was warped into the stream of the East River from Wells Wharf, and spread her sails anew for China: William Bell, supercargo, and Captain John Green, commander.[21]

XVI

The Long Limbs of Litigation

Even during the time the *Empress of China* was sailing on her second voyage to the Far East—even for years afterwards—the settlement of the first voyage's accounts continued to haunt those who had been duped and nearly ruined by Daniel Parker. Samuel Shaw and John Holker had been the two touched most seriously: Shaw, who died at sea off the Cape of Good Hope on May 30, 1794, never did receive the satisfaction to which he had been entitled; while John Holker, the late supercargo's survivor by twenty-eight years, continued all that time to fume at the ill-treatment he felt he had suffered at the hands of his partners in Daniel Parker & Company.

When Shaw returned to New York from China in May 1785 he had two strikes against him, both of which derived from misplaced trust in Parker and culpability for following dubious oral commands: the matter of the missing specie and the competitive lading of additional Oriental goods into the ship *Pallas*. To the ordinary citizen not personally concerned with the venture, Shaw personified the heroic enterprise it represented. His long letter of May 19, 1785 to Secretary of Foreign Affairs John Jay evoked a generous response wholly typical of the public mood: "That Congress feel a peculiar satisfaction in the successful issue of this first effort of the citizens of America to establish a direct trade with China, which does so much honor to its undertakers and conductors."[1] The language may sound strange to the modern ear but the sentiments were sincere. By the beginning of the new year, despite what could have been a bright future under his old friend Knox in the War Department, Shaw angled for another option and was "honored by Congress with their commission of Consul at Canton, when Mr. Randall also received that of Vice-consul."[2] No salaries, fees, or emoluments of office accompanied the positions. "You see this business is to cost Congress nothing," Shaw chuckled to Winthrop Sargent, "but Randall and I hope nevertheless to turn it to very handsome account."[3]

On February 4, 1786, three days after John Green's second sortie from New York to Canton began, Shaw and Randall also sailed from New York, this time in the ship *Hope*, Captain James Magee, bound for Canton by way of Batavia.

Impending litigation, however, hung heavily over his head even as he sailed. "I think I mentioned to you," he had written the previous autumn to Sargent, "the circumstances of some deficiencies on the part of Mr Parker in fitting out the *Empress of China*. His affairs, and consequently those of Holker his partner, being exceedingly embarrassed, he detained twenty three hundred dollars of the money that was to have been put on board notwithstanding the bills of lading were figures for an amount in which this sum was included. Parker mentioned this matter and told me that he would make the necessary entries in his books, so that justice should be done to the other owners and I be borne harmless from any consequences that might ensue,— and that he wished me not to mention the matter to Captain Green. I could not object to this, or any other measure Mr Parker might have thought proper to take, as he had given me my instructions in the name of the owners, and I knew no person but him in the business. Besides, there was something in his manners that stilled suspicion to sleep—I had been conversant only with the honest part of mankind and I even omitted taking a receipt or any kind of written voucher for the transactions.

"On our arrival at Canton, Randall and I took the necessary precautions to ascertain the exact sum of money on board, and that there was no more than what was set forth in the declaration by us made, subscribed and attested under oath, on the spot. This we thought necessary to prevent any difficulty which might arise from the want of a receipt, in case of any accident to Mr Parker or to me. Since the return of the ship, all this is corroborated by the certificate of oath of Mr Johnson, who was book keeper and cashier to Mr Parker, and had himself counted and put up the money sent to Canton— Mr Morris, as owner of half the ship and cargo, has obliged Holker, the partner of Parker, to account with him for this deficiency, and one hundred percent more as profits that should have been made thereon. Holker looks to me to make him good, and refers to Parker, who he says might make me whole—I refuse this, and a suit is commenced against me, for the deficiencies and damages.

"Mr Morris says I must stand the suit, and has entered bail for me to that effect. My lawyers, Lewis and Wilson, tell me all I have to do is prove the facts—Mr Parker was my master—I had no control over him—and he alone must be answerable for his own acts—that the law is clearly in my favor. They have given me this as their opinion, in writing, and subscribed their names to it. In equity and honor, the facts are sufficiently established—and I am taking such measures as will amply confirm them in law—What a disgrace to mankind that these are not one and the same principle! Let us quit the cursed subject—I must patiently wait the event. . . ."[4]

The flight of Parker to Europe, together with the appointment of Thomas Fitzsimons as trustee to settle the affairs of Daniel Parker & Company, had hugely complicated Shaw's original agreements with the owners (see following pages).

To Morris and Fitzsimons, he sent a proposal by which an equitable distribution might be made:

Gentlemen

As the division of the return cargo of the ship *Empress of China* has been made between the owners, each taking such part as belonged to him, a sale of the whole has not and cannot take place upon the principles of the agreement made with me by the owners,—and as some other mode of settlement must consequently be adopted, I do myself the honor to submit the following to your consideration,

To the amount of the homeward cargo, 76566½ dollars,
that a centum be added, which will make the sum of 153133

Also, the sum for which the ship has
been sold since her return   6250
                                                           ─────── 159383

From this sum, deduct the outfits of the ship
    and cargo from America   120000
        Also, a further sum, for the
balance of wages due the ship's company, duties,
and other contingencies on the ship and cargo
since her return   10000
                                                           ─────── 130000
                                                                   ───────
                                                                   29.383
                                                                   ───────

By the aforegoing statement there appears to be a profit on the voyage of 29383 dollars, one tenth of which, as stipulated in the agreement, is for the supercargoes.

1784	To Cash paid the following sums—vizt		Dollars 720^{ths}
from	Disbursements of the ship as per account of		
September	particulars	2309.360	
to 25 Dec,	Contingent expences for the factory at Canton		
	as per particulars	315.180	
	Cost of China for factory use, not included in		
	contingent expences	23. 54	
	Expence of merchandize including measurage		
	of the ship, pilot charges and rent of the		
	factory, as per account of particulars	4858.680	
	Comprador's accounts of supplies to the ship at		
	Wampo and for the factory at Canton, from		
	September last, including stores for the		
	passage to America	3591.542	
	Compensation to the officers, for the loss they		
	sustained by their ginseng being included		
	in the sales of the cargo—as per account		
	sales of that article and their receipts	1124.360	
	Commission, 2½ per cent, paid the house of		
	Desmoulins Terrier & Co. on the sales		
	of the Ginseng and on the purchases of		
	teas, porcelain, and Nankins, as per		
	their account current	3242.268	
	Amount of Invoice of the return Cargo		
1785	Expences at Canton after closing Desmoulins	76560.255	
	accounts, and homeward contingences to 11		
	May	671. —	
			92696.539
	Balance due the Owners		421.571
			93118.390

Dr Owners of Ship Empress of China   —   (Philadelphia Account—

To allowance for commission, by agreement, ten per cent on the
profits, estimated as follows—vizt

Cargo cost per invoice	76560.225		
One pipe Wine returned	256.584		
Balance of Canton account	421.571		
	77238.660		
Doubled by agreement, as			
supposed amount of sales	77238.660		
	154477.600		
Sales of the Ship at New York	6250.	160727.600	
Deduct-Ship and cargo outwards, as per			
agreement	120000		
Allowed for homeward expenses,			
duties &c	10000	130000. —	
	Profits	30727.600	
	One tenth of which is		3072.564

		Dollars—720ᵗʰˢ
By amount of the sales of the cargo from America as per		
particular account of each article	vizt	
Genseng 60238.360		
Do 954.	61192.360	
Cordage	7098.160	
Tar and Turpentine	449.360	
Lead	2736.540	
Tin	1071	
Tin ware	102	
Iron wire—lace & binding	90	
Cloths	609	
Wine	1138	
Furs	167	74653.700

One pipe Madeira Wine OEC. to go back to America
One pipe Brandy
One pipe Jamaica rum) taken for ship's account
Boards and Plank—Part taken for ship's account, and the remainder
                  sold by Capt Green, for which he is to account
                  with the owners on the ship's return ———
By Cash received from the ship 17700 dollars. In the invoice and
   bills of lading 20000 are said to have been put on board,
   but sufficient vouchers are produced to prove there
   were no more than seventeen thousand seven hundred

	17700.
By profits on old dollars	25. 50
By cash received of Capt Green for sundries he sold belonging to the ship	577.360
By cash for sundries credited in Mr Shaw's account of homeward contingencies	02.
By an error in charging a watch lost in Mr Shaw's factory contingencies	60.
	93118.390

---

in account with Samuel Shaw   Cʳ

By balance due them on Canton account	421.571		
advance thereon—double	421.571		
		843.422	
Balance due S. Shaw		2229.142	
			3072.564

Philadelphia 28 Octo. 1785.
Errors excepted
S. Shaw[5]

All things taken into consideration, I hope it will not be found that I have over-rated the value of the return cargo; and in the allowance of 10000 dollars for contingencies &c, it is presumed that every expence must be fully comprehended. I shall be happy if this idea of a principal on which a settlement may be founded should meet your approbation—if it does not, I will acquiesce in such an one as you shall be pleased to advance.[6]

During mid-January, not long before his departure in the *Hope*, Shaw travelled to Philadelphia again in an attempt to conclude the business. "An idea that a compromise might be affected with the ship *Empress of China*," he wrote to Winthrop Sargent, "induced me, at the pressing insistances of my friends, to go their again. It has terminated, agreeably to my expectations, *in nothing*. I have therefore procured bail and the law is to decide. I could curse the author of this trouble to me—but I have not time for such foundless employment."[7]

Daniel Parker, ever since his lightning defection from Philadelphia in mid-summer 1784, all the while had been busying himself in London laying the groundwork for better and even more grandiose commercial fantasies than ever before. "I do believe that I shall succeed here," he crowed to his confidant, Dr. Andrew Craigie.[8] Parker was always preening about such things.

Craigie, formerly Apothecary General of the Continental Army, had been one of the members of the Society of the Cincinnati who had accompanied the *Empress of China* out of New York Harbor as far as Sandy Hook when she sailed on her first voyage. His and Parker's friendship had gone back many years to their common background in and around Boston. Craigie was an apothecary, financier, and speculator in lands, particularly those west of the Allegheny Mountains. His friendship with Parker was so firm that he offered to represent his American interests while Parker remained abroad. Correspondence between Parker in London, Amsterdam, or Paris and New York, where Craigie was then situated, flourished for the better part of a decade.

Parker's schemes in London, which he never specified in correspondence to Craigie but instead entrusted for verbal transmission by his brother, Dr. Benjamin Parker, and other allies shuttling between Europe and North America, involved, among other things, a trade in tobacco through Amsterdam and a plan which sounded suspiciously as if he intended to relieve a member of the British nobility of a sum precisely equal to Parker's own, current requirements.

Ever the dreamer and the purveyor of hollow optimism, Parker's deals rose and fell as the moon and stars. Most of the time, he was flat broke yet

69. Andrew Craigie (1754-1819), apothecary, financier, and speculator, was born in Boston.
A close friend of Daniel Parker, Craigie represented his interests in America after Parker's
defection to Europe. Parker, conversely, acted for a time as the London agent of the Scioto
Company, a speculation in Ohio lands in which both Craigie and William Duer were
interested. Portrait by Archibald Robertson (1765-1835).

always remained supremely confident that the next business venture would resolve his present embarrassments. Correspondence was not to be sent directly to him but under separate cover to John Appleton at the New York Coffee House, London, or to Grigsby's Coffee House near the Royal Exchange, or to several other addresses that changed from time to time.

"I'm sensible of the necessity of my presence to oppose the Calumnies & Aspersions that envy, disappointment & dispair will falsely circulate," he wrote to Craigie on New Year's Day 1785, "let what will be said (& God knows, the Unfortunate are very rarely excused by common report from the worst of Crimes)."[9]

By late summer 1785, legal probes launched by Holker and Morris in Philadelphia penetrated the wild North Atlantic as far as London and gave Daniel Parker a bad turn. "I beg you," he wrote on August 20 to an unspecified correspondent in America, possibly brother Benjamin, "to deliver *my* books to *no* person but Doctr Craigie, in this I intreat you not to deviate— I perceive that if the Books are in the State of New York they will be taken by the officer & placed in the hands of the Trustees who may be appointed to settle my affairs—to prevent this you will not bring or suffer them to be brought into that State—I pray you to continue possession of them untill my return, when you shall be paid amply for your Services by me—If you must leave them, Dr. Craigie is the only person to whom I would have them delivered."[10]

Samuel Shaw had written to Parker in November 1785, one supposes, for the lack of the letter itself, to request exoneration of blame for the missing specie. "It is with unspeakable satisfaction," Parker replied at the beginning of 1786, "that I find myself in a situation not only to answer your letter of the Novr last but to give you the aid you require and this notwithstanding your belief that I had taken with me a property in States Securities was entirely without foundation for I declare to you upon my Honor and before God, that I did not bring with me or in any manner secure to myself any Property of any *kind whatsoever* excepting One hundred and twenty pounds I brought with me for my expences . . . I pray you my dear friend to keep the Contents of this Letter entirely to yourself and not to communicate to anyone that you know of any connection or acquaintance between me and the Gentleman who will deliver this to you. . . ."[11]

Parker loved secrecy and to sow misleading information. It kept people off balance; that way no one could really tell what he was feeling, thinking or planning. No clearer example of his furtive mind can be found than in a letter written to Andrew Craigie from Amsterdam in early February 1786.

Within a month, he claimed, predicting success of yet another of his pipe-dreams, "I shall be able to send orders for the payment of all Demands against me in America, the person who will be charged with this business will have orders to converse with you & I *pray* you to keep *all secret* untill he arrives, this I must injoin on you in the most positive terms—notwithstanding the malicious representations that my enemies in America have made both here & in London, yet I have formed *the best* Connections in both places . . . I shall not return to America before all demands against me are paid & Holker & Duer settled with—but this I would not have known, as it is my wish to have them expect me in America early in the Spring, & this you will en-deavour to have reported."[12]

Neither orders to Craigie to pay the demands nor payment itself was ever more forthcoming than intentions and promises. As the year wore on, Parker pressed Craigie to see what compromise could be struck: "I wish I could obtain from Holker & Duer an offer of a sum, which they would take for a final settlement of the affairs of DP & Co . . . Will you sound Duer on such a plan? & let me know the answer. . . ."[13]

"My wishes are," he wrote the next month, "to offer Holker & Duer a fixed sum to exonerate me intirely from all demands whatever in consequence of the concerns of DP & Co, & to secure me against all engagements of DP or DP & Co on Bills of exch'ge, notes of hand, or any other demands which are in their possession, or that they have secured the payment of, & such sum as they should agree to receive should be applied to the payment of demands that yet remain unpaid if such there are, or if they have assumed & paid the whole of such demands, in that case the money should be paid to them . . . be assured my good friend that I shall have property enough in a short time, & the connections I have in Europe are in all respects of the best kind, prospects are very pleasing, the more so, as I believe that I shall be able to retire *wholly* from business with a satisfactory independency."[14]

The realization of this "independency" was no closer in May 1787 than it had been nearly a year before. Just then, he received alarming news from Craigie: Holker was threatening to seek Parker's arrest in London. "The instant I can get possession of any property," Parker replied by return of post, "I will come forward for a settlement. This I wish you to assure H[olker] & to know decidedly if possible, what steps he has taken or intends to take—if he will agree not to arrest either my person or property for two years, & to have such agreement legally confirmed—I will not shrink back in any degree whatever, but will meet every demand & settle them properly, which at that time I shall, if not molested, have property enough to do . . . at all events let me know if they have sent orders here or to Holland to arrest my person—untill I receive this information I shall keep myself as much as possible out of the way. . . ."[15] He sincerely wished that Thomas Fitzsimons could be replaced as Trustee of Daniel Parker & Company's affairs. "I greatly fear," he had written earlier to Craigie, "that the proceeds of the *Empress of China* has been very unjustly disposed of & the Solidity of Mr Fitzsimons is very much questioned in this Country."[16]

More than a year and a half after Samuel Shaw had sailed for the second time to China, and still remained in the East, the litigation pending between John Holker and himself came to a head. Thomas Randall, on Shaw's behalf, solicited the assistance of Henry Knox to obtain a deposition from another old confidant of Parker's, George Joy, affirming Parker's removal of the $2,300 in specie.[17] To date, neither Shaw nor Randall had received as much as sixpence for their services as supercargoes in the *Empress of China*. The specie remained the bone of contention.

Early in November 1787, the cases of Holker *vs* Shaw and of Shaw *vs* Holker were heard simultaneously in the Court of Common Pleas. The actions began at four o'clock in the afternoon and continued for seven hours, when the Court was adjourned and the jury charged to return its verdict at three o'clock the following afternoon. When that time came, it had not been able to agree; nor had it by eleven o'clock on the morning of the third day. Eight members of the jury were in favor of ordering Shaw to pay Holker $2,300 plus interest; the remaining four thought that amount ought to be doubled![18] With no apparent possibility of agreement, the jury was dismissed and the action was declared a mistrial.

Soon afterwards, Shaw's attorney, William Lewis of Philadelphia, drafted a statement in Parker's name, which he hoped Parker could be induced to sign:

I certify that I was part Owner of and also Agent for fitting out the Ship *Empress of China* which in February 1784 sailed from New York for Canton in China under the command of Captain Green, That previous to the sd Ships Departure as aforesaid and after the bills of lading were signed I was under the disagreeable necessity of withdrawing the sum of twenty three hundred Dollars for the use and benefit of the owners without which their Interest would have been materially injured—In justice to myself I must declare that this was done entirely for the sake & Benefit of the Owners and that at the time of taking out the sd 2300 Dollars I had the most moral certainty of replacing them previous to the sailing of the sd Ship but was disappointed.[19]

"If Mr Parker will subscribe the Certificate," Lewis explained to Henry

Knox, "I think it will effectually serve Mr Shaw whose case is a cruel hard one. If Mr Parker can add to the Certificate that his necessities to take out this money arose from Mr Holker not having advanced his part of the money to be shipped or to answer any Demands against the concern I think it must make an End of the Business and therefore I wish you to write him in the most pressing manner to add to the Certificate a few words to this purpose if such is really the case. . . ."[20]

Nothing more on the subject was heard from Parker. Two years passed, during which time Shaw returned to America and made plans to go back to China yet a third time. No compensation for the first trip had ever been seen in all that time. On February 27, 1790, Shaw again wrote to Parker who still remained expatriated abroad. It was a long, long epistle but summarized admirably the years of apoplectic frustration that first voyage in the *Empress of China* had caused him.

"After so long an interval [it read] it is painful to me, at this late period, to be under the necessity of troubling you on the affairs of the late ship *Empress of China*. You well know that the owners of that ship not only refused paying Mr Randall and me our consideration for transacting her business, upwards of three thousand dollars, but that they also instituted an account against us for 2300 dollars, appropriated by you from their funds committed to us—and for 884 dollars, which, by your order on us in New York, we paid Captain Green on his arrival in Canton. On this amount 3184 dollars, they charged a cent damages, making the whole Six thousand (6368) three hundred sixty eight dollars, and instead of paying us our balance, passed it to the credit of this account, and sued us at law for the remainder.

"Of all the particulars of this business I acquainted you very fully in two letters towards the close of the year 1785, in a firm belief that you would extricate us as soon as possible from every embarrassment; especially as the most unlimited confidence in your integrity and honor had occasioned us to be thus involved. Your answer, avowing the whole of the circumstances and promising to indemnify us, did not arrive till after I sailed a second time for China. On receipt of that letter, Mr George Joy, your agent, offered to pay to my good friend General Knox one thousand dollars on said account, which the General declined receiving, as the suit was then defending and was expected to terminate in our favor—but the action was lost, as the jury could not agree before the term expired, eight being for and four against us.

"In the mean time, the affair remains unsettled—my friends have become my bail—a new suit is commenced—and after almost five years, I am a third time going to China, without having received a single dollar of the balance for my services the first time. On my arrival last July, Mr Andrew Craigie, your agent, told me that the business should be closed some how or other before I again left this country, but nothing definitive has yet been done. He has at length advised that I shall draw a bill on you for three thousand dollars, towards liquidating this account, which, under certain stipulations with my friends General Knox and Mr N Hoffman of New York, he will endorse. I accordingly make the draft, and conjure you, by every thing that is honest and sacred among men, that you duly honor it. How far the total neglect of this business by you, since your acknowledging yourself responsible for it, and the proposal of Mr Joy for paying 1000 dollars can be reconciled with your acknowledged goodness of heart, I am at a loss to determine. The world, by which I mean a few people only who know the transaction, are astonished at it—and more so, that I, who with Randall, have been so much injured, still continue to be your advocate. They do not hesitate to charge you with knavery and me with folly. Mr Parker, say they, is now a man of property and *ought to be made to pay*—a suit therefore should be immediately commenced against him in England, and the whole affair, with all its attendant and consequent circumstances, be published to the world.

"This is the opinion also and advice of my lawyers, but I wish to terminate the matter amicably. Gen. Knox and Mr Hoffman, my very good friends, have full powers to act for me in all cases, more especially in the present, and have in their possession every paper and voucher relating to it. They as well as I, have a regard for your reputation, but their welfare is now interested. They are my bails in the just, and must in their own defence, pursue the matter in England, in the most rigourous and public manner, unless your payment of my draft in favor of Mr Craigie should prevent. For Heaven's sake, Mr Parker, my once good friend, and as such let me still consider you, do not, my good friend, suffer this matter to have any further consequences. Consider the great, very great injury it has already been to me and to Mr Randall—reflect that our sufferings have proceeded solely from my unbounded reliance on the rectitude and honesty of your character—and do not longer delay doing us justice. Compensation for the distress of mind it has occasioned me you cannot make nor do I ask it. Be you just and I will be contented and so God speed you, as you deal with your friend / S. Shaw."[21]

Ultimately, Parker provided Shaw with a statement of indemnification, but it bore only Parker's signature; the mass of it was composed by and in the handwriting of Shaw. Signed and sealed in London at the very end of December 1791, it must have arrived in the United States at almost the same moment Shaw himself came home to court Hannah, daughter of the pros-

70. The *Alliance* was sold out of the Continental service during the summer of 1785, when she was purchased by Robert Morris and converted for use as a large China trader. After a relatively undistinguished merchant career, she was laid up and went to pieces on Petty's Island in the Delaware River.

perous Boston merchant William Phillips, whom he married in August 1792, only twenty-one months before he succumbed at sea off Cape Town to a long illness of the liver. The indemnification read:

Whereas the Ship *Empress of China*, commanded by Captain John Green, did on the 22 day of February 1784, sail from New York in North America, on a voyage to Canton in China, under the direction of Samuel Shaw, as agent or supercargo for said voyage, who received his instructions from me, as one of the proprietors in said expedition, and agent for all the others. And whereas in the bills of lading for said cargo the sum of Twenty thousand Spanish dollars was included as being part thereof,

Now be it known that by reason of my not having been supplied by the owners of said ship with a sum sufficient to complete the said Twenty thousand dollars, and not having the ability of myself to do it, no more than seventeen thousand seven hundred dollars were put on board said ship; and that the deficiency of twenty three hundred dollars was owing entirely to the aforegoing causes—and that under the idea till the moment of the ship's departure, that I should be furnished with the means of making up such a deficiency, the said bills of lading remained unaltered, and the ship proceeded to Sea on her voyage with only seventeen thousand seven hundred dollars, anything in the said bills of lading to the contrary notwithstanding.

In solemn attestation of the foregoing, I do hereby set my hand and seal, in London, this thirtieth day of December one thousand seven hundred and ninety one

(signed)   Danl Parker   (SEAL)

Signed, and
sealed in presence
of Michl Mahony[22]

Andrew Craigie, all the while, had been attempting to resolve the differences between Parker and John Holker and William Duer. On October 21, 1788, he had been able to report apparent success.

"I am just returned from Philadelphia," he informed Parker from New York, "where I concluded an Agreement between Holker and the Creditors of the Company there . . . I have not time by this Opportunity to give you a detail of my Negotiations nor of the Motives & reasons which led me to put your signature to the present instrument—what I have done has been from a conviction that your interest would be essentially served & secured in the place agreed on. If I am mistaken the fault is my own."[23]

Craigie had done well for Parker, faced as he had been with mushrooming hostilities and an incredibly complex tangle of conflicting financial statements, incomplete records, and volatile political considerations. "I had the pleasure before I left Philadelphia," he told Parker, "of drinking your health with Mr Holker & the Creditors—it was Mr. Holker's toast."[24]

John Holker would have done well not to have toasted Daniel Parker at all, for as late as 1813 Parker still had neglected to settle the accounts.[25] Holker's wrath remained unabated throughout the intervening decades, but the documentation leading to the definitive proofs necessary for settlement had become virtually impossible to obtain. In 1813, Holker was sixty-eight years of age and had but nine years of life left to him. When it all began, in 1783, he had been but thirty-eight. Robert Morris wound up in a Philadelphia debtor's prison and died in 1806. Duer had been committed to debtor's prison, too. He died in 1799. Parker seemed to float like a disembodied spirit through thick and thin, his fate as intangible as his strange, twisted personality. Shaw went to his reward in 1794, at the age of thirty-

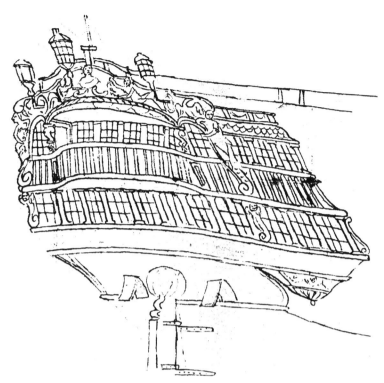

71. In November 1787, Samuel Shaw and Thomas Randall contracted for an 800-ton China trader. Designed by William Hackett, the architect of the *Alliance*, and built at Germantown, Quincy, Massachusetts, the ship *Massachusetts*—the stern of which is illustrated here—sailed from Boston to Canton in March 1790. Upon opening hatches in China, however, it was discovered that "the inside of the ship was covered with blue mould an inch thick." An offer by the Danes to purchase her was quickly accepted.

nine. Captain John Green followed him two years later. William Constable died in 1803, Dr. Robert Johnston in 1808, Thomas Fitzsimons and Thomas Randall in 1811, and John White Swift in 1812. No one with personal knowledge of the total financial ramifications of the *Empress of China*'s maiden voyage remained save Holker himself, Andrew Craigie, and the incorrigible Parker. Clearly, John Holker was finally outnumbered and his case became forever moot.

As for the *Empress of China*, Constable, Rucker & Company had bought her in July 1785 for a paltry $6250 and had dispatched her back to China, Captain John Green again in command. She sailed from New York on February 1, 1786, returned on May 4, 1787, and was again sold.[26]

Now known as the *Edgar*, within three months she sailed to Bordeaux in

France on a routine commercial voyage, but during her return passage to America in the winter season of 1787/88, she was so wracked by the stress of storm and wave that a plan to send her to China a third time had to be abandoned.[27] The old *Empress of China*, which by this time had been given the lowly condition rating of "E-1" by Lloyd's of London, was reduced to a trader plying the waters between New York and Belfast, Ireland.[28]

On March 13, 1790, she was reregistered in New York as the *Clara*, Captain Mark Collins commanding; John Shaw, a merchant of that city, the owner. Her end was near.[29]

On Washington's Birthday 1791, seven years to the day that she turned down the East River, her yards manned, and saluted the Battery as the first American ship ever to attempt the trade with the Chinese, the *Clara* became a total wreck and sank off the harbor of Dublin, Ireland. All hands were saved.[30]

APPENDICES

APPENDIX A

A *Fragmentary Abstract Log of the*
EMPRESS OF CHINA

In Record Group 27 at the National Archives, Washington, DC, may be found the following fragmentary abstract log. The original, the whereabouts of which has not been discovered, evidently was copied during the late 1840's or early 1850's for Lieutenant Matthew Fontaine Maury, USN, Superintendent of the Depot of Charts and Instruments of the Navy, in Washington. Maury's countrywide project of abstracting details from hundreds of ships' logbooks and journals, past and present, led to the production of his remarkable and innovative Wind and Current charts.

The entries for March 17 and April 1, the first mentioning the ship's doctor and the second the need to make spruce beer for the sick, strongly suggests that the author of the piece was Andrew Caldwell, Surgeon's Mate.

The log—perhaps more precisely a journal—adds much to other known accounts by John Green and Samuel Shaw. Owing to the complexity of the abstract's format, the notations of daily positions, winds, and the like, have here been tabulated separately on page 257.

FEBRUARY 1784

Sunday, 22. Weighed anchor and made sail out of the East River in company with 3 ships and one brig. As the ship passed the Fort, a multitude of spectators who were collected on the Battery and wharves gave her three cheers. Capt. Green ordered the ship to be manned and returned three cheers, then saluted the Fort with thirteen guns, which was returned with an equal number. The Capt. gave a parting gun and made more sail. At 5 PM anchored in Sandy Hook Bay.

Monday, 23. Wind light. At 9 AM got under way. At 1 PM thermometer 27°. Friends took leave. Gave them 3 cheers, which they returned. Then Captain saluted them with 9 guns. At 8 o'clock (PM) much cloud with some snow. Winds light and the night dark. At 3 (AM) a fresh breeze from the NW. Ship standing to the South and East, a rough sea.

Tuesday, 24. At 6 (PM) lighthouse on Sandy Hook bore NW, distance 12 miles.

Wednesday, 25. First part fresh gales and cloudy. Latter part, moderate winds and cloudy weather. Set topgallant sails. Saw a number of porpoises playing about the ship. Standing to the South and East.

Thursday, 26. First part light variable airs with small rain. Middle part, wind from North and East fresh. Took in topgallant sails. At 5 PM a fresh gale. Sent down topgallant yards. Close-reefed the topsails. Heavy rain. Latter part, a gale. Wore ship to the westward. Heavy rain with sharp flashes of lightning.

Friday, 27. Fresh gales and squally weather. Ship making a great deal of water in the upper works. At 6 (PM) hauled up the foresail. A hard squall with heavy rain. At 8 (PM) somewhat moderated but still squalls with hail. A heavy sea running.

Saturday, 28. First part moderate gales. Ship under double-reefed topsails. Gale moderating. Ship continuing to leak in her upper works. Found that the tiller, which was of iron, had worked aft into the rudder head which made it difficult to steer. Handed the main- and mizzen-topsails, hauled up the foresail and hove the ship to. Latter part squally weather with frequent showers of rain. Secured the tiller. Shook the reefs out of the topsails and made sail on our course.

Sunday, 29. Moderate gales and cloudy weather. Set the mainsail and jib. Latter part squally with rain. Took in the fore- and mizzen-topsails, hauled up the mainsail and close-reefed the main-topsail. A heavy sea running and the ship laboring much.

MARCH 1784

Monday, 1. First part fresh breezes and squally weather with frequent showers of rain. Middle part, the gale increasing. Battened down the hatches, the people living in the Round House and lower cabin. Saw a sea gull and another bird, name unknown, but seldom seen except in storms. Latter part, fresh gales with a high sea.

Tuesday, 2. Strong gales with severe squalls and heavy showers of rain and hail. Shook one reef out of the topsails. Continues squally and rain with occasional hail.

Wednesday, 3. Fresh gales and cloudy weather.

Thursday, 4. First part, moderate gales with squalls of rain. Latter part, wind moderate, fair and pleasant weather.

Friday, 5. Pleasant weather with moderate gales. Set the studdingsails. Latter part, hazy weather.

Saturday, 6. First, moderate gales with hazy weather. Saw a Portuguese man of war and a quantity of Gulf weed. Middle part, strong gales. Latter part, moderating. Set the mainsail, main-topmast and mizzen staysails. Weather hazy.

Sunday, 7. Moderate breezes and pleasant weather. Sea smooth. Latter part cloudy, breeze steady.

Monday, 8. Clear pleasant weather with moderate breezes. Middle part, weather hazy with a mild sea.

Tuesday, 9. Cloudy weather with pleasant breezes.

Wednesday, 10. Moderate breezes and pleasant weather. Caught a fish commonly called a Portuguese man of war.

Thursday, 11. Fair and pleasant weather. Light breezes.

Friday, 12. Pleasant weather. Light breezes.

Saturday, 13. Ditto   Ditto   and calms.

Sunday, 14. First part cloudy with light rain. Latter part, fair. It being Saturday evening, according to custom drank sweethearts and wives in "cherry punch"—capital tipple. Songs by those who could sing. All appeared very happy (could it have been the punch?) An albacore weighing 20 lbs. caught. Last turkey killed for tomorrow's dinner.

Monday, 15. Moderate breezes and pleasant weather. At 10 AM discovered land, which proved to be the island of Palma, one of the Canary isles. Here, the gentlemen closed their reckonning. Some of the gentlemen were within six miles. Capt. Randall was within 30 miles. Here we take a fresh departure.

Tuesday, 16. First part, light breezes and pleasant. Latter part, moderate and pleasant.

Wednesday, 17. Clear and pleasant weather with moderate breezes. This being St. Patrick's Day, all the officers dined in the Round House, most luxuriantly on codfish and potatoes, roast pork with applesauce &c and drank a few bottles of wine to the memory of the Saint and his offspring. The Doctor must have been something of a "bon vivant," as he always records with much gusto when they had a good dinner. Having crossed the Tropic of Cancer this morning, the sailors afforded us some amusement by receiving on board Neptune and his wife, for the purpose of adopting and shaving, according to their custom, those who had not crossed the line before.

Thursday, 18. Commences with clear pleasant weather. Middle part, hazy. Passed a large shoal of porpoises. People employed drying corn and salt that had become wet; also employed making fenders for the pinnace. Ship under royal and topgallant-steering-sails.

Friday, 19. Light breezes and hazy weather. At 3 (PM) the wind hauled aft. Hauled up the spank[er] and squared the yards. People employed setting up the rigging. Carpenters, coopers, &c. employed at their various avocations.

Saturday, 20. Moderate breezes and clear pleasant weather. The people were mustered and quartered at the great guns and braces, Mr. Swift appointed to command the Marines, and each man told his station. Saw a large and most beautiful jellyfish; also a tropic bird for the first time. Many porpoises playing about the ship but at too great a distance to be harpooned. Crew variously employed.

Sunday, 21. Light breezes and hazy weather. At 1.30 PM, made the island of Bonavista bearing WbS, distance about ten leagues. At 6 (PM), Bonavista bore SWbS, the most southern end of the western part of the island WbS, distance five leagues. Made the island of Salt bearing NNW½W, 8 leagues distant. At 7 (AM) discovered the island of St. Jago bearing SWbS, distant about 13 or 14 leagues. Same time saw St. Nicholas bearing NW, distance 7 or 8 leagues. At 10, St. Nicholas bore NW½N about 11 Leagues and Bonavista bore East about 8 or 9

leagues. People employed handing the cables and clearing the anchors.

Monday, 22. Weather fair and pleasant with moderate breezes. People employed getting the anchors off the bows. Got up the fore and main yard tackles. At 8 (PM) southern part of Isle of May bore east, distance about 4 or five leagues. The southern part of the island of St. Jago bore WSW about 4 leagues distant. Hove to under the main- and mizzen-topsails with the foresail aback. Wore ship at 12 and stood to the southward. At 6 (AM) made sail and stood in for the land. At 7 (AM) fired a gun for a pilot, who came off. At 9.30 came to with the small bower anchor in 8 fathom water in the harbor of Port Spraya [*sic*], the fort bearing NW½N. It was in this port where the Commodore Johnston had the miserable fight with Commodore Suffrin in which it was a disputed point which got the better of it. It appears that Commodore Suffrin had greatly the advantage in position from the situation of the harbor. The people of this island who were spectators speak in the most favorable terms of both commodores being at a loss to know which deserved the greatest praise for his conduct and valor. They give it as their opinion that Commodore Suffrin was bested.

Saturday, 27. 7 o'clock PM got under way with a fresh breeze from the NE.

Sunday, 28. First part, moderate breezes and fair. Latter part the same and cloudy.

Monday, 29. First part, fair weather; middle and latter steady breezes and cloudy.

Tuesday, 30. First part moderate breezes and hazy.

Wednesday, 31. Capt. Green observed a small shark close under the stern of the ship, he ordered a hook to be baited and thrown over. The ravenous fish immediately seized it and was brought on deck. A suck-fish was sticking to his belly. I have preserved this curious fish in spirits. It's extraordinary with what firmness the fish applies itself to any solid body. The crew employed getting the potatoes on deck and picking them over. They find that more than one half of them rotten and threw them overboard.

Thursday, 1. Light variable breezes and cloudy. Ship under larboard fore-topmast and topgallant-steering-sails. Middle part squally with rain. Took in the studding-sails, topgallant sails, and took one reef in the topsails. Latter part, heavy squall with much rain. Informed Capt. Green that spruce beer was necessary for the sick, who immediately ordered a barrel of the same to be made.

Friday, 2. Variable breezes and cloudy weather. At 5 tacked ship and hauled up the fore and main sails, shook the reef out of the mainsail, set main-topgallant and royal, fore and main topmast-studding sail, lower and main topgallant studding-sails, shook one reef out of the mizzen-topsail and set mizzen-topgallant and royal and spank[er]. Middle and main topmast-staysails, fore staysail, jib, and fore topgallant and royal. Latter part pleasant breezes and clear weather.

Saturday, 3. Moderate breezes and cloudy. All sail set. Middle part, squally appearances with rain. Reduced sail to double-reefed fore- and main-topsails and single-reefed mizzen. Thunder and lightning at a great distance. Latter part, light breezes and hazy weather, with dark clouds.

Sunday, 4. Light breezes with heavy rain, thunder and lightning. End with moderate breezes and cloudy with rain. Ship under reduced sail.

Monday, 5. Variable winds with hazy sultry weather. People employed making mats for backstay, points for fore-topsail, and making a water sail. Overhauled a hogshead of ginseng taken from between decks; found some of it mouldy. Headed it up again owing to the appearance of rain having taken some of it out, in order to see what effect the sea air would have in moulding it. It effected it. Latter part, foggy. Caught a shark about three feet in length, weighing about 30 pounds with two sucker fish sticking to his belly. It appears that these little fish are a constant attendant on the shark. This is a disputed point whether this fish is an enemy of the shark or not. Some think that by its sucking qualities it draws away the shark's moisture. The seamen are of the opinion that it is seen to attend on him for more friendly purposes. Perhaps to point him to his prey or to apprise him of his danger. This, to me, does not appear reasonable, the sucking fish being very inactive and disposed to stick to the first body it meets with.

Tuesday, 6. Light and variable breezes and dark cloudy weather. People variously employed. Ends with light breezes and cloudy weather with a remarkable smooth sea. A large number of bottle-nosed porpoises about the ship. Could not harpoon any of them.

Wednesday, 7. First part of this 24 hours calm and pleasant. Latter part, light breezes. At 11.30 PM took in the topgallant and royal studding-sails and mizzen-topgallant sail.

Thursday, 8. First part, light and variable winds and cloudy weather. At 11 (PM) tacked ship to the South and West. People employed making points; carpenter caulking the yawl.

Friday, 9. First part pleasant and steady breezes and cloudy weather. People variously employed. Latter part, variable winds and cloudy weather.

Saturday, 10. First part, moderate breezes and pleasant weather. At 6 (AM) set the main-topgallant-staysail, royal, spritsail, and spritsail topsail. Carpenters employed fixing blunderbusses in the gunwales fore and aft.

Sunday, 11. First part, pleasant breezes and cloudy. At 3 (PM) squally with rain. Clewed up the topgallant sail and hauled down the staysail. At 5 AM set them again. Latter part, fresh breezes and dark cloudy weather and frequent squalls

Date	Latitude at Noon	Longitude at Noon	Variation Observed	Temperature	WINDS First Part	Mid Part	Latter Part
		New York Sandy Hook					
February							
22					NW	NNE	Calm
23					NNE	Calm	SW
24	39.08N	72.11W		34	NNE	Southd	NW
25	37.36	70.14		40	NW	WNW	NW
26	36.30	70.09		44	Variable	West	
27	35.34	66.30		44	NW	WNW	WNW
28	35.33	64.24		53	WNW	WNW	SW
29	35.22	59.47			NW	West	West
March							
1	35.34	55.36		52	WbN		WbN
2	35.54	51.16		52	WbN	WNW	WNW
3	34.46	46.40		61	WbN	WbN	WbN
4	34.07	42.28			WbN	West	West
5	33.46	38.21		67	WbN	WbN	WbN
6	33.07	34.24		66	WSW	WSW	WSW
7	32.21	30.30		68½	WSW	Variable	Variable
8	31.56	27.08		65	SW	SW	SW
9	30.09	24.33		69	SWbS	SWbS	SWbS
10	29.04			68.5	SWbS	Variable	Variable
11	28.17	20.51		68	Variable	SSW	SSW
12	28.40	20.30		69	WNW	Variable	Variable
13	28.38	19.57		68.5	Variable	South	South
14	28.13	18.55		68	Variable	N & E	North
15	25.41	19.29		68	North	NNW	NNW
16	23.55	19.55	Ampl.14.12W	69	North	North	West
17	21.29	20.27		69	West	WbN	WbN
18	19.54	20.53		74	N & W	N & W	N & W
19	18.13	21.31		70	N & W	N & E	N & E
20	16.36	21.51		71½	N & E	N & E	N & E
21	15.40	23.28		73	S & W	S & W	South
22				74	NE	NE	NE
28	12.46	22.39		75	NNE	NE	NE
29	10.01	20.47		77	ESE	ENE	ENE
30	7.36	19.38		78	NEbE	NE	NbE
31	6.35	19.22			ESE	ENE	Variable
April							
1	5.26	19.22	9.52W	82	Variable	N & E	S & E
2	4.32	19.27		84	S & W	S & W	S & E
3	3.44	19.10		82	South	S & E	N & E
4	3.23	19.22		80	Variable	S & E	S & W
5	2.57	19.06	Ampl.9.00W	83	N & W	S & W	South
6	2.03	19.22		84	S & E	S & W	S & W
7	1.21	18.41		86	S & E	S & E	S & E
8	1.25	18.42	Ampl.13.00W	84	S & E	S & E	S & E
9	0.04S	19.19	Ampl.10.00W Azm.9.36W	84	S & E	S & E	Variable
10	1.32	19.28	Azm.9.52	84	S & E	S & E	Variable
11	3.10	19.30		84	S & E	S & E	S & E
12	5.10	19.49		85	S & E	S & E	S & E
21	25.18	22.40	Azm.2.02E	77	S & E	S & E	S & E
22	27.18	20.55		76	East	N & E	N & E
23	28.38	19.46	Ampl.16.00E	75	N & E	N & E	N & W
24	29.49	19.17		74	N & W	N & W	N & W
25	30.24	17.35	Ampl.1.30W	73	N & W	N & W	N & W
26	31.25	14.50		72	N & W	N & E	N & E
27	32.37	10.43		74	N & E	N & E	N & E

attended with rain. At 10 AM set the jib and spanker.

Monday, 12. Commences with moderate breezes and cloudy weather. Set all sails. Got up the hammocks and aired bedding. Ends with steady breezes and pleasant weather.

Wednesday, 21. Moderate breezes and clear pleasant weather. People employed making points and fitting a coat for the bowsprit and making hammocks. Latter part, fresh breezes and dark cloudy weather.

Thursday, 22. Weather pleasant and fine with a steady breeze. Saw a bird called a Matrass. Ends pleasant.

Friday, 23. Light breezes inclining to be calm. Ends pleasant.

Saturday, 24. Moderate breezes and good weather. People variously employed. Ends pleasant.

Sunday, 25. Pleasant weather and cloudy. Ends pleasant.

Monday, 26. First part, light breezes and clear weather. Latter part, fresh breezes and cloudy.

APPENDIX B

F. Molineux's Accounts of Purchases at Canton

Among the holdings of the Rare Book Room of the University of Pennsylvania is a small cloth-covered volume measuring four inches in height by six and an eighth in breadth. The inscription on the cover reads "RECEITS," followed by Chinese characters. The book was acquired by the University from the library of Frank Godey in 1928. An inscription within reads:

F. Molineux
Receipts
Canton in China
October 8th, 1784

Frederick Molineux was the Captain's Clerk on the *Empress of China*'s first voyage and evidently not only assisted John Green with the ship's business but also his private "adventures," the subject of Appendix C. Molineux's receipts identify the individual Chinese merchants with whom they traded. The second half of the receipt book is largely the work of Samuel Hubbart and pertains to Green's second voyage to Canton in the *Empress of China*. The latter is included here, although reduced to tabular form.

Both portions already have been reproduced in Samuel W. Woodhouse, "The Voyage of the *Empress of China*," *The Pennsylvania Magazine of History and Biography*, no. 63 (1939), pp. 30-36, and is retranscribed and reproduced here by permission.

Rece'd at Canton October 9th of
F. Molineux for Accot of Capt. Green ten
Dollars being in part of a Contract for
several Ombrellas

_____
10 Dollars   [Chinese characters]
Woy-sang—Ombrella maker
the upper part of Hog Lane

Rece'd at Canton October 14th 1784 of
F Molineux for Accot. of Capt; Jno Green
ten Dollars being in part for making of
sattin Breeches at 1½ Dollars p' pair

_____
10 Dollars   [Chinese characters]
Apan [or Assan],
Taylor on the lower Bridge

Reced at Canton October 20th 1784
of F. Molineux for Accot of Capt. Green
twenty Dollars on Accot. of Sattin Breeches

_____
Dollars 20   [Chinese characters]
Apan [or Assan],
Taylor, on the lower Bridge

Rece'd at Canton October 28th 1784 of
F Molineux for Accot of Capt. Green Fifty
Dollars being in part & on accot. of Sattin
Breeches having deliverd Forty Eight Pair
this day

_____
50 Dollars   [Chinese characters]
Apan [or Assan],
Taylor on the lower Bridge

Rece'd at Canton November 13th 1784 of
F. Molineux twenty six Tael, three Mace five
Candereens being thirty five Dollars & One
Mace the Amot, in full for an Invoice Box of
Lacquered ware for Capt: Green

35 Dollars 1 Mace
                              [Chinese characters]
                              Echong lacquer man

Reced at Canton Novr. 13th 1784 of
F. Molineux for Accot of Capt Green
twenty Dollars on accot of Sattin Breeches
having Delivered in all seventy six pair in
part of the hundred

20 Dollars
                              [Chinese characters]
                              Apan [or Assan],
                        Taylor on the lower Bridge

Rece'd at Canton Novr. 17th 1784 of
F. Molineux for Accot Capt: Green One
hundred Dollars for six hundred Mitts in full
say Ladies silk Mitts

100 Dollars   Jackwae
                              [Chinese characters]
                                    China street

Rece'd at Canton November 14th 1784 of
F. Molineux sixty nine Dollars and a half in
full for making One hundred & thirteen
Pair of Sattin Breeches I say received

69½ Dollars
                              [Chinese characters]
                              Apan [or Assan]
                        Taylor on the lower Bridge

Reced at Canton Novb 18th 1784 of
F Molineux for Accot of Capt Green Thirty
Eight Dollars in full for a box of Chow Chow
Articles bought this day

38 Dollars   [Chinese characters]
                              Tyune, Image Maker

Reced at Canton Novr 18th 1784 of
F Molineux for Accot of Capt Green One
Hundred & twelve tael Eight Mace Nine
Candereens six Cash being in full for a
small Invoice of Merchze equal to

150½ Dollars   [Chinese characters]
                        Simon Andres   China street

Rece'd at Canton Novr 20th 1784 of
F. Molineux for Accot of Capt Green One
hundred & twenty seven Dollars & two thirds
for an Invoice of Sundry Merchandize in full
                              [Chinese characters]

127 2/3ds Dollars
126 18/90ths Dollars   Tucshing, China street
see Charge Pr Book

Reced at Canton November 19th 1784 of
Fredk Molineux for Accot, of Capt Green
twelve hundred & twenty Dollars being the
Amount of an Invoice of Silks in full
bought of me—I say reced Pr me

1220 Dollars   [Chinese characters]
                              Poonqua, silk Mercht

Reced at Canton Novr 27th 1784 of
F. Molineux for Accot of Capt Green four
hundred & thirty seven Dollars six Mace five
Candereens four Cash being in full for several
Invoices of China Ware

437:6:5:4   [Chinese characters]
9 Cns 8 Cash Change &
never received   Exchin
                                    China Merch

Reced at Canton November 26th 1784 of
F. Molineux for Accot of Capt: Green
Eleven Dollars in full of all Accots of
Taylors work to this day having before
Received twenty Dollars, making in the
whole thirty One Dollars

11 Dollars & 20 Do   [Chinese characters]
make 31 Dollars
                              Aphong, Taylor

Reced at Canton Decr 2d 1784 of
F Molineux for Accot Capt: Green five
hundred & thirteen Dollars & three fourths of
a Dollar in full for an Invoice of Silks, I say
reced

513 ¾ Dollars   Poonqua silk Merch
                              [Chinese characters]

Reced at Canton Novr 30th 1784 of
F. Molineux for Accot of Capt Green Forty
two Dollars being in full the amot Sales of
two Barrells Tarr, to the Ship Le Necker,
Capt: Woolmore

42 Dollars   S. Shaw

Reced Caton [sic] Decr 2d 1784 of
F. Molineux for Accot of Capt: Green Eight
hundred & seventy three Dollars in full for
two Invoices of Silks say for two Boxes

873 Dollars   [Chinese characters]
                         Want Long, silk Mercht

Reced at Canton Decr 2d 1784 of
F. Molineux for Accot Capt. Green One
Hundred Dollars for Paper Hangings for
Robt Morris Esqr the Borders not being
included for   Eshing Paper Mercht

100 Dollars

                         [Chinese characters]
             The Clerk to Eshing paper Mercht

Reced at Canton December 7th 1784 of
F. Molineux for Accot of Capt Green, three
hundred & four Dollars four mace one Candn
being in full for two Invoices Nankeens &ca,
sol'd him I say reced for Lunque

Dolls	M	C	
304	4	1	Dolls
176			[Chinese characters]
180			Lunque, Hog Lane

Reced at Canton Decr 7th 1784 of
F. Molineux for Accot of Capt. Green One
hundred & sixty seven Dollars two Mace five
Candereens in full for sundry Merch sold him
P' Invoice

167 Dolls 2 M: 5 C   [Chinese characters]
                       Woysang, & Pouqua

Reced at Canton Decr 10th 1784 of
F Molineux for Accot Capt: Green One
Hundred & Nineteen & half Dollars in full
for an Invoice of Teas

119½ Dollars   for Conqua   [Chinese
                              characters]
Conqua
100

Reced at Canton Decr 13th 1784 of
F. Molineux for Accot of Capt Green three &
a half Dollars for Borders for Paper Hangings
for Mr. Morris

3½ Dolls   [Chinese characters]
                      Eshing paper Mercht

Reced at Canton Decr 13th 1784 of
F. Molineux for accot. of Capt. Green Eighty
four Dollars in full for Tayloring Accot

84 Dollars
                      [Chinese characters]
                      Apan [or Assan] Taylor

Reced at Canton Decr 14th 1784 of
F. Molineux for Accot of Capt Green One
hundred & twenty five Dollars in full for an
Invoice of China Ware of Sundries

125 Dollars   [Chinese characters]
                      Syngchon China Man

Reced at Canton Decr 15th 1784 of
F. Molineux for accot of Capt Green Four
hundred & Ninety two Dollars being in full
for an Invoice of Silks

492 Dolls   [Chinese characters]
                      Asseng silk Mercht

Reced at Canton Decr 15th 1784 of
F. Molineux for Accot Capt Green Seventy
six Dollars & 1 mace in full for an Invoice of
Sundries

76 Ds 1 mace   [Chinese characters]
                      Tyune Immage Maker

Reced at Canton Decr 16th 1784 of
F Molineux for Accot of Capt Green twenty
four Dollars for Cordage say three hundred
Wt, at Eight Dollars Pr as sold the Ship
Empress of China

24 Dolls   Abel Fitch

Reced at Canton Decr 16th 1784 of
F Molineux thirty Dollars for Accot of Capt
Green being in full for an Invoice of Fans for
Mr. A'Bunner

30 Dollars
                      [Chinese characters]
                      Simon Andres

Reced at Canton Decr 16th 1784 of
F Molineux for Capt Greens Accot, six
Dollars for six pr sattin shoes Ladies

6 Dolls
                      [Chinese characters]
                      Syung, shoe maker

Reced at Canton Decr 16th 1784 of
F. Molineux for Accot. Capt. Green thirty
Eight Dollars for Chop Boat & Duties, on
silks ombrellas &ca &ca

_____

38 Dollars
                              [Chinese characters]
                              Huqua Linguist

Reced at Canton Decr 17th 1784 of
F Molineux for Accot of Capt Green Eight
Dollars One Mace five Candereens as the
ballance of Accots in full

_____

8 Ds-1m-5   [Chinese characters]
                              Ayow, Compradore

Reced at Canton Decr 18th 1784 of
F Molineux for Accot of Capt Green Seventy
four Dollars & a half in full for China Ware to
this day

_____

74½ Dolls
                              [Chinese characters]
                              Exchin China Mercht

Reced at Canton Decr 18th 1784 of
F. Molineux for Accot of Capt Green forty
seven Dollars five mace two Candns five Cash
being in full for sundries Pr Bill

_____
         M C C
47 D: 5: 2: 5   [Chinese characters]
                              Waysang Pouqua

Reced at Canton Decr 18th 1784 of
F Molineux for Accot, of Capt Green fifty Six
Dollars in full for China Ware—for Souchin
Chowqua

_____

56 Dollars   [Chinese characters]
                              Anyong 56 Dolls

Reced at Canton Decr 18th 1784 of
F Molineux for Accot of Capt Green Forty
Nine Dollars & 5 Candereens in full for a
dressing Box & four Lacquerd Fans for Mrs
Morris

_____

49 Dolls   [Chinese characters]
                              Howqua Lacquer Man

Reced at Canton Decr 18th 1784 of
F Molineux for Accot. of Capt Green twelve
Dollars in full for a Glass & Painting same for

a dressing Box for Mrs Morris

_____

12 Dollars   [Chinese characters]
                              Puqua painter on
                              Glass &ca &ca

Reced at Canton Decr 18th 1784 of
F Molineux for Accot of Capt Green forty
three Dollars 6 Mace 5 Candereens in full for
an Invoice of China Ware

_____

43:6:5   Winchong   [Chinese
                  China Man   characters]

Reced at Canton Decr 18 1784 of
F Molineux for Accot of Capt Green
Nineteen Dollars in full for two tubbs of
China Bowls & One Dish Do

_____

19 Dollars   Layhoun   [Chinese
                  China Mercht   characters]

Reced at Canton Decr 18th 1784 of
F Molineux for Accot of Capt Green thirty
five Dollars & half in full for an Invoice of
Cassia & Flowers

_____

35½ Dolls   [Chinese characters]
                              Want Long silk Mercht

Reced at Canton Decr 19th 1784 of
F Molineux for Accot of C. Green thirty five
Dollars in full for Cloaths and making for
Capt Green & his son in full

_____

35 Dollars   [Chinese characters]
                              Achong Taylor

Reced at Canton Decr 19th 1784 of
F Molineux for Accot, of Capt Green Seventy
Eight Dollars & a half in full for Sundry
China Ware for Mr Syngchong China Mercht

_____

78½ Dollars   [Chinese characters]
                              Chew—for Synchong

Reced at Canton Decr 19th 1784 of
F Molineux for Accot of Capt Green three &
half Dollars for the Duty on a Glass for Mrs
Morris Dressing Box & half Do for Duty on
two Bundle Bamboo silks Mounted Window
blinds

_____

4 Dollars   [Chinese characters]
                              Huqua Linguist

There follow additional accounts from the *Empress of China*'s second voyage. The format and style is identical to the foregoing; however, they are summarized below:

Date	From whom received	Amount	Article	Provider
25 July 1786	Samuel Hubbart	$100.00	280 pr. satin breeches	Apan, tailor, lower bridge
5 August	John Green	80.00	Satin breeches & vests	Appan, tailor
6 August	Samuel Hubbart	84.50	Porcelain	Souchin Choqua, China Street
11 [August]	J. Green	12.00	Two coats, one camblett	Assong, tailor
13 August	John Green	35.00	24 short sets of China containing 480 pieces. 154 Cattee Sago packed with the china	
15 August	Samuel Hubbart	11.00 + 3 mace	China	Yick, China Street
15 August	Samuel Hubbart	57.00 + 1 mace	China	Manchin, China Street
16 August	John Green	50.00	Satin breeches & silk vests	Soyhing, Hog Lane
31 August	Samuel Hubbart	20.00	100 pr. black satin breeches	Appan, tailor
31 August	Samuel Hubbart	10.00		Asong, tailor
4 September	S. Hubbart	120.00	Satin breeches	Acung, tailor
5 September	Samuel Hubbart	48.00	Pictures painted on glass	Apan, tailor, lower bridge / Cinqua, limner
8 September	Samuel Hubbart	20.00	20 pr. satin shoes of different colors	Tucshing, shoe maker
8 September	Samuel Hubbart	21.00 + 5 mace	19 pr. "Gugletts" & basins enameled and a short set tea china enameled	Soyhing, Hog Lane
12 September	Samuel Hubbart	51.00 + 2 mace	Tailoring accounts	Apans
12 September	John Green	560.00	1000 pieces Nankeens	Esing
14 [September]	John Green	870.00	1500 pieces Nankeens	Esing
15 September	John Green	29.00	2 coats & 2 pr. breeches	Affong, tailor
15 September	John Green	12.00	Duty on 2 boxes of glass	Pinqua, linguist
15 September	Samuel Hubbart	23.00	24 mother-of-pearl mounted fans & 2 feather brushes	Tackyen
15 [September]	John Green	18.00	6 paint boxes & paints in watercolor	Wayhoun, China Street

Date	From whom received	Amount	Article	Provider
16 September	John Green	4.00	6 pr. Ankeen breeches	Apan, tailor
16 September	Samuel Hubbart	10.00 + 4 mace	12 catee china tub	Retailer along shore
16 September	John Green	60.00	Sextant & apparatus	[Signature illegible]
18 September	John Green	54.00	6 Chinese paintings on glass representing Empress at Nobels(?)	Punqua, painter
(?)	John Green	58.00	Pagodas & 4 Chinese images	Attin, image maker
19 September	John Green	75.00	2 pieces white silk with gold & silver spriggs	Toyong, embroiderer
20 September	Samuel Hubbart	50.00	Satin breeches	Affong, tailor
7 October	Samuel Hubbart	65.00	2 pieces of embroidered silk	Podey, embroiderer
7 October	Samuel Hubbart	231.00	Net proceeds of 167 pieces of gauze sold in America on account of Messrs Febeires of Canton	
9 October	John Green	60.00	36 paper fans, 30 silk fans, 7 pieces of mother-of-pearl with the names of 7 sorts of (?)	Charles Norris
10 October	Samuel Hubbart	45.00 + 7 mace		
10 October	Samuel Hubbart	23.00 + 5 mace	Tailoring	Onshing, Hog Lane
18 October			A child's clothes: three jackets, 2 pr. ankeen trousers	Ackong, tailor
18 October	John Green	70.00	100 pr. satin breeches	Appan (?)
19 [October]	John Green	31.00	Sundry bamboo blinds 30 green ones, 2 pr. candlesticks	Appan
22 October	John Green	1000.00	Sundry merchandise	Lunqua, Hog Lane
23 October	Samuel Hubbart	5.00	A tea set china for Mrs. Wilkinson, a set mother pearl counters for Mrs. Bunner, & 6 tooth brushes for John Green	Essing
25 October	Samuel Hubbart	63.00 + 2 mace, 5 cand.	100 pr. satin breeches	John Green
25 October	Samuel Hubbart	84.00	Several pieces Madras longcloth	Apan, tailor
26 October	Samuel Hubbart	29.00 + 2 mace, 3 cand.	Box of lacquered ware marked "IG"	John Green; Chongqua, China Street

Date		Amount	Purchase / Description	To
26 October	Samuel Hubbart	53.00 + 2 mace, 5 cand.	Table set Nankin blue & white China 170 pieces marked "HW Nº 1"	Hopyeck, China Street
4 November	John Green	40.00		Charles Norris
3 November	John Green	85.00	Tea chest made of silver	Tuhopp, silversmith
3 November	John Green	36.00 + 3 mace, 6 cand.	6 jars of sweetmeats, rattans & matting	Akee
6 November	Samuel Hubbart	10.00	Settlement of accounts	Jo Nimmo (?)
14 November	Samuel Hubbart	48.00	12 sets china	Chinqua
15 November	Samuel Hubbart	155.00 + 3 mace, 5 cand.	Settlement of accounts	Lunqua, Hog Lane
15 November	Samuel Hubbart	417.00 + 5 mace, 1 cand., 5 cash	Settlement of accounts	Young Sam Jack
16 November	John Green	805.00 + 1 mace, 5 cand.	Settlement of accounts	Syngchong
16 November	Samuel Hubbart	243.50	China ware	Exchin, china ware man
16 November	Samuel Hubbart	104.75	Settlement of accounts	Eshing
18 November	Samuel Hubbart	215.00	China ware	Souchin Chiouqua
23 November	Samuel Hubbart	20.00	Settlement of accounts	Charles Norris
23 November	John Green	176.50	Settlement of accounts	Eshing
24 November	John Green	56.00		Woysang
25 November	John Green	50.00	2 quarter casks of wine for Richard Dale	William Bell
25 November	John Green	74.50	For account of Richard Dale, to be paid to Sainqua, silk merchant	Charles Norris
26 November	John Green	193.00		Samuel Hubbart
25 November	John Green	26.00 + 2 mace, 5 candareens	Settlement of accounts	Charles Norris
27 November	John Green	67.00		Aphong, tailor
4 December	John Green	20.00	Duty on spirits imported on *Empress of China*	Charles Norris
6 December	John Green	(119 tael, 2 mace)		Gowqua, linguist
28 November	John Green	29.00	Settlement of accounts	Samuel Hubbart
28 November	John Green	6.00 + 2 mace, 5 candareens		Apan, tailor, lower bridge
10 December	John Green	56.00	To pay debts of Charles Norris	James Gilchrist
11 December	John Green	24.00	Duty on 3 oil pictures and 12 glass ditto	———, linguist

Manifest of Cargo on board the Ship Empress of China Jno Green Master — ℅ from Canton

Marks	Whole Chests Bohea Tea	Half Chests Do.	Quarter Chests Do.	One Eighth Chests Do.	One Sixteenth Chests	Oblong & Square bxs	Chests Hyson Tea	½ Hyson Skin	Do. Singlo	Chests Souchong	Chests China	Tubbs Do.	Cases Nankeens	Bales Cotton Cloths	Cases Silks	Pipe Wine	Cases Cassia	Bales Do.	Boxes Merchandize Chests Gum Camphor &c	Consigned
EC	510	55	25	30	60	689													1	Constable Rucker & Co.
EB	"	"	"	"	"	"	661													
EH	"	"	"	"	"	"	10			1				1						
EO	"	"	"	"	"	"		40	55	50	1			3					1	
BC	"	"	"	"	"	"					17									
EPB	"	"	"	"	"	"				88	8									
En	"	"	"	"	"	"						36								
Variety	"	"	"	"	"	"							21							
OEC	"	"	"	"	"	"								1	1					
AG	"	"	"	"	"	70														Constable Rucker & Co.
BG	"	"	"	"	"	"								"		"		14		
AG	"	"	"	"	"	20														
BG	"	"	"	"	"	"								"		"		10		
AG	"	"	"	"	"	30														
NFG	7	"	"	"	"	"						7								
JGS	"	"	"	"	"	"								7						
IXG	"	"	"	"	"	"									1					
JG	"	"	"	"	"	"				5	6									John Green
GH	"	"	"	"	"	"								4						
JG	"	"	"	"	"	63								"						
CG	"	"	"	"	"	"					2			50	"	"		1		Robt. C. Livingston
JC	"	"	"	"	"	"				2										Fredk. Mollineux
PH	"	"	"	"	"	"								1	4					Doctr. Johnson
RH	"	"	"	"	"	12			6	17	4				1	6	1			John Swift
EWS	"	"	"	"	"	1					2							12		Robert M. Hauer & Co.
RMC	"	55	25	30	60	690				4								8		Andrew Caldwell
AC	"	"	"	"	"	3												17		Abraham Fritch
AF	"	"	"	"	"	2												1		
	517	55	25	30	60	689	885	40	55	56	137	20	43	25	25	1	6	6	2	61

Robert Morris — 1 Case China Freighted at Philadelphia by Mr. Mollineux —
1 Packages Samuel Shaw —

SBC / LT / PB — 1 Box China Samuel Breck Boston by Mr. Mollineux
2 D.

Signed
John Green
Copy

APPENDIX C

*Captain John Green's Accounts of Purchases at Canton
and his Abstract Manifest of the Return*

Among the Captain John Green Papers at the Philadelphia Maritime Museum
are thirty pages of accounts pertaining to Green's private purchases in Canton
as well as others he was commissioned to undertake by acquaintances and friends
back home. It is felt that to reproduce these pages in type would detract from
their historical and scholarly importance. Cargo marks in the margin, for example,
could not be reproduced faithfully by such means. Each page, therefore, is reproduced photographically from the original, facing pages being kept in the
original sequence.

The abstract manifest of the return cargo, illustrated on the opposite page, also
comes from the Green Papers at the Philadelphia Maritime Museum.

An index of the merchandise specified in Appendix C appears on page 298.
Its entries are not repeated in the main index.

Sales of Merch.dize for Acco.t Mess.rs Ten Eyck, Seaman, Schermerhorn Wong: at Canton

Dat. 1 No.		Th. Dolar T M c c m Dut.	
	3½ Pipes of Wine .... Capt. Wolmore		
	at 90 Stars .... 15/Pip.	315	
	4 Tons Barr Lead .... Lunqua, Chinese March 5		
	Jap. 63.	m. c c	
	Say 69: 70: Chinese M.t ...... a 1 Tael P Pecul ..... 1.2.0 2/0 8 .. .. .. or	376	
	Total Amo.t Sales	Dollars 691	

Investment of 691 dollars the Amot of Sales for Acct of
Ten Eyck, Seaman, Schermerhorn & Comp: at Canton

			T.	M.	C.	C. or	Dollars
J G }	No 1 & 4 - 4 Boxes China ware Amt as ⅌ Invoice						135 ⁴⁴⁄₉₀
J G }	No 1 & 4 - 4 Tubs China bowles Do ⅌ Do						25 —
J G	1 Case of Cassia & Cassia flowers						35 ⁴⁴⁄₉₀
G	6 Chests Hyson Tea ⅌ Invoice						208 —
J G	No 5 — 1 Box of China ware ⅌ Do						28 —
	1 Cask of Batavia Arrack ⅌ Dt						10 —
J G	No 7 — 1 Box of China ware & Sago ⅌ Do						40 ¹²⁄₉₀
J G	1 do of Nankeen Merchdze ⅌ Do						110 ⁴⁸⁄₉₀
J G	No 8 — 1 do of Tea China ⅌ Invoice						32 —
	100 headed & ferrell'd Wangees						25 —
	100 ferrill'd Wangees without heads						15 —
	6 large Umbrella's ⅌ Invoice						15 —
	6 small ditto ⅌ Ditto						9 —
			Dollars				691 ³⁴⁄₉₀

270

Sales of Merch.se for Acct of Mr Thomas Russell Merch.t Boston ... at Canton

Date	Marks & Nos.		Tr. Dollars of Valo Date	Tr. MCC or Dollars
1784 Nov.r	J G No. 1 a 10	10 Boxes f.t Arms, Containing 228 stand — to Capt. Winslow —		513 .—
		Valo Dat 2½ Dollars Stand —		
	J G No. 1 a 4	4 Cask Barr Lead .... to Sunqua Chinese Merch.t		
		W.t 2 0 57 lb. French W.t		
		Tt. 30 46 lb.		
		20 Peculs 5 10 3 lb.		
		Pt. 6.c Tar. T M C O 7 M C O		
		0 4 1 18 at 4 Peculs 165. 9.2 — or 230 30/90		
			Dollars	743 30/90

Investment of 743 Dollars, The Amot Sales for Acct of Mr
Thos Russell of Boston Mercht Viz ——— Canton

		T	M	6	6	or Dollars
	1 Sett 140 Fish Counters pearl —					10
J G S	No 3 — 1 Box Silks ⅌ Invoice —					479⁶⁰⁄₉₀
G	6 Chests Hyson Tea ⅌ Do —					208
	11 Large Silk Ombrella's ⅌ Do —					29³⁰⁄₉₀
	11 Small Do — Do ⅌ Do —					16⁴⁴⁄₉₀
					Dollars	743⁵⁴⁄₉₀

Sales of Merchandize for the Acco.t of Sam.l Breck Esq.r of Boston — at Canton

		T	M	6	6	or	Dollars
1784	17½ Pipes Wine — to Capt Woodman a 90 Doll.s ? Pipe —						1575.
Nov.r	1 — Ditto — D.o — Dutch Supra Cargoes —						160
	1 — D.o — D.o — Capt. M.c Intosh —						120
	2 — D.o — D.o — M.r Matthews a 90 p Pipe —						180
	One ½ cask D.o — M.r Southerland —						30
	Two ½ casks D.o — M.r Seliere —						42
	Dollars —						2107

Investment of 2107 Dollars The Amot Sales for Acct

of Saml Breck Esqr of Boston ___ at Canton

		T	M	C	C or Doll
SBC	One Box contg China ware . Viz:				
	1 Sett Cypher'd Table China 256 ps	64	—	—	—
	1 Do ___ Do Tea China 35 ps	6	—	—	—
	20 sett Patty pans ⅌ Sett 3 ⅌ 2..4 ⅌	4	8	—	—
	2 doz Custard cups 48 ps 8 ⅌	1	9	—	—
	8 Flower Potts Cypher'd a 2..3..5 ⅌	18	8	—	—
	T	95	5	equal	127 30/40
	1 Piece Silver Sprig'd Embroider'd				
	White Lutestring (for Mrs Breck)				30 —
JG S	No 1 ___ 1 Box qt Silks ⅌ Invoice				681 —
Do	4. 1 Box qt Do ⅌ Do				461 —
G	20 Chests Hyson Tea ⅌ Invoice				689 40/40
JG	2 Rolls contg 3 ps Garden Flower Potts				12
JG	1 Box Merchtze ⅌ Invoice				68 30/40
JG No 3 & 4	two Tubs China ware ⅌ Invoice				28 —
	1 Sett Mother pearl Counters (Cypherd)				10
	Dollars				2107

Sales of Merch.[andise] for Acc.t of Monsieur De La Tombe, of Boston at Canton

		T.	M.	C.	C.	to Dollars
					Dollars —	234 —

1784
Novemr 2 Cases Champaign Wine —

Containing together 156 Bottles a 1½ dollar ⅌ —

Investment of 234 Dollars the Amo.t of Sales for Acco.t
of Mons.r De La Tombe of Boston ---- at Canton

		T	M	C	C	or	Dollars
LT PB	N.o 1 & 2 --- 2 Boxes China ware, ---						
	Containing each 1 sett of Table China						
	Cont.g 172 p.s p/ Sett – a 16 tael p.-	32	—	—	—	equals	42 $\frac{48}{72}$
	2 Venus paintings on Glass (the pair) ---	---	---	---	---		18 -
	— 3 Chests Hyson Tea p/ Invoice -	-	-	—	-		104 —
	N.o 12 One box China ware p/ Invoice -	-	-	—	-		28 —
	--- 3 Pieces Lutestring - - -	---	-	---	---		42 —
				Dollars –			234 $\frac{48}{72}$

Sales for Account of Mr. Joseph Barrell Merchd. Boston

Date		Nos.					Dollars
		T	M	o	C	o r	
1784							
Nov.r	BVG — 23 Casks Ginseng ...... Shenkingpal & Co. Mercht: —						
	Wt 27:2: 0 150 Dollars the Peat						4053
	One Cask Beari						14
	5 Cases of Claret .... come to a bad Market & allow'd for it Prime Cost						125
	Total Amo. Sales Dollars						4192 —

Investment of 4192 Dollars for the Amot Sales for
Accot of Wᵐ Joseph Barrell Merchᵗ Boston. Viz'

		I	M	C	C	or	Dollars
GH	Nº 1 — 1 Case contᵍ Silk Gauzes ⅌ Invoice						731 ²²⁄₉₀
J G S	Nº 2 — 1 Dᵒ contᵍ Romall Silk Handᵏfs						660 —
Dᵒ Nº 5 — 1 Dᵒ Sundry sorts of Silk							224 ²²⁄₉₀
Dᵒ Nº 6 — 1 Dᵒ Assorted Lutestrings							745 —
Dᵒ Nº 7 — 1 Dᵒ Plain & stripᵈ Dᵒ							523 —
L M	1 Small box contᵍ Ladies Mitts						108 —
G	20 Chests Hyson Tea ⅌ Invoice						693 ³⁰⁄₉₀
	248 Malacca Canes (together)						90 —
	40 Headed & ferrilld Wangees						20 —
	One Small box Containing						
	Mother Pearl Necklaces 25						
	& a sett Dᵒ Cyphred Counters 10						35 —
	One Small box of Musk						15 —
	113 ⅌ Sattin Breeches a 2½ ⅌						282 ²⁵⁄₉₀
L H	1 Matted Bale contᵍ Ladies Chip Hats						25 —
	24 Silk Waistcoats madeup ⅌ Invoice						48 —
					Dollars —		4192 ³⁰⁄₉₀

Sales Merch. for Acct of Mr. Andrew Bunner March 15 Philad.

Shankingus Chinese Merch.

1 Cask Gunning for
7¼ 1 " 29 — a 150 Dollars ℔ Pecul

Dollars 193

Investment of 193 Dollars the Amot. Sales for Acct. of
Mr. Andrew Bunner Mercht. Philad —

		Æ	M	C	C	or	dollars
JG S	Nº 5 — In a box of this discription. Viz:						
	1 Piece Garnet Sattin ..... 22 Doll.						
	1 Piece Black twilled Dº . 18 Dº —						
	1 Pt. Dº. 8 th.d Taffaty .... 15 Dº						
	1 Pt. Dº Striped Dº ...... 16 Dº						
	1 Pt. White Dº Lutestring — 13½						
	1 Pt. Pink — dº 13½						
	1 Pt. Brown ..... dº 16						
	1 Pt. Clarett Strip'd dº ..— 16.						
	1 Pt. White flowd Dº 16						
	1 Pt. thin Pink plain Dº ... 6¾						152¾
AB F	A Small box fanns Contain g.						
	700 brown Nankean fans a 3. 3 ₰	23	1	—	—	or	30¾
	2 Large Silk Ombrella's a 2½ ₰	—					5 —
	3 lesser Dº .. ditto a 1½ ₰	—					4½
					Dollars ..		193.

Each Piece mark'd D. B.

Investment of 1000 Dollars for Acco.t of Nixon Foster &

		T	M	C	C	in dollars
NFG — N.º 187	7 Chests Bohea Tea ——— W.t Vis.t —					
	N.º 1 — 407 — 59					
	2 — 415 — 61					
	3 — 426 — 62					
	4 — 428 — 63					
	5 — 422 — 60					
	6 — 422 — 61					
	7 — 427 — 61					
	2947 — 427					
	tare 427					
	Nett 2520, or 18.90 a 15 ₫/p.l	283	5	—	—	
	the dollar being paid at 72 Candareens ——— equal to					393 50/72
J.G S	N.º 5 — In a box of this discription Viz.t					
	3 Pieces Lutestrings at 13½ —— 40½					
	6 P.cs Taffaty .. a d.o ... 81 —					
	4 P.cs d.o .... a 12 .... 48 —					169 36/72
NFG N.º 187	7 Bales best Nankeens Cont.g —					
	660 Pieces ... a 4:4 ₫ piece	290	4	0	0	
	the dollar paid at 72 candareens ... equal to					403 24/72
	8 Large Silk Umbrella's - a 2½ D.$ —	—	—	—	—	20
	9 Lesser Ditto Ditto — a 1½ d.$ —	—	—	—	—	13 48/72
	Dollars					1000 6/72

Investment —   Dollars for Acco.t of W.m Morris Philad.—

		T	M	C	C	= dollars
W.m Morris Esq.	One Box China Ware cont.g ... Viz.t					
	1 sett Cypher'd table China 254 p.s a 6 ⅄ p. is	64	—	—	—	
	1 Sett d.o ... Tea d.o ... 49 D.o a 6 ⅄ p. is	6	—	—	—	
	8 sett patty pans .... 3 p.s a 2.2 is	1	7	6	—	
	2 doz Custard Cups .... 48 p.s a 6 ⅄	1	4	4	—	
	The Dollar paid at 7/5 Candareens say ...	73	2	equal to		97 52/90
d.o D.o	One box cont.g 2 sett Paper Hangings & borders	—	—			103 44/90
d.o D.o	One d.o cont.g a Ladies dressing box	—	—			49 16/90
Glass						
d.o D.o	One box cont.g Glass for dressing box	—	—			15 48/90
d.o D.o	One Small lead box solder'd & containg					
	5 Tael W.t of Musk a 32 tael ⅄ Cattie	10	—	equal to		13 43/90
	One sett of Mother pearl Counters Cypher'd (M.M)	—	—	—	—	10 —
W.m Morris 14.15	4 Small boxes cont.g 4 Images (Chinese)	—	—	—	—	16 —
Morris Esq.	One box cont.g a Marble stone Pagoda	—	—	—	—	25
d.o D.o TEA	N.os 1 & 3 — 3 Small boxes Tea ⅄.r Invoice	—	—	—	—	105
	1 Piece Gold Flower'd Lustring (W.m Morris)	—	—	—	—	30.
	1 Piece light Coloured Lustring Embroider'd					
	Pattern Suit of Cloaths (W.m Morris)	—	—	—	—	45

Investment of 20 Dollars for Acco.t of Mr. James Read.

IR	One Small box Cont.g China Ware viz.:	S	m	6	6 or Dollars
	12 Nank B&W Cups & Saucers breakfast	2	1	6	
	12 d.o — d.o — D.o Coffee D.o	2	—	4	
	12 d.o — d.o — D.o Chocolate D.o	2	1	6	
	2 Tea potts		1	—	
	1 Sugar Dish		—	3	
	1 Coffee or Chocolate Pott		—	7	5
	6 Small painted bowles		—	6	
	3 Blue & White d.o		—	3	6
	3 D.o Painted — d.o		—	3	6
	1 Blue & White q.t bowle		—	2	5
	2 Painted D.o — D.o				
	2 Soft Muggs		—	1	3
	2 Slop bowles & Stands		—	5	—
	2 Cream Cups		—	2	
	The Dollar paid at 75 Candarins		12 — 4 — 8 equal to		16 5/9
	1 Large Copper mounted Silk Umbrella				2 4/9
	1 Small D.o D.o D.o				1 6/9
				Dollars —	20 5/9

Invoice of Merch[t] for Acc[t] of Ten Eyck. Seaman & C[o].

		T	M	C	C	Dollars
J G	N[os] 1 & 4 — 4 Boxes China ware. Viz[t]					
N[o] 1	Cont[g] 300 N[o] Burnt China breakfast					
	Cups & Saucers — 3 patterns a 1 Mace	30	..	—	—	40.
2.	D[o] 300 D[o] D[o] pint bowles					
	of 3 patterns .... a 6:5..	19	..	—	—	
	& 15 Sett of Patty pans			M	C	C
	3 p[r] Sett .... a 2.2:0.	3	3	—	—	
	T	22	3	—	—	29 66/90
3.	Cont[g] 100 Blue & White Nankeen					
	Breakfast Cups & Saucers a 1.8:0	18	—			
	185 Blue & White Comm[n] D[o]. a .8:0	14	8			
	T	32	8	—	—	43 66/90
4.	Cont[g] 300 Blue & White pint bowles a 6:0.	18	—	—	—	
	& 5 sett patty pans ...... 2:0.0.	1	..	—	—	
J G	N[os] 1 & 4 Tubbs China ware Viz[t]	19	—	—	—	25 30/90
N[o] 1.	Cont[g] 15 B & W q[t] Bowles ..... a 2.5:0	3	7	5	0	
2.	Cont[g] 15 burnt China D[o] D[o] ..... a 3:0:0	4	5	0	0	
3.	Cont[g] 30 B & W Quart bowles .... a 1.5:0	4	5	0	0	
4.	Cont[g] 30 Burnt D[o] D[o] ..... a 2:0:0	6	2	—	—	
		18	7	5	—	— 25..
J G	One Case Cont[g] Cassia & Flowers d[o]					
	4 P[t] 66[c] Quil Cassia a 18 p[p] 19 6/90					
	& 82 Cattie Flowers D[o] a 20 p[p] — 16 36/90					35 42/90
G	6 Chests Hyson Tea avridged together					
	to weigh 50 Cattie each a 34 p 90					208 —
J G	N[o] 5 Cont[g] China ware Viz[t]					
	6 Sett B & W Breakfast China 20 p[r] Sett					
	a 3 p	18	—	—	—	
	6 Sallad Dishes ..... a 5 Mace p	3	—	—	—	
		21	—	—	—	28 —
	Amo[t] Carried over		Dollars			435 42/90

Invoice of Merch.ze for Acco.t Ten Eyck, Seaman &c.o Continued

		I	M	C	O	Dollars
	Amo.t brought forward - - -					435 ¾
	A Cask cont.g 20 Gallons Arrack - - -					10
J G — N.o 7 - -	1 Box cont.g China ware &/ago viz.t					
	10 Sett Flower Potts 5 p/ Sett a 3 doll — 30					
	95 Cattie Sago best sort a 10 7/8 p — 10 62/90					40 ½
J G - - - - Contents Nanke.n	1 Box cont.g as follows —					
	20 Pieces Col.d Nankeens a 45 c of a Dollar — D.t 10					
	80 Work'd Waistcoat Patterns 30 c/ p.t — 100					
	12 Nankeen Fans - - - a 4 th 90 - 48 th 90					110 48/90
	6 Large Ombrellas - - - - a 2 45 th 90 p doll.					15
	6 Lesser Ditto - - - - - a 1½					9
	100 headed & fenilld Wangees a ¼ p d.r					25
	100 fenilld Wangees (without heads) together -					15
J G - - N.o 8 - -	1 Box cont.g Tea China viz.t					
	8 Setts of 48 pieces p/ Sett a 4 doll p					32
	Dollars					691 9/90

Invoice of Merch.ze for Acco.t of Mr. Thos. Russell &Co.

				Dollars
JGS	No.3 — One Case Cont.g Silks Viz.t			
	3 pices Black			
	3 Do. White			
	5 Do. Pink			
	5 Do. Ash Col.r			
	3 Do. Pea Green			
	2 Do. Sea Green			
	3 Do. Laylock			
	1 Do. Olive Green			
	1 Do. Changeable			
	1 Do. Brown			
	1 Do. Blue			
	1 Do. light Blue			
	29 p.s Lustrings a 13 1/4 $ 395 $63/90			
	1 p.s Pink flow.d Do. a --- 16 45/90			
	1 p.s White d.o --- a --- 15 65/90			
	1 p.s Pea Green d.o --- a --- 16 --			
	1 p.s White d.o --- a --- 16 --			
	1 p.s Sattin flow.d laylock a 17			479 68/90
G	6 Chests Hyson Tea aweigh'd togather			
	to Weigh 50 Catt.s each a 34 60/90 $			208 --
	11 large Copper mounted Silk Umbrellas 2 4/90 $			29 30/90
	11 Small Do. Do. Do. a 1 45/90			16 45/90
	1 sett Mother Pearl Counters Cyphers TR			10 --
			Dollars	743 53/90

Invoice of Merch^re for Acco^t of Saml Breck Esqr Viz^t

		T.	M	C	C	Doll^s
SBC	One Box China ware cont^g ⸺					
	1 Sett Table China Cyphe^rd S B &					
	Consisting of 254 Pieces a ⸺ 64 ⅌ Sett	64	⸺	⸺	⸺	
	1 Sett tea China, 35 Pieces a 6 ⅌ D^o ⸺	6	⸺	⸺	⸺	
	20 Sett Patty pans 3 ⅌ D^o Sett a 2:4 ⅌ Sett	4	8	⸺	⸺	
	2 doz: Custard Cups a ⸺ 0:8 ⅌ doz	1	9	⸺	⸺	
	8 Flower Potts cyphe^rd S B a 2:2:5 ⅌	18	8	⸺	⸺	
		95	5	⸺	or	127
	1 Piece White silver Sprig Embro^d					
	Best Lutestring ⸺ a ⸺	⸺	⸺	⸺	⸺	30
	1 Sett Cyphe^rd Mother of Pearl Counters					
	140 ⅌ Sett ⸺ a ⸺	⸺	⸺	⸺	⸺	10
J G	N° 1 & 2 ⸺ 2 Rolls Containing three					
	Sett Garden flower potts a 4 ⅌ ⅌	⸺	⸺	⸺	⸺	12
J G	N° 6 & 7 ⸺ 2 Boxes China ware &					
	Cont^g together as follows ⸺					
	15 Large Painted bowles a 1⅓ ⅌ 20 D^o					
	2 Sett Even^g Tea China Consisting of					
	49 Pieces ⅌ Sett ⸺ a 4 ⅌ ⸺ 8 ⸺	⸺	⸺	⸺	⸺	28
G	N° 20 Chests Hyson Tea w^t together					
	each 50 Catti a 34 ⅌ 90 D ⅌ Chest ⸺	⸺	⸺	⸺	⸺	689
J G	1 Box Cont^g Merch^re ⸺ Viz^t					
	50 Pieces Coloured Nankeens at ½ doll^rs 25					
	10 D^o D^o twilled Cotton a 1 ⸺ 10					
	20 Pieces Blue Canton D^o Cloths 1 ⸺ 20					
	2 D^o White D^o D^o Fines 5 ⸺ 10					
	4 doz Nankeen fans ⸺ 3 30/90	⸺	⸺	⸺	⸺	68
					Dollars	965

Invoice of Merch.ize for Acco.t of Sam.l Buck Esq.r &c. Continu.

		T	M	C	C
J G S	No. 1 .. 1 Case Containg. Silks Vizt. —				
	20 p.rs Paunch Asort.d Col.s a 5 $D .. 100				
	10 p.rs Romall Hkfs a 44 D.o $ .. 440				
	5 D.o Lutestrings a 14½ p .. 72 90				
	4 D.o Moreens asort.d Col.a 9 $ .. 36				
	3 Pieces Peelongs .. a 3 D.t $ .. 9				
	3 Cattie black hair Ribbon a 4½ $ .. 13 45/90				
	2 D.o best sewing silk a 5 $ .. 10 —				681 —
J G S	N.o 4. A Case Cont.g Silks Vizt.				
	5 Pieces White flower'd				
	1 D.o D.o strip'd				
	2 D.o pink flower'd				
	3 D.o D.o striped				
	2 D.o D.o silver'd				
	2 D.o Ash flower'd				
	1 D.o D.o D.o				
	3 Pieces light blue d.o				
	1 D.o Claret d.o				
	2 D.o Pea Green d.o				
	1 D.o D.o Silver'd				
	2 D.o Laylock flower'd				
	25 p.rs flower'd Lutestrings a 16½ $ 412 45/90				
	1 Piece White flow'd Sattin a 15 45/90				
	1 Piece black Silk Sambletee — 15.				
	3 Cattie Sewing Silk a 4½ $ .. 13 45/90				
	1 D.o Black Hair Ribbon a 4 45/90				461.
	Amo.t Dollars				1142

N.B. N.o 1 Case to Contain 2 Strings Flowers D.o Laylock Lutestring not inclod.d in this Invoice which are Mark'd for Mr. L. My. Own —

Invoice of Merch.ze for Acco.t of Mons.r De La Tombe

		T	M	C	C	Dol.s
LT PB }	N.os 1 & 2 --- 2 Boxes China Ware .. Viz ..					
N.o 1.	Containing 1 Sett Blue & White Table China					
	Consist.g of 172 p.es p.Sett a .. 16 tael.s	16	--	--	--	
2 ..	Containg. 1 Sett D.o D.o D.o a D.o	16	--	--	--	
		T.	32 --	equal to		42½
	2 Venus Paintings on Glass the pair	--	--	--	--	18.
G _	3 Chests Hyson Tea — Wt. together on an					
	Average — 50 Cattie each a 34 44/72 p.C.t	--	--	--	--	104.
J G	N.o 12 ... 1 Box China Ware — Cont.g					
	5 Setts Tea China 34 p. p.Sett a 3 p. 15.					
	3 d.o D.o ..... 52 p.es p.r. a 6 2/12 .. 13					28.
	3 p.ces Lutestring . . . . . . a 14 D.o p.					14½
			Dollars	--		234

Invoice of Merch.ze for Acco.t of Mr. Jos.l Barrell &c.o

			Dollars
G H	N.o 1. 1 Case Silks Containing Viz.t		
	117 pieces of Gauze .. a 6 /3 p P.e		731 22/90
JG S } N.o 2 Cont.g 60 pieces Silk Armalls a 6 /9 p P.t			660 —
JG S } N.o 5. Containing 23 p.es light Lutestring a 7 /6			
	9 Cattie Sewing Silk a 5 /r Do 172 40/45		
	1/2 Do Hair Ribbon a 4 /9 p 6 6/9		224 22/90
Do N.o 6 Cont.g Silks Assorted — Viz. —			
	1 Piece Defer		
	1 Do Crimson		
	1 Do Cherry		
	3 Do Blue		
	5 Do Ash		
	7 Do White		
	2 Do Celladen		
	2 Do Lilly		
	3 Do Straw		
	4 Do Puce		
	1 Do Jenne		
	30 Pieces plain Lustrings a 14 1/2 p p.d Dollars --- 435 —		
	10 p.s Do Black .. a 14 p.r --- 140 —		
	10 Do striped Do .. a 17 p.r --- 170		745 —
G ...	20 Chests Hyson Tea W.t together on an Averidge 50 Cattie p .. a .. 34 60/90 p		693 3/9
	Amo.t Carried Over ___		3053 75/90

Invoice of Merchdze for Accot of Mr Jos. Barrell & Co (Conte a)

		Dollars
	Amot brought over	3053

J G &
S. No 7. A Case of Silks cont g — Viz
doll

A — 10 pieces striped Lustring 16½ p⌐ — 165.

B — 1 piece D⁰ D⁰ a 17.

C — 2 p⌐ D⁰ D⁰ a 17½ p⌐ 35.

D — 1 Ditto D⁰ D⁰ a 17 p⌐ 17.

20 pieces plain D⁰ a 14 p⌐ 280

2 Cattie sewing silk a 4½ p⌐ 9 ... 523

LM — 1 small Box cont g 600 p⌐ Ladies silk Mitts a 45/40 d⌐ p⌐ ... 100

LH — 1 D⁰ Bale c g 100 Ladies best Chip Hats a 12/½ p⌐ ... 25

J G — 1 D⁰ Box cont g 20 bunches M. P⌐ Necklaces 1/½ 25. } Doll 1
& 1 Sett Mother pearl Counters Cyphered BB — 10 ... 36

D⁰ ... 1 small box cont g 5 Tael wt of best Musk a 3 Doll p Tael ... 15

D⁰ — 1 Trunk, cont g 113 p Sattin Breeches 2/½ p⌐ ... 282

248 Malacca Canes together — — — 90

40 headed & ferrulld — — a ½ Dol p⌐ 20

24 Silk Double breasted Waiscoats a 20 p⌐ 48

Dollars — 4192

Invoice of Merch⸺ for Acc⸺ John Green ⸺

	T	M	C	C	Dollars
1 Sett Mother pearl Counters Cypher'd 1 $					10 –
2 D⁰ Comm⁰ D⁰ ⸺ D⁰ figur'd a 2½ $					5 –
6 D⁰ short ⸺ D⁰ ⸺ D⁰ ⸺ a 1 $					6 –
2 $ High Tootenag Candlesticks & Snuffers					10 ⁴⁵⁄₉₀
2 Small chamber bells					1 ⁴⁵⁄₉₀
1 Bamboo Baskett					1 –
2 bundles floor Matts					11 –
A box cont⁰ Lacquer'd Ware Vizt	T	M	C	C	
1 Dressing box &ca	6 . 0 . 0 . 0				
1 Nest boxes 5 $ D⁰	4 . 1 . 2 . 0				
4 Small dressing boxes	4 . 8 . 0 . 0				
4 large Counter Boxes	2 . 6 . 0 . 0				
10 lesser D⁰ ⸺ D⁰	4 . 2 . 0 . 0				
1 Oblong Tea Tray or Server	0 . 4 . 5 . 0				
4 lesser D⁰ Servers	1 . 2 . 0 . 0				
4 Scollop D⁰ D⁰	1 . 2 . 0 . 0				
4 Octagon Servers	6 . 0 . 0				
8 D⁰ lesser D⁰	4 . 0 . 0				
6 Small red Glass Servers &⎫					
6 D⁰ Black D⁰ together ⎭	4 . 8 . 0	26 . 3 . 5 . –			35 ¹²⁄₉₀
26 Silk Waistcoats made up a 2 D⁰ $					52 –
A Box Containg 3 $ Small Chinese Images a 3 $					9
Amt Carr'd over Dollars					141 ¹²⁄₉₀

Invoice of Merch.d. Acco.t. John Green (Continued)

			I	M	C	C	Doll.
	Am.t brought Over		-	-	-	-	141
JG...N.o 4	1 small Box cont.g. Cannisters tea	Doll.r					
	W.t 7 - cattie Gunpowder	7					
	2 - D.o Hyson Gome	3					
	2½ D.o D.o D.o	2½					
	Cannisters	2					14
M.rs Green	10 cattie Hyson a 5 p.r b.t		5				
	11 d.o Gunpowder a 5.6 p.d.o		6	1	6		
	Boxes & Cannisters		1	4			
		D.o	12	6	-	or	18
	1 Chess & back Gammon box tea	10					
1 Bundle	12 pieces Bamboo Blinds	4					
	4 Long pipes	1 30/90					
	1 Sett pearl Counters	2 45/90					
	1 D.o D.o Cypher'd T.M.	7 45/90					
	1 small Ombrella (Nancy Green)	1 45/90					
	10 large D.o a 2 45/90 th.s p.c	25					
	11 small D.o a 1 45/90 th.s	16 45/90					68
	1 Small box cont.g. for M.r Schermerhorn	Doll.r					
	6 Marble figures Ornam.d	9					
	d.o for J.G. 6 D.o p.r D.o	4½					
	1 D.o Grotto	1½					
	8 Flower potts	3½					18
	Am.t Carried over Doll.r						268

Invoice of Merch^ze Acco't John Green (Continued)

		T	M	C	C	Doll
	Amount brought over					268 $\frac{23}{90}$
Jabbin nes	1 Chest Cont'g Table sett China Viz't					
	3 210 Pieces	30	-	-	-	40 -
G C	1 Box Cont'g Tea China Viz't					
	3 Sett Burnt Breakfast 52 P's P' 3.2	9	6	-	-	
	3 D° D° Even'g 49 P's 1:7	5	1	-	-	
G	1 Box Cont'g China Ware	14	7	-	-	19 $\frac{33}{90}$
	1 Sett 49 P's	3	3	-	-	
	3 D° 43 D° a 1:6:0:0	4	8	-	-	
G	1 Box Cont'g D° D°	8	1	-	-	10 $\frac{72}{90}$
	50 Breakfast Cups & Saucers	3	-	-	-	
	50 Even'g D° D°	2	-	-	-	
	2 Tea Potts	-	4	-	-	
	2 Cream Cups	-	3	-	-	
	6 Slop bowles & Stands	1	2	-	-	
	1 Sett Beefsteak Dishes	4	5	-	-	
	1 D° Muggs	-	4	5	-	
		11	8	5	-	15 $\frac{72}{90}$
	1 Roll Cont'g 72 Flatt desert Plates	3	6	-	-	
	1 d° Cont'g 60 Sup D° D°	3	-	-	-	
		6	6	-	or	8 $\frac{72}{90}$
G	N° 4 This Case beside Cont'g Merch're for the Acco't of Sam'l Breck Esq'rs &c°					
	Contains also 1 P' Laylock Lutestring for Miss Green Doll a 14 $\frac{1}{2}$					29
	1 P' D° D° for Mrs Green					
	Amo't Carried over			Dollars		392 $\frac{22}{90}$

Invoice of Merch.ze Acco.t John Green (Continued)

			L	M	B	C	Dollars
	Amo.t brought Over						34
G.&B.	N.o 1&4 .. 4 Tubbs of China ware Vizt						
N.o 1 Cont.g	25 Burnt China bowles a 3/90 th $						8
2 d.o ..	26 d.o d.o .. d.o a d.o $						8
3 d.o ..	13 Large Bowles a 1/2 doll. $ 6.45/90						8
	6 Chocolate Cups a 1/4 d.o $ 1.25/90						
4 Cont.g	13 large bowles 1/2 d.o $ .. 6.45/90						4
	4 Chocolate Cups .. 1 —						
J.G. N.o 4	1 Box Cont.g China Ware Vizt						
	7 Sett Nank: B.&W Breakfast China						
	20 P.s in the Sett a 4 Doll. $ Sett						28
J G Stores	1 Tubb Containing						
	4 Factory painted Bowles a 5 1/2 $						22
	1 Small box Cont.g China ware &						
	intended for M.rs Schermerhorn ..						4
J.G. N.o 7 Cont.g	4 large China jarrs a 7 d.o $						28
Chow Chow	Cont.g Marble, Chinese & other figures for						40
J.G. N.o 10 Cont.g	10 Sett Breakfast China 34$:3 4$						30
J.G. N.o 11 d.o	9 Sett Breakf.t d.o 3 d.o $ .. 27 Doll.s						
	& 3 d.o of Salled Dishes a 1 $ — 3						30
G. ..	8 Chests Hyson Tea W.t together on						
	Averidge 50 Cattie each a 34.60/90 th $ Chest						247
	Amo.t Carried over Doll.rs						884

Invoice of Merch.ᵗˢ Acct. John Green (continued)

	T	M	C	C	Dollars
Amo.ᵗ brought Over	—	—	—		884 ⁷⁵⁄₉
12 Pieces White Bengal Cotton Cloth a 6 D.ᵒ p.¹					72
1 Piece painted Gauze for a Ladies Toilette					12
24 D.ᵒ D.ᵒ for Skreens a 16 D.ᵒ p.ˢ					4
24 Fishing rods a ¼ doll.ˢ p.ˢ					6
10 P.ʳ Nankeen Sattin Breeches a 3 Doll.ˢ p.ˢ					30
14 Silk & Nankeen Vests & D.ᵒ					20
20 pair best Crystial Spectacles a ½ D.ˢ					10
100 Gallons Arrack a D.ᵒ p.ˢ					50
4 Feather brushes a ¼ D.ˢ p.ˢ					1
3 Masques a ½ D.ˢ p.ˢ					1 ⁴⁵⁄₉
1 Large Chest					14
1 D.ᵒ Trunk (Green)					5
2 Rose wood Paper Boxes					7
1 small box cont.ᵍ 6 Cannisters tea					10
9 P.ʳ Nankeen Breeches & Vests					4
2 Pair Small candlesticks					2 ⁵⁰⁄₉
2 small Paint boxes					4
6 small jarrs sweetmeats & the jarrs					10
2 large D.ᵒ D.ᵒ D.ᵒ					15
4 boxes candy.ᵈ Oranges (Preserv.ᵈ)					5
1 Tubb cont.ᵍ 34 Cattie Sugar candy					4
GH. N.ᵒˢ 2 to 4 - 3 Boxes Merch.ᵉ Viz.ᵗ					
N.ᵒ 2 Cont.ᵍ 115 p.ˢ Gauze a 6½ — 747 ⁴⁵⁄₉					
3 D.ᵒ 114 D.ᵒ D.ᵒ a D.ᵒ 741					
4 D.ᵒ 24 D.ᵒ D.ᵒ a D.ᵒ 156	—	—	—		1644 ⁴⁵⁄₉
Dollars					2519 ⁶⁵⁄₉

CG
S —

No. 4 One Case of Silks particularly —

				Dollar
18 Yd 1 piece Blue striped Lutestring				17½
18 Do 2 Do Rose	Do	Do a 17½		35 —
15 Yd 3 Do Black	Do	Do a do		52½
15 Do 2 Do Cherry	Do	Do a 14¾		29½
15 Do 2 Do Rose	Do	Do a Do		29½
18 Yd 2 pieces plain Black	Do a 12$			24 —
18 Yd 1 Do Ash Col best Sattin a				21¼
18 Yd 2 Do Straw col:	Do a 21¼			42½
18 Do 2 Do Cherry Do		a do		42½
18 Yd 2 Do Puce Do		a d:		42½
18 Yd 2 Do Light Puce Do		a do		42½
18 Yd 2 Do Lellay Do		a do		42½
18 Yd 1 Do Crimson Do		a do		21¼
18 Yd 1 Do D'feu Do		a do		21¼
18 Yd 3 Do Light Blue Do		a do		63¾
18 Yd 3 Do White	Do	a do		63¾
18 Yd 1 Do Rose	Do	a do		21¼
18 Yd 20 Do Black	Do	a 18 . 360 —		

Dollars
973 —

52 pieces P. Invoice

Invoice of Merchze

			T	Mẽe	Dollars

A/G } No 1 & 120 – 120 Chests Hyson Tea Wt together

in the Gross – 10156 ℔s English

tare —— 2100

Nett 8050 ℔ or 60–37. a 42/ pe box — 2535 3 4 0

for Nonpayment in Old Dolls Agio 2 pc 50 13 1 0 — 3494 20/90

B/G } No 1 & 24 – 24 Chests Gun powder Wt together

in the Gross – 2727 ℔.

tare —— 432 —

Nett 2295 ℔s or 17. 21 a 56/ pt box ᴵ — 963 7 6 0

for Nonpayment in Old Dollars Agio 2 pc — 19 2 7 5 1328 22/90

C G / S — } No 1 & 10 – 10 Cases of Silk each Contg as follows

No 1 Contg 70 pieces black Canton Sattins —

in 35 pieces of 15 Yds p say rolls a 8/p doll p ... — 595 —

2 Contg 50 pieces Black Canton Sattin in

25 pieces of 15 Yds Do — a 8/p doll p ... — 425.

3 Contg 60 pieces Black Sinchaws (Chinchews)

in 30 pieces of 14½ Yds a 7¾ p ... — 465.

4 Contg 52 pieces Silks (the particulars)

pr Invoice opposite together — — — 973 —

5 Contg 25 ps black Padasoas

24¾ Yds a 16½ Dollars p ... — 412 40/90

6 Contg 50 pieces plain Lutestrings

Say Black 18 Yd p a 12/ pe ... — 600

7 Contg 50 pieces Black Canton Sattin

in 25 ps 15 Yd p — a 9/ p ... — 450

*9 Contg 50 pieces Peelongs assorted a 14¾

– d at 4½ Do p piece ..... 225 —

50 Do Inferior 14 Yd p a 2¼ 112½ 337 40/90

*8 Contg 100 pieces paunches assorted col: of

16 Yd p ..... a 4½ p ... — 450

10 Contg 40 pieces Stripd Flowerd Lutestrings

15 Yd p piece ..... a 16/ p ... — 640

Dollars 10,171 30/9

Merchandise Index to John Green's Account Book *(pages 267-297)*

Arrack, 268, 283, 294.

Baskets, bamboo, 290.
Bells, chamber, 290.
Blinds, bamboo, 291.
Boxes, backgammon and chess, 291.
  counter (lacquered), 290.
  dressing (lacquered), 290.
    ladies', 280.
    glass for, 280.
  nest of (lacquered), 290.
  paint, 294.
  paper, 294.
Brushes, feather, 294.

Candlesticks, 290, 294.
Canes, Malacca, 276, 289.
  W(h)angees, 268, 276, 283, 289.
Cannisters, tea, 291, 294.
Cassia and cassia flowers, 266, 268, 282.
Chinaware, 266, 268, 272, 274, 280-283,
  285, 287, 292-293.
  Bowls, 268, 281, 293.
    "Factory painted [with Hongs]," 293.
    Large, 285.
    Pint, 282.
    Quart, 282.
  Breakfast china, 282, 292, 293.
  Cups, cream, 281, 292.
    custard, 272, 280, 285.
  Cups and saucers, 282.
    Breakfast, 281, 292.
    Chocolate, 281, 293.
    Coffee, 281.
    Evening, 292.
  Dishes, Beefsteak, 292.
    Salad, 282, 293.
    Sugar, 281.
  Evening china, 292.
  Flower pots, 272, 283, 285, 291.
  Mugs, 281, 292.
  Patty pans, 272, 280, 282, 285.
  Plates, dessert, 292.
  Pots, chocolate or coffee, 281.
  Slop bowls and stands, 281, 292.
  Table china, 272, 274, 280, 285, 287,
    292.
  Tea china, 268, 280, 283, 285, 287, 292.
    Evening, 285.
  Tea pots, 281, 292.

Clothing, 280.
  Breeches, Nankeen, 294.
    Silk, 276, 289, 294.
  Handkerchiefs, 276, 286.
  Hats, ladies' chip, 276, 289.
  Mitts, ladies' silk, 276, 289.
  Vests, Nankeen and silk, 294.
  Waistcoats, silk, 276, 289-290.
    worked patterns, 283.
Counters, mother-of-pearl, 270, 272, 276,
  280, 284-285, 289-291.

Fans, 278, 283, 285.
Figures, marble, 291, 293.
Fire screens, 294.
Fishing rods, 294.

Grotto, 291.

Images, Chinese, 280, 290.

Jardinières (see "Flower pots" under "Chinaware").
Jars, 293, 294.

Lacquerware, 290 (see also "Boxes," "Servers," "Tea Tray").

Masks, 294.
Mats, floor, 290.
Mother-of-pearl, 270, 272, 276, 280, 284-
  285, 289-291.
Musk, 276, 280, 289.

Necklaces, 276, 289.

Pagoda, marble, 280.
Paintings on glass, of Venus, 274, 287.
Paper Hangings and Borders, 280.
Pipes, 291.
Porcelain (see "Chinaware").
Preserved candy and oranges, 294.

Ribbons, hair, 286, 288.

Sago, 283.
Servers, glass, 290.
  lacquer, 290.
Silver, 272.
Snuffers, candle, 290.

Spectacles, crystal, 294.
Sugar candy, 294.
Sweetmeats, 294.

Teas, 266, 268, 270, 272, 274, 276, 279-280, 282, 284-285, 287-288, 291, 293, 296.
Textiles, cloth misc., 266, 268, 285, 294.
　Cambletts, 286.
　Chinchews, 296.
　Cotton, twilled, 285.
　Gauze, 276, 294.
　Lutestrings, 272, 274, 276, 278-280, 284-289, 292, 295-296.
　Moreens, 286.
　Nankeens, 279, 283, 285.
　Paunches, 296.

Peelongs, 286, 296.
Satins, 278, 286, 295-296.
Silk, 266, 270, 272, 276, 284, 286, 288-289, 295-296.
　Sewing, 286, 288-289.
　Taffeta, 278-279.
Tray, tea (lacquered), 290 (see also "Servers").
Trunk, 294.

Umbrellas, 268, 270, 278-279, 281, 283-284, 291.

Wallpaper (see "Paper Hangings").
W(h)angees, ferruled and headed (see "Canes").

APPENDIX D

Eighty-Five Historic Imports and Exports of Canton*

AGAR-AGAR: a red algae or seaweed from Ceylon, New Holland, New Guinea, and adjacent islands. When boiled and cooked it becomes gelatinous. The Chinese used it for sizing paper and silk; from a derivative gum, they manufactured sweetmeats and transparent lanterns.

ALUM: a sulfate of potassium and aluminum exported to the Indian archipelago. It was used by the Chinese to purify river water for drinking.

AMBER: a fossil resin found in many areas but derived largely for the Canton market from the east coast of Africa. Transparent pieces containing insects, leaves, etc. were especially prized for the making of beads and ornaments. It was also used for incense.

AMBERGRIS: a yellow, black, gray, or variegated waxlike substance formed in the digestive tract of the sperm whale and found washed up on beaches or floating in the sea. A rare and costly item, it was used by the Chinese for nearly the same purpose as amber. It is also employed as a fixative for perfumes.

AMOMUM: seeds from the tree (*Amomum verum*) which grew in China and the East Indies. They have a strong smell and a pungent taste and were used by the Chinese to season sweet dishes.

ANISEED STARS: the fruit of a small tree (*Illicium anisatum*) which grew in China, Japan, and the Philippines. It has an aromatic taste and was used to season sweet dishes. Oil extracted from the seeds had medicinal uses.

ARRACK: a spirituous liquor distilled from such substances as molasses, palm toddy, coconut juice, and rice. The principal kinds came from Batavia, Goa, and Colombo.

ASAFETIDA: the foul-smelling juice of the roots of a Persian tree (*Ferula assafoetida*). It was used by the Chinese as a condiment and medicine.

BAMBOO: native plant used for building, clothing, food, paper, boats, masts, sails, ropes, medicines, sweetmeats, lampwicks, beds, fodder, canes, umbrella sticks, etc.

BEESWAX: brought mainly from the Indian archipelago and from Europe. The Chinese used it to form cases or envelopes for the tallow of the stillingia (tallow tree) during the manufacture of temple candles.

BETEL NUT: from the areca palm (*Areca catechu*) found in Java, Malacca, and Penang. The nut is chewed like chewing tobacco together with a leaf of the betel pepper (*Piper betel*) covered with quicklime.

BENJOIN (Benjamin): the resin gum from the pierced bark of a small tree (*Styrax benzoin*) brought from Borneo and Sumatra and used for incense.

BÊCHE-DE-MER (Tripang): sea slugs, or sea cucumbers, imported from Fiji and other South Sea islands. They were cleaned, dried, smoked, and eaten.

BIRDS' NESTS: a mucilaginous nest made by small swallows (*Hirundo esculenta*) found in Java, Sumatra, Macassar, and islands of the Sooloo group. They were collected, cleaned, dried, and shipped for making into a "soft, delicious jelly." The best birds' nests sold for nearly twice their weight in silver to the court at Peking.

BRASS LEAF: a thin, metallic decorative covering made by the Chinese for the Indian market.

CAMPHOR: the gum of the tree *Dryobalanops camphora* from Sumatra and Borneo used as a preservative against insects. The wood was often

* Adapted from *The Chinese Repository*, vol. II, February 1834, pp. 447-472.

used to make boxes, trunks, and small pieces of furniture.

CAPOOR CUTCHERY: a medicine and preservative against insects, from the root of a Chinese plant. It was exported to India and from thence to Persia and Arabia.

CARDAMOMS: a plant seed from the *Elettaria* and *Amomum cardamomum*. Those from India and Ceylon are different from those in China. The Chinese used the seeds for culinary purposes and Europeans also employed them for medicine.

CASSIA: the aromatic bark of the *Cassia lignea*, used for perfume, incense, and for cooking.

CASSIA OIL: distilled from the leaves of the cassia tree, it was used for medicines and flavoring.

CHINA ROOT: a climbing plant (*Smilax china*) used in China for medicines and export to India.

CHINAWARE (Porcelain): one of the principal exports to the West, Chinese porcelain often served as ballast on board ship.

CLOVES: the unopened flower bud from an evergreen tree (*Caryophyllus aromaticus*) found in the Moluccas and highly prized as a spice and as a preservative for foodstuffs.

CLOVE OIL: the oil distilled from cloves was used as a local anesthesia for toothache and for flavoring in medicines.

COCHINEAL: an insect (*Coccus cacti*) which lives on a certain species of cactus and is imported from Mexico and Central America to make scarlet, deep crimson, and deep purple dyes.

COPPER: the reddish, nonferrous metal (Cu).

CORAL: brought to China from islands in the Indian archipelago and made into ornaments. Buttons made from coral were used as an insignia of office in China.

COTTON: raw cotton was imported mostly from Bombay and Bengal. Some piece goods were brought to Canton from England.

CUBEBS: the fruit of a vine (*Piper cubeba*) growing in China, Java, and Nepal. They re-

semble peppercorns, have a pungent taste, and have an aromatic odor.

CUTCH (Catechu): an extract from the tree *Acacia catechu* of India, Burma, and Persia, used for brown and olive dyes, tanning, the tarring of fish lines and sails, and in medicines.

DAMAR: pine resin from the Malay peninsula used in the manufacture of varnish.

DRAGON'S BLOOD: a resinous red gum from the rattan *Calamus rotang* found in the East Indies and Malaya. It was used in medicine, for the coloring of varnish, and in painting.

EBONY: the dense, black wood of the tree *Diospyrus enenus* imported from Mauritius and other islands of the Indian Ocean.

ELEPHANT TUSKS: imported from South Africa, Siam, and Burma, and used by the Chinese for ivory carvings.

FISH-MAWS: the stomachs of various fish were brought in junks from the Indian islands and were considered by Chinese gourmets to be an article of great delicacy.

FLINTS: imported from Europe for a variety of expected uses.

GALANGAL: a plant root from the *Koempferia* and *Maranta galanga*, used in cooking. It has an aromatic smell and is peppery to the taste.

GAMBIER: the evaporated juice of a trailing plant (*Funis uncatus*) from islands in the Indian archipelago. It was used in connection with the chewing of betel nuts and also was used for tanning leather.

GAMBOGE: the evaporated gum resin of the tree *Stalagmitis gamogioides* found in Cambodia and Indo-China. It was used in medicine and for the production of a beautiful yellow pigment.

GINGER PRESERVED: candied sweetmeat from the ginger root (*Zingiber officinalis*) exported in jars by the Chinese.

GINSENG: the root of the *Panax quinquefolia*, much esteemed by the Chinese in tea or for chewing as a panacea or aphrodisiac. That which grew in Tartary was the property of the Emperor. Another species of ginseng grew wild in certain mountainous regions of North America. The bulk of the *Empress of China*'s cargo consisted of thirty tons of Appalachian ginseng collected in the deep woods of western Pennsylvania and Virginia.

GOLD: much of the gold imported into China came from Borneo.

HARTALL: an oxide of arsenic used in the manufacture of yellow paint.

HORNS and BONES: horn was imported and made into handles, buttons, and other decorative objects. Bone was transformed into lime.

INDIA INK: made from lamp black and glue, size, or gum. It was formed into cakes or sticks, which were frequently perfumed and gilded.

LACQUERWARE: large numbers of lacquered fans, trays, boxes, and small pieces of furniture were exported from China.

LEAD: pig and sheet lead was imported from Europe and, later, America. It was made into the linings of tea chests and, by oxidation, into exported red and white lead paints.

MACE: the crimson seed husk of the nutmeg from an evergreen tree (*Myristica fragrans*) native to the Moluccas.

MATS: from rush, rattan, bamboo, etc. The Chinese made large quantities of floor and table mats for domestic use and export.

MOTHER of PEARL SHELLS: largely the shell of the *Mya margaritifera* found in the Persian Gulf, the coasts of India, and among the islands of the Indian archipelago. The iridescent interior was made into toys, beads, seals, knife handles, spoons, boxes, and inlay for lacquerware pieces.

MUSK: the secretion of an abdominal gland of certain species of male antelope and deer from Tibet, Siberia, and China. Musk was rare and costly. It was used in medicine and as a fixative for perfume.

MUSK SEED: the fruit of the *Hibiscus abelmoschus* from China and other adjacent places, it is aromatic, musky, and bitter. The Arabians used it to flavor coffee, much as the French now use chicory.

MYRRH: the gum of a tree growing in Arabia and Abyssinia, which the Chinese used for incense and perfumes.

NANKEENS: a type of cotton cloth named for Nanking, where its reddish threads were originally made. Nankeens formed a large part of the Chinese export trade with the West.

NUTMEGS: see Mace.

OIL OF NUTMEGS: the essential oil was known as "Banda Soup" after the Banda Islands from which it came.

OLIBANUM: the gum of a large tree which grew in Arabia and India. It was known as frankincense by the ancients and was used as temple incense.

OPIUM: the dried juice extracted from the unripe capsules of a poppy (*Papaver somniferum*) grown in India and Turkey. A potent drug, the importation of which into China led to the Opium Wars of the 1840's.

PEPPER: the fruit of a climbing or rambling shrub (*Piper nigrum*) found in Sumatra, Malabar, and Malacca. The fruit was harvested and dried when it changed from green to red.

PUTCHUCK: a medicine brought from India and Persia, in color and odor similar to rhubarb.

QUICKSILVER (Mercury): mostly brought to China from Europe and oxidized into vermilion for painting on porcelain.

RATTANS: branches of the plant *Calamus rotang* that produces Dragon's Blood (q.v.). It was found throughout the Indian archipelago and was widely used for cordage, chairs, mats, beds, wickerwork, baskets, chair seats, and whole as walking sticks known as "Mallaca canes."

RHUBARB: a plant (*Rheum palmatum*) that grew in Tartary and China. A drug, made from the dried roots, was sent to Russia and Smyrna in Turkey.

RICE: a staple food crop throughout the Far East.

ROSE MALOES: from the hibiscus brought from Persia and India, it was a substance with the consistency of tar.

SALTPETER: potassium nitrate imported from India. It was used for the manufacture of gunpowder, fireworks, as a preservative of meat, and for medicinal purposes.

SANDALWOOD: the heart wood of a small tree (*Santalum album*) that grew in India and on the islands of the Indian and Pacific Oceans. The best variety came from the Malabar Coast of India. The Chinese used it as a fine powder for incense and as a dye. The oil is aromatic.

SAPAN WOOD: from the tree *Coesalpina sapan* which grew in India, the Philippines, and Burma. It is the same genus as Brazilwood. It was used as a red dye, for cabinet work, and inlay pieces.

SEA SHELLS: such as the nautilus, cabbage shell, trumpet shell, ducal mantle, etc. They were imported from the islands of the Indian Ocean.

SEAWEED: several species of *Fucus* were brought in junks to Canton where they were eaten raw or cooked by the poor.

SHARKS' FINS: collected from the Indian Ocean to the Hawaiian Islands, the chief supply was from Bombay and the Persian Gulf. They were fat, cartilaginous, and when cooked much esteemed by the Chinese as a stimulant and tonic.

SILK: one of the principal articles of export from China to the West.

SKINS: seal and sea otter pelts were in the greatest demand, followed by beaver, fox, and rabbit. A flourishing trade, almost completely monopolized by Boston, in sea otter pelts from the Northwest Coast of America grew up toward the end of the eighteenth century.

SMALTS: an impure oxide of cobalt united with potash. When ground fine, it is an azure (powder) blue and was used to color glass and porcelain.

SOY: the condiment made from soy beans.

SUGAR: from sugar cane (*Saccharum officinale*). That exported from China was mainly in a crystallized state and was called "Sugar Candy."

TEA: the principal article of export from China to the West. Tea was first popularized in England during the 1660's and later was introduced into the American colonies.

THREAD: gold and silver thread was imported from England and Holland for the ornamentation of clothing.

TIN: the best grades of tin, cast into ingots, came from the island of Banca and was called "Banca tin"; an inferior type known as "Straits Malacca tin." Plate tin was imported from England.

TORTOISE SHELL: from the hawk's bill tortoise (*Testudo imbricata*). The Chinese carved it into such articles as combs, boxes, and toys.

TURMERIC: the dried root of the *Curcuma longa*, a plant related to ginger and cultivated on all the Indian islands. It is an ingredient of curry and was also used as a yellow dye.

TUTENAGUE (China Spelter): an alloy of iron, copper, and zinc exported to India for the manufacture of boxes, dishes, and household utensils.

VERMILION: made by the oxidation of mercury and used for the painting of porcelain.

WHANGEES (Japan Canes): the product of a plant grown in China and made into walking sticks. The best were tough but pliable and tapering. Those that were bent at the head and had their knots at equal distances were preferred.

WOOLENS: broad cloths, long ells, cuttings, worleys, and camblets were imported from Europe in small quantities.

NOTES

I
Western Eyes Turn Eastward
(*pages 3-13*)

1. The account of the *Empress of China*'s departure is derived primarily from Captain John Green's "Journal of an Intended Voyage . . ." (Philadelphia Maritime Museum); the Abstract Log of the *Empress of China*, see Appendix A (National Archives, Washington, DC, Record Group 27); and Josiah Quincy, *The Journals of Major Samuel Shaw the First American Consul at Canton* (Boston: Wm. Crosby and H. P. Nichols, 1847).

2. The weather during the winter of 1783-1784 is described in David M. Ludlum, *Early American Winters, 1604-1820* (Boston: American Meteorological Society, 1966), pp. 64-66.

3. The identities of Messrs. Young and Schermerhorn are established from papers in Boxes I and VIII of the William Duer Papers, New-York Historical Society, New York, NY.

4. Winslow Warren, *The Society of the Cincinnati, A History of the General Society of the Cincinnati with the Institution of the Order* (Boston: Massachusetts Society of the Cincinnati, 1929).

5. *The Salem Gazette*, Salem, MA, March 4, 1784; report with New York dateline, February 26, 1784.

6. Thomas Moore, pseud., *Gaine's New-York Pocket Almanack for . . . 1784* (New York, 1784).

7. Rodman Gilder, *The Battery* (Boston: Houghton Mifflin Company, 1936), pp. 102-113. In its heyday, the Battery could mount almost 100 pieces of ordnance. During its long history the fort was occupied successively by the Dutch, British, Dutch, British, Americans, British, and Americans and had been variously named Fort Manhattan, Amsterdam, James, Willem Hendrick, James, William, William Henry, Anne, and George.

8. *The Independent Gazetteer; or the Chronicle of Freedom* (Philadelphia), no. 122, February 28, 1784.

9. General sources for the historical background of the East Indies and China trades are contained in such works as: William L. Langer, comp. and ed., *An Encyclopedia of World History*, revised third edition (Boston: Houghton Mifflin Company, 1952); William Bridgwater and Elizabeth J. Sherwood, eds., *The Columbia Encyclopedia* (New York: Columbia University Press, 1959); Hosea Ballou Morse, *The Chronicles of the East India Company Trading to China, 1635-1834*, 5 vols. (Cambridge, MA: Harvard University Press, 1926); Foster Rhea Dulles, *The Old China Trade* (Boston: Houghton Mifflin Company, 1930); Sir Evan Cotton, *East Indiamen* (London: The Batchworth Press, 1949); E. Keble Chatterton, *The Old East Indiamen* (London: Rich & Cowan, Ltd., 1933); J. H. Parry, *The Establishment of the European Hegemony, 1415-1715* (New York: Harper Torchbooks, 1961); and issues of *The Chinese Repository*, 1833-1841.

10. Dulles, *op. cit.*, p. 13n.

11. Russell Miller and the Editors of Time-Life Books, *The East Indiamen* (Alexandria, VA: Time-Life Books, Inc., 1980), pp. 88-89.

II
A Scheme of Furs and Ships
(*pages 14-30*)

1. John Holker Papers, 1777/1822, 41/4500F, Library of Congress, Washington, DC, hereinafter cited as Holker Papers (LC), microfilm reel 10, fols. 3846-3850. The LC collection is the largest single holding of Holker MSS; other Holker collections of note, however, are located in the William L. Clements Library, University of Michigan, Ann Arbor; "Miscellaneous Documents Relating to the First Voyage of the *Empress of China*," Holker Papers in the Benjamin Franklin Collection, Sterling Memorial Library, Yale University, New Haven, CT, hereinafter cited as Holker Papers (Yale); the Massachusetts Historical Society, Boston; and the Historical Society of Western Pennsylvania, Pittsburgh. One "Livre tour-

nois" was at the time worth about five shillings in Pennsylvania currency, or sixty-seven cents of a Continental dollar.

2. Jared Sparks, *The Life of John Ledyard, The American Traveller* (Cambridge, MA: Hilliard and Brown, 1828), pp. 126ff; "Ledyard, John," *Dictionary of American Biography*, vol. VI, pp. 93f.

3. Sparks, *Ledyard, op. cit.*, pp. 132, 137.

4. *Ibid.*, p. 129.

5. *Ibid.*, p. 130.

6. *Ibid.*, p. 131.

7. Biographical material on William Turnbull and Peter Marmie is from E. Earl Moore, "An Introduction to the Holker Papers," *The Western Pennsylvania Historical Magazine* (Pittsburgh: The Historical Society of Western Pennsylvania), vol. 42 (1959), pp. 227ff. The most concise biographical sketch of Holker is in Abraham P. Nasatir, *French Consuls in the United States: A Calendar of Their Correspondence in the Archives Nationales* (Washington, DC, 1967), Appendix F.

8. Biographical material on Daniel Parker is to be found in the Daniel Parker Papers at the Massachusetts Historical Society and at the Baker Library, Harvard University School of Business Administration. For William Duer, see the Duer Papers at the New-York Historical Society and his sketch in the *Dictionary of American Biography*, vol. III, pp. 486-487.

9. John Holker, fils to John Holker père, September 4, 1783. Holker Papers (LC), reel 11, fols. 4230-4232.

10. James Maury to Turnbull, Marmie & Co., October 21, 1783. *Ibid.*, reel 11, fol. 4336.

11. *Pennsylvania Packet* (Philadelphia), issue of September 9, 1783.

12. Samuel Eliot Morison, *The Maritime History of Massachusetts, 1783-1860* (Boston: Houghton Mifflin Company, 1941), p. 44.

13. Daniel Parker to Robert Morris, February 10, 1784. Parker Papers, Massachusetts Historical Society.

14. Holker Papers (LC), reel 15, fol. 6122.

15. The precise definition of "carpenter's measure" varied from region to region, thus causing confusion with exact tonnage figures. The various tonnages given for the *Empress of China* derive from the following sources: *360*—Quincy, Shaw, *op. cit.*, p. 134n; *368—Lloyd's Register*, 1791 (under *Clara*), see Chapter XVI; *368¼*—New York registration certificate no. 91, October 5, 1790, cited by Carl C. Cutler in a letter to D. Foster Taylor, Taylor/Peck

Papers, Peabody Museum of Salem, MA; *400*—certificate of insurance, Holker Papers (LC), reel 13, fol. 5351, and *ibid.*, Parker to LeCouteulx & Cie., March 10, 1784, reel 12, fols. 4801-4802. Others are given in the Congressional and New York State sea-letters, Green Papers, Philadelphia Maritime Museum.

16. Parker to LeCouteulx & Cie., March 10, 1784. Holker Papers (LC), reel 12, fols. 4801-4802.

17. Peck's obituary is in the *Independent Chronicle and the Universal Advertiser* (Boston), Thursday, May 6, 1790. Biographical material on him is also to be found in Howard I. Chapelle, *The History of American Sailing Ships* (New York: W. W. Norton & Co., Inc., 1935), pp. 134ff and the research files of D. Foster Taylor, Phillips Library, Peabody Museum of Salem, MA. Peck's *Minerva* of 1774 was described as "nearly as broad as long."

18. William Spence Robertson, ed., *The Diary of Francisco de Miranda: Tour of the United States, 1783-1784* (New York: The Hispanic Society of America, 1928), p. 132. The translation into English of the interview with Peck is found in "The Sojourn of Francisco de Miranda in Massachusetts and New Hampshire, September 16th to December 20th 1784," *Old-Time New England* (Boston), vol. XXVI (1935), no. 2, p. 44.

19. Daniel Parker to LeCouteulx & Cie., April 5, 1784. Holker Papers (LC), reel 12, fols. 4795-4798, 4866.

20. Joshua Humphrey's notebook, purchased September 28, 1927 from the Dreer Fund, is part of the larger Humphreys MS collection at the Historical Society of Pennsylvania, Philadelphia. John Charnock's often unreliable *Architectura Navalis* (London, 1798) lists the *Bellisarius*'s dimensions as 104'-0" on the lower deck, 91'-3½" on the keel, 27'-6" beam, and 10'-3" depth of hold.

21. Holker Papers (LC), reel 11, fol. 4275; Chapelle, *American Sailing Ships, op. cit.*, p. 59.

22. The Continental frigate *Hague* was built at Nantes, France, in 1777. Until 1782, she had been known as the *Deane*. The *Hague* and the *Alliance* were the only Continental frigates still in service at the end of the American Revolution.

23. James Swan to Daniel Parker, October 4, 1783. Holker Papers (LC), reel 11, fol. 4289. Biographical material on Swan is to be found in the *Dictionary of American Biography*, vol. IX, p. 234.

III
In Search of the *Panax quinquefolia*
(*pages 31-42*)

1. Holker Papers (LC), reel 10, fol. 4200.
2. That the importation of furs into Canton by American vessels became an important medium of trade is shown by the number of pelts shipped from 1805 through 1834: *Beaver*—241,334; *Fox*—137,198; *Nutria*—343,989; *Otter*—165,817; *Sea Otter*—148,340; *Seal*—1,605,091; *Muskrat, Rabbit, Sable*, and other small furs—100,191. *The Chinese Repository*, vol. III (April 1835), no. 12, p. 558.
3. *Ibid.*, vol. II (February 1834), no. 10, pp. 461-462.
4. Ben Charles Harris, *Ginseng: What It Is—What It Can Do for You* (New Canaan, CT: Keats Publishing Inc., 1978), pp. 31-34.
5. *The American Museum or Repository of Ancient & Modern Fugitive Pieces Prose & Poetical* (Philadelphia: Matthew Carey), vol. 7, p. 127.
6. Sarah Harriman, *The Book of Ginseng* (New York: Jove/HBT Books, 1973), pp. 65f.
7. A. R. Harding, *Ginseng and Other Medicinal Plants* (Columbus, Ohio, 1908), p. 43.
8. Adolph B. Benson, ed., *Peter Kalm's Travels in North America* (New York: Wilson-Erickson, Inc., 1937), vol II, p. 437.
9. Constable-Pierrepont Papers, Box 8, Shipping Papers, William Constable, "Proposed Voyages to China 1784-   ," New York Public Library. At the New-York Historical Society are a number of ledgers, letter books, day books, and journals of Robert, John, and Berendt Sanders (1748-1800) of Schenectady, NY, which detail the ginseng trade during those years in the Mohawk Valley.
10. Daniel Parker to Robert Morris, February 10, 1784. Parker Papers, Massachusetts Historical Society.
11. "Chronology of the Life of Dr. Robert Johnston," courtesy of Mrs. Alvan (Frances Johnston) Markle, III, Ardmore, PA; *Pennsylvania Archives*, vol. X (second series), pp. 172-173; "Memoirs of Brigadier-General John Lacey of Pennsylvania," *Pennsylvania Magazine of History and Biography*, vol. XXV (1901), p. 344. Dr. Johnston died near Waynesboro, Franklin County.
12. Holker Papers (LC), reel 11, fol. 4227; Turnbull, Marmie & Co. to Parker, *ibid.*, reel 11, fol. 4262.
13. Robert Johnston to Turnbull, Marmie &

Co., September 13, 1783, *ibid.*, reel 11, fol. 4252. The order in favor of Col. James Johnston is on reel 11, fol. 4255.
14. *Ibid.*, reel 11, fol. 4255.
15. *Ibid.*, reel 11, fols. 4280-4281.
16. *Ibid.*, reel 11, fol. 4295.
17. *Ibid.*, reel 11, fols. 4312-4313.
18. *Ibid.*, reel 11, fols. 4317-4318.
19. *Ibid.*, reel 11, fol. 4348.
20. *Ibid.*, reel 11, fols. 4380-4381.
21. *Ibid.*, reel 11, fols. 4411-4412.
22. *Ibid.*, reel 11, fols. 4402, 4472, 4489, 4506. Turnbull, Marmie & Co. charged 5% commission on purchases and 2½% on cash loans, drafts, and shipping insurance.
23. *Ibid.*, reel 12, fols. 4795-4798.
24. *Ibid.*, reel 11, fol. 4527. The blizzard is recorded in Ludlum, *op. cit.*, p. 65; and the length of the *Empress of China*'s passage from Boston is in *The Independent Journal or, The General Advertiser* (New York), no. 4, Monday, December 8, 1783, Bradford's Marine List, p. 3.

IV
Shedding the Fur Scheme
(*pages 43-56*)

1. "Ledyard, John," *Dictionary of American Biography*, vol. VI, p. 93.
2. Alan Villiers, *Captain James Cook* (New York: Charles Scribner's Sons, 1967), p. 279n.
3. Alexander Walker, *An Account of a Voyage to the North West Coast of America in 1785 & 1786*, Robin Fisher and J. M. Bumsted, eds. (Seattle: University of Washington Press, 1982); Samuel Eliot Morison, *The Maritime History of Massachusetts, 1783-1860* (Boston: Houghton Mifflin Co., 1941), pp. 46-48; Edmund Hayes, ed., *Log of the* Union: *John Boit's Remarkable Voyage to the Northwest Coast and Around the World* (Portland, Oregon: Oregon Historical Society, 1981).
4. Daniel Parker to John Holker. Holker Papers (LC), reel 11, fol. 4257.
5. Bradford Adams Whittemore, *Memorials of the Massachusetts Society of the Cincinnati* (Boston: The Society, 1964), pp. 543-544.
6. Samuel Shaw to Winthrop Sargent. ALS in MS Collection, Historical Society of Pennsylvania.
7. Holker Papers (LC), reel 14, fol. 5501. From this, one may surmise that William Duer provided John Ledyard with his letters of in-

troduction to Robert Morris and other Philadelphia speculators.

8. Robert Morris to Thomas Russell (Boston), John Langdon (Portsmouth, NH), William Burgess (Boston) et al., September 2, 1783. Charles P. Greenough MSS, Massachusetts Historical Society.

9. Henry Knox to George Clinton, December 4, 1783. Knox Papers, XVI-56, Massachusetts Historical Society.

10. Holker Papers (LC), reel 11, fols. 4501-4502.

11. *Ibid.*, reel 11, fol. 4543; Robert Morris to Daniel Parker, Knox Papers, XVI-86, Massachusetts Historical Society.

12. Holker Papers (LC), reel 11, fol. 4301.

13. Constable-Pierrepont Papers, Box 8, Shipping Papers, William Constable, "Proposed Voyages to China 1784-   ," notes on ginseng, New York Public Library.

14. Holker Papers (LC), reel 11, fols. 4506, 4592, 4622; reel 12, fol. 4698; reel 13, fol. 5064. Nicholson shortly afterwards commanded the Philadelphia ship *United States*, supposedly the first American vessel to put into an Indian port.

15. Green himself gives the year 1764 in a letter to Henry Laurens, February 17, 1782. John Green Letter Book, Philadelphia Maritime Museum, hereinafter cited as (PMM).

16. Lt. Cdr. Carrow Thibault, USNR, "Captain from the Country," typescript lecture about his ancestor, John Green, p. 2. PMM Library.

17. James S. Biddle, ed., *Autobiography of Charles Biddle, 1745-1821* (Philadelphia, 1883), pp. 46, 47.

18. George Lupton (Van Zandt) to William Eden, July 23, 1777, *Stevens' Facsimilies*, no. 259, Aukland MSS, Kings College, Cambridge, England, from William Bell Clark typescript in the John Green Papers, PMM.

19. Claypoole's *American Daily Advertiser*, Thursday, September 29, 1796.

20. George Lupton (Van Zandt) to William Eden, July 17, 1777, *Stevens' Facsimilies*, no. 181, Aukland MSS, Kings College, Cambridge, England, from William Bell Clark typescript in the John Green Papers, PMM.

21. *New York Gazette and the Weekly Mercury*, no. 1389, June 8, 1778.

22. Letter of June 11, 1778. John Bradford Letter Book, Library of Congress, Washington, DC.

23. Thomas Bell to John Paul Jones, November 3, 1778. John Paul Jones Papers, Library of Congress, Washington, DC, fols. 6879-6880.

24. Benjamin Franklin Papers, xvi, 208, 214; xv, 7, American Philosophical Society, Philadelphia; *The Public Advertiser* (London), no. 13962, July 8, 1778.

25. Benjamin Franklin Papers, lx, 37, *ibid.*

26. John Green to Thomas Digges, May 16, 1782; Green to James Burn, June 1, 1782; Green to David Hartley, June 2, 1783. John Green Letter Book, PMM.

27. *The Independent Gazetteer* (Philadelphia), no. 19, August 17, 1782.

28. Robert Morris Diary in Office of Finance, ii, 202, 211, 220-222, 228, 229, 240, 241, 256, 322, Library of Congress, Washington, DC; Robert Morris Agent of Marine Letter Book, pp. 129, 134, 140, United States Naval Academy, Annapolis, MD; John Green Letter Book, PMM; John Barry Papers, LC and PMM.

29. John Green to Joseph Swift, August 19, 1783, John Green Letter Book, PMM; Thibault, *op. cit.*, pp. 1, 7.

30. Robert Morris Agent of Marine Letter Book, *op. cit.*, p. 205.

31. Robert Morris Diary in Office of Finance, *op. cit.*, iii, 38, 49.

32. *The Independent Journal or, The General Advertiser* (New York), Monday, December 8, 1783, p. 4.

33. John Peck, research notes by D. Foster Taylor, Peabody Museum of Salem, MA.

34. Robert Morris Diary in Office of Finance, *op. cit.*, iii, 82; Robert Morris Agent of Marine Letter Book, *op. cit.*, p. 232.

v

Most Serene, Puissant, and Illustrious
(*pages 57-73*)

1. *Naval Records of the American Revolution* (Washington: Government Printing Office, 1906), p. 488; Craig Walter Green typescript of genealogical notes on the Green and related families, PMM; Constable-Pierrepont Papers, Box 8, Shipping Papers, William Constable, New York Public Library.

2. Craig Walter Green, *op. cit.; General Alumni Catalogue of the University of Pennsylvania* (Philadelphia: University of Pennsylvania, 1922); William Bell Clark, ed., "Journal of the *Empress of China*," *The American Neptune*, vol. X (April 1950), pp. 83ff; "Extracts

from the Letters of John Macpherson, Jr. to William Patterson," *Pennsylvania Magazine of History and Biography*, vol. 23 (1899), p. 53, and see also vol. 6 (1882), pp. 331-333 and vol. 30 (1906), pp. 130-152. The elder John Swift was at one time the Collector of the Port of Philadelphia.

3. Walter Craig Green, *op. cit.*; Letter of February 10, 1782; John Barry to Green, March 13, 1782; and Green to Alcie Green, March 23, 1782, John Green Letter Book, PMM; miscellaneous *Pigou* MS, J. Welles Henderson Collection, Philadelphia.

4. J. Robert T. Craine, comp. and Harry W. Hazard, ed., *The Ancestry and Posterity of Matthew Clarkson, 1664-1702* (n.p., J. Robert T. Craine, 1971), pp. 19, 29.

5. Clark, "Journal . . . ," *op. cit.*, pp. 83ff.

6. Thomas Westcott, *Names of Persons Who Took the Oath of Allegiance to the State of Pennsylvania* (Philadelphia: John Campbell, 1865), p. 98; Clark, "Journal . . . ," *op. cit.*, pp. 83ff; Molineux is mentioned occasionally in Green's correspondence from Mill Prison, John Green Letter Book, PMM where also there is a MS book of British naval signals, presented to Green at Mill Prison by Molineux and others as a token of esteem. Molineux's letter of June 19, 1785 concerning trade with the East Indies is in the Constable-Pierrepont Papers, Box 1, William Constable Letters, 1785, New York Public Library. His account book of purchases at Canton (see Appendix B) is in the Rare Book Room, University of Pennsylvania. A map of Erie, PA in the 1790's, presumably by him, is listed in *Evans*.

7. William Bell Clark and William James Morgan, eds., *Naval Documents of the American Revolution* (Washington: Government Printing Office, 1964-   ), 8 volumes published to date; *Naval Records of the American Revolution* (Washington: Government Printing Office, 1906).

8. Quincy, *Shaw, op. cit.*, p. 112; Shaw to Winthrop Sargent, December 24, 1783, ALS in MS Collection, Historical Society of Pennsylvania.

9. Whittemore, *Cincinnati, op. cit.*, pp. 501, 543-544.

10. Quincy, *op. cit.*, p. 38.

11. Jonathan Goldstein, "The Ethics of Tribute and Profits of Trade: Stephen Girard's China Trade, 1787-1824," typescript thesis, PMM; *Naval Records of the American Revolution, op. cit.*, pp. 327, 356, 400, 413.

12. Hannah Roach card file, American Philosophical Society, Philadelphia, citing the *Pennsylvania Packet* of March 23, 1782 and the *Pennsylvania Journal* of May 31, 1783.

13. Parker to Holker, December 13, 1783. Holker Papers (LC), reel 11, fols. 4501-4502.

14. Parker to Turnbull, Marmie & Co., January 15, 1784. *Ibid.*, reel 12, fol. 4678.

15. Ludlum, *op. cit.*, p. 65.

16. Parker to Holker, January 17, 1784. Holker Papers (LC), reel 12, fol. 4682.

17. ALS in MS Collection, Historical Society of Pennsylvania.

18. Holker Papers (LC), reel 12, fol. 4698.

19. Bills of lading for the wine, specie, and ginseng are in the Holker Papers (LC), reel 12, fol. 4695. Those for the tin, merchandise, cordage and cables are in the Holker Papers (Yale).

20. Both documents are in the John Green Papers, PMM.

21. *Ibid.*

22. Gouverneur Morris to Charles Thomson, December 30, 1783. Charles Thomson Papers, Library of Congress, vol. I, fols. 7726-7727.

23. The original sea-letters are in the John Green Papers, PMM.

24. Holker Papers (LC), reel 12, fols. 4727-4730.

25. *Ibid.*, reel 12, fols. 4733, 4743-4744.

26. News item with a New York dateline in the *Pennsylvania Gazette*, February 18, 1784.

VI

Aweigh at Last
(*pages 74-83*)

1. Randall to Knox, February 4, 1784. Knox Papers, XVII-4, Massachusetts Historical Society.

2. Ludlum, *op. cit.*, pp. 66-67.

3. Green to Swift, February 5, 1784. Hildeburn Papers, Historical Society of Pennsylvania.

4. *The New York Packet and the American Advertiser*, no. 361, Monday, February 23, 1784, p. 2.

5. *The Independent Gazette or the New York Journal Revised*, no. xxi, Thursday, February 26, 1784.

6. Francis Ross Holland, Jr., *America's Lighthouses, Their Illustrated History Since 1716* (Brattleboro, VT: The Stephen Greene Press, 1972), p. 11.

7. Green's Journal, with original spelling, symbols, and abbreviations, was annotated and edited by William Bell Clark and published in *The American Neptune* in five parts: vol. X (1950), pp. 83-107, 220-229, 288-297, and vol. XI (1951), pp. 59-71, 134-144. The journal, then owned by Carrow Thibault, is now part of the John Green Papers, PMM. Another fragmentary journal, possibly by Surgeon's Mate Andrew Caldwell, survives in a mid-nineteenth-century copy at the National Archives, Washington, DC. It is reproduced here as Appendix A.

8. William Falconer's *An Universal Dictionary of the Marine* (London, 1780) defines "round house" as: "A name given, in East Indiamen, and other large merchant ships, to a cabin or apartment built in the after part of the quarterdeck and having the poop for its roof. . . ."

9. Holker Papers (LC), reel 12, fols. 4758-4763.

10. *Ibid.*, reel 12, fol. 4841.

11. *Ibid.*, reel 12, fols. 4870-4871.

VII
An Unexpected Stopover
(*pages 84-102*)

1. Holker Papers (Yale) and Holker Papers (LC), reel 14, fol. 5541.

2. Holker Papers (LC), reel 12, fol. 5656.

3. *Ibid.*, reel 12, fols. 4797-4798.

4. *Ibid.*, reel 12, fols. 4801-4802.

5. Holker Papers (Yale).

6. Quincy, *Shaw, op. cit.*, pp. 134-136.

7. Holker Papers (LC), reel 12, fol. 5666.

8. *Ibid.* A letter in French from John Girard to his brother Stephen, in which the former mentions having received Randall's letter, is in the Girard Papers, American Philosophical Society, Philadelphia.

9. Holker Papers (LC), reel 12, fol. 5666.

10. Quincy, *op. cit.*, pp. 136-148.

VIII
Doubling the Cape
(*pages 103-114*)

1. Samuel Dunn, *A New Directory for the East-Indies* (London: Printed for Henry Gregory, 1780), pp. 375-376.

2. Holker Papers (LC), reel 12, fol. 5011 and reel 13, fols. 5158-5159. The latter is du-

plicated in the Holker Papers (Yale); the translation from the French is the author's.

IX
The Flight of Daniel Parker
(*pages 115-126*)

1. Samuel Shaw to Winthrop Sargent, November 10, 1785. ALS in MS Collection, Historical Society of Pennsylvania.

2. Holker Papers (LC), reel 12, fol. 4863.

3. William Duer Papers, Correspondence, Box 1, New-York Historical Society.

4. Holker Papers (LC), reel 16, fol. 6440.

5. William Duer Papers, Correspondence, Box 1, New-York Historical Society.

6. *Ibid.*

7. *Ibid.*

8. Holker Papers (LC), reel 13, fol. 5162.

9. *Ibid.*, reel 13, fol. 5157.

10. That Parker was in Philadelphia at the beginning of July is demonstrated by his letter of July 2 to James Swan in Boston. Holker Papers (LC), reel 13, fol. 5194.

11. *Ibid.*, reel 14, fols. 5554-5557.

12. *Ibid.*

13. *Ibid.*, reel 14, fol. 5868.

14. *Ibid.*, reel 14, fols. 5554-5557.

15. Quincy, *Shaw, op. cit.*, p. 150.

X
In the Sunda Strait
(*pages 127-145*)

1. Dunn, *op. cit.*, pp. 376-377.

2. *Ibid.*, p. 380.

3. John White Swift to John Swift, July 18, 1784, Hildeburn Papers, Historical Society of Pennsylvania.

4. Holker Papers (LC), vol. 27, fol. 5351 recto. Those portions of the policy printed here in *italics* signify manuscript portions of the original document. The translation from the French is by the author.

5. Quincy, *Shaw, op. cit.*, pp. 150-160.

XI
Canton Cumshaw and Commerce
(*pages 147-171*)

1. Holker Papers (Yale), expenses at Whampoa and Canton.

2. *Ibid.*, and Francis Warriner, *Cruise of the United States Frigate* Potomac *Round the World During the Years 1831-1834* (New York: Leavitt, Lord & Co., 1835), pp. 191-197.

3. Quincy, *Shaw, op. cit.*, pp. 163-164.

4. Hosea Ballou Morse, *Chronicles of the East India Company, op. cit.*, vol. 2, p. 94.

5. Quincy, *op. cit.*, p. 177n.

6. William C. Hunter, *The 'Fan Kwae' at Canton Before Treaty Days* (London: Kegan, Paul, Trench & Co., 1882) and reprint (Taipei: Ch'eng-wen Publishing Co., 1965), pp. 98-101.

7. John White Swift to John Swift, December 3, 1784, Hildeburn Papers, Historical Society of Pennsylvania.

8. Morse, *op. cit.*, vol. 2, p. 95.

9. Holker Papers (LC), reel 15, fol. 5888.

10. Constable-Pierrepont Papers, Box 8, Shipping Papers, William Constable, "Proposed Voyages to China 1784-   ," New York Public Library.

11. Quincy, *op. cit.*, pp. 160-167.

XII
Learning to Trade with the Hong Merchants
(*pages 172-188*)

1. Morse, *op. cit.*, vol. 2, p. 95.

2. Holker Papers (LC), reel 15, fol. 5889.

3. Holker Papers (Yale).

4. Hunter, *op. cit.*, p. 36, and Kenneth Scott Latourette, "The History of Early Relations Between the United States and China, 1784-1844," *Transactions of the Connecticut Academy of Arts and Sciences*, vol. 22 (August 1917).

5. Morse, *op. cit.*, vol. 2, p. 45 and appendix lists of yearly fiadors by ship. "Qua" has its equivalent in "Mr." or "Sir." The most famous hong merchant during the golden era of the China trade was Houqua (or Howqua); however, it is often overlooked that there were *four* hong merchants of that family business name, otherwise known as: (1) Wu Kuo-ying, 1731-1800, (2) Wu Ping-chien, 1769-1843, third son of Wu Kuo-ying, (3) Wu Yuan-hua, 1801-1833, fourth son of Wu Ping-chien, and (4) Wu Ch'ung-yueh, 1810-1863, fifth son of Wu Yuan-hua. The first Houqua had been a salt merchant and for a while was known as Puankhequa's Purser, but he finally joined the co-hong the year after the *Empress of China*'s first trading season. See Albert Ten Eyck Gardner, "Cantonese Chinnerys: Portraits of How-qua and other

China Trade Paintings," *The Art Quarterly*, vol. XVI (Winter 1953).

6. Quincy, *Shaw, op. cit.*, p. 193; Morse, *op. cit.; New Lloyd's List* (London), no. 1640, January 25, 1785.

7. Hunter, *op. cit.*, pp. 24f.

8. Quincy, *op. cit.*, pp. 167-188, 198-200.

XIII
Chinese Justice
(*pages 189-200*)

1. Holker Papers (LC), reel 13, fol. 5445; reel 14, fol. 5467; and reel 15, fol. 5879. The discrepancy in the quantity of the wine through leakage, and its subsequent reapportionment, is treated in great detail. Obviously, it was a major concern of the officers at the time; the shortage in the specie boxes then came as a crowning blow.

2. Holker Papers (Yale).

3. *Ibid.*

4. *Ibid.*

5. *New Lloyd's List* (London), no. 1678, June 3, 1785.

6. Morse, *Chronicles of the East India Company, op. cit.*, vol. 2, p. 99.

7. Quincy, *Shaw, op. cit.*, p. 186.

8. Morse, *op. cit.*, vol. 2, p. 100.

9. *Ibid.*, p. 102.

10. Quincy, *op. cit.*, pp. 188-190. Upon his return to the United States, Shaw wrote a lengthy recapitulation of his experiences and observations in China to John Jay, then Secretary of Foreign Affairs. With it went the Fuyuen's two pieces of silk for the inspection of the Congress. Shaw's letter to Jay, and associated correspondence, was published in various newspapers of the time; in *The American Museum, op. cit.*, vol. 1, pp. 217-221; in Quincy, Appendix A, pp. 337-341; and in *The Chinese Repository*, September 1836, no. 5, pp. 219-223.

11. Morse, *op. cit.*, vol. 2, p. 104.

12. Quincy, *op. cit.*, pp. 193f.

13. *Ibid.*

14. Morse, *op. cit.*, vol. 2, p. 105. Shaw, and the others on board, had no way of knowing the ultimate fate of the gunner. The incident, however, made an indelible impression and was relayed in the glow of pro-Chinese sentiment to the New York press upon the ship's return. The *Pennsylvania Packet and Daily Advertiser*, no. 1966, May 25, 1785, reprinted the story as it was originally reported by the *New York News*

Dispatch of May 21: "We are informed, that during the continuance of the ship *Empress of China*, at Canton, a salute was fired on some occasion, from one of the ships in the harbour, when very ignorantly, and most unfortunately it proved that the charge in one of the saluting guns had not been drawn, which proved fatal to two Chinese inhabitants, who were killed on the spot. This melancholy event brought on the resentment of 30,000 natives, who secured the gunner of an English ship, from whence the execution was done; but the commanders and ship companies of all the vessels from the various countries, British, French, Americans, Danes, Swedes, Dutch &c. combined to recover the captive gunner, and after a weeks cessation of business, and the man had submitted to a very equitable trial, was acquitted and enlarged, the ancient good humour of the Chinese returned, since they found, from a very candid investigation that the misfortune was not premeditated, but pronounced in their law courts as mere *Chance Medley*. It must be observed, that China is governed by most excellent laws, which are rigidly executed, otherwise what could be done by so many myriads of inhabitants as compose the immense empire of China?—The preceding general detail has been suddenly collected; should there be found any error, the Printer will gladly produce from more accurate and minute intelligence that may be offered him, a correct edition of this commotion."

XIV
Bound for Home
(*pages 201-219*)

1. Randall to Knox, December 26, 1784. Knox Papers, XVII, 156, 2449, Massachusetts Historical Society.
2. Hunter, '*Fan Kwae*,' *op. cit.*, pp. 101-102.
3. *Ibid.*, p. 103.
4. Jonathan Ingersoll to Elias Hasket Derby, April 8, 1785. Derby Papers, *Grand Turk*, Essex Institute, Salem, MA.
5. Issue of May 12, 1785.
6. Issue of May 14, 1785.
7. Quincy, *Shaw*, *op. cit.*, pp. 200-210.

XV
Sales and Selling Out
(*pages 220-234*)

1. Duer to Holker, December 7, 1784. Holker Papers (LC), reel 14, fol. 5463.
2. Holker to Duer, December 28, 1784. William Duer Papers, Box 1, Correspondence, New-York Historical Society.
3. Holker to Duer, January 1785. *Ibid.*
4. *Ibid.*
5. Among other newspaper accounts from farther afield of the *Empress of China*'s return were the following: *Loudon's New York Packet* (May 12); the *Pennsylvania Packet and Daily Advertiser* and the *Pennsylvania Journal and Weekly Advertiser* (May 14); the *Connecticut Courant* (Hartford), the *New York Packet*, and the *Pennsylvania Packet and Daily Advertiser* repeat from the *New York News Dispatch* (May 16); the *Pennsylvania Gazette* (May 18); the *Pennsylvania Packet and Daily Advertiser* repeat from the *New York News Dispatch* (May 23); and the *Connecticut Courant* (May 30, 1785).
6. Deposition sworn before James M. Hughes, Notary Public, May 13, 1785. Holker Papers (Yale).
7. Holker Papers (LC), reel 14, fols. 5511-5512, 5724. The latter is dated May 19, 1785.
8. *New York News Dispatch*, May 19, 1785.
9. The William Constable & Company partnership agreement is in the William Duer Papers, New-York Historical Society.
10. Emily Williams, "The Luck of the Irish: A Biographical Sketch of William Constable," Lewis County [NY] Historical Society *Journal*, vol. V (1975), nos. 2-3, pp. 3-33.
11. The *Pallas* left Macao on January 20, 1785, only three weeks after the *Empress of China*, and arrived in Baltimore on August 9. On the tenth, Thomas Randall wrote to Henry Knox: "I have the pleasure to inform you of my arrival here in the Ship *Pallas* which my friend Mr Shaw and myself purchased in China, we stopped some time at Batavia the capital of the Dutch settlements in the East Indies where the reception our flag met with was polite and friendly." Knox Papers, XVIII-69, Massachusetts Historical Society. According to the *New York Packet* of August 22, 1785, her cargo consisted of teas, china, silks, satins, gauzes, velvets, umbrellas, paper hangings, etc., "The sale of which is to commence at Baltimore on the 1st of October next, by public vendue and to continue untill the whole is disposed of, under

the following conditions: The purchaser immediately to pay ten per cent on the amount of whatever lots he may buy, and either give undeniable and satisfactory security for due payment of the balance, in two months, or leave the goods as a deposit until they are cleared out, which must be at the expiration of two months from the date of the purchase, otherwise, they are to be re-sold immediately on the first purchaser's account, who is to be answerable to the proprietor for any deficiency, and the expenses attending the second sale." Samuel Shaw's special-order Society of the Cincinnati porcelain was among the objects of the *Pallas* cargo. One item among the *Empress of China* material in the Holker Papers (LC)—reel 15, fol. 5981-a—mentions this porcelain in passing. An accounting of circa January 20, 1786 from Constable, Rucker & Co. for sales and expenses therein incurred on materials from the *Empress of China*, the document is headed "Amount of China per Invoice exclusive of the Cincinati is 2938 Dollars." Further, nothing more is recorded of it.

12. John White Swift to John Swift, June 1, 1785, Hildeburn Papers, Historical Society of Pennsylvania.

13. John White Swift to John Swift, June 13, 1785. *Ibid.*

14. Statement by Thomas Fitzsimons, Holker Papers (Yale). A nearly duplicate copy is in the Holker Papers (LC), reel 15, fols. 5897-5898.

15. William Constable to Thomas Fitzsimons, November 30, 1785. Holker Papers (LC), reel 15, fols. 5880-5881.

16. Holker to Fitzsimons, June 30, 1785. *Ibid.*, reel 14, fol. 5749.

17. Memorandum of Thomas Fitzsimons, Holker Papers (Yale).

18. Holker Papers (LC), reel 16, fols. 6253-6254. The accounts of the *Empress of China*'s purchases, sales, expenses and profits are by no means complete and largely refer to the theoretical half-share owned by Daniel Parker & Company. The following lists where the appropriate materials can be found, but in the author's opinion it would now be impossible to reconstruct a wholly accurate picture of the voyage finances.

(A) *Daniel Parker Letter Book*, no. 806 MSS:761 MS60-1741, Baker Library, Harvard University School of Business Administration. Primarily pre-*Empress* military contracts.

(B) *Daniel Parker Papers*, Massachusetts Historical Society. (D. Parker & Co. in account with D. Parker—"To ½ Ship *Empress [of] China* Cargo &c [$] 59,000.")

(C) *Joseph Barrell Papers*, no. 879 MSS:766 MS60-1490, Baker Library, Harvard University School of Business Administration. Waste Book (1770-1803) shows that by July 1785 at least four chests of Hyson tea from the *Empress of China* had been received in Boston. "Goods Received from China" were advertised the following month. See also Ledger (1784-1802).

(D) *John Holker Papers* (Yale) contain miscellaneous accounts, especially concerning Samuel Shaw and Thomas Randall.

(E) *John Holker Papers* (LC) (reel/folio numbers of the more important accounts).

(1) 11/4590 Daniel Parker & Co. in Account with Daniel Parker.

(2) 11/4592 Daniel Parker & Co. in Account with Daniel Parker.

(3) 11/4622 Daniel Parker & Co. in Account with Daniel Parker.

(4) 14/5497 "Recd from Constable Rucker & Co. of New York P Order of Mr. T. Fitzsimons," no date.

(5) 14/5563 "Owners of the Ships *Empress China, Columbia, & Comte de Artois*," no date.

(6) 15/5880-5881 William Constable to Thomas Fitzsimons, November 30, 1785: "Account of Sundries Shiped & delivered by order of Mr Thomas Fitzsimons on account of Danl Parker & Co. one Half of the *Empress of China*s Cargo from Canton."

(7) 15/5888-5889 Abstract of Sales in China, Purchases in China, Sales in New York, no date.

(8) 15/5980-5981-a "The Following Proportions of Goods Sold, Shipped & Delivered Damaged & remaining on hand of the *Empress of China*'s Cargo, are Carried to the Credit of Daniel Parker & Co Account Sales their One Half (Amount of China per Invoice exclusive of the Cincinati . . .)," January 20, 1786.

(9) 15/6045 "Messrs Daniel Parker & Co in Account Current with Constable Rucker & Co," December 31, 1787.

(10) 15/6086 "Abstract Sales of one half Cargo of Ship *Empress of China* for Account John Holker Esquire & Others," no date.

(11) 15/6090 "Account of the disposition of the C[?] Proceeds Cargo ship *Empress [of] China*," no date.

(12) 15/6097 "Adventure to Canton in the Ship *Empress of China* in acct with the [?]," no date.

(13) 15/6099 "Messrs Josiah W. & W. Gibbes in a/c with John Holker," no date but probably 1786.

(14) 15/6100-6101 "Messrs Josiah W. & W. Gibbs in a/c with John Holker," no date.

(15) 15/6200 "Sales of one half Cargo of the Ship *Empress of China* J Green Comr from Canton, consg of 161 Chests & 318 boxes Bohea Tea, 145 [445?] boxes Hyson, 20 Singloe, 12 Souchong Teas, 5320 pieces Nankeens 320 pieces White Cloths &c for Act J. Holker Esqr & others," December 23, 1787.

(16) 15/6204 "Messrs Daniel Parker & Co of New York their Account Current with Constable Rucker & Co," December 31, 1787.

(17) 16/6253-6254 Accounts of Parker & Co. with Mordecai Lewis & Co., June 1, 1788.

19. *The Independent Gazetteer; or the Chronicle of Freedom* (Philadelphia), no. 196, July 30, 1785.

20. *The Independent Journal or, the General Advertiser* (New York), Saturday, June 18, 1785; also the *Pennsylvania Packet*, June 21, 1785.

21. *New York Daily Advertiser*, January 20, 1786. John Green seems to have incurred the wrath of several of his former officers, including John White Swift, who wrote in late December 1785 or early January 1786: "Capt Green is a———man. If I don't make haste to conclude I fear he will leave me in the lurch. I find he does not intend to take any of his former officers with him this voyage." Draft in letter from Robert C. Livingston to John Swift, December 15, 1785, ALS in MS Collection, Historical Society of Pennsylvania. John Green, Jr. did go out as mate, however.

Some details and accounts of the *Empress of China*'s second voyage are to be found in the Constable-Pierrepont Papers, New York Public Library. The ship returned to New York in early May 1787.

Samuel Shaw, too, developed strong feelings of animosity against Green. The suspected cause is Green's probable suspicion of Shaw arising from the famous missing specie and from siding with Messrs. Morris and Holker who declined paying Shaw his wages in view of the discrepancy. From Canton, early in 1787, Shaw wrote: "Are you acquainted with Green, with whom I came here the first voyage? *Hic niger est—hunc tu, Amice caveto* ['This one is wicked; may you, O friend, beware of this one']. The line was never better applied, for he is a diabolical scoundrel. Had I time to tell you the whole story, you would be of the same opinion—*Longa est in-* *juria, longae ambages* ['Long is the injustice; long are the details']—and so I must refer you to Randall when you and he meet." Shaw to Winthrop Sargent, January 12, 1787, ALS in MS Collection, Historical Society of Pennsylvania.

XVI
The Long Limbs of Litigation
(*pages 235-250*)

1. *Journals of the Continental Congress*, June 9, 1785; Quincy, *Shaw, op. cit.*, Appendix A, pp. 217, 341.

2. Quincy, p. 219.

3. Samuel Shaw to Winthrop Sargent, February 1, 1786. ALS in MS Collection, Historical Society of Pennsylvania.

4. Shaw to Sargent, November 10, 1785. *Ibid.*

5. Shaw Accounts, Holker Papers (Yale), "No 11."

6. Shaw to Robert Morris and Thomas Fitzsimons, October 19, 1785. Holker Papers (Yale).

7. Shaw to Sargent, January 26, 1786. ALS in MS Collection, Historical Society of Pennsylvania.

8. For a biographical sketch of Craigie, see the *Dictionary of American Biography*, vol. II, pp. 497-498. Daniel Parker to Andrew Craigie, October 15, 1784. Craigie Papers, Box 8, Folder 6, Incoming Correspondence, Daniel Parker, 1782-May 1787, American Antiquarian Society, Worcester, MA.

9. Parker to Craigie, January 1, 1785. *Ibid.*

10. Parker to unidentified correspondent, August 20, 1785. *Ibid.* The recipient may have been Ephraim Grant, one of Parker's cronies, rather than his brother Benjamin.

11. Parker to Shaw, January 1, 1786. *Ibid.*

12. Parker to Craigie, February 9, 1786. *Ibid.*

13. Parker to Craigie, June 7, 1786. *Ibid.*

14. Parker to Craigie, July (nd), 1786. *Ibid.*

15. Parker to Craigie, May 2, 1787. About this time, he wrote to Craigie: "I have been my dearest Friend on board the *London* (an east india ship) now in the river just arrived from China, the captain informs me that he saw the *Empress of China* in the Streights of Banca, which are within 1 months sail of Canton, that he did not speak her, but that he saw her colours, & afterwards he stopd at the streights of sunda, where he found that she had water'd a few days before, he had the ships name & the

Captains in his log Book which he shew me. . . ." *Ibid.*

16. Parker to Craigie, April 1, 1787. *Ibid.*

17. Henry Knox to William Lewis, September 21, 1787. Knox Papers, XXI-12, Massachusetts Historical Society.

18. Alexander Fullerton to Knox, November 11, 1787, (5335) XXI-44, and Knox to Fullerton, November 15, 1787, (857) XXI-50. *Ibid.*

19. Lewis to Knox, May 29, 1788, (5379) XXII-46. *Ibid.*

20. *Ibid.*

21. Shaw to Parker, February 27, 1790, XXV-146. *Ibid.*

22. Knox Papers (2652) XXX-71. *Ibid.*

23. Craigie to Parker, Box 8, Folder 8, American Antiquarian Society.

24. *Ibid.*

25. Holker Papers (LC), reel 16, fols. 6440-6443.

26. William Constable to William McIntosh, April 26, 1788. William Constable Letter Book (June 11, 1782-November 10, 1790), p. 45, New York Public Library.

27. Constable, Rucker & Company engaged with John Peck, designer of the *Empress of China*, now working in the Portsmouth, NH / Kittery, ME area, to build the firm a 500-600 ton ship of southern live oak and cedar to replace the *Empress of China* in the China trade. *Ibid.* Peck's estimate of March 18, 1788 is in the Constable-Pierrepont Papers, Box 8, Shipping Papers, Misc. 1, New York Public Library.

28. The fact that she was renamed *Edgar* is revealed in letters from Sampson Fleming to William Fleming (in Ireland) of August 1, 1787 and December 28, 1787. Sampson Fleming Papers, New York Public Library. Her rating is as listed in *Lloyd's Register* (London) for 1791.

29. Forrest R. Holdcamper, comp., *List of American Flag Merchant Vessels That Received Certificates of Enrollment* [for coasting voyages] *or Registry* [blue water voyages] *at the Port of New York, 1789-1867* (Washington, DC: National Archives, 1968), 2 vols.

30. The *New-York Daily Gazette*, no. 712, Thursday, April 7, 1791. The sinking of the *Clara*, together with the information that she was formerly the *Empress of China*, was also reported in *The New York Journal, & Patriotic Register*, no. 28 of vol. XVL (cumulative no. 2548), Saturday, April 9, 1791.

SELECT BIBLIOGRAPHY

Manuscripts

Abstract Log Book of the *Empress of China* (National Archives)
ALS in MS Collection (Historical Society of Pennsylvania)
Joseph Barrell Papers (Baker Library, Harvard University)
John Barry Papers (Philadelphia Maritime Museum)
John Barry Papers (Library of Congress)
John Bradford Letter Book (Library of Congress)
Constable-Pierrepont Papers (New York Public Library)
Andrew Craigie Papers (American Antiquarian Society)
Elias Hasket Derby Papers (Essex Institute)
William Duer Papers (New-York Historical Society)
Benjamin Franklin Papers (American Philosophical Society)
Benjamin Franklin Collection (Sterling Memorial Library, Yale University)
Stephen Girard Papers (American Philosophical Society)
John Green Papers (Philadelphia Maritime Museum)
Charles P. Greenough Papers (Massachusetts Historical Society)
Hildeburn Papers (Historical Society of Pennsylvania)
John Holker Papers (Library of Congress)
John Holker Papers (Massachusetts Historical Society)
John Holker Papers (Sterling Memorial Library, Yale University)
Joshua Humphreys Papers (Historical Society of Pennsylvania)
John Paul Jones Papers (Library of Congress)
Henry Knox Papers (Massachusetts Historical Society)
Frederick Molineux Account Book (Rare Book Room, University of Pennsylvania)
Robert Morris Diary in Office of Finance (Library of Congress)
Robert Morris Agent of Marine Letter Book (United States Naval Academy)
Daniel Parker Papers (Massachusetts Historical Society)
Daniel Parker Papers (Baker Library, Harvard University)
John Peck / D. Foster Taylor Papers (Peabody Museum of Salem)
Charles Thomson Papers (Library of Congress)

Newspapers

Boston Gazette
Claypoole's *American Daily Advertiser* (Philadelphia)
Connecticut Courant (Hartford)
Independent Chronicle and the Universal Advertiser (Boston)
Independent Gazetteer; or the Chronicle of Freedom (Philadelphia)
Independent Gazette or the New York Journal Revised
Independent Journal or, the General Advertiser (New York)
Loudon's *New York Packet*

New York Daily Advertiser
New-York Daily Gazette
New York Gazetteer and Country Journal
New York Gazette and the Weekly Mercury
New York Journal, & Patriotic Register
New York News Dispatch
New York Packet and the Daily Advertiser
Pennsylvania Gazette
Pennsylvania Journal and Weekly Advertiser
Pennsylvania Mercury and Universal Advertiser
Pennsylvania Packet and Daily Advertiser
Salem Gazette (Salem, MA)

Books

Benson, Adolph B., ed., *Peter Kalm's Travels in North America* (New York, 1937)
Biddle, James S., ed., *Autobiography of Charles Biddle, 1745-1821* (Philadelphia, 1883)
Chapelle, Howard I., *The History of American Sailing Ships* (New York, 1935)
Charnock, John, *Architectura Navalis* (London, 1798)
Chatterton, E. Keble, *The Old East Indiamen* (London, 1933)
Clark, William Bell and William James Morgan, eds., *Naval Documents of the American Revolution* (Washington, DC, 1964-   )
Cotton, Sir Evan, *East Indiamen* (London, 1949)
Craine, J. Robert T., comp. and Harry W. Hazard, ed., *The Ancestry and Posterity of Matthew Clarkson*, 1664-1702 (np, 1971)
Davis, Ralph, *The Rise of the English Shipping Industry* (Newton Abbot, England, 1962)
Dulles, Foster Rhea, *The Old China Trade* (Boston, 1930)
Dunn, Samuel, *A New Directory for the East-Indies* (London, 1780)
Fairburn, William Armstrong, *Merchant Sail* (Center Lovell, Maine, 1945-1955), 6 volumes
General Alumni Catalogue of the University of Pennsylvania (Philadelphia, 1922)
Gilder, Rodman, *The Battery* (Boston, 1936)
Goldstein, Jonathan, *Philadelphia and the China Trade, 1682-1846* (University Park, PA, 1978)
Harding, A. R., *Ginseng and Other Medicinal Plants* (Columbus, OH, 1908)
Harriman, Sarah, *The Book of Ginseng* (New York, 1973)
Harris, Ben Charles, *Ginseng: What It Is—What It Can Do for You* (New Canaan, CT, 1978)
Hayes, Edmund, ed., *The Log of the* Union: *John Boit's Remarkable Voyage to the Northwest Coast and Around the World* (Portland, OR, 1981)
Holdcamper, Forrest R., comp., *List of American Flag Merchant Vessels That Received Certificates of Enrollment or Registry at the Port of New York, 1789-1867* (Washington, DC, 1968)
Holland, Francis Ross, Jr., *America's Lighthouses, Their Illustrated History Since 1716* (Brattleboro, VT, 1972)
Hunter, William C., *The 'Fan Kwae' at Canton Before Treaty Days* (Taipei, 1965)
Ludlum, David M., *Early American Winters, 1604-1820* (Boston, 1966)
Malone, Dumas, ed., *Dictionary of American Biography*
Miller, Russell, and the Editors of Time-Life Books, *The East Indiamen* (Alexandria, VA, 1980)
Morison, Samuel Eliot, *The Maritime History of Massachusetts, 1783-1860* (Boston, 1941)
Morse, Hosea Ballou, *The Chronicles of the East India Company Trading to China, 1635-1834* (Cambridge, MA, 1930), 5 volumes

Nasatir, Abraham P., *French Consuls in the United States: A Calendar of Their Correspondence in the Archives Nationales* (Washington, DC, 1967)

Naval Records of the American Revolution (Washington, DC, 1906)

New Lloyd's List (London, 1784. . . .)

Paine, Ralph D., *The Ships and Sailors of Old Salem* (New York, 1909)

Parry, J. H., *The Establishment of the European Hegemony, 1415-1715* (New York, 1961)

Quincy, Josiah, *The Journals of Major Samuel Shaw the First American Consul at Canton* (Boston, 1847)

Robertson, William Spence, ed., *The Diary of Francisco de Miranda: Tour of the United States, 1783-1784* (New York, 1928)

Sparks, Jared, *The Life of John Ledyard, the American Traveller* (Cambridge, MA, 1828)

Thomas, William Sturgis, *Members of the Society of the Cincinnati* (New York, 1929)

Villiers, Alan, *Captain James Cook* (New York, 1967)

Walker, Alexander, *An Account of a Voyage to the North West Coast of America in 1785 & 1786*, Robin Fisher and J. M. Bumsted, eds. (Seattle, 1982)

Warren, Winslow, *The Society of the Cincinnati, A History of the General Society of the Cincinnati with the Institution of the Order* (Boston, 1929)

Warriner, Francis, *Cruise of the United States Frigate* Potomac *Round the World During the Years 1831-1834* (New York, 1835)

Watrous, Stephen D., ed., *John Ledyard's Journey Through Russia and Siberia, 1787-1788* (Madison, WI, 1966)

Westcott, Thomas, *Names of Persons Who Took the Oath of Allegiance to the State of Pennsylvania* (Philadelphia, 1865)

Whittemore, Bradford Adams, *Memorials of the Massachusetts Society of the Cincinnati* (Boston, 1964)

Articles and Serial Publications

The American Museum or Repository of Ancient & Modern Fugitive Pieces Prose & Poetical (Philadelphia)

The Chinese Repository (Canton)

Clark, William Bell, ed., "The Journal of the *Empress of China*," *The American Neptune*, vol. X (1950) and vol. XI (1951)

"Extracts from the Letters of John Macpherson, Jr. to William Patterson," *Pennsylvania Magazine of History & Biography*, vol. 23 (1899)

Gardner, Albert Ten Eyck, "Cantonese Chinnerys: Portraits of How-qua and Other China Trade Paintings," *The Art Quarterly*, vol. XVI (1953)

Latourette, Kenneth Scott, "The History of Early Relations Between the United States and China, 1784-1844," *Transactions of the Connecticut Academy of Arts and Sciences*, vol. 22 (1917)

"Memoirs of Brigadier-General John Lacey of Pennsylvania," *Pennsylvania Magazine of History & Biography*, vol. 25 (1901)

Moore, E. Earl, "An Introduction to the Holker Papers," *The Western Pennsylvania Historical Magazine*, vol. 42 (1959)

Pennsylvania Archives

"The Sojourn of Francisco de Miranda in Massachusetts and New Hampshire September 16th to December 20th 1784," *Old-Time New England*, vol. XXVI (1935)

Ver Steeg, Clarence L., "Financing and Outfitting the First United States Ship to China," *Pacific Historical Review*, vol. XXII (1953)

Williams, Emily, "The Luck of the Irish: A Biographical Sketch of William Constable," *Lewis County Historical Society Journal*, vol. V (1975)

Woodhouse, Samuel W., "The Voyage of the *Empress of China*," *Pennsylvania Magazine of History & Biography*, vol. 63 (1939)

Miscellaneous

Goldstein, Jonathan, "The Ethics of Tribute and Profits of Trade: Stephen Girard's China Trade, 1787-1824," typescript thesis at the Philadelphia Maritime Museum

Green, Craig Walter, "Two Naval Captains . . . Capt. John Green, Sr. and Capt. James Craig, Jr." Typescript biographical and genealogical notes, Philadelphia Maritime Museum

Thibault, Carrow, "Captain from the Country." Typescript lecture, Philadelphia Maritime Museum

INDEX

On page 298, there appears a separate index to the merchandise acquired by Captain John Green in Canton, the subject of Appendix C. Its entries are not repeated in the main index below. Names of persons, however, will be found in the following compendium.

A

Achong, Canton tailor, 262.
Acung, Canton tailor, 263.
Aferdson, Peter, Swedish shipmaster, 214.
Affong, Canton tailor, 263.
Akee, Canton merchant, 265.
Albany, New York, 20.
Alexandria, Virginia, 38.
Alliance, Continental frigate (Capt. John Barry), 55; illustrations, 55, 247.
"American India Company," 23.
Amoy, Formosa Strait, 12.
Amsterdam Island, Indian Ocean, 121, 127.
Andres, Simon, 260-261.
Angelica, later *Empress of China*, ship, 25, 29, 56.
Anger (Anjer), Java, 139.
Ann, brig (Capt. Charles Biddle), 51.
Annapolis, Maryland, 70.
Anunghoy (Lady's Shoe), Pearl River, 148.
Anunghoy Fort, Pearl River, 202.
Anyong, Canton merchant, 262.
Aphong, Canton tailor, 260, 265.
Appalachian Mountains, 38.
Ap(p)an, Canton tailor, 259-261, 263, 265.
Appleseed, Johnny, 18.
Appleton, John, 242.
Arch Street Ferry, Philadelphia, illustrated, 233.
Arnold, Benedict, 52.
Ascension Island, South Atlantic Ocean, 30.
Asong, Canton tailor, 263.
Assan, Canton tailor, 259-261.
Asseng, Canton silk merchant, 261.
Atone, Canton merchant, 275.
Augusta, Virginia, 38.
Austrian Imperials, trade with China, 12, 178.
Ayow, Chinese compradore, 262, 275.

B

Baker, William, 40.

Baltimore, Maryland, 25, 38, 40, 42, 218, 230.
Banca, South China Sea, 145, 156, 167.
Banca, Straits of, 145, 209, 212.
Bancroft, Edward, 118.
Banks, ——, Dutch captain (ship *General de Klerk*), 210, 212-213.
Bantam, Java, 144-145.
Barber, Nathaniel, 25.
Barnes & Livingston, 230.
Barrell, Joseph, 20, 275-276.
Barrell, Joseph & Company, 288.
Barry, Capt. John (Continental frigate *Alliance*), xvii, 54 (illustration), 55.
Batavia, Java, 9, 128, 138-139, 141, 143-145, 205, 212, 218, 236.
Bath, Virginia, 37-38.
Beaulieu, ——, French captain (East Indiaman *Pondicherry*), 185.
Belfast, Northern Ireland, 250.
Bell, Capt. Thomas (ship *United States*), 207.
Bell, William, supercargo of *Empress of China*, second voyage, 234, 265.
Belle Ile, France, 53.
Bellisarius, ship, model for *Empress of China*, 27, 29; lines (illustration), 28; dimensions, 28, 306 note 20.
Bellona, British East Indiaman (Capt. James Richardson), 185.
Bengal, 167, 230.
Bensalem, Pennsylvania, 57.
Benson, Robert, 65.
Bentham, ——, Dutch supercargo, 212-213.
Betsy, schooner (Capt. Blunt), 41-42.
Biddle, Capt. Charles (brig *Ann*), 51.
Bil(l)iton, South China Sea, 145, 155-156.
Biram Gore, British East Indiaman (Capt. Maugham), 185.
Black Duck, coasting vessel (Capt. James Morgan), 42.
Blake, Thomas, 222.
Blatchford, Capt. —— (British East Indiaman *Foulis*), 174, 185, 207.
Blinds, bamboo, 264.
Blunt, Capt. —— (schooner *Betsy*), 41-42.
BoaVista, island of Cape Verdes, 91, 95, 255.
Boca Tigris, Pearl River, 148, 163 (illustration), 197, 202, 208.
Bogue, the, see Boca Tigris.
Bojadore, Cape, West Africa, 8.

Bombay, India, 195, 200.
Bonavista, see BoaVista.
Bordeaux, France, 249.
Boston, Massachusetts, 19-20, 25-26, 29, 36, 42-44, 49, 56, 58, 60, 62, 81, 84-85, 116-117, 120, 207, 233, 240, 247, 266; place where *Empress of China* built, 25.
Boston Tea Party, 29.
Bourbon, Continental frigate/U.S. merchant ship, 29-30, 50, 120.
Brailholtts, Claus, Dutch captain (ship *Concordia*), 139.
Breck, Samuel, 20, 266, 271-272, 285-286, 292.
Breck, Mrs. Samuel, 272.
Breeches, satin, 263.
Brest, France, 141.
Bristol, Pennsylvania, 56.
Brockholst, Capt. ——, of New York, 52.
Brothers, coasting vessel (Capt. Whiting), 42.
Brownlow, John, 39.
Brushes, feather, 263.
Bunker Hill, Battle of, 29.
Bunner, Andrew, 230, 261, 277-278.
Bunner, Mrs. Andrew, 264.
Burlington, New Jersey, 231.

C

Cabot, John and Sebastian, 9.
Calcutta, British East Indiaman (Capt. Thompson), 185.
Caldwell, Andrew, surgeon's mate of the *Empress of China*, 6, 58, 60, 253, 266.
Caldwell, James, 60.
Callender & Henderson, 39.
Canary Islands, Atlantic Ocean, 254.
Candlesticks, 264.
Cantey, Island of, 208.
Canton, China, 4, 7-8, 11, 15, 17-18, 30, 46, 49-50, 63-65, 67, 69-70, 75, 78, 87, 94, 118-119, 128-130, 141-142, 147-149, 152-153, 155, 159, 167, 170-173, 176-185, 188-189, 195-198, 200-201, 205-206, 208, 212, 214, 230, 233-234, 236, 238-239, 244-245, 247, 259-265, 299-302; illustrations, 168-169, 175, 191, 196.
Canton (Pearl) River, 149, 151 (map), 166, 207.
Caperita Point, South China Sea, 208.
Cap(e) François, Hispaniola, 91-93, 95-96, 100.
Cape Henlopen, Delaware, 52, 147.
Cape Horn, 19, 50.
Cape May, New Jersey, 52, 147.

Cape of Good Hope, 15, 18, 24, 36, 68, 94, 103-104, 127, 139, 141, 204-205, 207, 214-215, 218, 220, 235.
Cape Town, 9, 25, 204-205 (illustration), 247.
Cape Verde Islands, Atlantic Ocean, 67, 91-101, 103, 127.
Caribbean Sea, 205.
Carson, Capt. John (American brig *Rebecca*), 218.
Carthagena, 218.
Cartier, Jacques, 9.
Cassia, 262.
Catherine, Empress of Russia, 44.
Chadqua, artist, cover.
Chalmers, William, Swedish consulate, Canton, 159-160.
Charles II, King of England, 9, 12.
Charleston, South Carolina, 36, 52.
Chesapeake, Battle of the, 141-142.
Chew, assistant to Canton merchant, 262.
China Trade, 8, 10-12, 14ff, 18, 31ff, 104, 127-128, 152-153, 176-188, 201.
Chinaware, 260, 262, 265.
Chinaware merchants, 261-262, 265.
Chinese images, 264.
Chinese medicine shop, 178 (illustration).
Chinqua, Canton merchant, 265.
Choo-keang (Pearl) River, 149, 151 (map).
Chop, Grand, 201f, 203 (illustration).
Chow-chow articles, 260.
Chowqua, hong merchant, 174, 183.
Chowqua, Souchin, 262.
Christ Church, Philadelphia, 51.
Chuen-pee (Bored Nose), Pearl River, 148.
Chu-kiang (Pearl) River, 147, 151 (map).
Cincinnati, Society of the, 5-6, 36, 45, 141, 188, 240, 313-note 11.
Cincinnatus, Lucius Quinctius, 5, 8.
Cinqua, limner, 263.
Clara, ex-*Edgar*, ex-*Empress of China*, ex-*Angelica*, American ship (Capt. Mark Collins), 250.
Clark, William Bell, xv-xvi.
Clarkson, Gerardus, 58.
Clarkson, Matthew, 58.
Clarkson, Samuel (Rev.), midshipman of the *Empress of China*, xvii, 58.
Clinton, George, Governor of New York, xvii, 49, 64-66.
Clive, Robert, Baron Clive of Plassey, 23.
Clote, Island of, 67.
Cloth, clothing, 263-265.
Codman, John, 73.
Co-hong, see Hong merchants.

College of Philadelphia, 36, 57.

Collins, Capt. Mark (American ship *Clara*), 250.

Colombe, ——, French captain (East Indiaman *Fabius*), 142.

Columbia, American ship (Capt. Thomas Read), 29, 50-51, 56.

Columbus, Christopher, 9.

Comet, Pennsylvania privateer sloop, 58.

Compradore, 180, 202, 238, 262.

Comte d'Artois, American ship (Capt. James Nicholson), 6, 29-30, 50, 56, 72, 116.

Concordia, Dutch East Indiaman (Capt. Claus Brailholtts), 139.

Congo, Africa, 218.

Congress Island, South China Sea, 156.

Conococheague Valley, Pennsylvania, 36, 40.

Conqua, Canton tea merchant, 261.

Constable, Rucker & Company, 57, 228, 234, 249, 266.

Constable, William, xvii, 58, 228, 229 (illustration), 249.

Constable, William & Company, 228.

Constellation, United States frigate, 61.

Continental Army, 5-6, 23, 45-46, 228, 240.

Continental Congress, 23, 29, 69f.

Continental Navy, 3, 6, 29, 50, 52, 56, 58.

Contractor, American ship, 29.

Contractor, British East Indiaman (Capt. McIntosh), 185, 198.

Cook, Capt. James, 15-16, 44.

Cordeaz, ——, French second captain (East Indiaman *Triton*), 142, 162.

Counters, 264.

Craigie, Dr. Andrew, xvii, 6, 78, 240-244, 246, 248-249; 241 (illustration).

Craigie, Wainwright & Company, 230.

Crane's Third Continental (Massachusetts) Artillery, 60.

Cromwell, Oliver, 9.

Crossing the Line ceremonies, 89-90, 255.

Crowninshield, George & Sons, 27.

Cumberland, Maryland, 38.

Cumshaw and measurement, 152-153, 182f.

D

Dale, Richard, 265.

Davis, John, explorer, 9.

de la Neufville, John and Son, 142.

De la Tombe, 273-274.

DelaVille, ——, 105, 129, 132.

Delaware Bay and River, 4-5, 18-19, 55, 76, 147, 150 (map), 228.

Derby, Elias Hasket, 204-205, 207 (illustration), 214.

Desmoulins, ——, 170, 190, 193-194, 208.

Desmoulins, Terrier & Company, 238.

Djarkarta (see Batavia).

Doggers Bank, 167.

Dollars, trade, 199 (illustration).

d'Ordelin, ——, French captain (East Indiaman *Triton*), 142, 145, 153, 156, 159, 162-163, 167, 170, 185, 208, 212.

Dorea, ——, 93, 96.

d'Orvilliers, Duc, 141.

Dressing box, 262.

Dublin, Ireland, 250.

Duc de Lauzun, American ship (Capt. John Green), 55.

Duer, Lady Kitty, 58, 118.

Duer, William, xvii, 20, 23, 43-44, 46-48, 58, 86, 116-118, 120-124, 153, 220-224, 243, 248.

Dunn, Samuel, 67, 103-104, 127-128, 142.

Dutch Folly Fort, Canton, 175 (illustration).

E

Earl of Sandwich, ship, 174.

East India Company, British, 9-12, 24, 58, 154, 172, 174, 195, 205.

East India Company, Dutch, 9, 208, 215.

East India Company, French, 141.

East Indies, 8.

Echong, Canton lacquerware merchant, 260.

Edgar, ex-*Empress of China*, ex-*Angelica*, American ship, 249.

Edward, ship, 6.

Elfreth's Alley, Philadelphia, 232.

Elizabeth I, Queen of England, 9.

Elizabethtown, New Jersey, 226.

Ellis & Cockle, 221, 223.

Empress of China, ex-*Angelica*, American ship (Capt. John Green); cargo to China, 3, 65, 129; Society of the Cincinnati involvement, 5-6; risks, 12-13; origins of, 25; physical description, 25f, 67, 129; crew, 25, 65; armament, 25f, 65; place of construction, 26; basis of design, 27; ginseng cargo collected, 31-42; passage from Boston to New York, 42, 56; selection of officers, 46-47f, 57-58; selected for voyage, 49-50; preparations for sailing, 60ff; delays in sailing, 62; bills of lading, 62-63; documentation and sea-letters, 64 (illustration), 65, 66 (illustration), 67, 70, 71 (illustration); specie withheld by Parker, 64, 115, 189ff, 226, 244ff; Capt. Green's instructions, 67-69; Washington's Birthday celebrated on board, 73; insurance, 75, 84-88, 104, 129-133, 131 (illustration); seaworthiness, 42, 56, 79-81f, 86, 90; value of ship and cargo, 87; sails from New York, 3-8, 76-78, 253; stopover at Porto Praya, 91-101; sales of cargo at Canton, 154-155; cargo from China, 172-173; sales of cargo in America, 228, 232, 238-239; preparations for second voyage, 234; John Green's journal of voyage, 78-79, 81-83, 88-91, 93, 101-102, 105-114, 121-126, 133-140, 155-162, 208-211; Samuel Shaw's narrative, 89-90, 95-101, 126, 140-145, 162-167, 170-171, 176-188, 211-219; fragmentary abstract journal of voyage, 253-258; *Empress of China* fan, illustrated, 164-165; association objects, illustrated, 213, 216-217, 222-225.

Eshing, Canton paper merchant, 261, 265.
Esing, Canton merchant, 263.
Exchin, Canton merchant, 260, 262, 265.
Experiment, sloop, 231.

F

Fabius, French East Indiaman (Capt. Colombe), 139, 141-143.
Factories, foreign, see Hongs.
Falmouth, England, 53.
Fans, 261-264.
Febeires, Messrs., of Canton, 264.
Fiador, see Hong merchants.
Fiji Islands, 31.
Fitch, Abel, second mate of the *Empress of China*, 58, 103, 111, 138, 261.
Fitch, Abraham, 266.
Fitzsimons, Thomas, xvii, 117-121, 221-222, 226, 231, 237, 244, 249.
Flint, ——, 118.
Fogo Island, South Atlantic Ocean, 99.
Fort George, New York, 6, 7 (illustration), 76, 78, 253.
Foulis, British East Indiaman (Capt. Blatchford), 174, 185.
Franklin, Benjamin, 44.
Fredericksburg, Virginia, 39.
French Navy, see Royal Marine.
French's Island, Whampoa Reach, 180, 184.
Freneau, Philip, poem, xiii.
Fuh-keen, China, 173.
Furs, 16-17, 29, 31, 43-44, 49, 182 (illustration), 307-note III/2.

G

Galbert, ——, French interpreter, 197-200.
Gaspar, ——, 145, 156.
Gaspar Island, South China Sea, 148 (illus-

tration), 156-157, 162, 167.
Gaspar Strait, South China Sea, 148 (illustration), 167, 212.
General de Klerk, Dutch East Indiaman (Capt. Banks), 208-213.
General Elliott, British East Indiaman (Capt. McClew), 185.
George, Paul, 160.
Geowqua, hong merchant, 174.
Germantown, Pennsylvania, Battle of, 60.
Gilchrist, James, 265.
Ginseng (*Panax quinquefolia*), 3, 24f, 31-42, 50, 105, 154-155, 207.
Girard & Company, 91, 93, 96.
Girard, Stephen, 60, 91.
Gloucester, Massachusetts, 46.
Glove maker, Canton, 260.
Godey, Frank, 259.
Goldsborough, Maine, 59.
Gore, ——, British captain (East Indiaman *Nassau*), 185, 207.
Gowqua, Chinese linguist, 265.
Grand Chop, translation, 201f; 203 (illustration).
Grand Turk, American ship (Capt. Jonathan Ingersoll), 204-205, 207, 214.
Grasse, François-Joseph Paul, Comte de, 141-142.
Great (Grand) Ladrone, South China Sea, 158-159, 208.
Green, Alice, Alcie, Mrs. John, 75, 84, 231, 286, 292.
Green, Capt. John, captain of the *Empress of China*, xv, xvii, 3-8, 12, 25, 51-58, 62-63, 65-68, 70, 72, 74-75 (illustration), 76, 78, 84-85, 91-93, 103, 127-129, 143, 147-148, 162-163, 167, 170, 189-191, 193-194, 201, 204-207, 214-216, 220, 230-231, 234, 236, 239, 244-245, 247, 249, 253, 255-256, 259, 263-297; his journal of the voyage, 78-79, 81-83, 88-91, 93, 101-102, 105-114, 121-126, 133-140, 155-162, 208-211.
Green, John, Jr., xvii, 3, 57, 231.
Green, Miss, 286, 292.
Green, Nancy, 291.
Green Bank, New Jersey, 129.
Greencastle, Pennsylvania, 36.
Gridley's Regiment, Massachusetts Artillery, 60.
Grigsby's Coffee House, London, 242.
Groton, Connecticut, 15.
Guild, Benjamin, 25.
Guild, Benjamin & Company, 120.
Guinea, Africa, 218.

H

Hackett, William, 55.

Hague, ex-*Deane*, Continental frigate, 29.

Hai-lin-shan, South China Sea, 159.

Hallet, ——, American captain (sloop *Harriet*), 24, 205.

Harriet, American sloop (Capts. Hallet and Sturges), 23-24, 36, 205.

Harrison, Jr. & Company, 80.

Hartford, Connecticut, 16.

Haswell, William, 137.

Havana, Cuba, 55.

Havre de Grâce, France, 93, 95-96.

Hawaiian Islands, 15, 31.

Hawke, British East Indiaman (Capt. Rivington), 185, 212-213.

Hemmet, ——, British captain (East Indiaman *Ponsborne*), 185.

Henry the Navigator, 8.

Hingham, Massachusetts, 23.

Hispaniola, West Indies, 91.

Hodgkinson, Peter, second captain of the *Empress of China*, xvii, 57-58, 79, 82, 103, 111, 128f, 138-140, 143, 161, 163.

Hoffman, N., 246.

Hog Lane, Canton, 176.

Holker, John, Jr., xvii, 20, 22 (illustration), 23, 39, 43-44, 46-47, 49, 60-62, 71, 73, 80-81, 84-86, 104, 115-118, 120, 129-130, 220-223, 226, 231-232, 235-236, 242-245, 248-249.

Hong merchants, 153, 170, 174, 180.

Hongs, at Canton, 168 (illustrated), 175-176.

Hoorn, Dutch East Indiaman (Capt. Terence), 215.

Hope, American China trade ship (Capt. James Magee), 236, 240.

Hoppo, 149, 152-153, 174, 181-182, 186, 195, 199-200.

Hopyeck, Canton merchant, 265.

Howqua, Canton lacquerware merchant, 262.

Hubbart, Samuel, 263-265.

Humphreys, Joshua, 27f.

Hunter, William C., 152, 173, 175.

Huqua, Chinese linguist, 262.

I

Image maker, Chinese, 261.

Indian Queen Tavern, Philadelphia, 18, 49.

Ingersoll, Capt. Jonathan (American ship *Grand Turk*), 204-206 (illustration), 214, 218.

Iroquois Indians, 34.

J

Jackson, commander of a sloop of war, 51.

Jackwae, Canton glove maker, 260.

Jartoux, Jesuit Father, 34.

Java, 67, 127-128, 137-140, 142-143, 177, 201.

Jay, John, 235.

Jefferson, Thomas, 44.

Johnson, Seth, 225, 236.

Johnston, Col. James, 38, 40.

Johnston, Dr. Robert, xvii, 6, 36, 38-40, 58, 138, 156, 249, 266.

Johnstone, Commodore, 98, 255.

Johnstone, ——, 215.

Jones, John Paul, 44, 52.

Jones, Samuel, 51-52.

Jo Nimmo, 265.

Jorge, Señor, Portuguese supercargo, 213-214.

Joy, George, 244-246.

K

Kaign & Altmore, 231.

Kalm, Peter, 35f.

K'ang-hsi, Emperor, 12.

Keppel, Admiral Augustus, 141.

Killum, ——, American captain (coasting vessel *Sally*), 42.

Knox, Major General Henry, xvii, 45, 48 (illustration), 60, 74, 201, 235, 244-246.

Knox, Mrs. Henry, 74.

Kollock, Alice (Alcie), 51, 57; see also Green, Mrs. John.

Kollock, Hester, 57.

Kuhn & Risberg, 231.

L

La Brune, ship, see *Queen of France*.

La Cara & Mallet, 86.

Lacquerware, 260, 262, 264.

Lady Hughes, British East Indiaman (Capt. W. Williams), 185, 195-200.

Lafayette, Marquis de, 20, 141, 228.

Lafitau, Jesuit Father Joseph Francis, 34.

La Jengut (Jengat), French brig (Capt. Pécote), 93, 96.

Lankeet Island (Dragon's Den), Pearl River, 148.

La Prudent, British frigate, 53.

Latham, British East Indiaman (Capt. Robertson), 185, 208.

Layhoun, Canton chinaware merchant, 262.

Leavitt, Dr., ship *Grand Turk*, 214, 216.

LeCouteulx & Compagnie, 84-85, 88, 104, 116, 118-119, 129, 155, 221, 232.
LeCouteulx de Canteleu, Jean-Barthélemy, 84.
LeCouteulx de la Noraye, Laurent-Vincent, 84.
LeCouteulx de Verclives, Antoine, 84.
LeCouteulx du Moley, Jacques-Jean, 84.
Leda, ship, 27.
Ledyard, John, xvii, 15-19, 23, 29, 43-44, 47, 49, 56, 62.
LeFevre, ——, of Lisbon, 94, 100.
Le Necker (Neckar), British East Indiaman (Capt. Woolmore), 185, 260.
Lewes, Delaware, 51.
Lewis and Wilson, 237.
Lewis, Mordecai, 231.
Lewis, Mordecai & Company, 223, 231-232.
Lewis, William, 244.
Lexington and Concord, Battles of, 60.
Liberty, British cutter, 53.
Limner, Chinese, 263.
Linguists, 262-263, 265.
Lintao, China, 162.
Lintin Island, Pearl River, 148, 162.
Lion, ship (Capt. John Green), 53.
Lisbon, Portugal, 9, 94-95, 98-99, 100, 213.
Livingston, Robert C., 228, 266.
Livingston, Walter, 20, 23, 116.
Loderstrom, ——, 24.
Loire River, France, 53.
London, England, 9, 12, 15, 54, 72, 85, 87-88, 100, 118, 121, 240, 242-243, 248.
Long Island Sound, New York, 16.
Lorient, France, 53, 208.
Lunqua, Canton merchant, 265, 267, 269.
Lunque, Canton Nankeen merchant, 261.
Lydia, bark of Boston, 137.

M

Macao, Portuguese colony at mouth of Pearl River, 11, 67-68, 86, 147-148, 159, 160-161 (illustration), 162-163, 166, 177, 180, 185, 202, 208-209, 212.
McCaver, Robert, first mate of the *Empress of China*, 58, 82, 103, 111, 156, 162, 189, 266.
Macclesfield Shoal, South China Sea, 158-159, 209.
McClew, ——, British captain (East Indiaman *General Elliott*), 185.
McEldrie & McHendrie, 40.
McIntosh, ——, British captain (East Indiaman *Contractor*), 185, 198, 271.

Madras, India, 218.
Magee, Capt. James (American China trade ship *Hope*), 236.
Mahony, Michael, 248.
Malacca, Strait of, 129, 141, 167, 177.
Mallet, ——, 170.
Mancel, ——, French captain (East Indiaman *Provence*), 185.
Manchin, Canton merchant, 263.
Manila, Philippines, 176.
"Manor Livingston," 20.
Marmie, Peter, 20.
Marshall, James, seaman on the *Empress of China*, 122.
Martin Vas Island, 108.
Massachusetts, American East Indiaman, 249 (illustration).
Matthews, ——, 271.
Maugham, ——, British captain (East Indiaman *Biram Gore*), 185.
Maury, Lt. Matthew Fontaine, 253.
May, Isle of, Cape Verdes, 91, 255.
Middlesex, British East Indiaman (Capt. Rogers), 185.
Middletown, Connecticut, 117.
Mifflin, Thomas, 70.
Mill Prison, Plymouth, England, 53 (illustration), 54, 58.
Miranda, Francisco de, 26-27.
Molineux, Frederick, xvii, 58, 208, 259-266.
Monmouth, Duke of, 12.
Monroe, James, 70.
Montgolfier, Joseph Michel, 142.
Morgan, Capt. James (American coasting vessel *Black Duck*), 42.
Morgan, John, carpenter on the *Empress of China*, 206, 218; porcelain of, 222-225 (illustrated).
Morin, ——, French captain (East Indiaman *Sagittaire*), 185.
Morris & Nesbitt, 53.
Morris, Gouverneur, xvii, 46, 70, 227 (illustration), 228.
Morris, L. R., 67.
Morris, Robert, xvii, 5, 18-20, 21 (illustration), 23-24, 36, 39, 43-44, 46-47, 49, 51-52, 55-56, 61, 70, 72-73, 80-81, 84-85, 88, 115-116, 119-120, 226, 227 (illustration), 228, 236-237, 242, 248, 261, 266, 280.
Morris, Mrs. Robert, 262, 280.
Morton, Maria S., 230.
Mother-of-pearl, 263-264.
Munqua, hong merchant, 174.

N

Nagasaki, Japan, 9.
Nankeen merchant, 261.
Nantes, France, 129, 133, 160.
Nashaminy Creek, Pennsylvania, 56.
Nassau, British East Indiaman (Capt. Gore), 185.
Navigation Acts, 10-11.
Neptune, trial of sailors (1807), 196 (illustration).
Nesbitt & Company, 30.
Nesbitt, J., of Lorient, 208.
Nesbitt, Pennsylvania letter of marque, 53.
Netherlands, 9-12.
Neversink (Navesink), New Jersey, 219.
New Albion, 44.
New Directory for the East-Indies, by Samuel Dunn, 103.
New London, Connecticut, 29-30.
Newport, Rhode Island, 30, 55.
New York, 3-5, 14, 17-20, 27, 39-42, 49, 51-52, 56-57, 59, 62-63, 65, 67, 69, 73-74, 76, 78, 84, 87-88, 94, 118-119, 129-130, 142, 148, 191, 206, 219, 224-225, 228, 230-232, 234, 236, 238, 240, 242, 244-248, 250.
New York Coffee House, London, 242.
New York Packet, American coasting sloop (Capt. Wade), 231.
Nicholson, Capt. James (American ship *Comte d'Artois*), xvii, 6, 50 (illustration), 51, 56, 72, 78.
Nixon, Foster & Company, 279.
Nonsuch, British East Indiaman (Capt. Stevenson), 185.
Nootka Sound, Northwest Coast of America, 15 (illustration), 16, 44.
Norris, Charles, 265.
North Pacific Ocean, 18.
North Shore, Massachusetts, 23.
North Vietnam, see Tonkin.
Northwest Coast, 18, 29.
Northwest Passage, 9.

O

O'Donnell, Capt. John (East India ship *Pallas*), 185, 230.
Old China Street, Canton, 176.
Olney, Capt. Joseph, 52.
Orange, Prince of, 216.
Ostende, Belgium, 12.

P

Pagoda models, 264.

Pallas, chartered East India ship (Capt. John O'Donnell), 185, 201, 226, 228, 230, 235.
Palma, Canary Islands, 254.
Panax quinquefolia, see Ginseng.
Paint boxes and paints, 263.
Painter on glass, 262.
Painters, see Limner.
Paintings, oil, 265.
Paintings on glass, 263-265.
Pankekoa, see Puankhequa.
Paper hangings, 261.
Paper merchant, 261.
Parker, Daniel & Company, 6, 20, 23, 25, 29, 36, 44, 50, 61, 84-85, 115-116, 118, 120, 129-130, 222, 226, 231, 235, 237, 243-244.
Parker, Daniel, xvii, 5-6, 20, 23-25, 27, 29-31, 36, 39, 41-43, 45-49, 51, 60-64, 67, 69-71, 75, 78, 84-86, 88, 91-92, 94, 96, 100, 104, 115-121, 142, 155, 189, 191-193, 220-221, 223-227, 232, 235-237, 240, 242-246, 248-249.
Parker, Dr. Benjamin, 42, 240, 242.
Parker, James, 38.
Parker's Island, South China Sea, 156.
Partridge, George, 70.
Patriote, vessel (Capt. John Green), 53.
Paul, ——, Massachusetts ship builder, 27.
Pearl River, China, 11, 147, 149, 151 (map), 201.
Peck, John, xvii, 7, 26-27, 233.
Pécot(e), Capt., French brig *La Jengut*, 93, 96.
Peking, China, 142, 214.
Pennsylvania, map of, 37.
Pennsylvania Court of Admiralty, 58.
Pennsylvania Navy, 58.
Penrose, James, 56.
Pervis, ——, second mate on British East Indiaman *Latham*, 208.
Philadelphia, 18-20, 23-24 (illustration), 36-39, 41, 44, 46, 49, 51, 53, 55-58, 60-62, 69-72, 76, 80, 84, 91, 93, 117-120, 128-129, 147, 205, 207, 222, 224, 226, 228, 230-232, 233 (illustration), 238-240, 242, 244, 248, 266; Philadelphia merchant ship, 63 (illustration).
Philip II, King of Spain, 9.
Phillips, Hannah, 246.
Phillips, William, 247.
Pigou, American China trade ship (Capt. John Green, Jr.), 58.
Pigou, William Henry, chief of English factory, Canton, 170, 178, 186, 195.
Pinqua, Chinese linguist, 263.

Pinqua, hong merchant, 174.
Plymouth, England, 53.
Polly Bird, American coasting sloop, 231.
Polo, Marco, 8.
Pomona, ship (Capt. John Green), 52.
Pondicherry, India, 207.
Pondicherry, French East Indiaman (Capt. Beaulieu), 185.
Ponsborne, British East Indiaman (Capt. Hemmet), 185, 212.
Poonqua, Canton silk merchant, 260.
Porcelain, 263, see also Chinaware.
Porcelain, shipping of, 190 (illustration).
Porcelain shop, 191 (illustration).
Port-au-Prince, St. Domingo, 53.
Porter, ——, 5, 78.
Porto Praya, Cape Verde Islands, 91-92 (illustration), 95, 100-101, 103, 255.
Portsmouth, New Hampshire, 27.
Potoe, Island of, 208.
Pouqua, Canton merchant, 261-262.
Prager Liebart & Company, 86.
Pringle, ——, 40.
Provence, French East Indiaman (Capt. Mancel), 185.
Puankhequa, hong merchant, 174, 183, 195, 199-200.
Pulo Aor, island, South China Sea, 157, 211.
Pulo Condang, island, South China Sea, 139.
Pulo Condore, island, South China Sea, 157-158, 210.
Pulo Pisang, island, South China Sea, 157, 211.
Pulo Sapa(r)ta, island, South China Sea, 148 (illustration), 157-159.
Pulo Timon, island, South China Sea, 157, 167, 210-212.
Pulo Tingy, island, South China Sea, 157.
Puqua, Canton painter on glass, 262.
Pu-wei, Lü, 8.
Pythagoras, 8.

Q

Quebec, 57.
Queen of China (Empress of China), 42.
Queen of France, ex-*La Brune*, 52.

R

Randall, Thomas, second supercargo of the *Empress of China*, xvii, 6, 46, 55, 60, 62-63, 68, 74, 79, 82-83, 85, 91-93, 95-96, 98-100, 110, 134, 138, 141-143, 155-156, 159, 161-163, 167, 170, 184, 189-191,
194, 196, 199-201, 206-208, 211, 226-227, 230, 236, 244-246, 249, 254.
Randall, Thomas & Company, 60, 93.
Rattans and matting, 265.
Read, James, 281.
Read, Capt. Thomas (American ship *Columbia*), 50f, 56.
Rebecca, American brig (Capt. John Carson), 218.
Reid, John, chief of Imperial factory, Canton, 178, 194.
Rendon, Don Francisco, 55.
Resolution, H.M.S., 15 (illustration).
Retaliation, Continental brigantine (Capt. John Green), 52.
Richard(s), Peter, 122, 138-139.
Richards, Thoss, 122.
Richardson, Capt. James (British East Indiaman *Bellona*), 185.
Richardson, Capt. William (British East Indiaman *Triumph*), 185.
Ridley & Pringle, 14, 49.
Ridley, Matthew, 14, 49.
Rivington, ——, British captain (British East Indiaman *Hawke*), 185, 213.
Robertson, ——, British captain (East Indiaman *Latham*), 185.
Robinson, Capt., 208.
Rocky Hill, 20.
Rodney, Admiral George Brydges, 141-142.
Roebuck, A., of British factory, Canton, 170, 179.
Rogers, ——, British captain (East Indiaman *Middlesex*), 185.
Rose, ——, 170.
Rouen, France, 20.
Roundy, Capt. Charles (American China trade ship *Sumatra*), 202.
Royal Exchange, London, 242.
Royal Henry, ship, 209.
Royal Marine, French, 20, 23.
Rucker, John, 228.
Russell, Thomas, xvii, 20, 269-270.
Russell, Thomas & Company, 284.

S

Sagittaire, French East Indiaman (Capt. Morin), 185.
Sago packing, 263.
Sainqua, Canton silk merchant, 265.
St. Bartholemew, West Indies, 218.
St. Domingo, St. Jago, Cape Verde Islands, 99-100.
St. Eustatia, West Indies, 218.

St. Helena Island, South Atlantic Ocean, 30.
St. Jago, Cape Verde Islands, 91, 95-101, 128, 142, 255.
St. Johns Island, South China Sea, 159.
St. Louis, order of, 141.
St. Martin, West Indies, 219.
St. Mary's Island, 108.
St. Nicholas Island, Cape Verdes, 91, 255.
St. Paul Island, Indian Ocean, 67, 121, 127.
Saldanha Bay, 215.
Salem, Massachusetts, 23, 27, 204-205, 207, 214, 218.
Sally, American coasting vessel (Capt. Killum), 42.
Sally, sloop, 231.
Salt Island (Sal), Cape Verdes, 255.
Salt Island, South China Sea, 156, 167.
Sanciam Falso, South China Sea, 159.
Sandy Hook, New Jersey, 5, 77 (illustration), 78, 88, 240, 253.
Sargent, Major Winthrop, xvii, 46, 58, 62, 115, 236, 240.
Schenectady, New York, 228.
Schermerhorn, ——, 291.
Schermerhorn, Mrs., 293.
Schermerhorn, Peter, 5, 78.
Schuykill River, Philadelphia, 18.
Scioto Company, 241.
Seagrove & Constable, 228.
Sea otters, 16, 17 (illustration), 29, 181 (illustration).
Sears, Col., of Boston, 24-25, 36, 205.
Second Bar, Canton, 208, 212.
Shaunessy, James, 40.
Shaw, John, 250.
Shaw, Nathaniel, 59.
Shaw, Samuel, first supercargo of the *Empress of China*, xv, xvi, xvii, 6, 45 (illustration), 48, 58, 60, 62-64, 68, 74, 82, 85, 91-94, 115, 134, 138, 147, 149, 156-157, 159, 161, 174, 189-191, 193-194, 196-201, 206-208, 210-211, 225-227, 235-240, 242, 245-246, 248-249, 253, 266; narrative, 89-90, 95-101, 126, 140-145, 162-167, 170-171, 176-188, 211, 219.
Shaw, William, 59.
Shewall, Capt. Robert, 51-52.
Shinkienqua, Canton merchant, 275, 277.
Ship models, by John Green in Mill Prison, 53f.
Shippey, Josiah & Company, 228.
Shoes, 261, 263.
Shy Kingqua, hong merchant, 174, 186, 200.
Sibears, Messrs., 160.
Sibiere, ——, 271.

Silk, 262-264.
Silk culture, 193 (illustration).
Silk merchants, 260-262, 265.
Silver, 265.
Silversmith, Chinese, 265.
Simonds, Jonas, 5, 78.
Singkiang Province, China, 174.
Sinnot, Capt., 51.
Sinqua, hong merchant, 174.
Sixth Pennsylvania Battalion, 36.
Small, Capt., 49.
Smasham Rock, South China Sea, 157.
Smith, George, supercargo of the *Lady Hughes*, 195-198.
Smith, Melancton, 118.
Smith, Oliver, 117.
Smith, Richards, 230.
Snake root, 41.
Soarez, Señor, Portuguese supercargo, 213.
Souchin Chowqua (Chiouqua, Choqua), 262-263, 265.
South China Sea, map of, 146; 148 (illustration).
Southerland, ——, 271.
South Shore, Massachusetts, 23.
Soyhing, Canton merchant, 263.
Spanish Armada, 9.
Staple Act, 10.
Staunton, Virginia, 38.
Stevenson, ——, English captain (East Indiaman *Nonsuch*), 185.
Stirling, Lord, 58.
Sturges, ——, American captain (sloop *Harriet*), 205.
Suffren Saint Tropez, Admiral Pierre André de, 98, 255.
Sulivan, British East Indiaman (Capt. Williams), 185.
Sumatra, American China trade ship (Capt. Charles Roundey), 202.
Sumatra, 127, 139, 177, 201, 212-213.
Sunda Strait, 9, 67, 92, 101, 104, 127, 136 (map), 140, 153, 167, 201, 214; Bantam Point, 139; The Button, 139; Cantaya Island, 143; The Cap, 139; Carpenters Rocks, 137; Claps Island, 137; First Point, 128; Fourth Point, 138; Friar Rocks, 137; Java Head, 128, 135, 137, 140, 148 (illustration), 214; Krakatoa Island, 127, 214; Mew Bay, 128, 137 (illustration), 153; Mew Island, 137-138, 142-143; Mew Road, 137; North Island, 139, 212, 214; Point St. Nicholas, 139; Princes Island, 67, 128, 137-138, 140; Serigny, 138, 143; Third Point, 138; Thwart-the-Way Island,

Sundra Strait (*cont.*)
138-139; Trowers Island, 137; Two Sisters, 139-140; Welcome Bay, 138.
Sutherland, William, 26.
Swan, ——, 27.
Swan, James, xvii, 20, 29.
Sweetmeats, 265.
Swift, John, xvii, 74, 77.
Swift, John White, purser of the *Empress of China*, xvii, 57, 62-63, 75, 110, 128, 138, 142-143, 153-154, 159, 163, 189-190, 194, 212, 230, 249, 255, 266.
Symmetry, cartel vessel, 54.
Syngchon(g), Canton chinaware merchant, 261-262, 265.
Syung, Canton shoemaker, 261.

T

Table Bay, South Africa, 204, 214.
Table Mountain, Cape Town, 205 (illustration), 216.
Tackyen, Canton merchant, 263.
Tailors, 259-263, 265.
Tartarel, ——, 96.
Taylor, ——, 118.
Tea, 11f, 173.
Tea chest, 265.
Tea merchant, 261.
Tea packing, 187 (illustration).
TenEyck, Seaman & Company, 282-283.
TenEyck, Seaman, Schermerhorn & Company, 267-268.
Terence, ——, Dutch captain (East Indiaman *Hoorn*), 212-213.
Terrier, F., 194.
Thames River, England, 52.
They Island, South China Sea, 156.
Thomson, Charles, 70.
Thom(p)son, ——, British captain (East Indiaman *Calcutta*), 185, 207.
Tiger Island, Pearl River, 148.
Tigris (Pearl) River, 148-149.
Timothée, ——, 170.
Tonkin, Indo China, 12.
Toothbrushes, 264.
Torterelle, ——, 93.
Trinidad Island, South Atlantic Ocean, 108.
Triton, French East Indiaman (Capt. d'Ordelin), 138-139, 141-145, 153, 155-156, 158-159, 161-163, 167, 170, 185, 212.
Triumph, British East Indiaman (Capt. William Richardson), 185.
Trolliez, ——, supercargo of *Triton*, 142, 170.

Truxtun, Thomas, 55, 60, 61 (illustration).
Tucshing, Canton shoemaker, 260, 263.
Tuhopp, Canton silversmith, 265.
Turnbull, Marmie & Company, 20, 31, 36, 38-40, 42, 61, 80, 120.
Turnbull, William, xvii, 20, 32 (illustration).
Two Brothers Island, South China Sea, 157.
Tyune, Canton image maker, 260-261.

U

Umbrellas, 259, 262.
Unalaska, Aleutian Islands, 16 (illustration).
United States, American merchant ship (Capt. Thomas Bell), 207.
University of Pennsylvania, 36, 57.

V

Vancouver Island, British Columbia, 16.
Verranzano, Giovanni da, 9.
Ver Steeg, Clarence L., xvi.
Vieill(i)ard, ——, French consul at Canton, 160, 197, 200.
Virginia, letter of marque brigantine (Capt. Peter Hodgkinson), 57-58.
Virginia, 37 (map).

W

Wade, Capt. (American coasting sloop *New York Packet*), 231.
Wadsworth & Carter, 49.
Wallpaper, see Paper hangings.
Waln, Robert, Sr. and Jesse, 58.
Want Long, Canton silk merchant, 261-262.
Warm Springs, Virginia, see Bath.
Washington, American China trade ship (Capt. Peter Hodgkinson), 57.
Washington, Gen. George, 3, 5, 20, 45, 52, 73.
Watertown, Massachusetts, 20.
Wayhoun, Canton merchant, 263.
Waysang, Canton merchant, 262.
Weddell, Capt. John, 11.
Wells Wharf, New York, 234.
Welsh, ——, 51.
West Point, New York, 46.
Whampoa (Reach), China, 147-149, 152-153, 164-166 (illustration), 167, 172-173, 179-180, 182, 195-196, 198, 200-202, 204 (illustration), 205-208, 212, 238.
Whiteside, Peter & Company, 231.
Whiting, Capt. (American coasting vessel *Brothers*), 42.

Wilkinson, Mrs., 264.
Williams, ———, British captain (East India-
man *Sulivan*), 185.
Williams, ———, British commodore at Wham-
poa, 206.
Williams, Joseph Minnick, xvi.
Williams, Capt. W. (British East Indiaman
Lady Hughes), 185, 195, 197-198.
Williamson, Hugh, 70.
Willing & Morris, 51-52, 57.
Willing, Thomas, 51.
Winchester, Virginia, 40.
Winchong, Canton chinaware merchant, 262.
Window blinds, 262.
Woo-E Hills, China, 173.

Woolmore, ———, British captain (East Indiaman *Le Necker*), 185, 260, 267, 269, 271.
Woysang, Canton umbrella maker/merchant,
259, 261, 265.

Y

Yick, Canton merchant, 263.
Yorktown, Virginia, 141.
Young, Ebenezer, 5, 78, 117.
Young, Sam Jack, 265.

Z

Zantzinger, Adam, 231.

The Empress of China,
by Philip Chadwick Foster Smith,
was published under a grant
from the Andrew W. Mellon Foundation
by the Philadelphia Maritime Museum
and designed by Klaus Gemming, New Haven, Connecticut.
The typeface was first cast about 1796
in Philadelphia by Binny & Ronaldson.
In its recutting by Mergenthaler Linotype Company
it was named Monticello, since it was first used
for the fifty-volume *Papers of Thomas Jefferson*.
Princeton University Press set the text for
The Empress of China
in the new film version of Monticello.
The book was printed by
The Meriden Gravure Company, Meriden, Connecticut,
on Mohawk Superfine Text paper,
made by Mohawk Paper Mills, Cohoes, New York,
and was bound by
The Stinehour Press, Lunenburg, Vermont.